THE FOLDING SCHOONER

THE FOLDING SCHOONER

AND OTHER ADVENTURES IN BOAT DESIGN

by Philip C. Bolger

International Marine Publishing Company
Camden, Maine

Copyright © 1976
by International Marine Publishing Company
Library of Congress Catalog Card Number: 76-8779
International Standard Book Number: 0-87742-083-1

All rights reserved. Except for use in a review, no part of this book may be reproduced or utilized in any form or by any means, electronic or mechanical, including photocopying, recording, or by any information storage and retrieval system, without written permission from the publisher.

*Dedicated
to
W. T. Bolger*

CONTENTS

	Preface	viii
	Note on the Metric System	ix
1	The Elegant Punt	1
2	Surf	7
3	Teal	13
4	The Folding Schooners	19
5	A Cold-Water Sailboard	31
6	A Minimum Kayak	36
7	Navel Jelly	39
8	Toy Riverboat	43
9	Utility for Homebuilders	47
10	Cynthia J.	54
11	Black Skimmer	60
12	Blackgauntlet II	67
13	Rondo II	81
14	The Pari-Mutuel Schooner Project	88
15	Proa	91
16	Tiger Lily	99
17	The Plywood Trireme	102
18	Yacht Tenders	105
19	Little Superior	110
20	Vectis	115
21	Recreational Rowboat	119
22	Harbinger	122
23	Windfola	129
24	Dovekie	136
25	Ocean-Crossing Rowboat	146
26	Chicago Coble	150
27	Moccasin	155
28	Economy Motorsailer	167
29	California Lobsterboat	172
30	All-Weather Houseboat	176
31	Gill-Netter Type Houseboat	184
32	Resolution	189
33	Anchor	195

PREFACE

I have a true vocation; it's been upwards of thirty years since there's been a day in which it hasn't pleased me to think about boat design, many hours most days. So far, there's no sign of boredom setting in, which I take to be the test of the vocation.

I've reached working hypotheses different from the conventional wisdom. This book was produced out of the usual motives of profit and vanity, and its rationalization is mainly entertainment, but I wouldn't mind if it was regarded as an anti-textbook tending to subvert usual design doctrine in two respects.

The first, minor subversion, has to do with "planing," of which I say briefly and dogmatically that if a boat is light and powerful enough to plane well, she can't be prevented from planing; all the designer needs to worry about is her attitude and stability. Design features meant to generate exceptional lift always seem to degrade the boat.

The second doctrine I disagree with is the double assumption that a sail is hard, or easy, to handle in direct proportion to its area, and that drive per square foot is a fair measure of efficiency. Every living boat sailor has been indoctrinated in those ideas; the result is a standard rig for sailboats which is the most expensive and most laborious and dangerous to handle, *for its area,* of any in history. Both assumptions are plainly false and collapse the instant they're challenged, but the consequences of their having gone unchallenged for seventy years will be with us for a long time. Already there's been about a seventy-year gap in the development of sails that are powerful for their cost, handling effort, and effect on the stability of the hull.

We can go back to 1890 and start over, or make cautious modifications of conventional rigs such as lengthened booms, or try to design from first principles. Since most people are afflicted with strange superstitions about what the first principles are, this last generally ends in fiasco. I've been trying to combine the three methods in some reasonable balance of prudence and enterprise. I can recommend the results of an oath I took, now a good many years ago, with my right hand raised and my left on a copy of Claud Worth's *Yacht Cruising,* never to read a rating rule.

Philip C. Bolger
Gloucester, Massachusetts

NOTE ON THE METRIC SYSTEM

Briefly, not wanting to be a bore on the subject, and because it will be a dead issue long before this paper is brittle:

1. North America must change to the metric system if only because we'll be too lonely otherwise.

2. There's no possible doubt that it's superior, more convenient to use, than the English system. (It's a great pity the French scientists who devised the metric system in 1790-something didn't get it quite right, so it could be used for navigation along with everything else, but it's still closer than the statute mile, which is said to be a thousand double paces of an average Roman legionary soldier.)

3. The two metric designs in this book were both so designed by request of the builders: *Dovekie* by the far-sighted Peter Duff, who wanted to break in himself and his crew to use it; *Vectis* by Larry Dahlmer, who had built a boat before to metric plans and found it quicker and easier even at first trial.

4. It's an error leading to maddening frustration to try to translate from one system to the other. What's invested in the accustomed system is a mass of memorized images: As a child each of us was told that it was a mile to such and such a place, or that a sheet of plywood was 122 by 244 centimeters (that's the one you're used to, English-speaker). What Americans must do is find a Geological Survey map of their familiar surroundings and using the kilometer scale printed on the map pick themselves a familiar kilometer that will serve them and their children ever after. Then they must get a meter stick and memorize the metric dimensions of familiar objects, forgetting as fast as possible what their English dimensions are. Learn that fresh water freezes at zero Centigrade, that at minus-20 it's not smart to expose much skin to a fresh breeze; at plus-10 you'll want warm clothes unless you're working out strenuously; at plus-20 you're comfortable with long sleeves and a high neckline; and at plus-30 you'll sweat in bare skin if the humidity is normal.

Vectis and *Dovekie* are five meters and six-and-a-half meters long respectively. That's how long they are; never mind what it comes to in feet and inches.

1
THE ELEGANT PUNT

7'9" x 3'7"

Harold Payson, doing a little business selling boat plans on the side, figured that a very small and simple design would "give 'em confidence" to tackle something larger. The specification put me in mind of a design I made years ago for a box factory that wanted to try manufacturing boats; the proprietor gave the plans to his foreman when the shop opened at eight o'clock. He came back at noon to see what the foreman thought of the idea and found he'd built four boats. . . .

This shape and construction seem to me to make about as good a boat as anything it's practical to build out of wood; in fact, better than most of the more complex shapes. The single midships mold means that no two punts will come out exactly alike, as the sheer, rocker, and gunwale plan will all differ according to the way the sides happen to take the bend. The difference in looks and behavior is negligible.

These boats row and tow about as you'd expect. They sail much better than you might expect, especially in a light breeze and smooth water, on account of the high and powerful rig. I hear that Joy Payson, sailing one of these, caused her father some embarrassment by outsailing a much more pretentious boat (also my design) that he was demonstrating to a customer. The rig is cheap for its size by the elimination of superfluous items, such as a halyard and sheet blocks, to say nothing of stays and shrouds, which I've known people to put on such craft. Still, sail, spars, rudder, and leeboard cost about as much as the hull, a point to bear in mind if compact storage and the 70-pound weight of this hull aren't the critical factors.

*This plan and others bearing his name are printed by courtesy of Harold H. Payson, South Thomaston, Maine, from whom they're available, at a larger scale and responsibly up-dated.

The elegant punt with ideal racing crew.

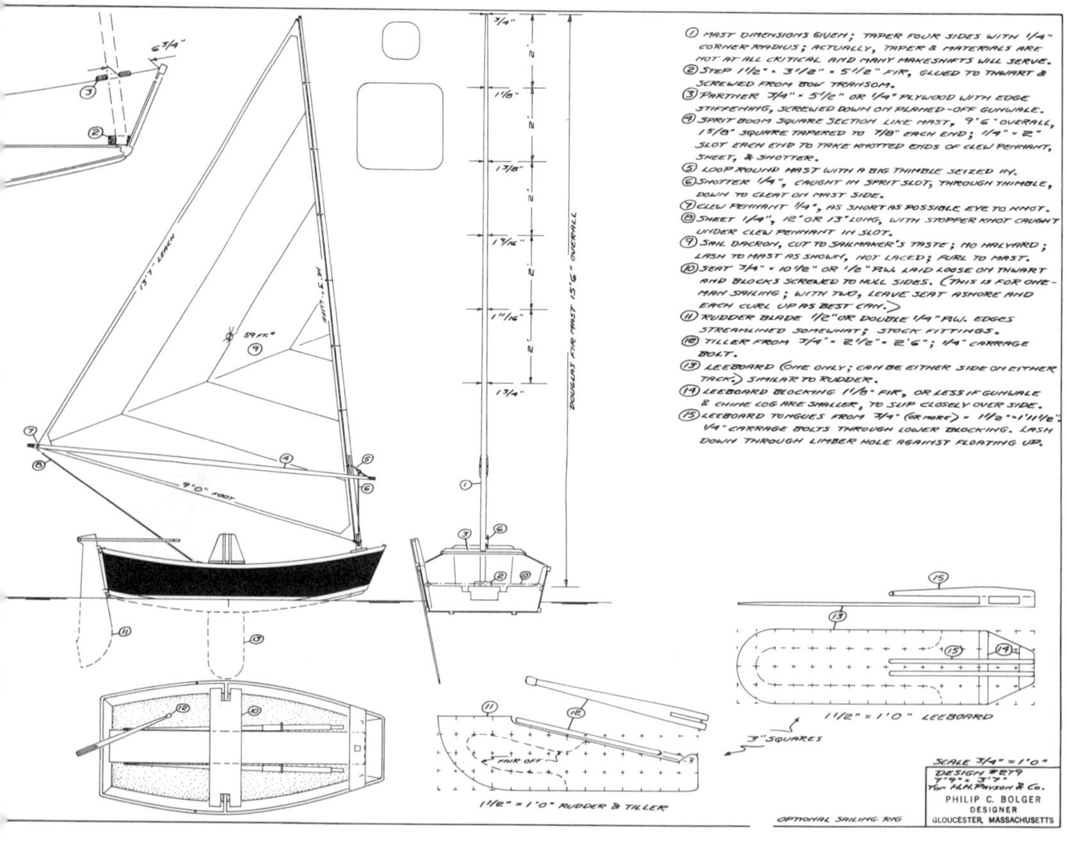

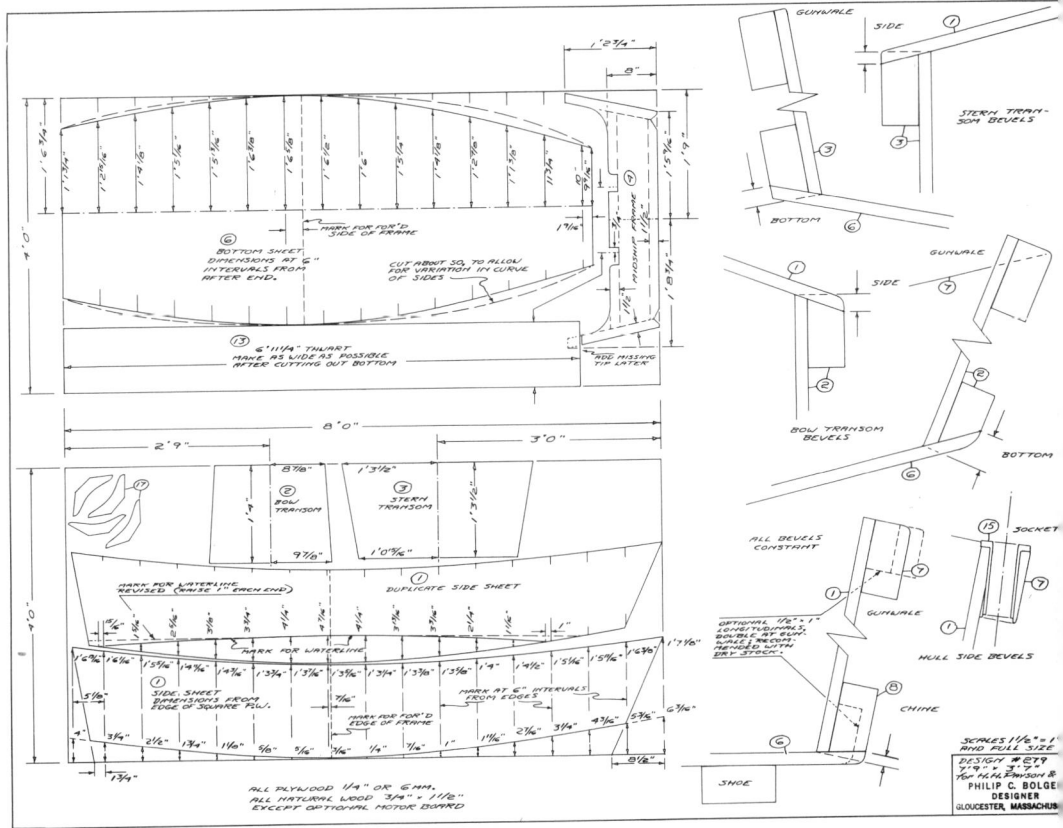

BUILDING DIRECTIONS AND KEY TO PLANS

Materials needed: two ¼" x 4' x 8' sheets of marine plywood; eight 8' lengths of ¾" x 1½" fir, mahogany, or other moderately hard wood of good gluing type, plus about 25' of the same in shorter lengths. Also one ¾" x 7½" x 12½" piece of the same for a motor board if wanted.

1. Mark plywood as diagrammed for side sheet and cut out; smooth up edges and use as pattern for other side; mark with ball-point pen, bearing down enough to score the sheet slightly for the waterline, and not forgetting that the waterlines should be on the outsides of the sheets as assembled, and the marks for the midship mold location on the insides.

2. Mark out bow transom from diagram and cut out; shape given is before bevelling; clamp, glue, and nail or screw fastening frame around edges; bevel bottom and sides as shown by the full-size sections; make sure the centerline marks are visible, especially at the bottom.

3. Stern transom made in same way as bow; if it's desired to have the boat take an outboard motor (maximum power 4 h.p.; maximum weight 34 pounds) add the motor board as shown; make sure centerline marks are there.

4. Midship frame made as diagrammed; note that the height given, 1' 2¾", is to the top of the side fastening frames — the plywood need not be carried above the 8" level except for looks; if it is carried to the top, as shown, the small piece missing due to lack of space on the sheet can be glued on later. Midship frame has no bevel anywhere. Note drainage openings at bottom, and cut-outs for seat stringers made wide enough to hold the oars in the top. Mark the centerline.

(Set midship frame upright on a more or less flat surface; stand one side up against it, lining up frame with mark on sheet; glue surface and nail, or merely nail, sheet to frame, keeping them as nearly at right angles as possible. Attach the other side sheet on the other side of the frame.)

5. Lightly tack a small block of wood each end of each side sheet, as shown on the drawing of the outside of the stern. Run a light rope all the way around the sides and across the ends and twist it up with a stick (Spanish windlass) to tighten and pull ends of sides together until they will grip the transoms; by tapping and pushing try to get the two sides to come in somewhat evenly.

(Line up the transoms with outsides of fastening frames exactly flush with ends of side sheets and with bevelled bottoms exactly level with bottoms of side sheets; if a discrepancy shows up in height, take it out of the top.)

6. Cut out bottom to diagram given, marking clearly for midship frame and centerline, and for the shoes (see #9).

(Turn sides-transoms assembly bottom-up; lay bottom sheet in place with centerline marks lined up on centerlines of transoms and frame, thereby evening curve of sides and eliminating any parallelogram shape. Tack or screw lightly in place; don't fasten it so you can't get it off, and don't trim its edges. Turn assembly back right-side-up.)

7. Attach gunwale stringers to outside of sides all around top edge; first clamp both stringers to sides at stern, then bring around sides with a clamp every two feet or less, till both are clamped at the bow; best bring in both at once if possible; unclamp one, coat it with glue, and clamp it back on, tapping for exact alignment with edge of sheet and using more clamps if necessary. Do the same for the other side. At leisure, drive a nail or screw every six inches or so, from the inside. If the material for the gunwales is very stiff and the bend seems too hard, the gunwales can be reduced in size, say to not less than ½" x 1".

8. Remove bottom and attach chine logs in same way as gunwales; note that if the chine logs are bevelled in advance, the edges of the sides should be also; the full-size section given shows bevel needed if logs are put on square and bevelled in place.

(Check bevel of chines and bottoms of transoms and smooth up to take bottom sheet; bottom can now be trimmed around edges to exact shape of outside of chine, again making sure centerlines are in line. Make sure position of shoes marked on bottom sheet inside and out. Glue and nail or screw bottom sheet in place, with a fastening about every four inches and extra ones at the corners, to transoms, midship frame, and chine logs; start fastening at one end and work to the other, or in the middle and work out to the ends, *not* trying to work from both ends to the middle.)

If bottom is to be fiberglassed, do it now; round off chines and tops of chine logs and use one layer of 10 ounce cloth of the common type with polyester resin, stopping glass on top of chine logs.)

9. Shoes can be attached at one end, fastening to transom, then to midship mold, then to the other transom, and finally at about 6″ intervals and staggered, from inside.

10. Install cleats on insides of transoms to take ends of seats.

11. Attach side stringers to thwart and check length to make sure stringers will fit within the end cleats.

12. Glue polyurethane foam blocks as shown to the underside of the thwart.

13. Put thwart in place and screw down (better not nail it as it might need to be removed sometime) on midship frame and end cleats.

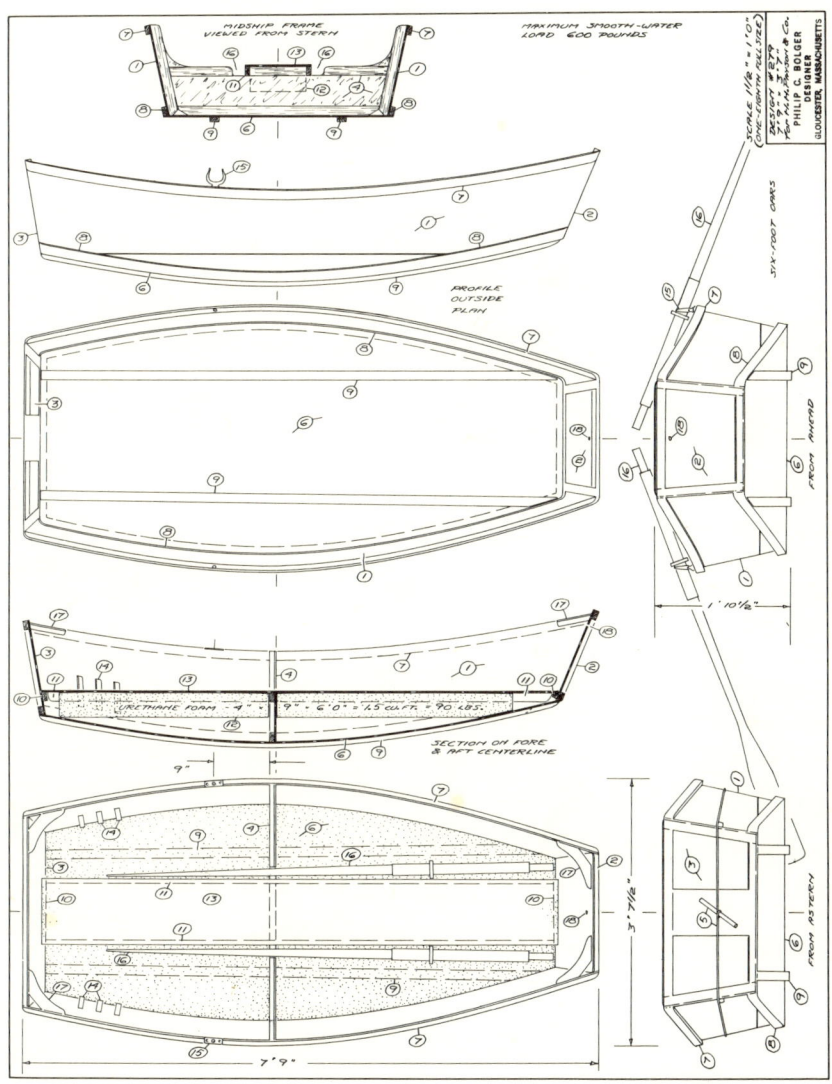

14. Foot braces can be $\frac{3}{4}''$ square (i.e., split $\frac{3}{4}'' \times 1\frac{1}{2}''$) by about $5''$ long; decide exact location, mark places, drill holes in side plywood for two or three screws or nails each, glue in place and drive fastenings from outside.

15. Standard $\frac{1}{2}''$ bronze rowlocks in flush sockets.

16. Six-foot spruce oars.

17. Quarter knees are mostly decorative and builder can leave them off or please herself about size and shape; if they're used they should be strong enough to support the weight of the boat, with at least four big nails or screws from gunwales each, plus gluing. As shown they're supposed to be plywood with backing underneath of left-over framing pieces, but if the builder happens on some natural crooks or feels like laminating them, so much the better.

18. Hole for painter about $\frac{3}{8}''$ (for $\frac{1}{4}''$ rope); hold painter with a stopper knot inside.

(Not shown, but to be considered; this boat can be carried very neatly on its side, with the carrier's shoulder taking the weight under the high side. As drawn it has to be held there by gripping the chine log on the high side with the off-hand; to have a free hand to carry the oars, cut about a four-inch diameter hole in the midship frame, not too near the edges, at a position found by trial, to slip through the forearm of the carrying arm.)

2
SURF

$15'6'' \times 3'7''$

Having remarked that the cost of the Elegant Punt's rig seemed to be out of proportion to the cost of the hull, I suggested to Harold that he add an equally simple, but stretched hull for the same spars and sail, since he had a set on hand. In effect, we just took the punt and stuck four feet of taper on each end, plus the affectation of the ornamental false head for the fun of it. Result: an improvement in looks and capability out of all proportion to the added cost and weight; also, space for some really effective positive buoyancy, so much that it ought to be an easy business to get her dried out after a misadventure.

About the only drawback is that the rudder has moved off into the middle distance from where a singlehander ought to sit. I thought of an extension tiller and of tiller lines carried forward under hooks or fairleads out at the sides; neither is very satisfactory compared with taking somebody with you for ballast and, it's to be hoped, good company.

The slot in the end of the bowsprit is to hold the mooring pennant, or a light anchor could be carried there dangling, to be let go from abaft the mast. Harold shimmed up the slot between the bowsprit and the top of the false head, to stiffen the bowsprit. Having done so, he inquired why I'd left it open on the drawing. By that time I'd completely forgotten why, but answered after hasty thought with the sophistry that it was to let the bowsprit spring and so ease the jerks on the anchor line; I still don't recall what I was thinking when I drew it, and maybe that really was the idea. . . .

The crab skiff in action.

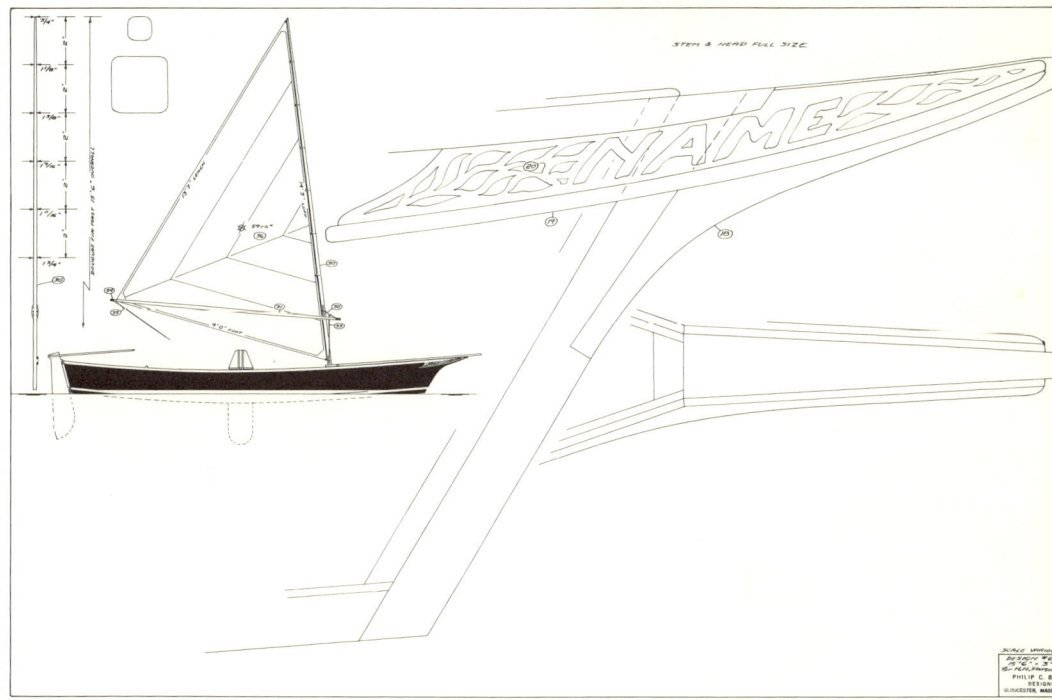

BUILDING DIRECTIONS AND KEY TO PLANS

All plywood, as designed, is ¼" in 4' x 8' sheets (four required), preferably marine grade, though exterior will serve if the core voids are located and plugged as far as possible. Various combinations of sheet length and thickness are permissable and desirable from some points of view but will in all cases be either heavier or more expensive, usually both. Natural wood, understood if not labelled plywood, may be almost any timber hard enough to hold nails and not too oily, acidic, etc., to hold glue; e.g. not balsa or teak. Except where otherwise specified all of it is from ¾" x 1" stock.

1. Hull sides marked out from diagram to given dimensions; assemble with rivets, clinch nails, or even staples or tacks if otherwise firmly held while the glue sets up, on 6"-wide butt straps.

2. Transom can be a single slab of natural wood ¾" x 7" x 15⅛", or plywood that size with a fastening frame like the bulkheads either inside or out.

3. After bulkhead marked out and cut out of plywood to given dimensions (no plank thickness deductions) with fastening frame on after side; drain holes ½" x 1½" as shown.

4. Midship frame web 7½"-high plywood, 19 5/16" half-breadth on top edge, 17¾" at bottom; fastening frame top and bottom; side frames from ¾" x 2½" x about 15½"; drainage as shown.

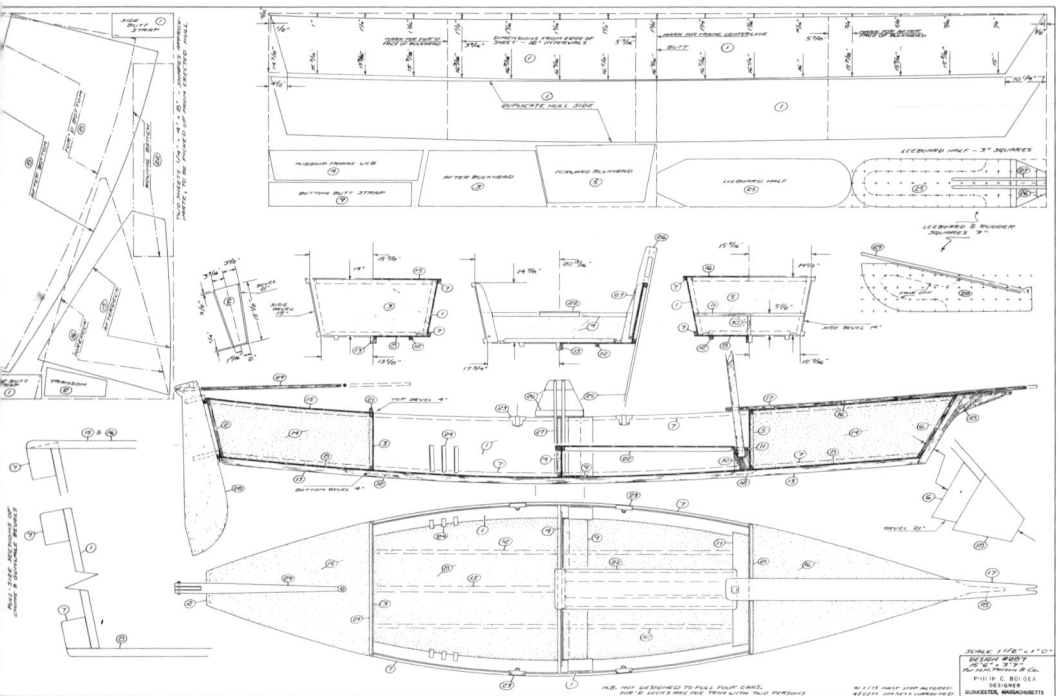

5. Forward bulkhead similar to after one.

6. Stem from ¾" x 2" x 18"; see full size section; secure to one of side-sheets.

(Stand sides bottom up; glue center frame and carefully nail on station marks with 1" #14 bronze ring nails. Put forward and after bulkheads temporarily in place. Build stern from ¾" spruce, fir, or something and back inner face with ½" plywood so that the 1¼" #10 bronze screws of the gudgeons will have enough holding power. When nailing transom and stern in place, clamp backing pieces of scrap on the sides to stop them from slipping inboard.)

7. Make and attach with glue and nails the chine logs and gunwale stringers, allowing for bevels as shown full size.

8. Using shape of erected sides as pattern, cut out bottom sheets.

9. Bottom butt strap 6" wide but offset forward to have about 1½" lap over after sheet (to clear midship frame).

10. Mast step from ¾" x 3¾" x about 4⅞"; cut down about as shown to give some bury to mast heel; use glue and three 2½" screws from bulkhead; shape so hull bottom will bear on it closely.

11. Mast heel thwart from ¾" x 4" x 2'4¾"; glue and screw with about ten 2½" or longer screws through bulkhead, plus some nails from sides.

(Clean up bevel of chine logs and side plywood to get a good bearing for bottom all around; line up bulkhead, transom, etc., centerlines with a straightedge plank to get about the same curve in the two sides; glue and nail bottom in place.)

12. Bottom skids ½" x 1", glued in place and nailed from inside.

13. Shoe 1½" square, glued and nailed from inside.

14. Fill ends of hull with expanded foam or cut blocks of foam, making sure there'll be a good bearing to support the decks.

15. Afterdeck cut to shape from hull. Bevel down sides and gunwales to get a good bearing as shown, and nail in place.

16. Cut foredeck to shape from hull.

17. Bowsprit-mast partner ¾" x 5½" x 6'4½", glued and nailed to top of deck before installing deck. The slot in the end of the bowsprit is a chock for mooring pennant or anchor warp; belay to mast or mast partner.

18. Cutwater sided 2" and bevelled to about ¾" forward face; take shape from full-size pattern furnished, or modify to taste; install with nails from stem before placing foam and deck.

19. Trail knees ½" square, bent in flat to hull side and cutwater with a ½" wedge to fair out the angle in the rabbet.

20. Trailboards ¼" carved and painted to taste; may be different or omitted entirely at owner's option.

21. Coamings ¾" x 1".

22. Rowing bench plywood, 10" x 3'9" (to lie flat in after part of cockpit when sailing); four ¾" x 1" stiffeners underneath; two cross-cleats at after end to form lips gripping midship frame so it can be secured without fastenings.

23. Rowlock sockets standard ½"; locate by trial; oars 6'6".

24. Foot braces ¾" x 1", glued to sides.

25. Leeboard (one only, can be either side on either tack) double ¼" plywood as diagrammed, or ½" or (best) ¾" plywood if a suitable piece of scrap of plywood can be had economically.

26. Leeboard blocking 1⅛" (to ship board closely over gunwale).

27. Leeboard tongues from ¾" (at least) x 1½" x 1'11½"; ¼" carriage bolts through lower blocking; pin against floating off through holes shown, or lash through drain hole.

28. Rudder blade unfortunately can't be placed on the four sheets of plywood; look for a scrap of ¾" plywood; ½" plywood has served for years in some rudders of this size and type but several such have broken across core voids. Rudder and leeboard can also be built up of edge-nailed ¾" x 1" strips or rodded planks and this construction stands alternate wetting and exposure to sun better than plywood. In any case streamline edges as much as patience allows.

29. Tiller from ¾" x 2½" x 3'7" (this length will be most convenient to stow but longer would be pleasanter to use; hole at grip end is to take bolt of an extension tiller by way of compromise); ¼" bolt to rudder.

30. Mast dimensions as given (thicknesses about minimum); taper four sides with about ¼" corner radius; actually taper and material are in no way critical and many makeshifts will serve, especially as dismastings on this scale aren't apt to be lethal.

31. Sprit boom is square section like mast, 9'6" overall, 1⅝" square tapered to ⅞" each end (or different as convenient); ¼" x 2" slot each end to take knotted ends of clew pennant, sheet, and snotter.

32. Loop around mast with a big thimble seized in.

33. Snotter ¼", caught in sprit slot, through thimble, down to cleat on side of mast.

34. Clew pennant ¼", as short as possible eye to knot.

35. Sheet ¼", 12' or 13' long, with stopper knot caught under clew pennant in sprit slot.

36. Sail dacron, cut to sailmaker's taste, not necessarily with up-and-down mitre shown on plan for prettiness; no halyard; lash to mast as shown, not laced; not to have any battens; furl to mast.

3
TEAL

12'0" x 3'6"

I was tempted to arrange this book strictly in the order the designs were made. If it were a textbook that would be the way to do it, showing the learning process on various themes and highlighting the afterthoughts. It's also a nice question, what a designer ought to do about a design that's extant and usable, and makes a respectable boat, but which he's sure he could improve if he took the time to reconstruct it.

The design number 310 makes this one very recent; May, 1975, to be exact. Like the crab skiff, it was made for Harold Payson and was meant to use the same rig, out of the original Elegant Punt. The proposal lay around for months; I'd look at it every so often, finding myself discontented each time with whatever I'd sketched the time before. I doodled flat-iron skiffs and long punts, and a skiff with identical pointed ends like a miniature *Navel Jelly* (see design #296, Chapter 7). They all seemed nondescript in looks and behavior, or else wasted plywood, or both.

Eventually it penetrated my limited wit that the pointed ends didn't have to be the same length. I think the result is extremely nice; unobtrusive and unaffected, but exactly right for what she is. She sails well, rows well, tows well; a paragon of all the virtues if you accept that one adult or two smallish children makes an overload in anything but perfectly smooth water.

She's built out of the same two sheets of plywood as the 7'9" punt and uses nearly the same amount of other lumber, fastenings, and equipment. The labor time can't be much different either, nor the skill needed for a good outcome. She'd be little or no heavier if the same plywood thickness were used, as it could be; I went to $3/8''$ thinking to make her good and strong, and because I hear that it's easier than $1/4''$ to come by in a good quality.

Two or three years of sporadic mental effort produced a good-looking twelve-foot boat out of the same pile of material as the cute but homely eight-foot-minus boat. Does this make the latter obsolete? She's more com-

14 TEAL

The 12-foot double-ender on trial. Quite a pretty shape for two sheets of plywood!

pact, which might be handy at times. Otherwise, it's a good illustration of the question designers (and their clients) have to learn to live with: "Why didn't you do it right the first time?"

KEY TO PLANS

1. Midship frame from ¾" x 2½"; gussets ⅜" plywood 8½" x 14" x 17¾"; note drain limbers port and starboard.
2. Temporary molds each end from ½" x 2½" and ½" x 1½"; these jam up against outer (i.e., toward the ends) edges of side butt straps; give them a sharp bevel so the edges will bear right in the angle of the strap and side plank.
3. End posts from 1½" square; see full-size diagrams for bevels.
4. Side planks straight-sided 16" wide, assembled as diagrammed into 12' 7⅜" long on gunwale edge, 11' x 2¼" on chine edge; mark as diagrammed, on opposite sides (relative to butt straps) for midship frame.
5. Side butt straps ⅜" x 4" x 16"; make sure they're exactly 4" wide and exactly centered on the butt, otherwise the molds will be out of position and the whole shape of the boat will be more or less different.
6. Gunwales ½" x 1½" sprung on when sides are in place on the molds;

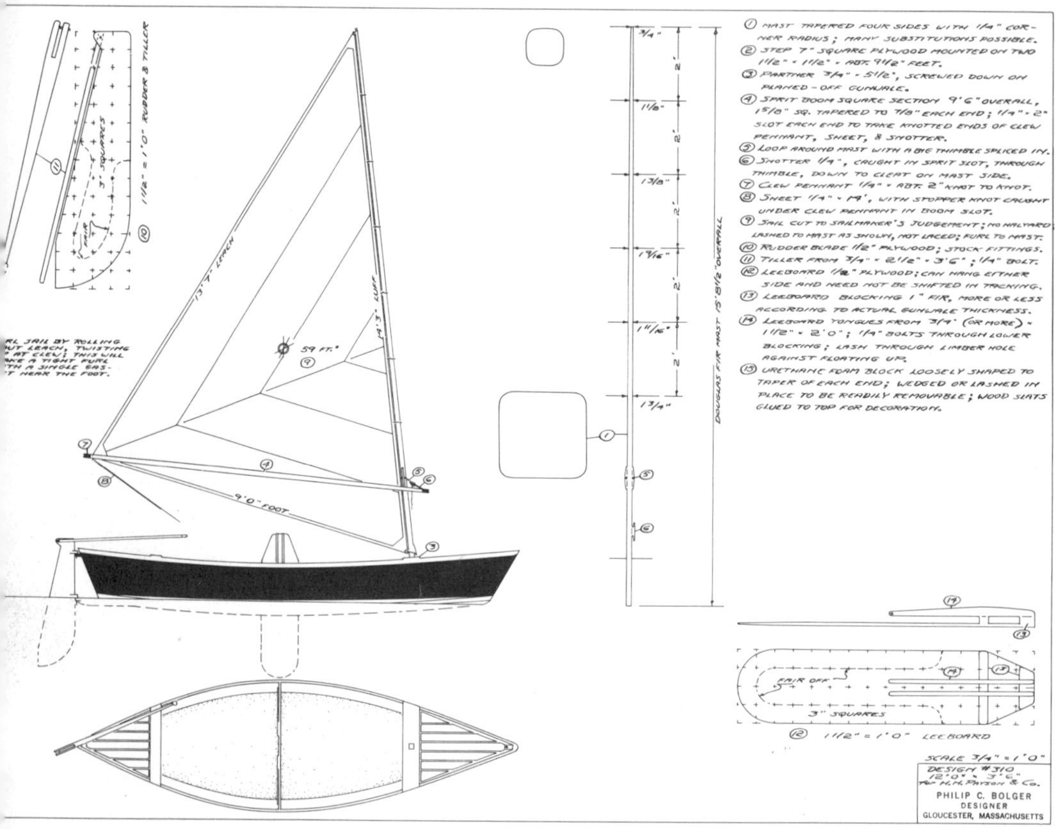

16 TEAL

Harold Payson fits the bottom to the first 12-footer.

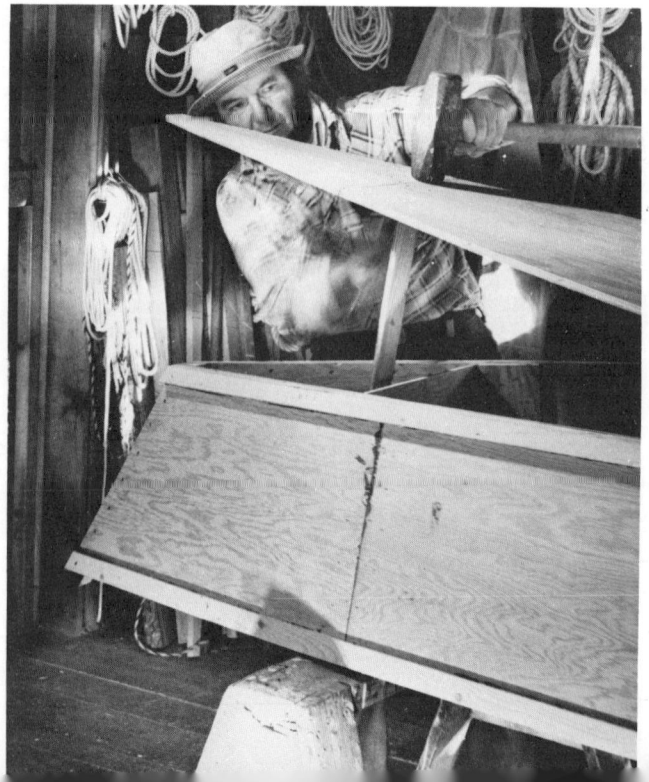

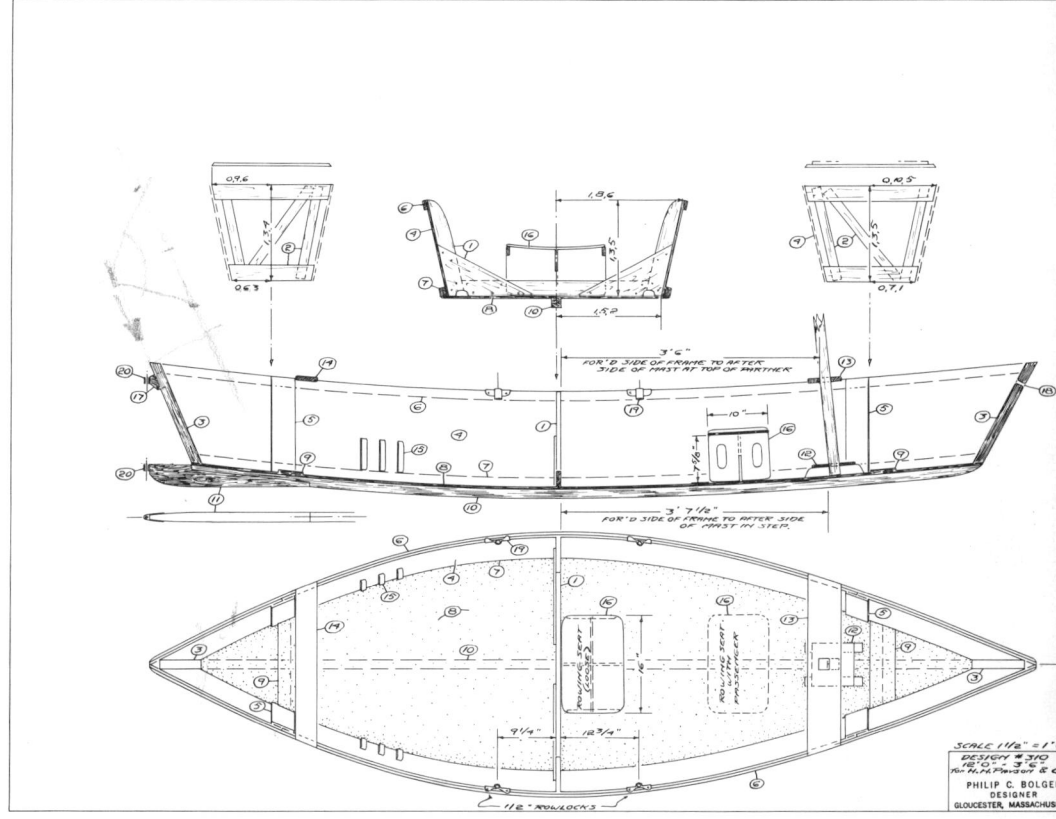

better check first against rough-cut bottom to make sure they're bent about as intended; gunwales can be doubled later if they seem too limber, but on test hull better wait on this till bottom and partner are in place.

7. Chine logs double $\frac{1}{2}''$ x $1\frac{1}{2}''$ sprung on and fastened from inside except for end fastenings to end posts from outside.

8. Bottom $\frac{3}{8}''$ plywood cut out to diagram but leaving about $\frac{1}{2}''$ all round for fitting to actual form of chines; assemble on butt straps after a trial fitting.

9. Bottom butt straps $\frac{3}{8}''$ x $4''$.

10. Shoe $1\frac{1}{2}''$ square or (if too stiff) double $\frac{3}{4}''$ x $1\frac{1}{2}''$.

11. Skeg from $1\frac{1}{2}''$ x $3\frac{1}{2}''$ x about $2'2''$.

12. Mast step, see rigging sheet item 2.

13. Partner, see rigging sheet item 3.

14. After thwart $\frac{3}{4}''$ x $3\frac{1}{2}''$ x about $2'3''$.

15. Foot braces $\frac{3}{4}''$ square x about $5''$; locate by trial.

16. Rowing seat $\frac{3}{8}''$ plywood; note $\frac{1}{2}''$ concavity of seat and rounding of all lower edges (which could also be padded) to avoid scarring bottom.

17. Block about $1\frac{1}{2}''$ x $2\frac{1}{2}''$ square, carved to fit over sternpost and take upper rudder gudgeon.

18 TEAL

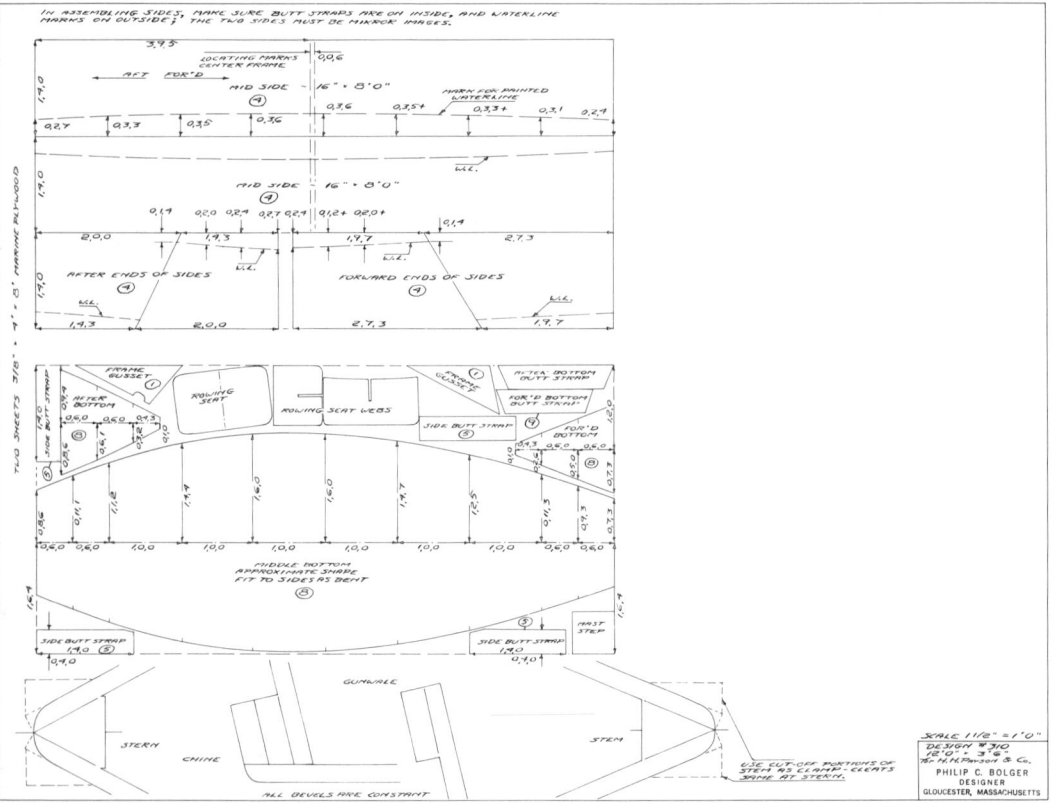

18. Hole through stem to take painter with stopper knot inside.

19. Stock 1/2" rowlock sockets, preferably bronze.

20. If stock strap gudgeons can't be found, they can be made by welding or brazing straps to a machined block, or screw-eyes will serve.

21. If more positive buoyancy is required or wanted, I'd recommend filling the spaces between the partner and stem, and thwart and stern, with styrene foam blocks carved to fit the whole spaces but kept 3" or 4" up clear of the bottom (to stow ends of oars among other things); top of foam can be sheathed with cloth and epoxy to keep the gulls from eating it, and marked "NO STEP!" (That would be around 200-220 pounds positive buoyancy, which should be plenty to allow bailing her out if swamped, and the location will let her float deep on her side and make it easy to right her from bottom-up.)

(This was what Harold Payson had to work from: he has prepared an elaborate every-single-hammer-blow set of instructions, heavily illustrated, to go with the large-scale plans he sells.)

4
THE FOLDING SCHOONERS

$$\boxed{31'0'' \times 5'0''}$$

A local man got up a pseudo-traditional race limited to gaff-rigged schooners over twenty-five feet on the waterline. This, of course, started me musing on something cheap and easy to file away, that would meet the restrictions. At first I had in mind hooking two sailboards together, but the open skiffs used less material and looked more impressive, besides being more comfortable if possibly not as safe to sail over a fifteen-mile open-sea course. Immensely tickled at my own ingenuity, I had Harold Payson build one. He did it in 154 hours of labor, with around $450 worth of materials, thanks to such economies as making the masts out of a couple of trees that happened to be standing in his back lot.

She sailed very pleasantly, and everything worked after some tinkering; the supplement to the specs will give a good idea of how many mistakes I made, and what kind, but fundamentally she seemed quite sound. Originally there were no latches at the chines, the ends being held down by gravity. This worked in smooth water, but in a certain length of wave the bow would bounce up and fall back with a disconcerting bump; also, once going through a narrow canal in the wake of a string of heavy motorboats, she jackknifed spectacularly in a trough (Amy Payson once said she ought to be called *Switchblade*) and gave me a great fright. The first set of latches failed almost immediately; the second design is shown and seems to be just adequate. The stress on them isn't enormous on paper, but in practice, if they have any play they're quickly jarred to destruction.

I trailed her around a thousand miles behind an Opel Kadette without problems, sailing on Penobscot Bay, Long Island Sound, and points between. We came seventh of fourteen entries in the race she was built for and would have done two or three places better if I hadn't made a string of tactical errors. (The superb Murray Peterson-designed schooner *Agamemnon* was the winner.)

20 THE FOLDING SCHOONERS

Folding schooner ready for the road.

I once folded and unfolded her singlehanded, on challenge, but I dropped her pretty hard at the end of each maneuver and don't recommend it. She's not a sensible choice for a singlehander in the first place, though one man can sail her easily enough by leaving off the jib, which doesn't seem to contribute much for windward work in any case. In strong winds she handles well with reefed mainsail and full foresail. Capsized, she goes clean bottom-up, but can be righted and bailed out afloat, and can be sailed, after a fashion, full of water. This last capability certainly saved the lives of a couple who dumped her in forty-degree water about the end of December.

Her speed makes her wet as sharpies go. Between that and the flimsy bottom she's not to be recommended for open-water work, though there's a man in Alaska who apparently has sailed his in all kinds of horribles without breaking her, so far. Another Alaskan made a cruise down the Yukon River and found her quite appropriate. Lakes and rivers are suitable habitats.

Several have been built using thicker bottoms, and at least one has a ½" thick bottom and ⅜" sides. This makes a less disposable boat. The heavier ones appear to sail at least as well as the light ones, but they cost more and are that much more of a lift to fold up.

Several owners have complained about a lee helm and of trouble tacking. I don't know what caused it in each case, as the first one was perfectly hung, but the recommended extra foot on the main boom will do no harm because the rudder is so far aft that she can stand any amount of weather helm, even sailing to windward under mainsail alone.

The racing rule offered is phrased to provoke, but I'm ready to defend it is an example of a function-based rule (the singlehanded and other crew-limit races are another example), the only legitimate type in my opinion barring a cost-limit rule enforced by claiming races.

The folding schooners are toys and conversation pieces. They're not meant for people who take themselves very seriously, which can be taken as a claim or as an admission according to temperament. The joke is not a sick joke, and a good many people can enjoy it at once considering the storage space it takes up.

The schooner rig was "given" in this case, but I'll observe that it is in fact suitable for long hulls. The main advantage of the rig is that a large part of its area will stand without stiff staying. If you're going to stay it stiffly, as in a staysail schooner, it's generally best to eliminate the foremast and have a cutter. Starling Burgess, who designed the first staysail schooner for rule-cheating reasons, pointed this out about 1926, and I've seen a drawing of that schooner, the *Advance*, rigged as a cutter with huge economies in weight, windage, and cost, and not a solitary drawback except that she would have been excluded from a certain racing class. A secondary advantage of the schooner in its classical form is that the largest sail is aft where it can be hoisted first and lowered last, at relative leisure, without so much tendency for the vessel to start charging around her mooring. It can even be left set fairly safe for hours at anchor. This is why it was the predominant rig among commercial coasters and fishermen, and is still worth considering in sizable coastwise-cruising yachts.

PROPOSED RULES FOR GLOUCESTER SCHOONER CLASS

1. Boats are to be capable of being stored inside a space not more than 15'8" long, by 5'2" wide, by 4'4" high, with no component projecting.
2. Boats, including all components, must be capable of being transported

The designer and Walter Fredrick on Annisquam River. Ought to give the main peak halyard a small pull.

by a highway trailer, and launched from the trailer on any ramp in common use for trailer boats of any type without special equipment or help from non-crewmembers. Races may be required to start from a fully-stowed position on the trailer and clear of the water whenever demanded by any contestant.

3. No component incapable of being separated from the rest shall weigh more than 150 pounds.

4. Boats may be required to demonstrate a capability of being righted and bailed by their crews after being completely swamped, including being re-rigged if the rig must be demounted in righting.

5. Boats protested for inadequate structural strength shall be tested by one kick from the bare toes of the protester at a point of his own choosing, any resulting damage to be the penalty of the protestee for the excessive lightness.

6. If any contestant is detected using his engine, all other contestants may use theirs.

7. Class Secretary (designer until further notice) will issue numbers on receipt of photographic evidence of boat's existence; no variation in design of rig, hull, or construction will be considered grounds for refusal if the above rules are claimed to be met.

KEY TO PLANS

Throughout, "plywood" signifies $\frac{1}{4}''$ thick 4' by 8' sheets of fir or mahogany exterior grade; if marine grade (not supposed to have interior voids) is available, it should be used and the premium paid; if not, voids should be plugged wherever found, and all sheets tested by flexing before installation to show up major defects in the interior veneers.

"Fir" signifies natural wood, and may actually be any stock offering good gluing properties, as for instance mahogany, pine, cedar, or spruce as well as Douglas fir; oak, hard yellow pine, ash, and teak should be avoided. The dimensions noted are supposed to correspond in most cases to standard "dressed lumber" sizes, and are minimum in all cases; they may be increased by an eighth of an inch wherever convenient, allowing for the difference at the bevelled edges shown.

"Screw" signifies, ideally, large diameter bronze or Everdur wood screws, for which other types of screws, or the barbed or ringed nails of various types, may be substituted satisfactorily if the gluing is properly done without holidays due to drying up.

"Glue" must be a waterproof, gap-filling, marine type, resorcinol or epoxy, and must be liberally applied in all joints throughout the construction.

The assembly method described permits the boat to be built without complete lofting or accurate building jig, or more flat area than is needed to lay down an eight by four sheet of plywood. (It's the old and traditional method for building flat-iron skiff hulls, incidentally.) It has the defect that mismeasurements by designer or builder will in many cases not be apparent until assembly is attempted; also that alterations, as for instance a different frame spacing, can not be planned by the builder. A complete set of offsets for conventional lofting

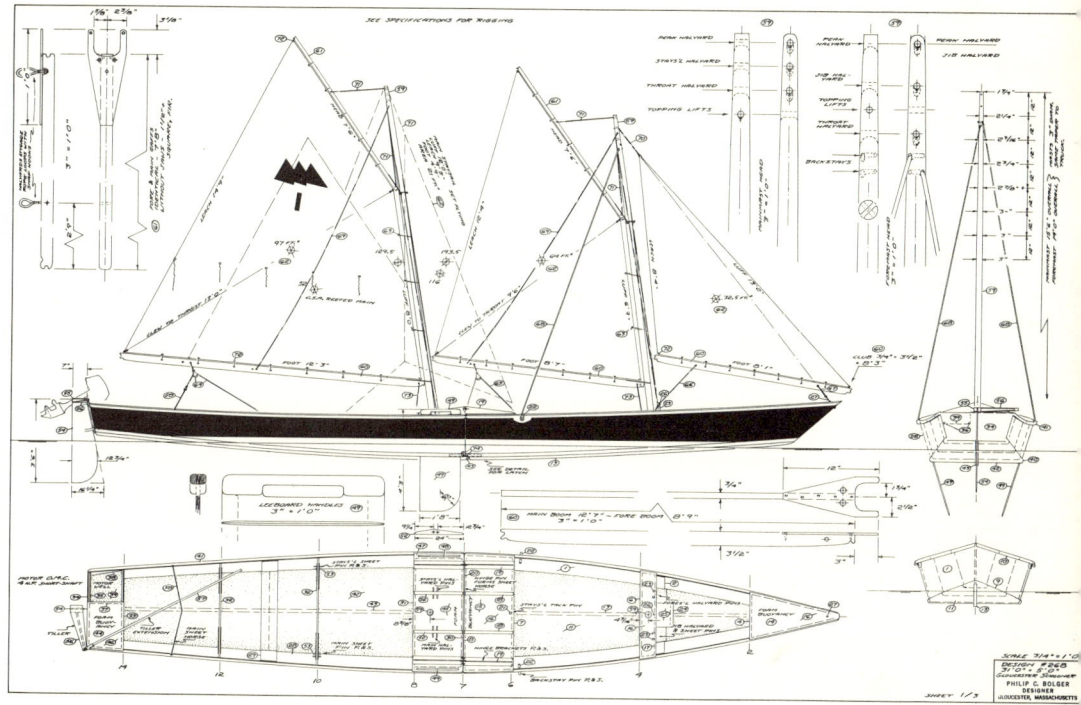

is therefore provided and its use is recommended, especially to anybody not planning to follow the design exactly in materials or arrangements.

1. Forward hull sides made up to pattern from two 2' x 8' sheets each; mark clearly for position of bulkheads, the given marks being for the after side, bevelling being on the forward side in the forward hull.

2. Butt straps 8"-wide plywood, glued and riveted or clinch-nailed.

3. Stem from 1½" x 1½" x 2'8¼" fir; section as shown full size; secure to one of the hull sides with glue and ¾" screws.

4. Bulkhead at station 2, plywood with ¾" x 1½" fir fastening cleats on all sides.

5. Drainage and vent openings at chines in all frames and bulkheads.

6. Bulkhead at station 4, plywood with opening about as shown; ¾" x 1½" cleats sides and top, 1½" x 2½" on bottom; two ¼" bolts near bottom centerline as shown.

7. Bulkhead at station 6, plywood with opening about as shown; ¾" x 1½" cleats all round.

8. Transom of bow hull plywood with ¾" x 1½" cleats on bottom and sides, 1½" x 2½" at top; no opening and no limber holes!

(Bevel bulkheads and stem as given full size on the plan; fasten the second side sheet to the first at the stem, being most careful with alignment as a small mismatch here will be very inconvenient at the other end. Bring the two sides in around the prepared bulkheads and fasten to the transom with glue and 1" screws. Tap the bulkheads into exact position on their marks and into line with

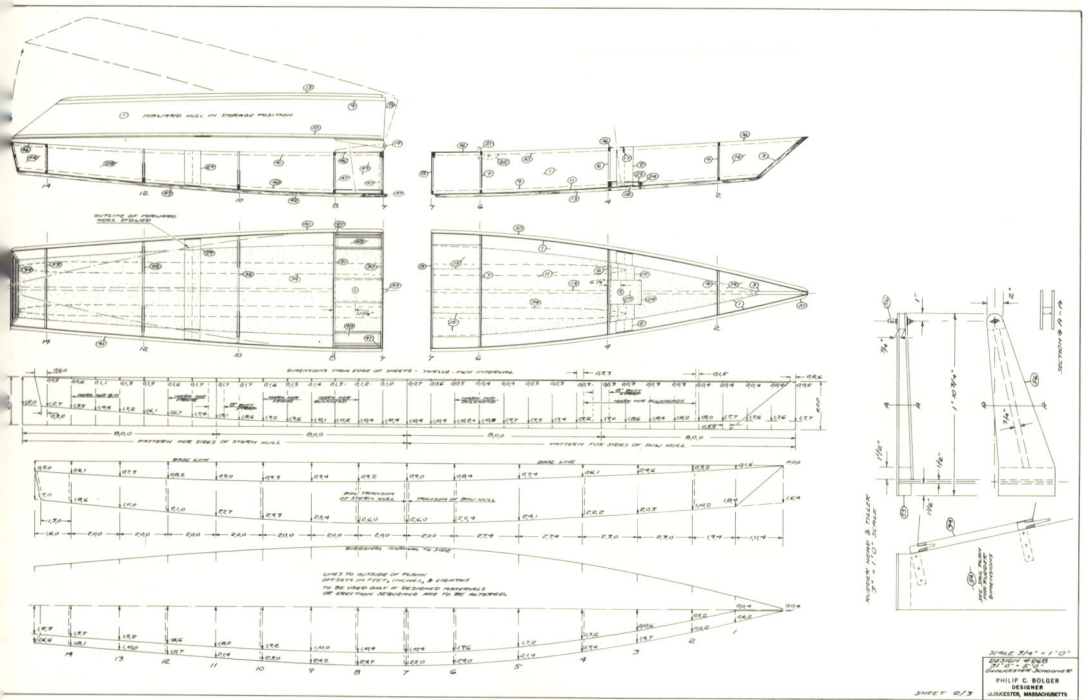

the bottom of the sides, and fasten permanently as with transom.)

9. Chine logs of forward hull ¾" x 1½" fir, bent around over the plywood sides, clamped in place and secured with glue and ¾" screws spaced about four inches or less as needed. Bevel the underside to take the hull bottom sheets.

10. Gunwales from 1½" square fir, bent round outside of side sheets and secured with glue and screws from inside.

11. Forward hull bottom from two lengths of plywood, marked in place for approximate shape, removed, butted, and secured to chine logs, transom, bulkhead cleats, and heel of stem with glue and 1" screws.

12. Bottom butt strap 8"-wide plywood.

(Bottom may be sheathed with one, two, or more layers of 10-ounce glass cloth and polyester resin at builder's or owner's option, or it may be of thicker plywood or two layers of plywood if strength and rigidity is judged more important than light weight.)

13. Shoe 1½" square fir, on centerline from stem to about 1¾" short of transom; one ⅜" x 5" carriage bolt up through the bulkhead bottom cleat at station 4 as shown; 1" screws from inside, and glue, along the rest of the length. (The bolt is to take the thrust of the foremast.)

14. Forepeak filled solid with expanded foam or with blocks cut to fit.

15. Blocks of foam 12" x 12" x 24" or equivalent each side between transom and bulkhead at station 6.

16. Decking plywood; see full-size section for the way the gunwales are bevelled to take the decks; glue and 1" screws as elsewhere.

17. Beam to support forward edge of mast partner $3/4''$ x $2\frac{1}{2}''$ fir.

18. External stiffeners on for'd hull after deck $1\frac{1}{2}''$ square fir; secure these before the deck is installed on the hull, with glue and $1''$ screws from below on not more than about $2''$ spacing.

19. Hinge brackets welded from $1/4''$ x $4''$ steel plate, galvanized; see detail diagram; two $3/8''$ x $4''$ bolts through transom-top cleat, two $2''$ round-head screws to bulkhead #6 top cleat, and six $1/4''$ x $1\frac{1}{2}''$ stove bolts through the deck between.

20. Hinge pin $1/2''$ galvanized rod upset at one end, pinned at the other, running from side to side (about $4'2''$ overall on the plan but fit to placement of brackets) to form foresail sheet horse.

21. Staysail tack pin from $1''$ x $1\frac{1}{2}''$ oak or ash, $1''$ square through deck.

22. Backstay pins $1''$ square oak, ash, or metal, a drive fit through hull side and $1\frac{1}{2}''$ x $2\frac{1}{2}''$ x $9''$ fir padded under gunwale stringer and glued and screwed to side.

23. Pins for foresail halyards and for jib sheet and halyard $3/4''$ x $1\frac{1}{4}''$ oak or ash; $3/4''$ square through deck (see shape on $1\frac{1}{2}''$ scale drawing of bow), a loose fit in the deck.

24. Forward mount of foremast step $1\frac{1}{2}''$ x $1\frac{1}{2}''$ x $12''$ fir, glued to and screwed from the hull bottom.

25. Foremast step $12''$ x $17''$ plywood, glued and screwed down each end.

26. Hole in foremast partner; $1/4''$ rope passes through with stopper knot underneath, eye splice around a thimble close down to the deck on top to form a lead for the jib sheet.

27. Hole through deck and stem with rope eye, similar to #26, for snap hook of jib club pivot rope.

28. After hull sides made up same as forward sides.

29. Butts as in forward hull.

30. Forward transom of after hull identical to after transom of forward hull except that the fastening cleats are on the opposite side.

31. Bulkhead at station 8, plywood with $3/4''$ x $1\frac{1}{2}''$ fir cleats all round; opening about as shown.

32. Frames at stations 10 and 12, each three sections of $3/4''$ x $2\frac{1}{2}''$ fir with double $10''$ plywood chine gussets.

33. Bulkhead at station 14, plywood with $3/4''$ x $1\frac{1}{2}''$ cleats all round; (Note that the dimensions are given to the underside of the deck, but that it is not decked on the port side; i.e. its top should stand about $1/4''$ below the gunwale there when finished; in any case, any inexactness in the matching of frames and bulkheads to the pre-shaped sides should be taken out at the deck or gunwale, leaving the bottom exact.)

34. Stern transom plywood with $3/4''$ x $1\frac{1}{2}''$ fir cleats, including an intermediate cleat to take the heel of the motor well flat.

35. Pad for motor clamps $3/4''$ x $3\frac{1}{2}''$ x $12\frac{3}{4}''$ fir, glued and screwed to transom.

36. About $1/2''$ drain holes through the transom.

37. Motor well inboard side $3/4''$ fir.

38. Cleat on hull side $3/4''$ x $1\frac{1}{2}''$ fir, to take outboard edge of well flat.

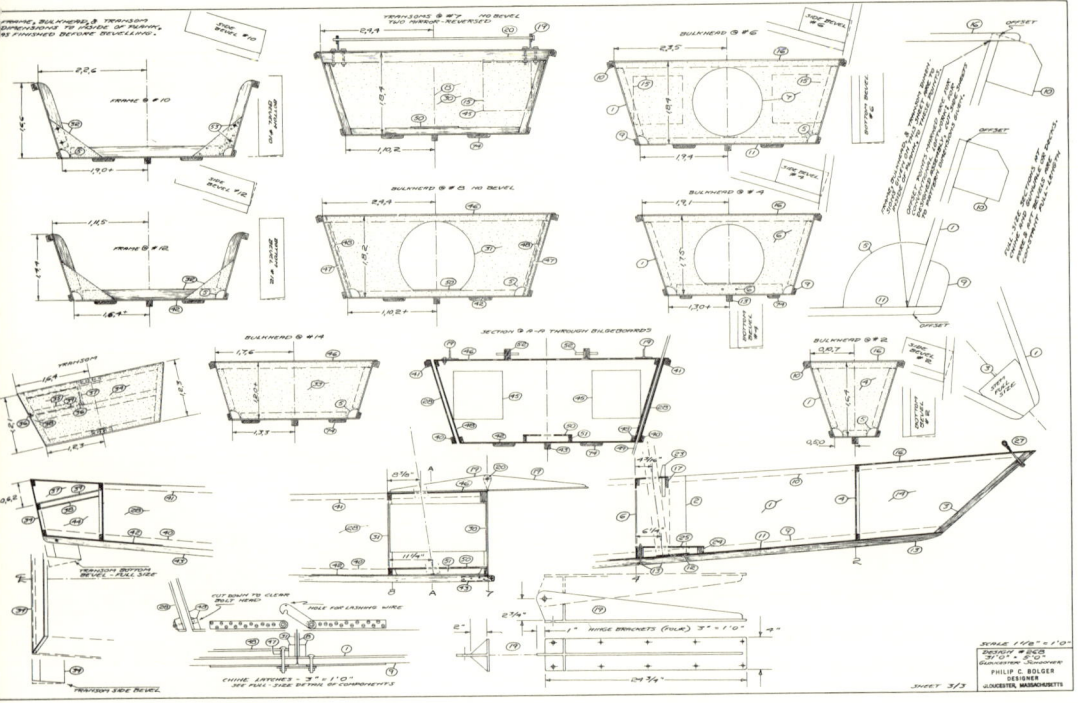

39. Well flat plywood; glue and screw to lower edge of inboard side piece (#37) before installing either.

(Assemble sides on bulkheads and transoms as with forward hull, taking some care to prevent distortion into a parellelogram shape to any noticeable extent.)

40. Chine logs same as in forward hull.

41. Gunwales same as in forward hull.

42. After hull bottom plywood, butted and placed as with forward hull, but should be marked with a clear centerline at right angles to the forward end and used as a square to true up the assembly by making marked centerlines of transoms, bulkheads, and frames match the bottom centerline.

43. After hull shoe $1\frac{1}{2}''$ square fir from stern to $1\frac{1}{2}''$ projection shod with $\frac{1}{16}'' \times 1'' \times 8''$ galvanized straps to engage the trailer winch hook.

44. Space abaft bulkhead at station 14 filled with expanded or cut foam.

45. Foam blocks each side corresponding to note #15 of forward hull.

46. Decking as in forward hull, see #16.

47. Headblocks of bilgeboard cases $\frac{3}{4}'' \times 1''$ fir, glued and screwed to inside of topsides on each side, hard up against transom and bulkhead at station 8.

48. Inboard walls of bilgeboard cases plywood with $\frac{3}{4}'' \times 1\frac{1}{2}''$ fir cleats top and bottom, allowing for bevel; glue and screw to headblocks, and from bottom and deck. (Hull sides form outboard walls of cases.) It might be best to install these cases before the bottom; builder decide on the spot.

49. Bilgeboards double ¼" plywood (may be ½" but the chance of breaking them across an undiscovered core void is greater and the built-in centerline is convenient for fairing and edges). Bilgeboards 1'8" wide and 4'3" long overall; see diagram on sail plan sheet.

50. Mainmast step 12" x 24¾" plywood, glued and screwed with about six 1½" screws at each end to transom and bulkhead frames.

51. Stiffening cleats on each side of step ¾" x 1½" fir, cut away at ends to trap no water.

52. Deck stiffeners from 1½" fir, shaped about as shown on sail plan sheet to take ¾" oak or ash halyard pins.

53. Oak or ash pins for main and staysail sheets each side.

54. Rudder blade same construction as bilgeboards; standard pintles and gudgeons.

55. Blocking at top of rudder 1½" square.

56. Tiller two pieces of ¼" plywood with a spacer as diagrammed on the lines sheet; ¼" x 2" shoulder-eye bolt at the end.

57. Tiller extension 1¼" square spruce, about 7' long, with a spring socket of the type sold for spinnaker poles to engage the tiller eye-bolt.

58. Main sheet horse ½" dacron rope rove through a hole in the gunwale each side, held by stopper knots; leave about a foot of slack.

59. Masts 3" diameter, preferably spruce but may be fir (i.e., anything), tapered at head and drilled for running and standing rigging as shown on the sail plan.

60. Fore and main booms, and jib club, all from ¾" (make ⅞" if readily available, especially if the spars are spruce) by 3½" spruce or fir; lengths and end details about as shown.

61. Fore and main gaffs not less than 1½" or more than 1¾" square spruce or fir; lengths and details, shape of plywood jaws, about as shown on the sail plan sheet.

62. Sails lightweight dacron, cut across or up-and-down according to sailmaker's advice; no roach, no battens; reef points in main spaced as shown, not closer. Secure to gaffs and booms with separate ties, not lacings.

63. Grommets of ⅜" dacron rope instead of mast hoops; use no more than the three and two shown.

64. Main sheet ⅜" dacron about 20' long; snap hook to traveller horse; plastic-shell 2¼" sheave-diameter block on rope sling to boom.

65. Foresail sheet same as main.

66. Jib sheet ¼" x 12'; knot or eye splice to club, through thimble on pennant #26, to pin #23.

67. Jib club pivot rope ⅜", spliced loop seized between club and snap hook to pennant eye near stem.

68. Foremast backstays ⅜" x 14' dacron; stopper knots at holes in masthead; belayed on pins #22; about 6' x ¼" tail with a snap hook to an eye plate (not shown) on or near bulkhead at station 4 to secure the lee (slack) backstay. (Backstays are needed only to set up the jib against sagging when working to windward; the mast will stand without them on all points of sailing.)

69. Topping lifts of foresail and mainsail ¼" dacron, each in one piece

28 THE FOLDING SCHOONERS

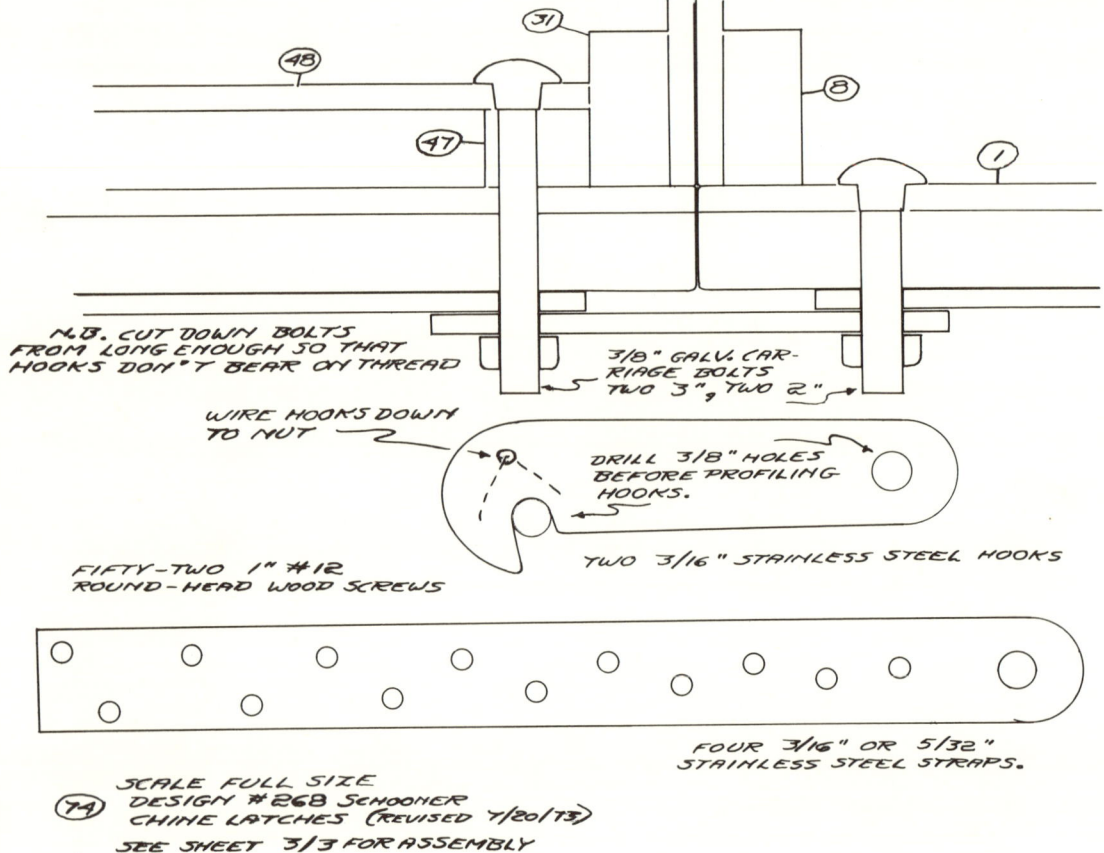

with stopper knots each side of masthead hole and at the ends to hold and adjust the lifts through holes in the booms.

70. Jib halyard $3/8''$ dacron.

71. Fore and main throat and peak halyards, and main staysail halyard, $1/4''$ dacron, running in well-faired $3/4''$ diameter holes in the mastheads as shown; belayed on pins as shown. Main staysail sheet also $1/4''$, single, to be brought around when the sail is lowered for tacking.

72. Outhauls, throat and tack lashings, etc., all $3/16''$ braided nylon.

73. Downhauls $1/4''$ from booms to pins or cleats at bulkheads at stations 4 and 8.

Revision notes (refer to Plans Key)

Instruction note following #6: Side bevel is shown backwards; bevel should come off plywood side.

#8: Some builders may find it easier to secure forward sides first at transom rather than at the stem; note the necessity of a marked centerline at right angles to the end of the bottom sheet, to use the bottom as a square to true up the alignment with marked centerlines on transoms and frames.

#11 and #42: Bottom of unsheathed ¼" exterior plywood is extremely flexible, with eventual fatigue failure possible; see added note #74 and drawings for exterior reinforcement for ¼" bottoms. One layer of glass cloth is recommended, carried to the tops of the chine logs; apply glass before installing shoe (#13) or reinforcing planks (#74).

#20: Sharpen pin end of hinge rod to make installation easier.

#22: Make all pins round.

#26: Set stopper knot to bring eye as close to deck as possible.

#30: Forward transom of after hull should have a very slight bevel to the forward face (i.e., after side biggest) of not more than $\frac{1}{16}$".

#35: Insert ¾" x 3½" x 15" fir doubling pad inside motor-mount area (designed transom top is too thin to take up motor clamps, and plywood buckled at inboard edge of hull side fastening cleat).

#43: Abolish this fitting; stop shoes flush with transoms; haul up to a hook fitted to *after* end of after hull shoe.

#52: Fasten stiffeners from below at not over 3" intervals, besides glue to top of deck.

#54: Sharpen trailing edge of rudder about the same as leading edge (square trailing edge chatters if pintles are loose in gudgeons). Also make sure rudder is mounted high enough for end of tiller to have ample clearance in swinging over transom; recess bolt head #56 into tiller end to help in this.

#56: Optionally, two spacers, at edges of plywood, to make a box section; less liable to be damaged.

#58: Make horse rope ⅜".

#61: Cut back jaw plywood so that friction with mast is taken by the end of the gaff when peaked up; not to lift veneers in lowering.

#63: Fit ties with a stopper knot each side of luff grommets and secure with a reef knot on forward side of mast (see note on #71).

#64 and #65: Sheets may be ¼" and blocks smaller.

#69: Splice a rope loop through the two topping lift holes in each boom; put a snap lock in the ends of the lifts each side, so the lifts can be detached from the booms while the masts are stepped.

#70: Jib halyard to engage head of jib with a snap hook, or a knot, to be easily detached; make halyard not less than 24' long.

#71: All halyards to engage loops on gaffs with snap hooks as shown on gaff detail. (It's necessary to be able to detach sails, booms, and gaffs from the masts easily and quickly as otherwise a horrible tangle results which delays re-erection. System should be: 1. lower sails; 2. detach topping lifts, halyards, and luff ties; 3. collect ends of halyards, backstays, and topping lifts, tie them together to make complete loops, and lash them all loosely to their masts; 4. furl sails in separate bundles on their booms and gaffs; and 5. lift out masts and, for trailering, stow in after hull, starboard side. It's helpful in rigging if the various lines are color-coded with thread or paint so they can be identified without looking aloft for the lead.)

#72: Indications are that performance would benefit by adding a foot to the foot of the mainsail, making foot dimension 13′3″, the clew-to-throat diagonal 13′9″, mainsail area 103 square feet, the boom 13′7″, and leach 15′1″.

#73: The downhauls seem to be unnecessary.

#74: Bottom reinforcing planks: ¾″ x 5½″, laid with inboard edges 8″ outboard of centerline (i.e., 16″ apart); on forward hull about eight feet long; on after hull about 15′2″ long, with ends tapered about as shown; glue to bottom and screw from inside with ¾″ screws spaced 3″ or 4″ apart and well staggered. This reinforcement is unnecessary if ⅜″ plywood is used for bottoms but is a more efficient solution than the thicker bottom both in rigidity and protection. In increasing structural weights, avoid adding weight to the forward end of the forward hull where it will increase the effort of folding and unfolding; on trial the designed structure proved perfectly rigid except for "give" in certain areas of the bottom when walked on heavily.

Unfolding: should not be done on the trailer. The boat should be slid off the trailer still folded, preferably straight into the water; when afloat, turn her around with the "middles" toward the shore, haul up as far as convenient, and then unfold her; reverse process for folding.

5
A COLD-WATER SAILBOARD

15'9" x 3'11"

This doesn't look much like a sailboard, but it did start with a request for a sailboard to use in cold water, to keep one's bottom dry, in fact. The obvious thing to do was to make it bigger and higher-sided, but that made it too heavy, the weight of the deck being the problem in all such designs. It's not supported by water pressure like the hull bottom, so it has to be either thick or stiffly framed. Or foamed, of course, but foam weighs something (I wonder how a unicellular foam blown up with hydrogen instead of air would behave?) and it's not free.

It occurred to me that if the decked, watertight volume were kept to a short length in the middle, there'd be enough buoyancy and stability. The rest of it could be just shrouding to smooth up the water flow around a four-by-eight raft. The ends would bail themselves pretty dry under way with suction bailers. At rest there'd be standing water, but not much of it. With the scuppers plugged, there'd be a high-sided open boat with any amount of room. If water got into her it could be bailed out the usual way, or allowed to run out the drains by tipping the ends up — stand aft to drain the bow, forward to drain the stern. She couldn't be completely swamped like an open boat, but the people could usually keep dry and it wouldn't be so easy to slide off her as it is in a flush-decked board.

I think the plumb ends and vertical sides are the most efficient in this type of boat. Flared sides and raked ends don't seem to do any good except for looks, and for a slightly more economical use of plywood. I usually do use some flare and rake for the same reason I gave this one some sheer: I couldn't stand the looks of the functionally correct sheer which would be dead straight and level. I guess I could save one sheet of plywood by using a straight sheer, which makes me uneasy but not enough so to do it for publication.

The boomed spritsail not only offers a large sail area on short spars

On the edge of the Mississippi.

(cheap to buy, handy to store) but puts the area where she can carry it best. I've found that these rigs without halyards work very well, except that they can't be effectively reefed unless you go into some such contortions as for the arrangement in *Dovekie* (see Chapter 24). Boats in this class never seem to reef anyway; if they can't lug whole sail, they don't go out. Dropping the peak will ease them suddenly, but they won't sail on the wind with it down.

The mast with long axis athwartships seems promising to me from an aerodynamic standpoint. The large detail shows how it's supposed to work, and it seems obvious that it fairs the air flow into the sail better than any other non-rotating shape. Unfortunately for science, the boat is in Minnesota; I'm in Massachusetts. Dr. Messick, who built her, says she seems fast, and probably that's all I'd be able to say if I went out there myself with tufting, smoke trails, and all. She could hardly help being fast, considering her proportions and sail area.

Material cost was $215 in 1975, not counting the sail; say about half that of a store-bought sailboard of similar performance and a good deal less capacity.

A COLD-WATER SAILBOARD

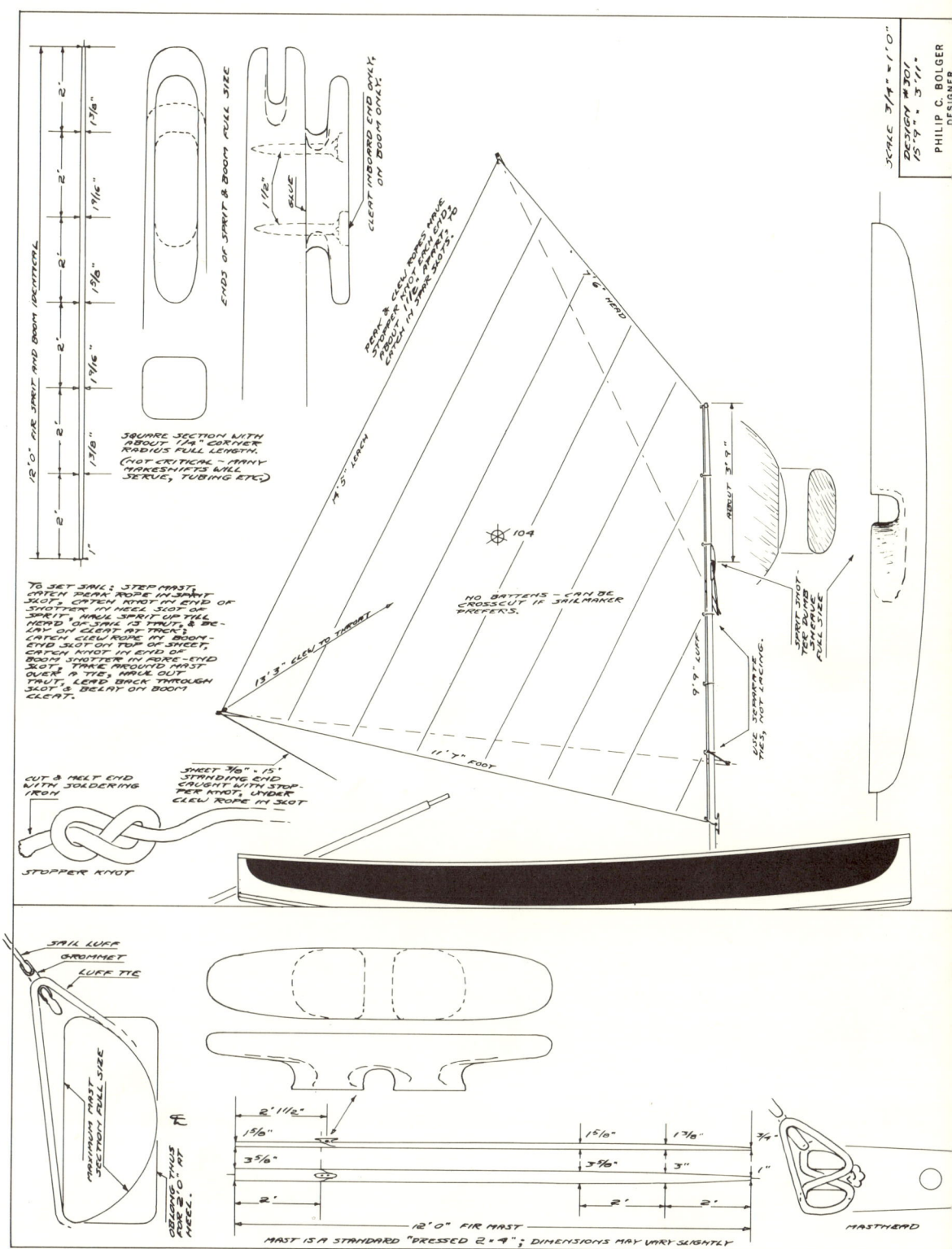

A COLD-WATER SAILBOARD

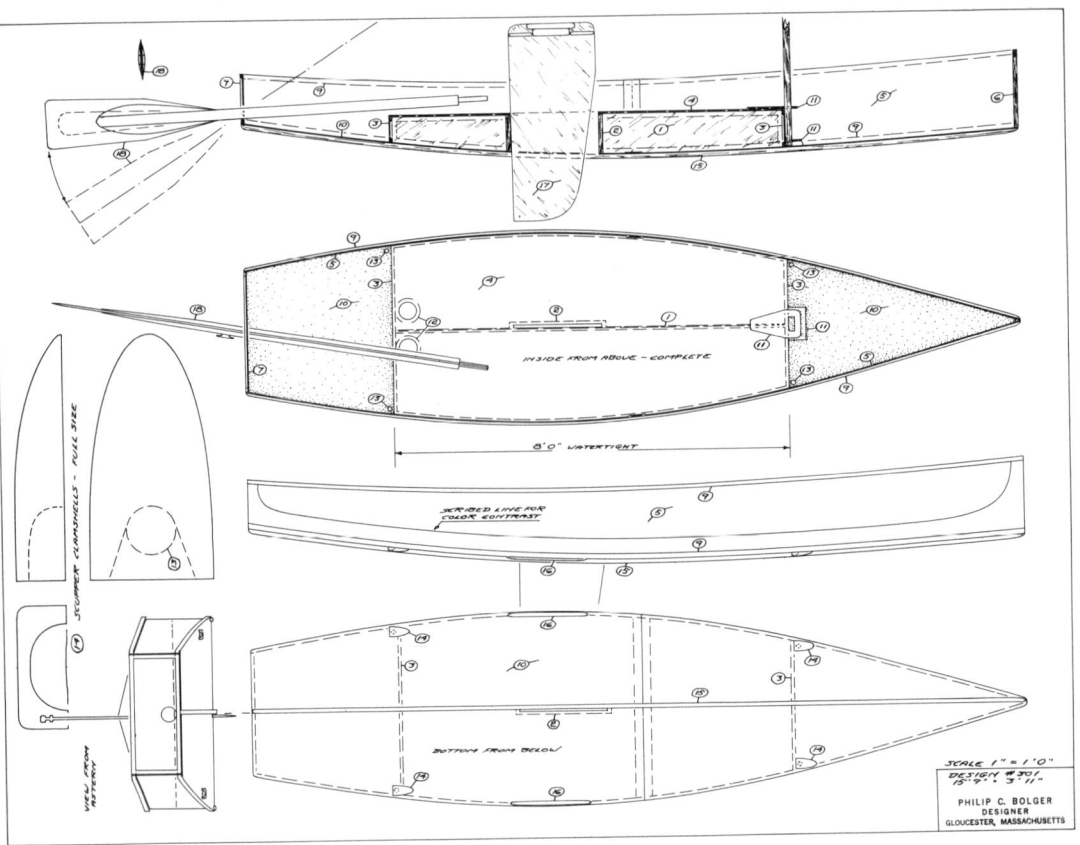

KEY TO PLANS

1. Center web ¼" plywood to given dimensions; ½" x 1" fastening frame all around on starboard side.
2. Daggerboard trunk ¼" plywood; ½" x 1" framing on side away from center web; ¾" x 1" headblocks from spacers to web; mount on port side.
3. Bulkheads ¼" plywood; ½" x 1" framing.
4. Deck ½" plywood; ½" square fastening frame sprung around sides. (Nail bulkheads to ends of center web; nail and glue deck to top of assembly; bare side of center web should come on marked centerline.)
5. Sides ¼" plywood with 4" butt straps as diagrammed.
6. Stem ½" x 1", secured to one side plank and bevelled.
7. Transom ¼" plywood; ½" x 1" framing on outside; 3½" diameter hole for steering sweep.
8. Spring sides around deck and bulkheads; nail and glue to them; pull in, nail and glue to transom, and fasten together at stem.
9. Chine log and gunwale clamp ½" x 1"; glue and nail to sides.
10. Put ¼" plywood bottom in place; mark out shape at sides, remove, assemble on 4" butt strap, and glue and nail in place. (N.B. — bottom can be

A COLD-WATER SAILBOARD

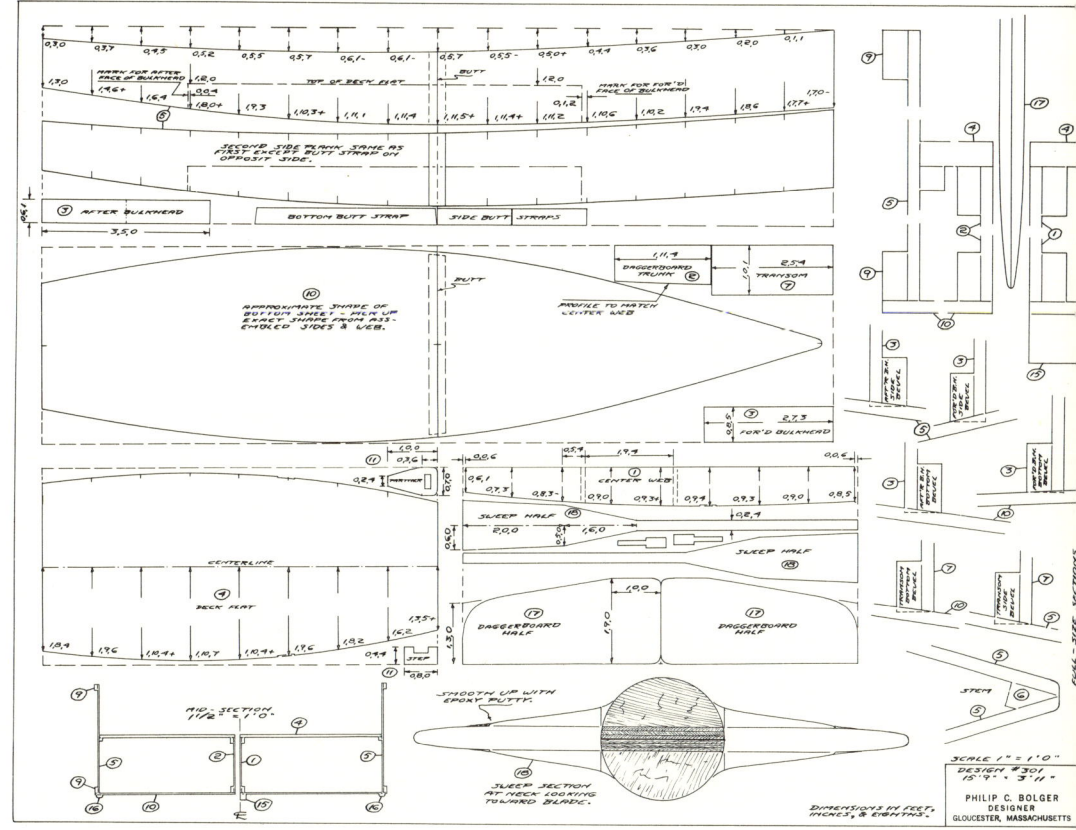

⅜" if preferred; if so, other components on same sheet can be so as well.)

11. Mast partner and step ½" plywood; step rests on 1" square cleats.

12. Access holes, preferably at least 6" diameter; can be screw plates or something like plastic coffee-can covers.

13. Scuppers about 1" diameter; can be fitted with corks or plugs to make ends of boat dry and buoyant in absence of spray or rain.

14. Aft-facing scoops for self-bailing; shown full size.

15. Shoe 1" square hardwood.

16. Protective cleats ½" x 1".

17. Daggerboard double ¼" plywood, sharpened on exposed edges, with ½" grip and stops at top; drill holes to suit for pins to hold board at various raised points to taste.

18. Steering sweep double ¼" plywood full length of nine feet; 1" x 2½" stiffeners and fairings each side, rounded off and faired about as shown; all glued up; edges of blade faired somewhat. (N.B. — steering is done by twisting the grip, not by pushing or pulling it like a tiller; this sweep can be used with blade and grip in a wide range of positions to suit heeling angle, etc. It'd be just as well to have a lanyard with a snap hook somewhere on the sweep so it can be released without being pulled inboard.)

6
A MINIMUM KAYAK

> 11'5" x 1'11"

This was made to sell as a plan to the likes of a high-school woodworking student: minimum material cost and working time for a result that could be used with some real satisfaction. I notice that practically everybody is intrigued by the appearance of a kayak* and tempted to try one.

They do frighten people as well, and with some reason. Types that you can't get out of easily, or any kayak used far offshore or in cold water, leave a fairly small margin for carelessness. I make a point of sobriety in them myself. I think, though, that the danger is so obvious that few people get trapped by it, and since I taught myself to sit loosely above the waist and let the boat roll around under me I've not had any close calls that I'm aware of. That's the reason, by the way, why a boat of this type should never have a back rest or anything of that nature that would tend to pull your upper body over with the roll of the boat; for two or three hours of paddling (that's about as long as most people would want to sit down), the back doesn't seem to get stiff or tired, perhaps because the paddle tends to pull it forward.

At any rate, this design with its big open cockpit is meant to be used in warm water, or if the water's somewhat cold, at least where it's smooth, shallow, and close to shore, so if the occupant loses her balance she can bail out at once and swim for it. This leaves me with a somewhat better conscience than furnishing a diagram on how to do the Greenland Roll. Anybody interested in pursuing expertise could do well to get in touch with Bart

---

*The late L. Francis Herreshoff used to insist that the word "kayak" applied only to a fabric-stretched-on-a-frame type; this boat he would call a decked double-paddle canoe. I tend to agree, but the phrase is too clumsy and the distinction too nice to hold.

"How does a commercial fisherman try a kayak?"
"Nervously."

Hauthaway, 640 Boston Post Road, Weston, Massachusetts 02193, who teaches kayaking and builds kayaks and related items, and is a, if not the, leading expert on the subject. While you're at it write the Superintendent of Documents, U.S. Government Printing Office, Washington, D.C. 20402 USA, and see if he still sells *The Bark Canoes and Skin Boats of North America* (Smithsonian Institution Bulletin 230) for $3.50 as he did for awhile. If so, get it, because it's a large, hardbound book full of fascinating drawings (including a diagram on how to do the Greenland Roll) by Howard Chapelle, and at that price you may take it that you've already paid a good part of the money, in taxes, that the book cost to produce and publish, and you may as well pay the small remainder and get something good for your money.

As I'm writing this I hear that the U.S. Coast Guard is thinking of prohibiting the sale of kayaks because they're afraid they'll be blamed if some citizen should chance to drown herself in one, as no doubt she would in some quarters. This kind of government concern tends to make one think of emigrating, except that every other country I've tried myself, or have heard of, is worse. Come to think of it, I suppose the present overpowering public concern for safety of the body is no more nuisance than former concern for the soul, so maybe the present fashion will also pass.

A MINIMUM KAYAK

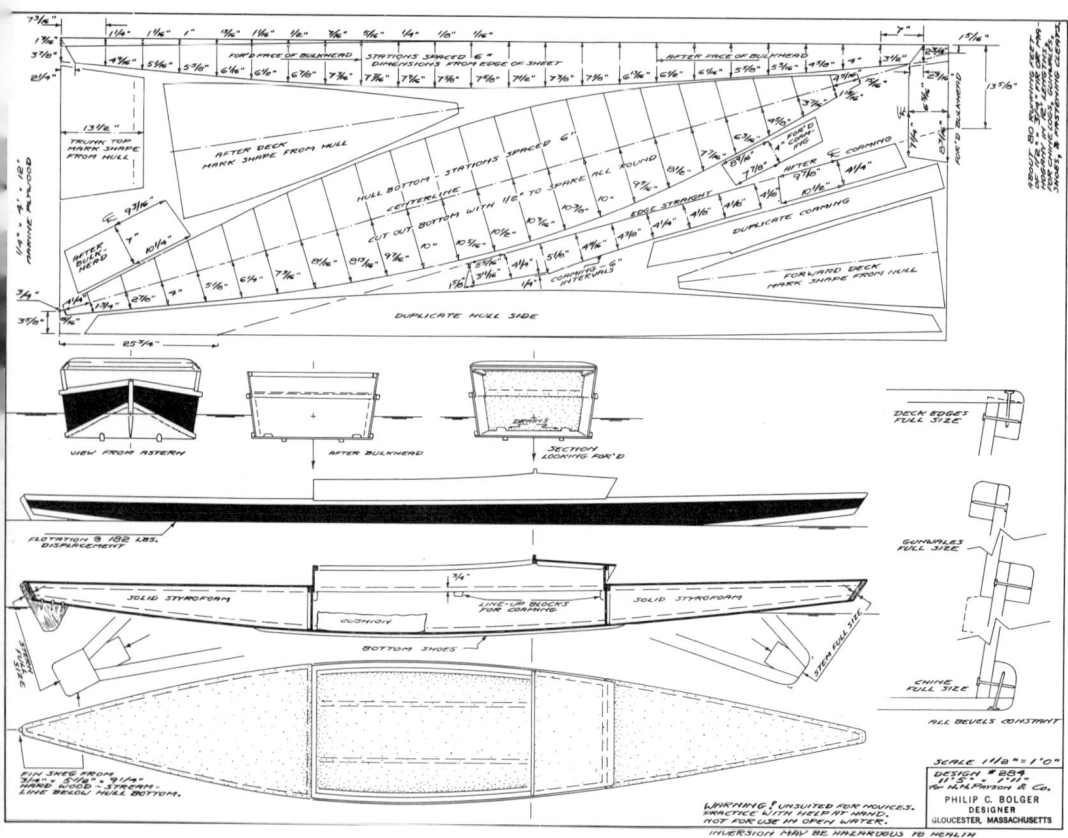

7
NAVEL JELLY

31'0" x 4'3"

Gary Gerber called me on a Friday, to see if I'd lend him my folding schooner to compete in The Great Race at Westfield, Connecticut. It seemed that this race involved running some distance to the river, rowing or paddling downstream and off to a certain island where a bag of trash of specified size had to be collected (I gathered there was no question of a shortage of trash) and brought back upriver to a "recycling center." Gary and his friends reckoned that a numerous team could collect the trash faster, and that the long schooner could carry them all easily. I thought the schooner was too heavy for the purpose, and had sold her by that time in any case, but I offered to design them a disposable racer they could throw together cheaply for a split of the prize money. He went away to discuss it with his crew.

Sunday he called back to agree to the proposition. Having ruminated about it in the meantime I went straight to work. Thursday I sent them this drawing and the key that follows; Friday they got it and studied the scheme; Saturday they bought the materials in local stores; Saturday night they began work; Monday the boat was launched into Gary's swimming pool for a trial; Tuesday they rowed on the river and made some adjustments and alterations; Wednesday they handsomely won the race against a motley field of ninety-odd teams.

The boat weighed 182 pounds and cost about a dollar a pound, all materials bought retail. It averaged nearly four and a half miles per hour over a seven-mile course, carrying more than six times its own weight. The second finisher, a big canoe with three paddlers, was only six-odd minutes behind, but it was generally agreed that the three had worked harder than the seven.

The ten-foot, two-handed oars shown on the drawing were not to be found for sale in time (judging from some manufactured oars of that length

40 NAVEL JELLY

Victory in sight.

I bought later myself, it was just as well; every one in the pile was warped, and a crooked oar is a heart-breaking thing to work with) I hurriedly designed some makeshift oars but time ran out. Seven-foot oars could be bought or borrowed; somebody on the team saw that with plank outriggers laid diagonally across the gunwale for bow and stroke oars they could pull six pairs. It could well be that with this arrangement she was faster than she would have been as designed. I understand one man alone can get her along quite well if it's dead calm and smooth.

That was a highly satisfactory episode, good for the egos of: Peter Kappel (captain), Harry Groves, Bob Bourke, Jim Richardson, Gary Gerber, Arvid Brondstrom, and Bill Ricketts. Also that of the designer. It leaves a kindly feeling for the Schlitz Beer Company, who put up the prize.

ASSEMBLY SEQUENCE

Materials required: six sheets of $1/4''$ x 4' x 8' exterior AA fir plywood; about two hundred running feet, more or less according to wastage, of $3/4''$ x $1\frac{1}{2}''$ (dressed 1 x 2) spruce or fir; about fifty feet of $3/4''$ x $5\frac{1}{2}''$ (dressed 1 x 6) preferably fir; about twenty feet of $3/4''$ square fir; five gross of $7/8''$ #12 Anchorfast nails or equivalent; one gross of $1\frac{1}{4}''$ #12 nails; about five quarts (a wild guess as quantity varies wildly with wastage) of resorcinol marine glue or the equivalent epoxy (better but more expensive). Also four ash oars not less than eight feet and preferably nine or ten feet, two five-foot paddles, and three or four large plastic buckets.

Cut out hull sides from diagrams and assemble on butt straps into two streight-edged planks 16" wide and 31'5" long; butts may be glued only, or may use copper clinch nails or small bolts.

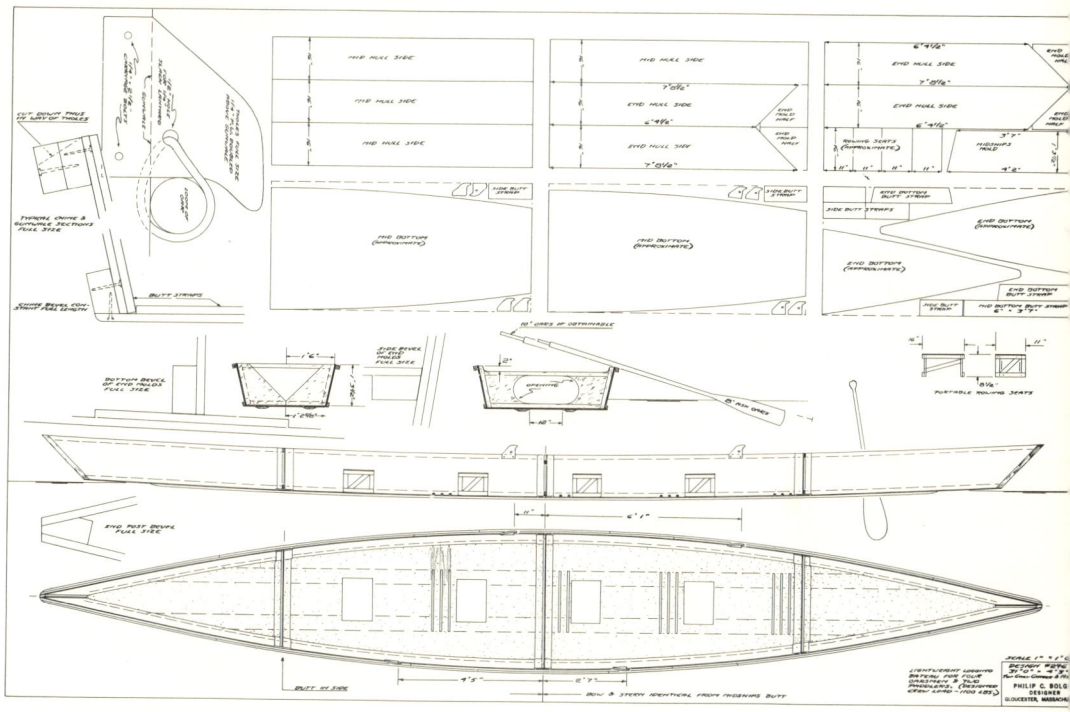

Bevel end posts from full-size diagram and nail and glue each to one side plank.

Make up midship mold and two identical end molds from diagrams; dimensions given are overall and allow for thickness of butt straps; see full-size diagrams for bevel of end molds.

Set up sides on edge parallel on each side of midships mold and nail them to the mold, with mold centered on plywood butt.

Bring ends together simultaneously, inserting end molds with plywood (larger) face towards midships and lined up with side butts; nail and glue sides to molds and to each other at end posts.

Spring gunwales around top edge of sides in two courses of 3/4" x 1 1/2" as shown, staggering butts well clear of each other and of plywood butts; clamp, nail at about 6" intervals, and glue. (In this process, take pains to see that the hull stays symmetrical; mark a centerline on each mold and check frequently that the centerlines of the molds, and the end posts, are lined up; the plywood will be very limp and the gunwales will hold any distortion introduced.)

Spring chine logs around in same way as gunwales but in one course only (get the butts in these logs as tight as possible; should really be scarfed) and bevelled to full-size diagram given.

Turn assembly bottom-up (handling it *gently* with many hands); mark out bottom sheets to actual shape, cut out and install; nail to chine logs on not more than 6" spacing and don't spare the glue here as it is the most critical joint in the structure; she will leak and may break up if there are holidays. (The bottom

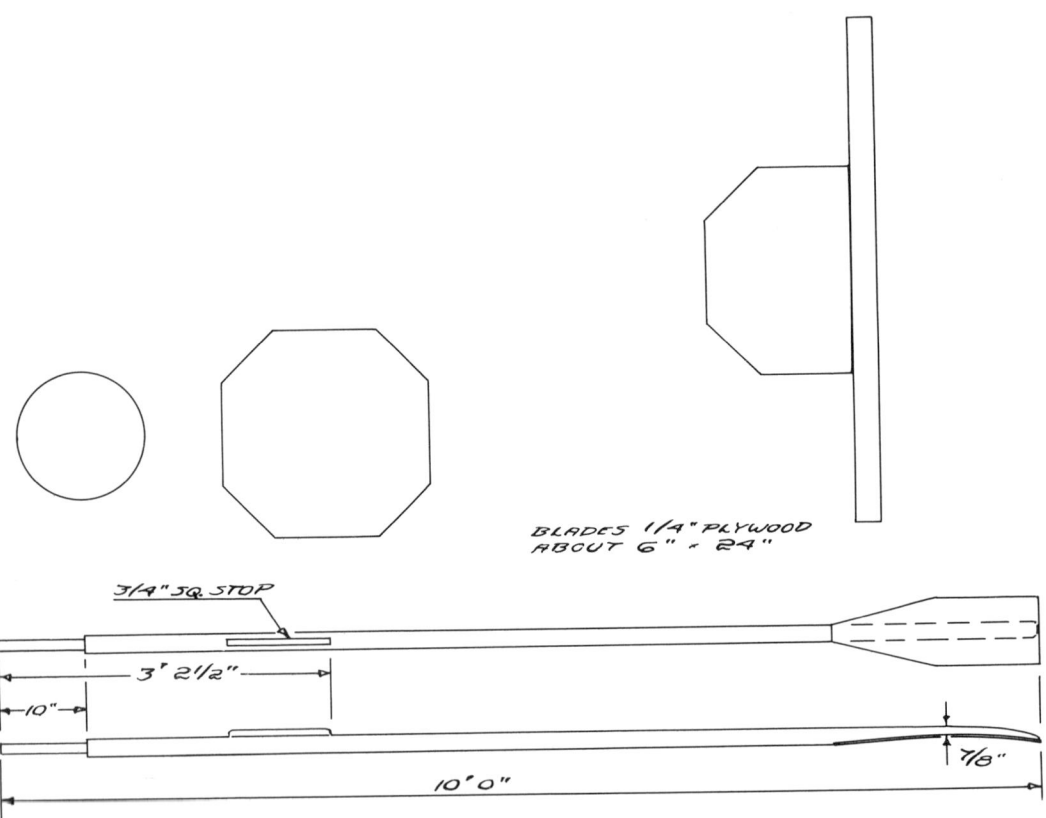

butt straps can either be made first and nailed to the molds, or the bottom sheets can be assembled on them; I think the former would be best.)

Make up bottom shoes, bevelled about as shown, and glue on with nails from inside on about 6″ spacing, well staggered. (Gluing here can be slap-dash but some glue is essential as these are meant for local stiffening as well as overall tension members.)

Make and place tholes, which are double ¼″ plywood glued and bolted to sides; see full-size pattern.

Rowing seats can be plywood tops with ¼″ x 1½″ legs and bracing about as shown, or could be camp stools cut down to a suitable height, or some cardboard boxes with glued-in stiffening, or inverted buckets, or whatever suggests itself. The thing to keep in mind is to avoid having the weight of the rower concentrated on a small foot on the ¼″ hull bottom; the seats should have fairly long skids or the equivalent and should as far as possible rest on the areas backed by the external shoes.

The foot braces are just ¾″ square cleats fastened down into the bottom shoes with a screw at each end; screws are used so they can be moved if necessary to suit the individual oarsmen.

This boat should be stepped into only when she's afloat, and as far as possible the crew should avoid stepping heavily near the chines especially.

8
TOY RIVERBOAT

$$20'5'' \times 8'0''$$

This conversation piece was meant to carry paying passengers on a dammed-up stretch of the Ipswich River, a stream barely out of the brook class, but pretty to look at. She's the aquatic equivalent of a carnival merry-go-round, a toy for small children and nostalgic adults.

The hull assembly went together neatly; a nice, imaginative job was made of the gingerbread and joinery, better than the plans show in detail. The diesel engine was replaced by an electric motor and battery system designed by Transportation Systems Laboratories of Bedford, Massachusetts, a firm that produced impressive electric automobiles. The bearings and gears were neatly worked out. Then for some reason not told to me she was placed on the riverbank, covered with a tarpaulin, and never launched. So I don't know if she would float, let alone how well my blind stabs at wheel diameter, paddle dip and area, and gearing ratios might have worked out.

I thought she might make four miles per hour at thirty rpm's at the

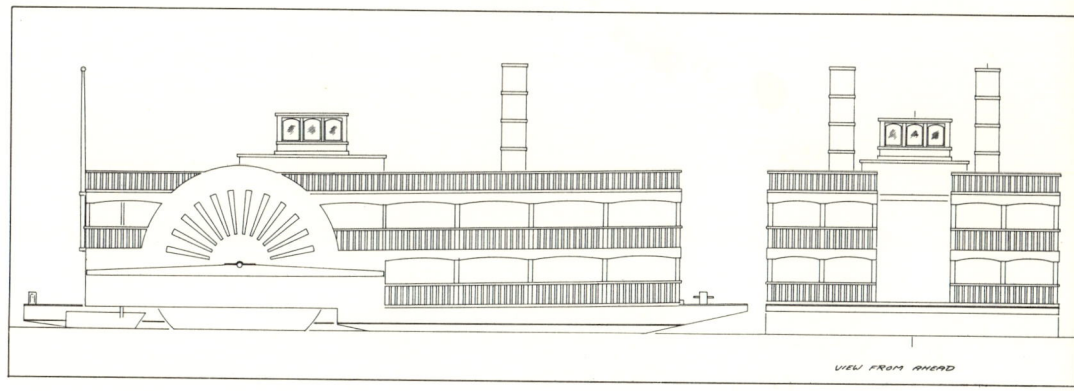

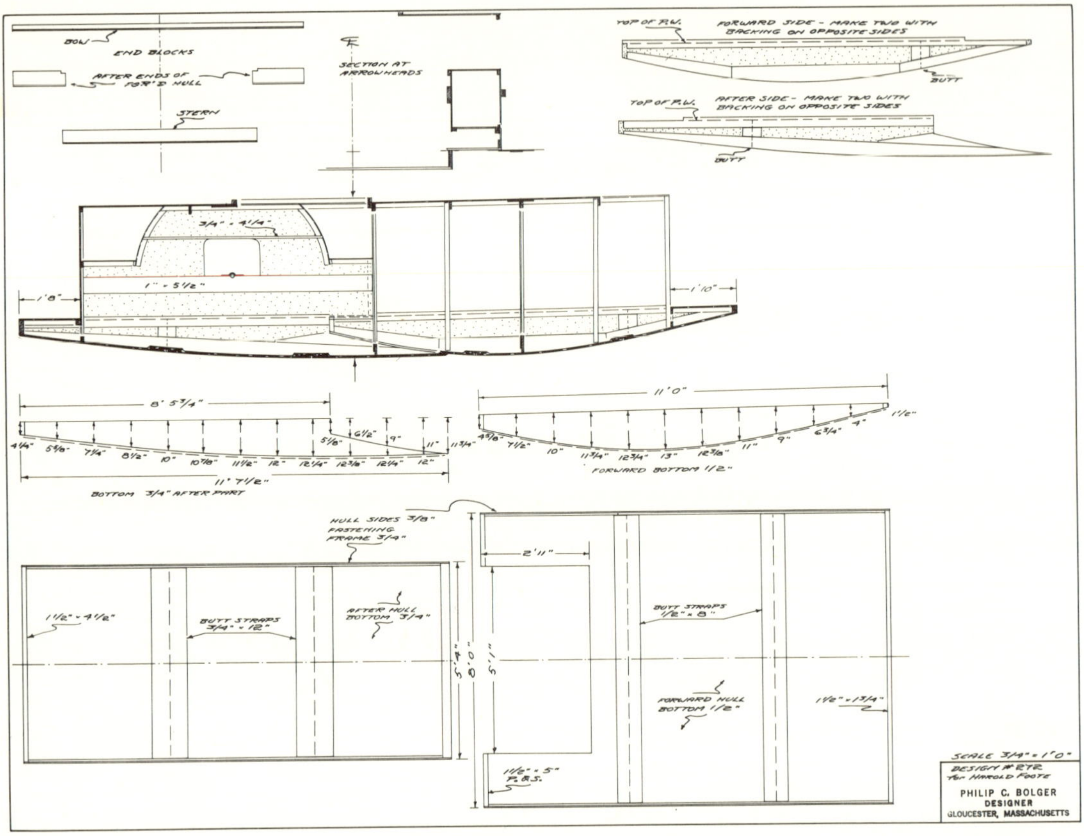
BOW
END BLOCKS
AFTER ENDS OF FOR'D HULL
STERN
SECTION AT ARROWHEADS
TOP OF P.W.
FORWARD SIDE - MAKE TWO WITH BACKING ON OPPOSITE SIDES
BUTT
TOP OF P.W.
AFTER SIDE - MAKE TWO WITH BACKING ON OPPOSITE SIDES
BUTT
3/4" × 4 1/4"
1" × 5 1/2"
1'8"
1'10"
8' 5 3/4"
4 1/4"
5 5/8"
7 1/4"
8 1/2"
10"
10 7/8"
11 1/2"
12"
12 1/4"
12 3/8"
12 1/4"
12"
5/8"
6 1/2"
9"
11"
11 3/4"
11' 7 1/2"
BOTTOM 3/4" AFTER PART
11'0"
4 5/8"
7 1/2"
10"
11 3/4"
12 3/4"
13"
12 3/8"
11"
9"
6 3/4"
4"
1 1/2"
FORWARD BOTTOM 1/2"
HULL SIDES 3/8" FASTENING FRAME 3/4"
1 1/2" × 4 1/2"
BUTT STRAPS 3/4" × 12"
AFTER HULL BOTTOM 3/4"
5'4"
8'0"
5'1"
2'11"
BUTT STRAPS 1/2" × 8"
FORWARD HULL BOTTOM 1/2"
1 1/2" × 1 3/4"
1 1/2" × 5" P.&S.
SCALE 3/4" = 1'0"
DESIGN #272 for HAROLD FOOTE
PHILIP C. BOLGER
DESIGNER
GLOUCESTER, MASSACHUSETTS

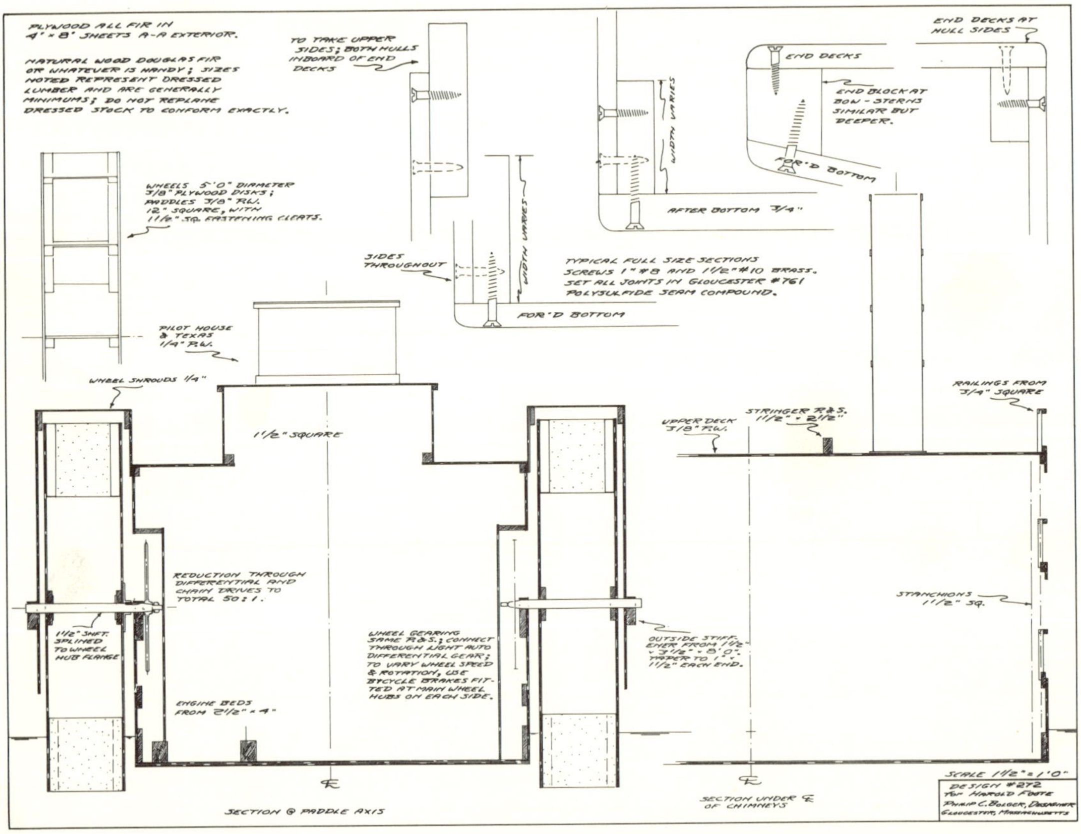
PLYWOOD ALL FIR IN 4' × 8' SHEETS A-A EXTERIOR.
NATURAL WOOD DOUGLAS FIR OR WHATEVER IS HANDY; SIZES NOTED REPRESENT DRESSED LUMBER AND ARE GENERALLY MINIMUMS; DO NOT REPLANE DRESSED STOCK TO CONFORM EXACTLY.
TO TAKE UPPER SIDES; BOTH HULLS INBOARD OF END DECKS
END DECKS
END DECKS AT HULL SIDES
WIDTH VARIES
END BLOCK AT BOW - STERNS SIMILAR BUT DEEPER.
FOR'D BOTTOM
AFTER BOTTOM 3/4"
WHEELS 5'0" DIAMETER 3/8" PLYWOOD DISKS; PADDLES 3/8" P.W. 12" SQUARE, WITH 1 1/2" SQ. FASTENING CLEATS.
SIDES THROUGHOUT
WIDTH VARIES
FOR'D BOTTOM
TYPICAL FULL SIZE SECTIONS SCREWS 1" #8 AND 1 1/2" #10 BRASS. SET ALL JOINTS IN GLOUCESTER #761 POLYSULFIDE SEAM COMPOUND.
PILOT HOUSE & TEXAS 1/4" P.W.
WHEEL SHROUDS 1/4"
1 1/2" SQUARE
REDUCTION THROUGH DIFFERENTIAL AND CHAIN DRIVES TO TOTAL 50:1.
1 1/2" SHFT. SPLINED TO WHEEL HUB FLANGE
WHEEL GEARING SAME P.&S.; CONNECT THROUGH LIGHT AUTO DIFFERENTIAL GEAR; TO VARY WHEEL SPEED & ROTATION, USE BICYCLE BRAKES FITTED AT MAIN WHEEL HUBS ON EACH SIDE.
ENGINE BEDS FROM 2 1/2" × 4"
OUTSIDE STIFFENER FROM 1 1/2" × 3 1/2" × 8'0" TAPER TO 1" × 1 1/2" EACH END.
SECTION @ PADDLE AXIS
UPPER DECK 3/8" P.W.
STRINGER P.&S. 1 1/2" × 2 1/2"
RAILINGS FROM 3/4" SQUARE
STANCHIONS 1 1/2" SQ.
SECTION UNDER ℄ OF CHIMNEYS
SCALE 1 1/2" = 1'0"
DESIGN #272 for HAROLD FOOTE
PHILIP C. BOLGER, DESIGNER
GLOUCESTER, MASSACHUSETTS

TOY RIVERBOAT   45

wheels, with five brake horsepower, the last figure being the really dubious one. I was ready to be mildly apologetic if I were proved to be 25 percent wrong.

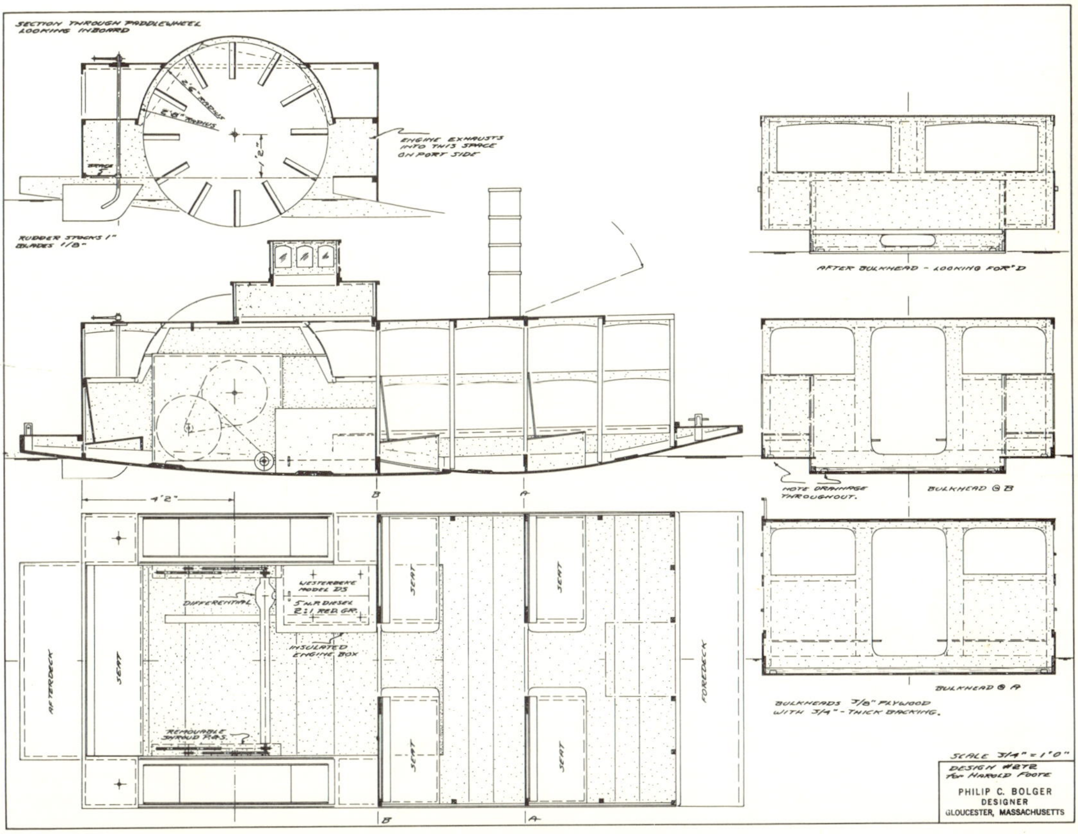

Sidewheelers do have a certain fascination. I have some general drawings somewhere of a really advanced one, the *Commonwealth,* a five-thousand-ton twenty-two knot coastwise passenger steamer built in 1908; she must represent about the peak of high-water for the type. Once in a while I get

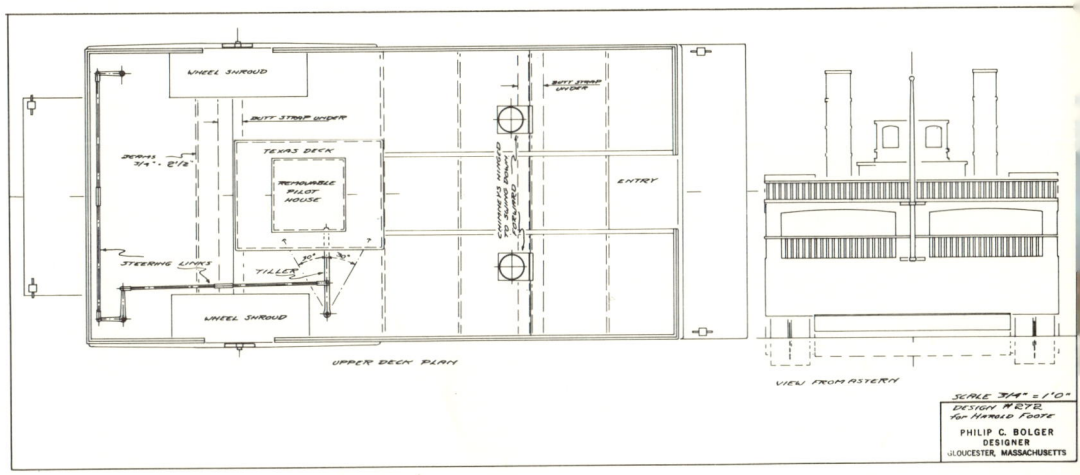

them out and see if I can't justify a yacht or excursion boat on some such lines; the shallow-water functioning looks very attractive. It won't do, though; the wheels have to be capable of working independently or you don't get the maneuvering benefits, but they also ought to be interconnected for reliability; the gearing defeats me. Using a hydraulic motor for each wheel would seem the likeliest approach, though maybe two steam engines driving from the same boiler system would be worth a look. I've had just enough to do with steam engines to know that they don't give good results unless you've learned a lot more about them than I, or most of the people who talk about reviving them, have.

The Volkswagen differential was a good device of the owner-builder of the toy boat here; brakes on each wheel allow the pilot to control the speed of each wheel, including stopping one completely and diverting all the power to one side. It doesn't seem likely that this arrangement would work on a much bigger scale. Besides, the real point is that a single stern-wheel will do the job, and even that seems relegated to history by developments in vertical-axis propellers and more recently with low-velocity, high-volume jets. No harm in thinking about it, though: how about a side-wheel surface-effect machine?

9
UTILITY FOR HOMEBUILDERS

$$22'0'' \times 7'6''$$

This boat was designed to the order of a stillborn amateur-building magazine. She was meant to *look* easy to build and, somewhat secondarily, to be so as far as possible. She's another one laid out to be assembled from diagrams drawn on the plywood, without lofting or a flat base; this particular one hasn't been tested so there may be a bad offset or two lurking in the underbrush. The "instructions" below explain how I thought she could be put together without having to turn her completely over, which, with an object this heavy and bulky, will be nice if it works well.

The promoter sent me a clipping of a little fiberglass British workboat as an idea of the kind of styling he thought would be liked. I took the chance to use the plumb bow and vertical sides; combined with the deep-V bottom, I judge this will produce a good behavior in rough water. She may be on the wild side running down a steep sea, her forefoot being an ugly shape when it's deeply immersed, but an overhanging bow and flaring sides would make it worse, not better. If I had one of these I'd go gingerly into a rough inlet but be easy in mind about anything else she'd be likely to meet with suddenly.

The instructions follow, including my pitch to prospective builders.

GENERAL REMARKS AND KEY TO PLANS

The assembly has been carefully planned on a proven principle and should go quickly and easily if fully understood and followed. If substantial changes are planned it would be best to loft her full size and erect her bottom-up in the usual way, so that mistakes of designer or builder will appear before much wood has been cut. She should still be quick to build for her capabilities. The vertical stem, sides, and transom were adopted not only because they simplify assembly but because they result in the best performance for the materials needed and space occupied.

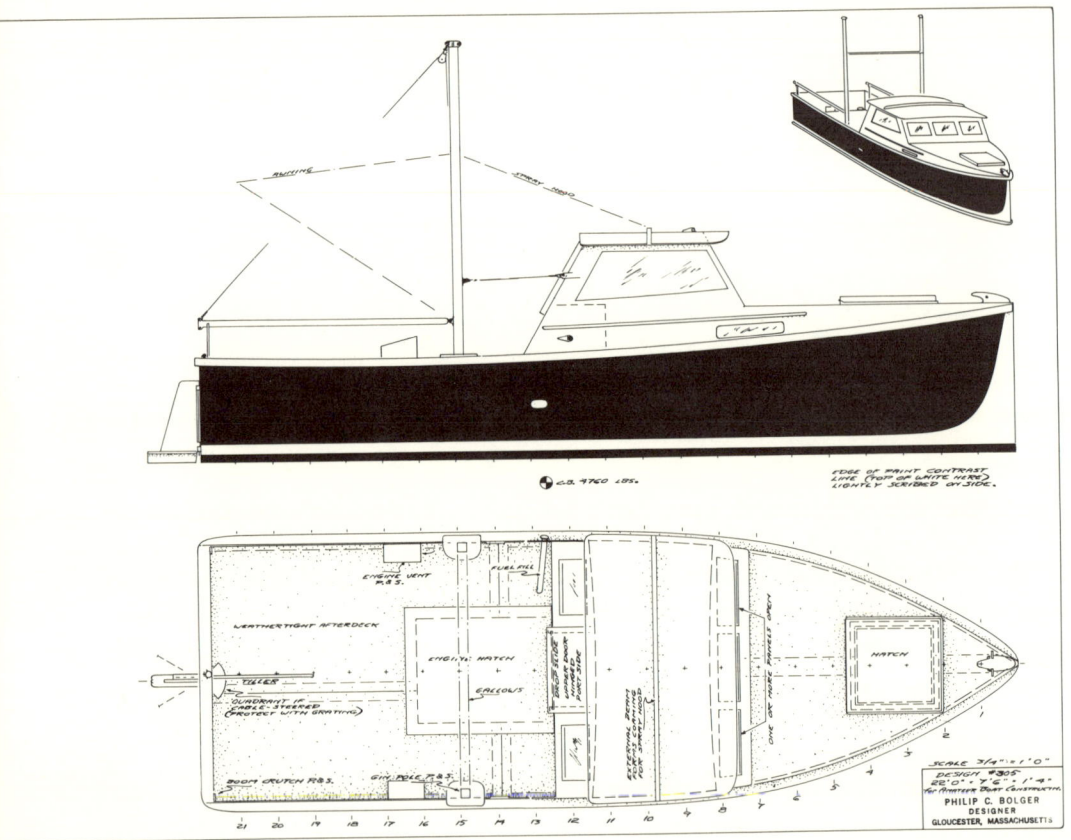

The Westerbeke Pilot 20 diesel specified is the designer's choice and will give ten to twelve knots according to weight and other factors. The boat will behave decently with still smaller engines, especially if fitted with reduction gears to swing a reasonably large propeller. With larger engines she is capable of considerably more speed but is likely to be rather inefficient (that is, slow in proportion to weight and power) at speeds above about 15 knots. No engine weighing more than about 900 pounds should be used, and reduction gearing should be adapted to not more than 17″ or less than 14″ prop diameter. Most engines will require some shaft angle and many will need a raised engine hatch. Power range of outboard motors installed in the tunnel as sketched may be 9.9 h.p. to 50 h.p. or more; twin outboards will require elimination of the tunnel and substitution of a raked transom with full-width slop well, and this modification lies in the category that should be conventionally lofted. High-powered motors will require installation of transom trim tabs, not only for fore-and-aft high-speed trim, but for transverse stability; these can be fixed wedges sized by trial and error, or some adjustable type; they should be located as far outboard as possible.

The natural wood used (understood if not specified as plywood) can be any of the usual species suitable for glued structures; Douglas fir is good; softer woods such as cedar or spruce, or harder ones such as mahogany, are suitable; oak, yellow pine, and teak tend to take glue badly and may be too stiff for some of the bends.

Glue may be resorcinol or epoxy. Fastenings are meant to be Anchorfast or other barbed nails, though bronze screws are better and galvanized wire nails will serve. The model is adaptable to the "sewn" system in which the joints are wired together and secured with glass tape, but more molds will be needed to produce a fair shape without the wooden longitudinals. Glass cloth, Dynel, and other sheathings may be used but the designer is inclined to doubt cost-effectiveness. The WEST System epoxy treatment seems at this writing to be worth considering; a pamphlet explaining it is available from the suppliers, Gougeon Bros., 706 Martin St., Bay City, Michigan 48706, for $2.00 as of February, 1975.

The design is laid out to make economical use of 4' x 8' (122 x 244 cm.) plywood sheets. Marine plywood (not supposed to have large interior gaps) should be used if it can be had at any price; if not, test exterior-grade sheets by flexing and tapping and fill voids found with glue, polyester slurry, and/or wood plugs; also try to locate known voids in flat areas of the hull. The boat may be built of thicker plywood than specified throughout; for example, ¾" bottom and ½" sides; this would be wise in high-powered versions; designed thicknesses are meant to be minimums for lowest first cost and best fuel economy.

Wide variations to builder's taste is possible in parts not very explicitly specified.

1. Bulkheads and transom ⅜" plywood with ¾" fastening frames; see drawings for dimensions and bevels; note 1½" square cleats on 'D' and transom to take afterdeck.

2. Frame 'B' made up as shown from ¾" x 3½".

3. Hull sides ⅜" plywood assembled to diagram; two identical except that ⅜" x 6" plywood butt straps and the locating marks for bulkhead, afterdeck, and guard placement come on opposite sides.

4. Stem from 1½" square nailed and glued to port side sheet.

(Set port side sheet up on edge, on horses to bring straight bottom edge at least 15" off the floor; put transom and bulkheads 'D' and 'E' in place against the side on their marks, wedging them or the sides up or down to get the exact correct height; glue and nail the sides to them.)

5. Afterdeck ⅜" plywood; note off-center fore-and-aft butt strap to use full width of one sheet; ¾" x 1½" fastening frame around edges and 1½" x 2½" frame abaft hatch opening; fore-and-aft beams ¾" x 2½".

(Put afterdeck in place, resting on transom and Bulkhead 'D' cleats, fore-and-aft beams resting on top of Bulkhead 'E', and port edge against inside of side sheet; nail and glue in place. Now put up starboard side sheet in place on the assembly and nail and glue it in place. Bring forward ends of sides together, inserting 'C', 'B', and 'A' as you go, roughly on their marks but not permanently secured; nail and glue starboard side sheet to stem. Now tap the three bulkheads exactly to their marks, or to a position that produces a fair sweep in the sides, and nail and glue them permanently one by one.)

6. Deck clamp ¾" x 1½" sprung round inside top edges of sides.

7. Guard moldings double 1½" x 2½" (i.e., to finish 2½" x 3") bent in on marks, glued, and nailed from inside.

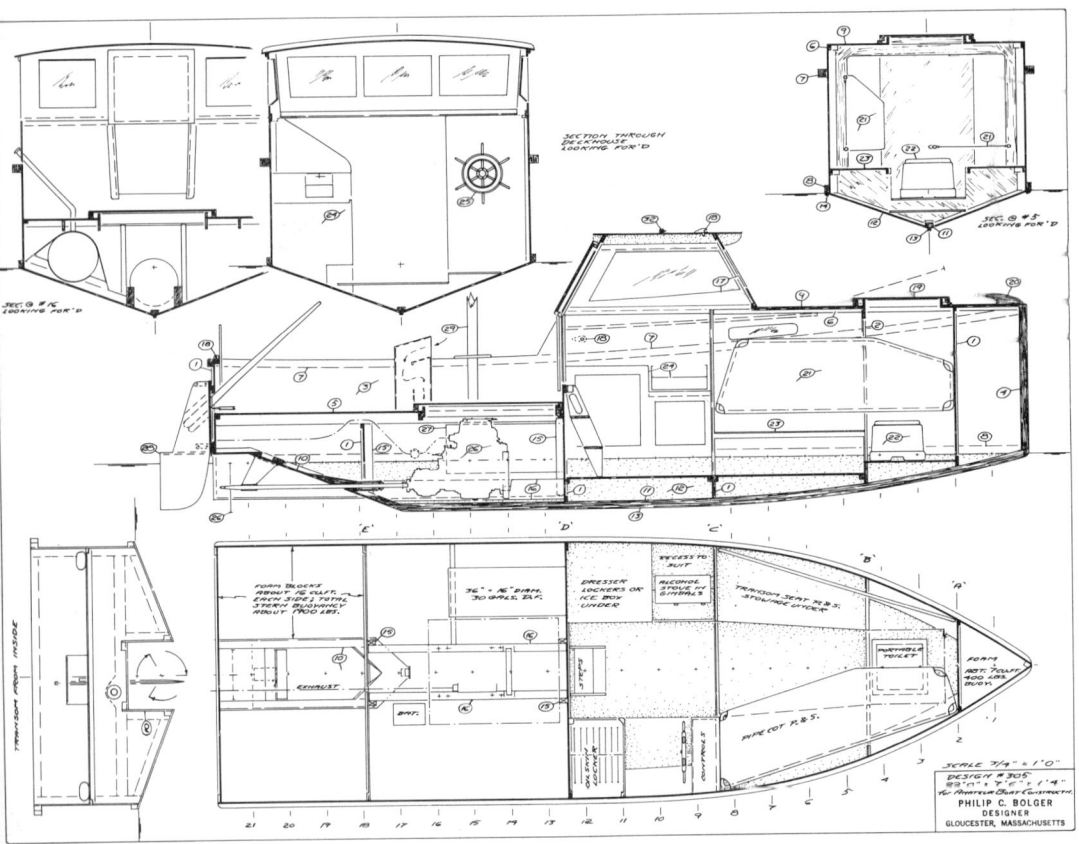

8. Chine logs 1½" x 2½".

9. Foredeck ⅜" plywood.

10. Tunnel ½" plywood with fastening frames from 1½" x 2½" as shown, and shaft log as shown or as modified to suit some other engine. Better leave excess at forward edge to allow for assembly or design errors. Glue and nail to transom and bulkhead 'E', checking alignment carefully. (Assembly is now supposed to be rigid enough to be rolled up on its side; either side as convenient.)

11. Keel from ½" x 2½".

12. Bottom ½" plywood, one side lapping the other over the keel, then bevelled to take the shoe.

13. Shoe ¾" x 1" oak or other hard wood (or may be shod with metal) secured with screws, not glued, to be replaceable.

14. Spray rails ¾" x 1½" run from stem to about amidships.

15. Posts to take ends of engine beds 1½" x 2½", glued and bolted through bulkheads.

16. Engine beds sided 2½", molded about 6½" (different profile for different engines); would actually be good to place these before the bottom sheets are installed.

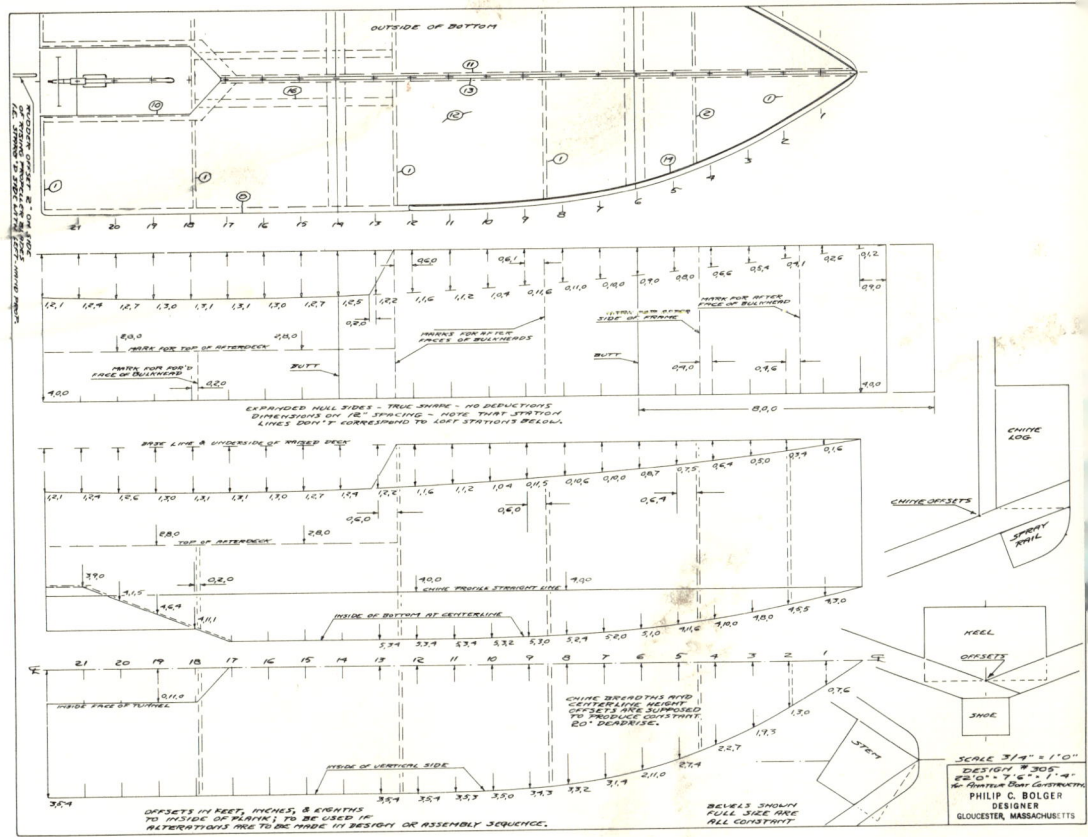

17. Wheelhouse ⅜" plywood (top may be ¼"); ¼" clear plastic windows screwed to outside; one or more sections of windshield may be framed and hinged; note that front of house forms the girder supporting the after edge of the deck.

18. Navigation lights.

19. Forward hatch ⅜" plywood with double coamings; may be hinged or removable, and may be fitted with a Skyvent or other ventilator.

20. Mooring cleat bolted through deck and centerline butt strap.

21. Steel or aluminum pipe-frame berths.

22. Portable toilet.

23. Transom seats ⅜" plywood; may be built as lockers or omitted.

24. Galley to suit.

25. Controls to taste; outboard motor type like Teleflex will serve; rudder connections should be taken aft above afterdeck.

26. Engine shown: Westerbeke Pilot 20 with 2.5:1 reduction gear; exhaust with condensation trap and loop, muffler to suit; 1¼" bronze shaft; strut welded up from ⅜" stainless steel, or cast bronze type, with Cutless bearing in any case; propeller 16" diameter, 16" pitch three-blade for about 1200 r.p.m. (See remarks above for comments on options.)

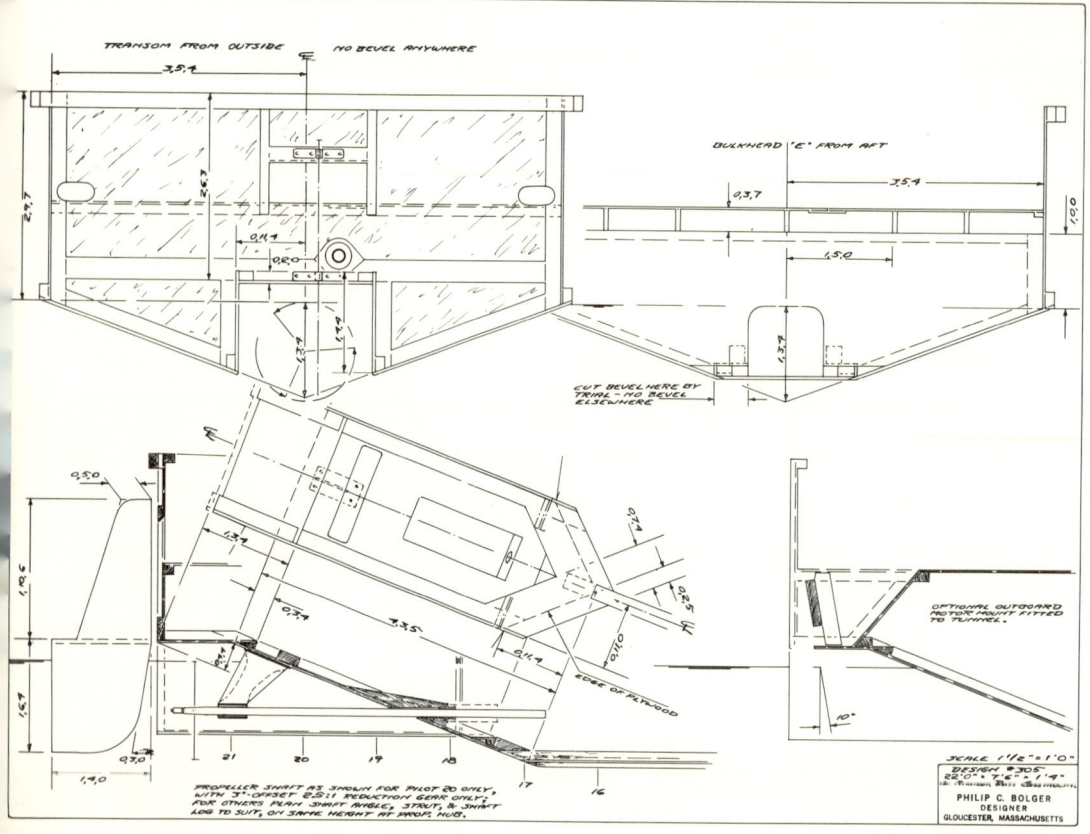

27. Tank as shown or as convenient; should not be moved much.

28. Rudder 1″ thick of double ½″ plywood; underwater edges roughly sharpened; ¾″ x 1″ stiffener each side at tunnel-top level; box on port side to form socket for removable tiller; bronze or stainless steel strap gudgeons on rudder and transom to take ⅜″ x 24″ rod pivot.

29. Gin poles about 3″ square; can step in partners as shown or simply bolt to hull side; connect with 1½″ x 3″ gallows.

30. Booms 2″ square or can be tubes; rest in crutches at stern to form railings.

31. Lifelines with pelican hooks protect gangways ahead of gin poles.

32. Spray hood snaps to beam on top of wheelhouse; rolls up under gallows when not in use.

33. Awning similar to hood, but with a stiff spreader or batten at after end, supported by raised booms.

34. Plywood boxes form water-trap ventilators; if a gasoline engine is used there must be two outlet vents, one ducted to the bilge under the engine; these can be in the form of boxes set against inside of transom, with a baffle built in; latter should be as high as possible above waterline.

UTILITY FOR HOMEBUILDERS

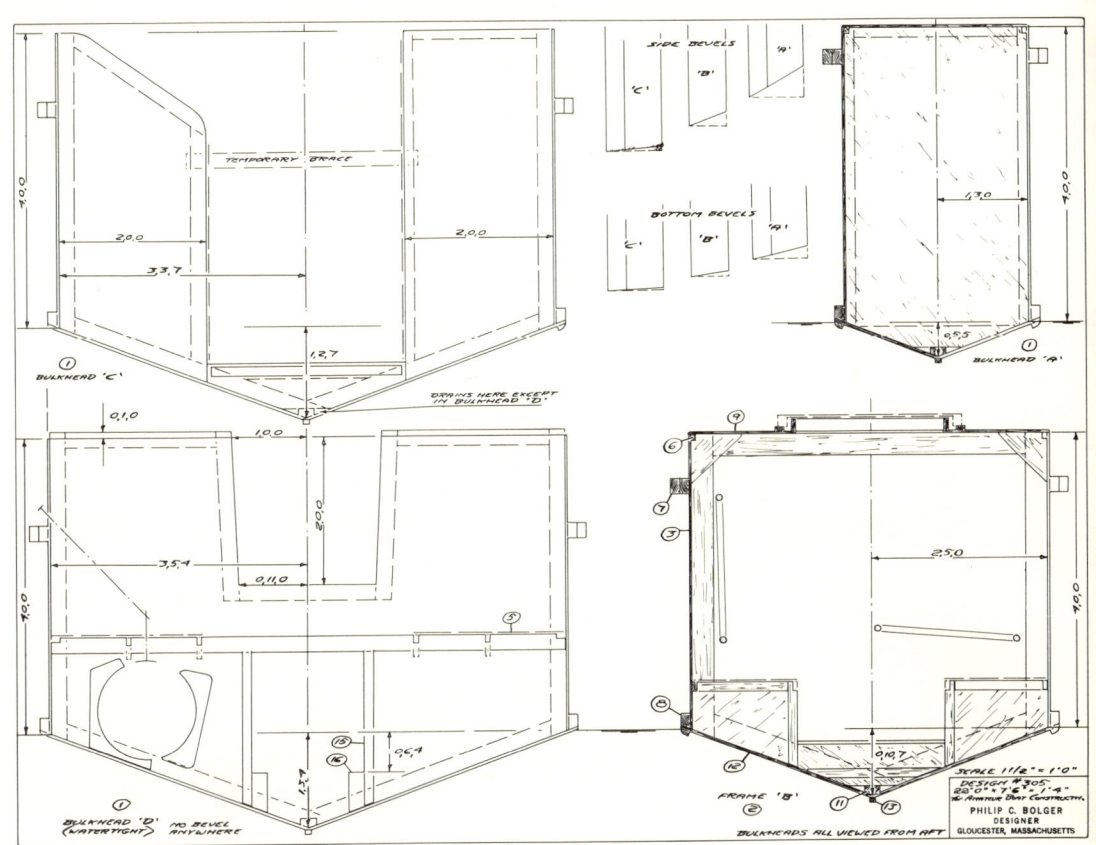

10
CYNTHIA J.

| 14'6" x 5'6" |

Rick Ramsey built this tiny boat for trailer-sailing on the lakes and rivers of Indiana. It would be stretching the truth to call her a cruiser, but she does have the first prerequisite, a place long enough to lie down, with a tight deck over it. For the deck to do much good in a rainstorm the open stern would need to be tented over, as otherwise the water would run forward under you from the cockpit. Such a tent would be reasonably easy to arrange: it's possible that with some ingenuity and a few extra grommets the sail could be made to serve. In any case, the cuddy is handy, even if a night is never spent in it, for locked storage and to provide some shelter to the cockpit.

The large amount of deck and high sides all around ought to make her an easy boat on the nerves compared with most of her size and weight. Being in a boat rather than on top of it is quite rare nowadays — a clear luxury. She can heel very far before she ships any water, and further still, in a quick knockdown, before she ships so much that she won't recover. Her normal sailing angle is well upright, wide as she is for her depth and weight, so there's a big margin between her usual attitude and the point of no return.

She is another case of a boat that's much bigger than her length might suggest. The sheet-use diagram gives away the cost: ten sheets of plywood, including a good deal more wastage than I'm proud of.

I've had no performance report on her, but I think her sailing will be a surprise to a good many people. She has a big rig for her weight, stability to carry it, and, in smooth water, not much to stop her. She won't like a sharp chop at all, especially to windward, and her maximum speed is obviously not very high compared with a good sailing dinghy, but most of the time she'll be a creditable performer and all the more satisfactory because she doesn't look she would be. She'll also do good work without her crew having to put out a lot of effort or get very wet.

KEY TO PLANS

Plywood needed is noted on the drawing, and can be fir or mahogany, marine grade if at all possible. Fastenings, except where otherwise noted, are assumed to be Anchorfast or other barbed nails, as long as bury allows, mostly 1". Glue may be resorcinol or epoxy and should be lavishly used. Natural wood, understood if not specified as plywood, may be any available timber of reasonably good gluing and nail-holding properties, as Douglas fir or mahogany; sizes are supposed to correspond to standard dressed lumber dimensions and may vary slightly as convenient, preferably on the large side, especially if of softer wood such as soft pine, white cedar, or spruce.

1. Hull sides cut out to given dimensions, marked for moldings and for frames and bulkhead locations.
2. Side butt straps 7" wide; assemble sides flat, glued and riveted or clinch-nailed on butt straps; note that straps come flush with bottom of side sheets but stop about 5/8" below top edge to clear raised deck stringers.
3. Transom: dimensions given are those of plywood inside; framing goes outside; bevel as diagrammed.
4. Frame #4 from 3/4" x 2 1/2".

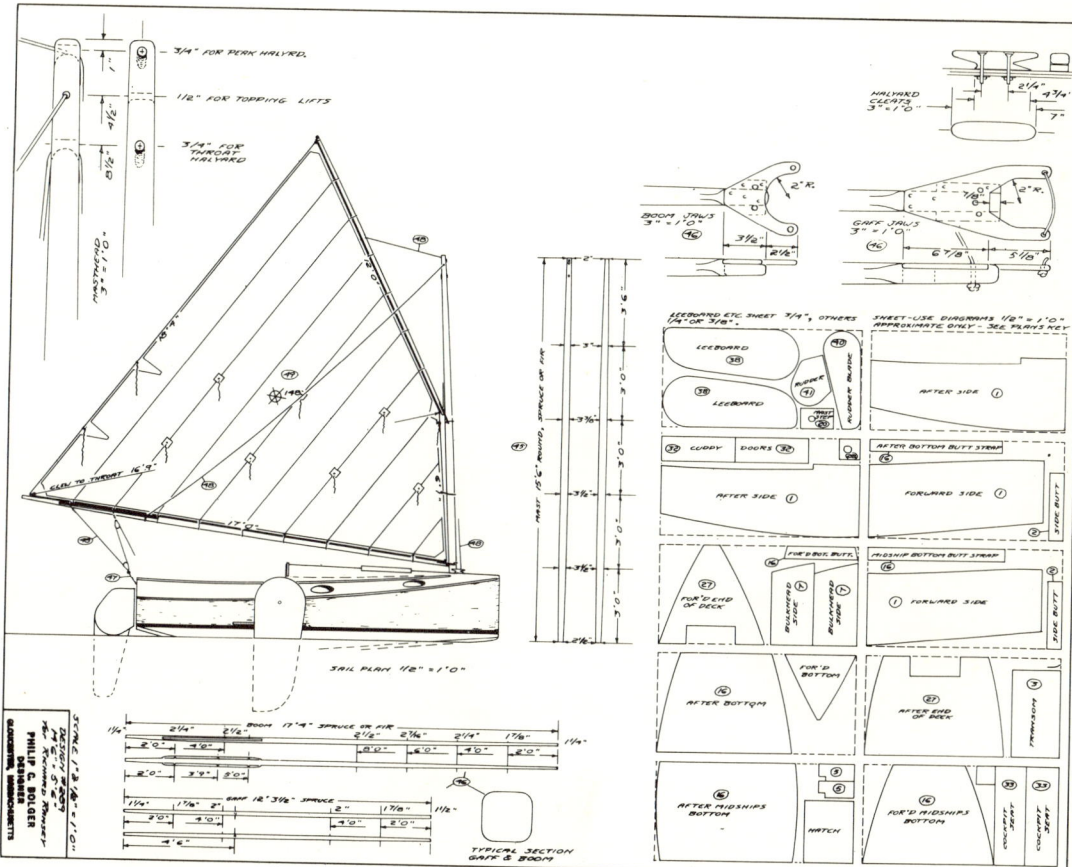

5. Frame #4 gussets 8¼" x 17" plywood; cut down at sides to take seat carline.

6. Limber holes in all frames about 1".

7. Bulkhead at #3 plywood 1'8¾" wide each side, with ¾" x 2½" fastening frame.

8. Arch beam from ¾" x 2½" spans opening.

9. Frame at #2 from ¾" x 2½"; plywood gussets about 9" on each side against planking.

10. Deck beam from ¾" x 5½" with crown cut off top edge.

11. Frame at #1 from ¾" x 2½" including deck beam; double up bottom frame to take ¼" bolt through bottom shoes; gussets similar to #2.

12. Stem bevelled to full-size pattern from 1½" square; secure to one of side sheets.

(Stand side sheets on edge each side of bulkhead; nail to bulkhead. Run a light rope in a complete loop around the sides and across ends, and twist up the rope to bend ends of sides in together. Insert frames and transom; nail side to them and at the stem; stem and transom must be glued as well as nailed; glue can be omitted from frames if desired. Turn hull bottom-up; line up frame centerlines with a sprung plank for a straightedge.)

13. Raised deck clamps from ¾" x 1"; insert inside plywood sides in slots of frames and bulkhead; butt against stem; make sure they stand high enough to get a good bearing for the deck when bevelled to the crown; nail and glue to sides.

14. Chine logs and side stringers ¾" x 1"; glued to and nailed from side sheets; check early on if the chine logs are limber enough to take the edge-set toward the stern; if they're too stiff soak them in hot water till they can be forced to approximate shape on the floor or against a wall, and let them dry out a few days while held in the curve.

15. Inside cockpit rail clamp ¾" x 1".

16. Place bottom in four-foot sheets starting from stern, taking exact shape from assembled sides. Six-inch butt straps can be installed as each sheet is placed, or the whole thing can be shaped in place, removed for assembly, and replaced. Take great pains with the glue, especially at the chine joints, as a holiday equals a small leak at once and probably bad failure later.

17. Bottom shoes from ¾" x 2½", glued, and nailed from inside; run them as far fore and aft as possible and cut off flush with sides and transom, rounding up forward ends somewhat.

18. Trailer shoe ¾" x 1"; may be shod with metal strip or half-oval. (Turn hull right-side-up.)

19. Inside bottom stiffening cleats, in cabin only, ¾" x 2½"; glue down and nail from outside.

20. Mast step ¾" x 10" x 16" plywood; glued and nailed to frame and through bottom to center shoe.

21. Plywood padding for deadlights.

22. Deadlights ⅛" clear plastic, screwed to inside of sides with seam compound.

23. Block of styrofoam or urethane foam wedge-shaped, about 16" fore and

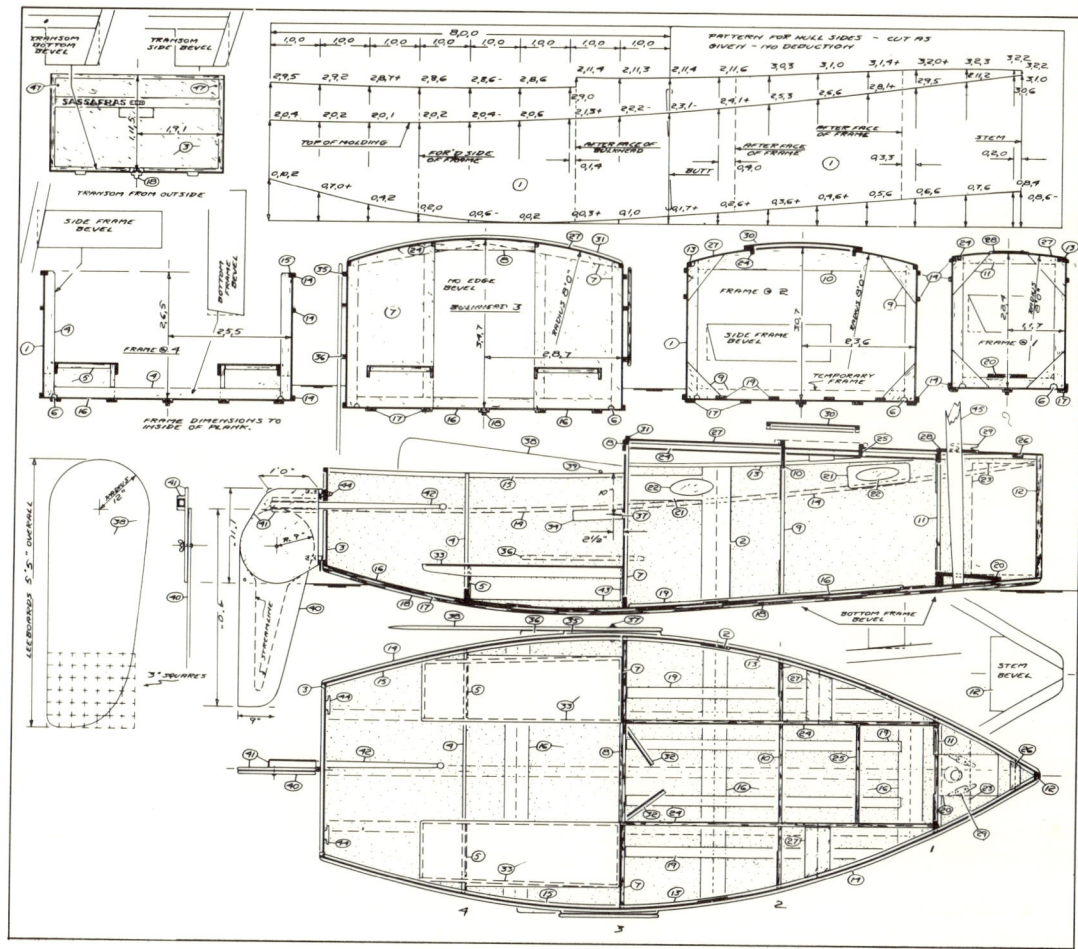

aft, 18″ across the back, and 2′3″ top to bottom, or as much larger as will fit; cleat it in place to keep it clear of the mast (makes 270 pounds positive buoyancy).

24. Raised deck stringers ¾″ x 1″; should come dead straight if alignment is correct.

25. Hatch beam from ¾″ x 2½″.

26. Foredeck butt strap from ¾″ x 2½″, planed to slight crown, nailed from sides.

27. Deck plywood, in two 4′ sections plus a small patch at the stem; 6″ butt straps abreast the hatch opening; glued and nailed down all around.

28. Plywood pad glued to top of deck forms partner about 10″ square.

29. Jam halyard cleats about as detailed; two ¼″ x 2½″ brass flat-head stove bolts each through deck with large washers underneath. (These cleats are supposed to be able to take both halyards, peak over throat, so hoisting can be done from weather side of hatch.)

30. Hatch plywood with ¾" x 1" frame; glue up hatch and frame while sprung to a slightly harder curve than the deck crown; provide a couple of hooks to hold the hatch in place from inside; it will usually be stowed below when sailing.

31. Coaming ¾" x 1".

32. Cuddy doors plywood; ¾" x 1" frame; hinged to swing clear around against bulkhead on the inside; light hasp and padlock.

33. Cockpit seats plywood 1'4" x 4'0"; bulkhead cleat and after end frame ¾" x 1"; side frames ¾" x 2½".

34. Inside pad for leeboard pivot bolts ¾" x 2½" x about 12".

35. Pad out moldings #14 to get leeboard bearings exactly parallel.

36. Lower leeboard guards built up from ¾" x 1" x about 2'10".

37. Leeboard pivot bolts ½" x 4" bronze carriage bolts, heads inside, nuts a loose fit over two large washers each.

38. Leeboards ¾" plywood or double ⅜", sharpened for about 4" at edges below lower guard.

39. Hole and pin to hold board raised; if lowered board has too much tendency to float up, it can be held down the same way, or else ballasted with 10-12 pounds of lead.

40. Rudder blade from ¾" or double ⅜" plywood, with edges more or less sharpened to reduce chattering; ½" x 2½" bronze carriage bolt pivot with washer and wing nut to set up tension (so it will stay down, or partly down, without ballast).

41. Rudder ¾" plywood; standard bronze or stainless steel pintles and gudgeons; box on side to take tiller from ¾" x 1½" with ¼" plywood cap, made with a slight taper so tiller can jam in tight and not slop.

42. Tiller from 1½" square by 3'6".

43. Buoyancy foam blocks styrene or urethane, about 8" x 12" x 36", each side under cockpit seats, slung in fabric bags tacked or hooked to seat frames. (Total positive buoyancy of these two blocks and the one in the bow is about 500 pounds, making it possible to sail the boat while flooded, but observe that if capsized she may go all the way bottom-up, in which case it will take about 150 pounds crew weight and the leverage of a leeboard to right her.)

44. Two six-inch cleats, mainly to hook main sheet under (lee side) when beating and reaching.

45. Mast as shown; should be an easy fit at step and partners, without wedges; halyards keep it from hopping out, but take care about glue and fastenings in the bottom shoe near where the mast bears on the bottom, as these and the bolt mentioned in item #11 take the thrust of the halyard tension.

46. Boom and gaff as detailed; the jaws are ⅜" or ¼" but should be screwed to the spars without glue as they'll suffer frequent breakages; the parrel of the gaff jaws can be about 3/16" nylon set up so it's quite slack when the gaff is horizontal for hoisting and lowering but comes fairly taut when peaked up. Note how veneer of jaws is protected from rubbing on the mast by a slight set-back from ends of spars.

47. Traveller horse ¼" nylon, held by stopper knots inside transom.

48. All running rigging is dacron (preferably, with manila for second choice)

¼″ diameter, including sheet about 60′ running through two plastic-shell blocks at least 1¼″ sheave diameter; topping lift about 32′, running freely in masthead hole and knotted under boom, set up to carry boom at a convenient height with gaff lowered; and throat and peak halyards each about 30′.

49. Sail cut to sailmaker's judgment, not necessarily as shown; the number of reef points shown is sufficient, as is the single luff tie. Lash to boom and gaff with separate ties as shown, do not lace. In designer's opinion this sail should be of somewhat lighter cloth than usual for its area.

11
BLACK SKIMMER

> 25′3″ x 7′0″

Skimmer is a predecessor of *Blackgauntlet II* (see next chapter), designed a couple of years later for a particular experienced owner rather than as "plans for sale." We judged she was small enough to be held up somewhat by her crew, and thus carry her sail more upright and so need less ballast and stand more breadth for her length than the bigger sharpie. She has just enough ballast to make her self-righting in conjunction with the buoyancy of her high, raised deck. The sliding seat is not meant very seriously; we thought it might be fun on the occasion of a brush with some other boat. No doubt it'll help her a lot in a breeze of wind, given somebody ambitious to use it.

The cuddy is similar to that of my *Pointer,* in which I've managed to make myself at home for as much as a month. It's dry and well ventilated, with good sprawling space if nothing else.

The rig is also much like *Pointer*'s, which started as a cat but acquired a mizzen cannibalized from an experimental sailing dinghy. It's a convenient rig, powerful for its cost. The only important drawback is that if you jam the masthead sheave, as once happened, it's a long way up to clear it. I also used to loathe the day when it came time to step or unstep the mast, though I hoped that the partners shown would make it easier; at least it doesn't have to be coated or caulked at the partners. Most people with sailing cruisers seem to put up with as bad or worse; at least this rig, having no wire, doesn't scream like a banshee in the night when the wind blows.

The leeboards are hung by an old Flemish method, extremely simple compared with the complex Dutch-geometry mounts of *Blackgauntlet II.* The trick is to place the rope loop so it'll tighten itself as it goes down, and to make it easy to take up the tension. The drawback is that no matter what you do or how much trouble you take there's always some slop in it; running before the wind, both boards will be broken-winged off the hull;

Built by Mike's Boat Shop, Gloucester Point, Virginia.

then if you bring her suddenly to the wind, or jibe, there'll be a skid and a great jerk as the board swings back in and brings up on its guard. You want to keep an eye on the condition of the loops, by the way; there's a leeboard like one of these lying somewhere off Gloucester to this day, on account of my impression that the loops would go through a full season.

Perhaps this is as good a place as any to run through the answers to the standard questions about leeboards: no, they don't have to be handled every tack — leave them both down all the time; no, don't build them asymmetrical or toed-in, you'll overdo it if you try it at all; yes, they're noisy and collect driftwood and pot-warp; yes, they do need to be that big and especially that wide and they also need at least that much ballast; yes, I agree that they're ugly.

62 BLACK SKIMMER

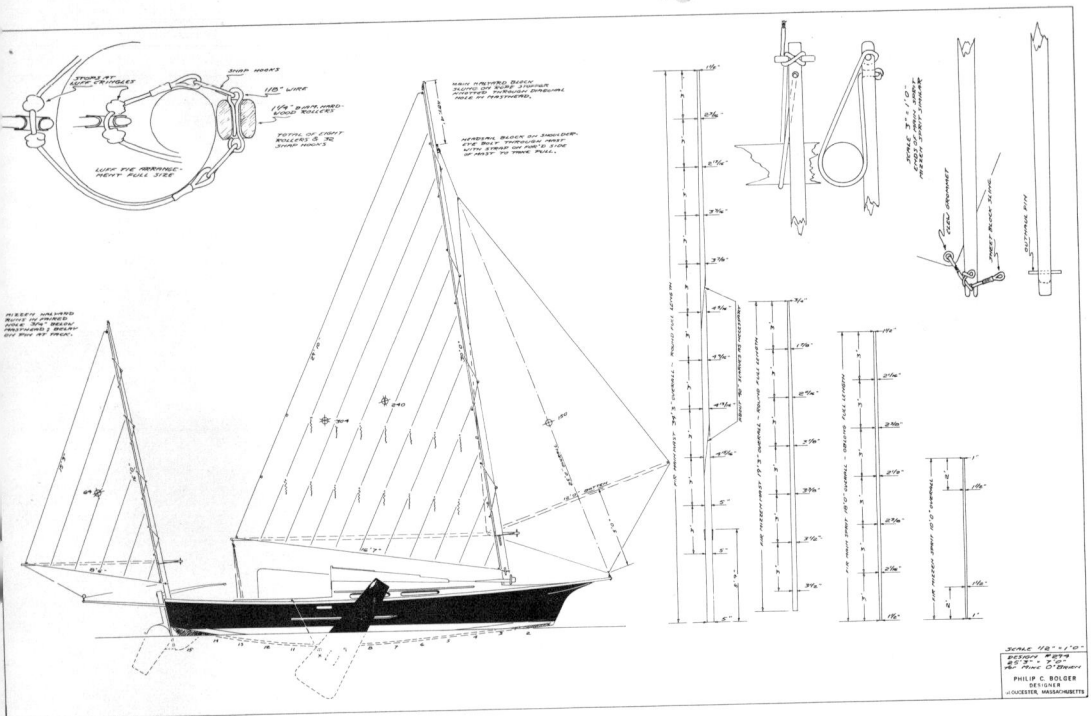

KEY TO PLANS

All plywood is marine grade, ½" thick, in 4' x 8' sheets; natural wood may be fir, mahogany, or any locally available, moderately hard wood having good gluing properties; sizes are intended to conform to standard dressed lumber and may vary slightly as convenient. Fastenings may be bronze screws or Anchorfast or other barbed nails. Glue and finish is intended to be WEST System epoxy from Gougeon Bros., P.O. Box 384, Bay City, Michigan 48706.

1. Frames, bulkheads, and transom plywood, assembled and bevelled to given dimensions; fastening frames are ¾" throughout, using widths 1½", 2½", and 3½" more or less as shown.

2. Plywood side sheets assembled to diagram on 8"-wide butt straps; if butts are shifted from indicated positions, make sure they clear frames.

3. Stem from 1½" x 2½", bevelled as shown and secured to one of side sheets.

(Stand side sheets up on edge, bottom-up, on each side of midship frame; bring forward ends together and after ends to transom, simultaneously by having two or more people or Spanish windlass or both; tie or brace together and insert other frames and bulkheads on their marks to check fit. Glue and nail to stem and transom. One by one, glue and nail other frames and bulkheads, taking special pains to have no holidays in the glue of #3 and #15.)

4. Chine logs from 1½" x 2½", glued to and nailed from sides.

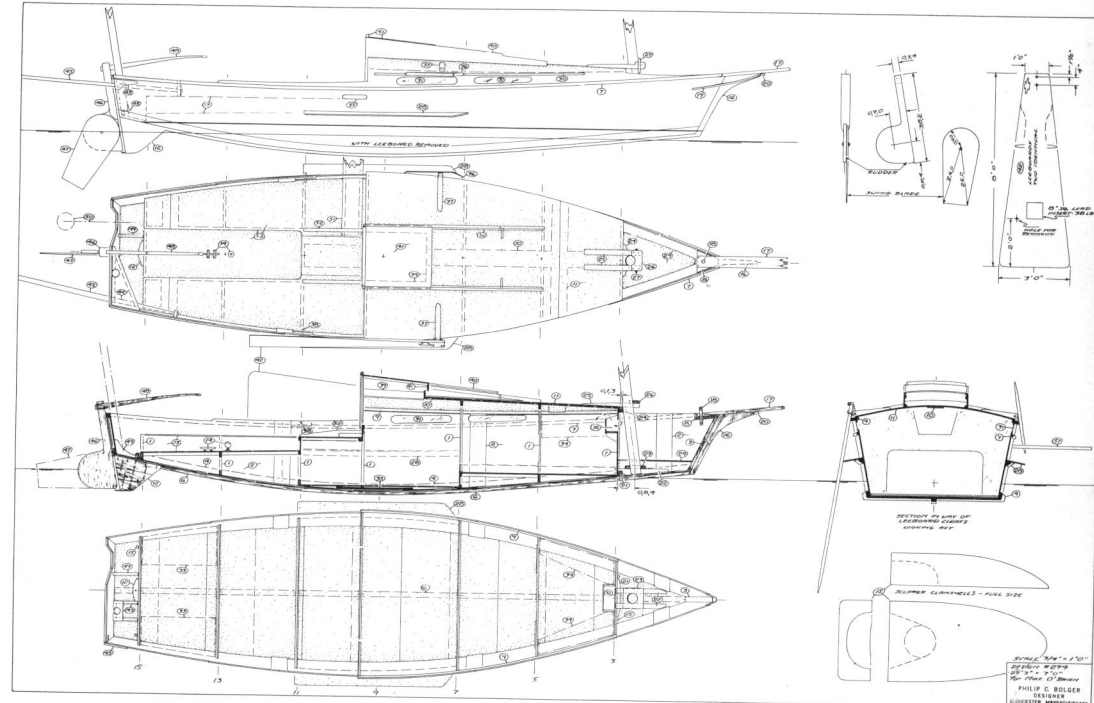

5. Bottom double plywood with staggered butts as shown; slather the glue as holidays will attract rot.

6. Shoe 1½" x 2½". (Hull can now be turned right side up as gently as possible.)

7. Main sheer molding 1½" half-round.

8. Breasthook from 1½" x 10½" or backed plywood.

9. Raised deck clamp from ¾" x 1½". (This timber has the only varying bevel in the boat and must be fitted cut-and-try.)

10. Centerline deck butt strap 8"-wide plywood, planed to deck crown.

11. Raised deck plywood, butted on centerline and forward of frame #5.

12. Skeg sided 2½", faired to 1½" at edges with leading edge further streamlined; 3" screws from hull bottom plus one ½" bolt through 2½" x 2½" x 12" block inside; metal tab on bottom after edge under heel of rudder about as shown.

13. Afterdeck and foot well plywood with ¾" x 1½" fastening cleats.

14. Single swivel block and 8" cleat for main sheet.

15. Drains for bow and stern wells 1" diameter holes through bottom with small aft-facing clam-shells outside to produce suction.

16. False head built up from 2½" siding, glued and bolted to stem.

17. Bowsprit from 1½" x 5½" x 3'8", glued and bolted to head and to breasthook.

18. Mooring pin 1½" diameter hardwood.

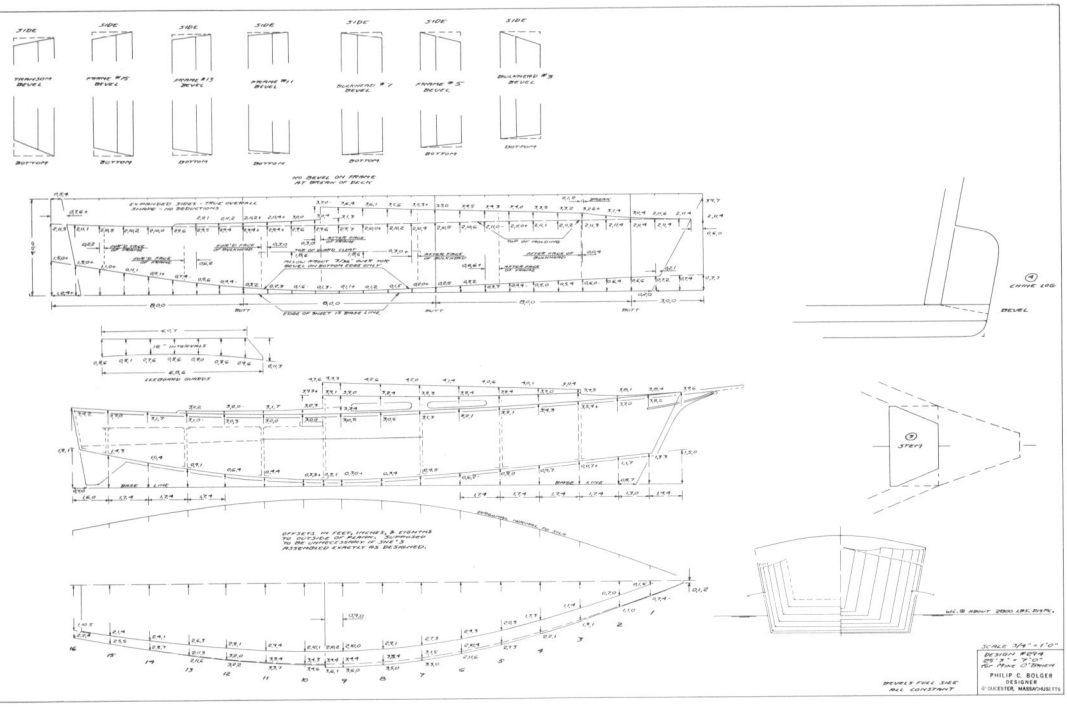

19. Trail knees ¾" square kneed out in angle of head and planking as much as necessary to take the bend cold.

20. Figurehead or scroll to taste.

21. Mainmast step floor 1½" x 2½" x 19", bolted or screwed to bulkhead.

22. Step feet 2½" x 3½" x 2'1"; note cross drains at after ends; nail up through bottom from outside.

23. Step collar 1½" x 10" square.

24. Partner block from 2½" x 3" x 16".

25. Partner arms from 2" x 2½" x 2'5".

26. Semi-collar from 1½" x 3½" x 10"; four ¼" bolts to arms.

27. Halyard belaying pins 1" square, 7" long.

28. Leeboard guards plywood to diagram; supporting stringers 2½" square, bevelled about as shown.

29. Well floorboard plywood or slats, laid loose; 15-pound yachtsman anchor stows under.

30. Trim molding 1" half-round.

31. Windows ⅛" clear plastic screwed to outside of plank.

32. Ventilation hole 6" x 12", screened, with trap box inside.

33. Buoyancy blocks under after deck urethane foam cut to fill bays about as shown; should amount to about five cubic feet each side for total 600 pounds buoyancy.

34. Forward buoyancy blocks shaped to fill angle of deck and sides with edges faired in to fit frame #5; total buoyancy about 250 pounds. (Optional; intended to

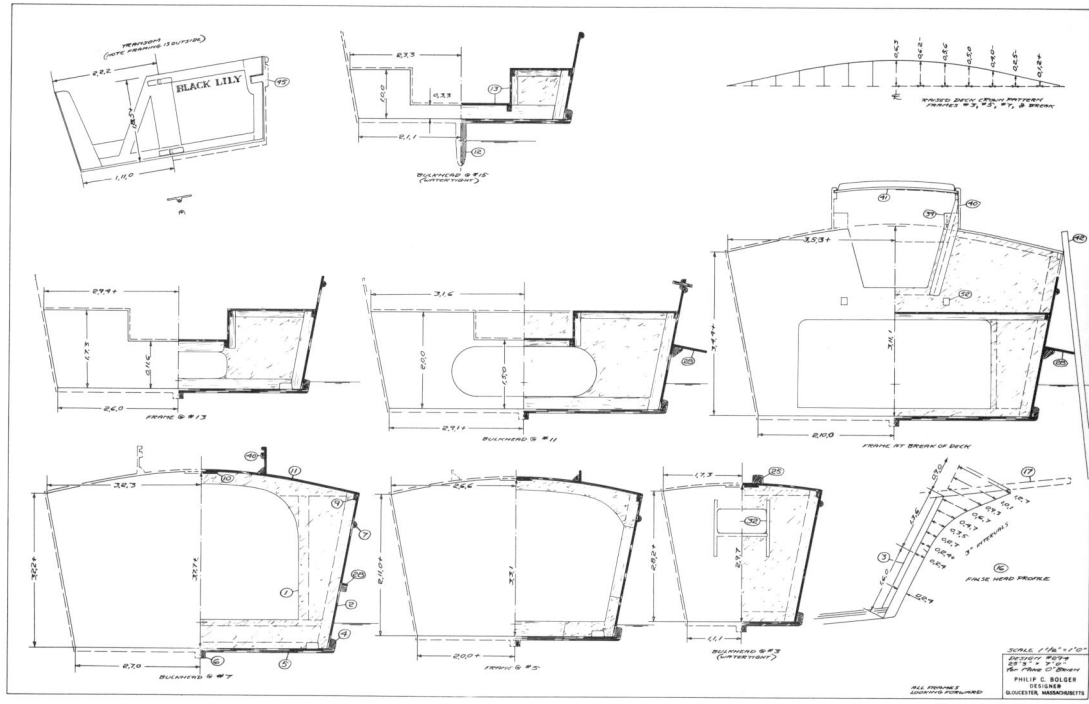

produce self-righting when completely flooded; she's unsinkable without them, and self-righting without them unless a good deal of water gets in the cuddy.)

35. Ballast: three 3/4" x 12" x 5'6" steel plates, galvanized or enamelled; one 3/8" bolt each through bottom of hull; total weight about 500 pounds.

36. Upper leeboard blocking shaped from 1½" x 3½" x 2'5", to bring top bearing of boards parallel with hull centerline. (If toe-in is demanded, one degree might be about optimum.)

37. Leeboard mounts from 2½" x 2½" x 1'7½", glued and with at least four 3/8" bolts through deck; 5/8" diameter hole for pivot line well rounded-off. Pivot line ½" diameter braided polypropylene held by stopper knot at top of board, passes through hole in mount, out through lower hole in board, and sets up to 8" cleat on board; the idea is that it tightens itself as the board swings down.

38. Leeboard pins 3/4" diameter hardwood.

39. Hatch coamings 3/4" x 3½".

40. Slide runners plywood with 3/4" square and 3/4" x 1½" rails at top, 1½" x 1½" stringers on deck (these are deck girders as well as hatch members; fasten well from below and with glue).

41. Hatch slide plywood; about 1" crown held by sawn members at ends; no side frames.

42. Leeboards 1½" thick; may be triple plywood, glued strips, or edge-drifted planks; edges well streamlined from about 4" from edge.

43. Mizzen mast step consists of a 1½" square by 7¼" cleat bolted to tran-

som and hollowed to take heel of mast; two 1½" x 3½" x about 12" shoes, and a plywood sheet about 5" x 10" with a 3½" diameter hole.

44. Mizzen partner a plywood web knee with ¾" x 1½" frame about as shown.

45. Mizzen sheet outrigger 1½" x 2½" x 8'0", tapered to 1" x 1½" outboard; set in slot in transom inside planking, with a ¾" x 5" x 12" reinforcing pad on outside of hull; heel end in a 1½" x 3½" bracket on inside of planking.

46. Rudder sided 1½", same construction as leeboards; cheeks up stock portion 1½" x 3½" each side; special cast bronze gudgeons on transom and rudder to take ⅜" pintle rod.

47. Rudder blade ¾", plywood or strip, with edges sharpened (if not sharpened it will chatter); pivots on a ½" bronze bolt set up with a (preferably oversize) wing nut.

48. Tiller 4'5" overall, to jam into 1½" x 2½" slot in rudder head.

49. Motor knee sided 1½".

50. Motor 5 to 7 horsepower.

51. Hiking board 10" x 6'4"; ½" plywood top and bottom staves with ¾" x 1½" spacers each edge; runs loose in brackets and side slots.

52. Hiking board brackets from 1½" x 3½" x 2'7"; forward end held in hole in bulkhead; glued and bolted to afterdeck (these also serve as foot braces, and to stiffen afterdeck).

12
BLACKGAUNTLET II

33'6" x 7'7"

I had the 33-foot leeboard sharpie *Pointer* built in 1959 and used her myself for eleven years. A year or two later I designed *Blackgauntlet* for Peter Duff, as an improvement on *Pointer*, and have sailed in her occasionally since. I wasn't so satisfied with either of them that I wanted them duplicated, but now and then I'd sketch at a new version with an eye to making a popular stock plan. Eventually I did it, producing this design.

A heavily ballasted sharpie like this makes an excellent boat in some ways. She goes to windward well in light and moderate weather and is fast reaching and running; by way of comparison I sailed (singlehanded, by the way) *Pointer* in four match races with a respectable Pearson Triton. She got the better of me each time on the beat, but I won all the races by speed on the reaches and runs. *Pointer*'s best timed run was seven hours in a rising wind from Highland Light on Cape Cod to Eastern Point on Cape Ann, forty-two miles broad-reaching; she must have come close to eight knots during the last part.

In a head sea these boats go softly, and keep so dry that I never wore oilskins on them except for rain. They handle so well and turn so quickly that *Pointer* had no engine the last several years I owned her. I used to sail full-tilt a boat-length to leeward of my mooring and put the tiller down hard when the buoy came abreast of the mast; she'd pivot on her leeboard and stop short with her bow on top of the buoy. The reverse of the coin was that she wouldn't shoot any distance and did not at all like being pinched.

The convenience of drying out upright is obvious; I found in *Pointer* that if the tide left her two or three hours dry, she never got foul. I had room to maneuver because nobody else wanted such a mooring.

Such boats wander and sail around their anchors horribly. Hence the full-batten mizzen, which can be left set without slatting itself to bits.

Blackgauntlet II *laid out flat.*

Blackgauntlet II *assembled; she may be one-quarter finished, or less.*

Blackgauntlet II *ready for launching.*

Sheeted down flat, it tames her. Because these boats pound and splash noisily at anchor, I've found no way to sleep well but to hunt up some smooth little creek.

The rudder is much like the New Haven type. It's said they were built to drop down a foot or so below the bottom of the boat, supposedly to give more reliable steering in heavy weather, but I once designed and tried such an arrangement and found that the steering was much worse with the rudder in the lowered position, obviously because of eddies over the top of the blade that the hull blocks when the rudder is in the position shown.

A heavy sharpie, like this one, too big to be held up by crew weight, has to be narrow for her length and weight, or, perhaps better put, long for her breadth and weight. The old rule of thumb, confirmed by my experience, is six times as long overall as wide on the bottom. If she's much wider (or shorter) than that, she'll be very slow to windward, especially if it's at all rough. But regardless of her length, a boat that is deep-bodied for her breadth, and doesn't carry her ballast on a deep fin, will be tender under sail. She has to be sailed on her side and her crew must get used to normal sailing angles of twenty, thirty, and more degrees of heel. That's why they don't pound under sail, incidentally, but the heeling is often uncomfortable and can be terrifying the first time it's encountered.

Now it's a fact that while motorboats and multihull sailboats can have hard chines without any special effect on performance, a chine always degrades a single-hull sailboat's performance at least slightly, and a deep and harsh chine, as here, has quite a bad effect. The separate set of lines and offsets, page 73, shows about what the shape ought to be. It's the form that Commodore Ralph Munro evolved out of the working sharpie. It has all the same virtues and vices, but more virtuosity and less viciousness.

The flat-bottom true sharpie is much quicker to build, especially by the prefabrication method specified here. But the material cost is no less and can be more as plywood is not an inherently cheap material. The cost of rigging is the same in one hull as the other; so is the cost, including labor cost, of the deck and interior joinerwork. The engine and tanks cost the same, as does the ballast. The economy in the sharpie is in *labor time only*, of the hull *underbody only*. That saving can be considerable in a professionally-built boat, and it can get a backyard boat afloat in a relatively short time, but it will infect any other investment made in the boat when she comes up for resale.

I'd suggest that the hull ought to be the last place to economize. That's not saying it shouldn't be done, but that rig, power plant, and cabin should all have the money wrung out of them first, in whatever order seems good to the individual. *Black Skimmer* and *Rondo II* were rigorously put through

Peter, Margaret, and Ian Duff on Buzzards Bay a long time ago.

this process. *Blackgauntlet II* was not quite so consistently conceived, and I think she's a borderline case if not actually right over the line where you can't ever get your money back out of her. Peter Duff has made *Blackgauntlet I* a good investment, but he did it by keeping her, steadily used and very carefully maintained, right through a period of galloping inflation, for around fifteen years. If he'd sold her sooner, he'd have taken a beating.

By the same token, if you see a not very old boat like this offered for sale, you might be looking at a great buy, if you're willing to make her acquaintance patiently and work with her eccentricities and not against them.

KEY TO PLANS

"Plywood" signifies fir or mahogany, marine grade if available, otherwise exterior grade AA tested for internal voids by flexing and edge voids plugged as carefully as possible. "Fir" signifies natural wood, and may be Douglas fir, any type of mahogany, or other timber of good screw- and glue-holding prop-

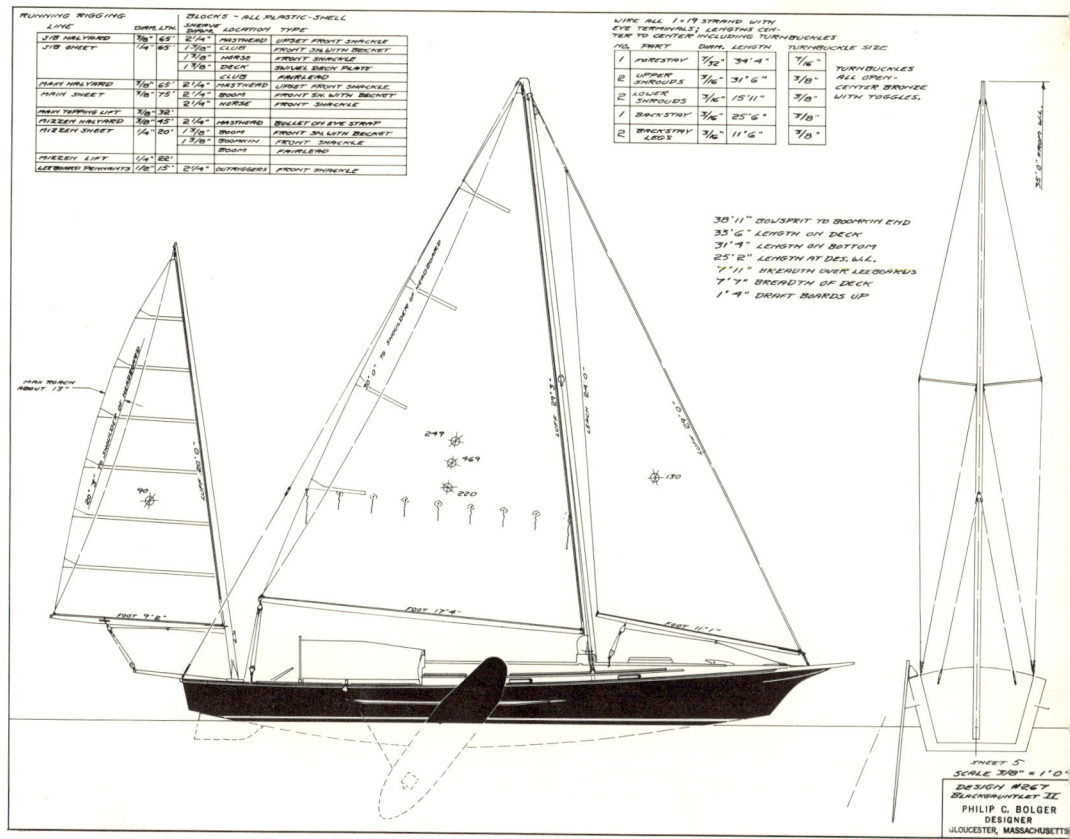

erties; white cedar, spruce, and other very soft and light woods may serve if the gluing is adequate; oak, yellow pine, and teak should be avoided if possible due to poor gluing properties. "Screw" signifies any fastening, preferably large-diameter bronze or Everdur wood screws, but other types of screw and the various barbed or ringed nails will serve if the gluing is good; should be as long as there is backing depth in all cases. "Glue" may be resorcinol or epoxy, waterproof, low-pressure-setting, and gap-filling.

1. Hull sides ½" plywood in three twelve-foot sheets to a side, cut out to diagram given and assembled flat.

2. After butt straps double ¼" plywood, 12" wide against sheets with 6" backing strap; glue and screw to sheets with ⅝" screws from first strap, ⅞" from backing strap; forward straps the same except that the first strap is 16" wide at the top to come back to the chain plate attachment points at the deck.

3. Stem from 2½" x 3½" fir, bevelled to 1½" face; glue and screw to one of side sheets with 1½" screws.

4. Bulkhead #1, ½" plywood with ¾" fastening frame.

5. Clamp openings in all bulkheads, except for the upper clamp at bulkhead #4, which must fit closely, cut out on 2" to 3" radius to be well clear of clamps as placed.

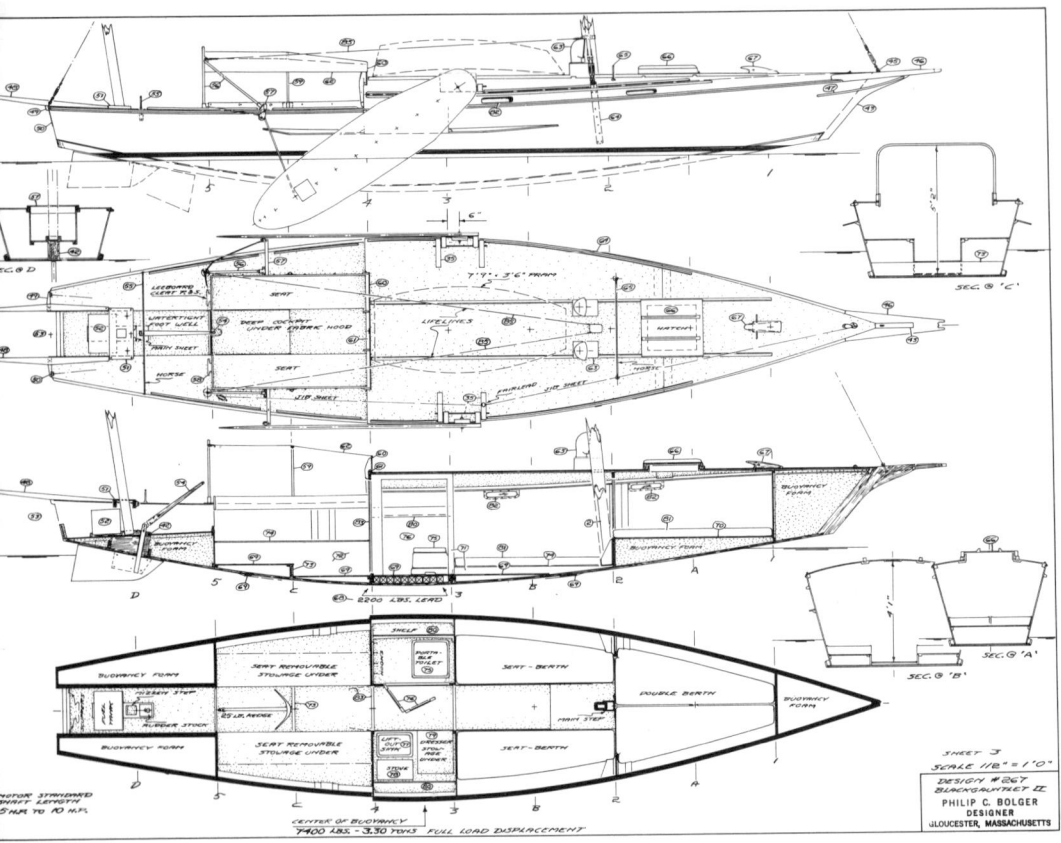

6. Drainage openings at the chine in all bulkheads; size varies somewhat according to arrangement, especially at bulkhead #2, where they should be low enough to drain under the berth flat, not onto it; these openings are shown into foam-filled spaces to take off condensation and provide minimal ventilation.

7. Bulkhead #2, ½" plywood with ¾" fir fastening frame about as shown in broken lines on the 1½"-scale drawing; opening to double berth as shown or to taste; note reinforcement where the mast step will come.

8. Bulkhead #3, ½" plywood with ¾" fir fastening frame; opening as shown; across bottom on the after side a 1½" x 3½" fir timber to take three or four ¼" bolts when the bottom is put on by way of resisting any tendency to sag under ballast weight.

9. Bulkhead #4, ½" plywood with ¾" fir fastening frame, door opening about as shown; cleats ¾" x 1½" to support and secure ends of after decks, cockpit seats, and galley dresser; 1½" x 4½" timber across bottom on forward side.

10. Bulkhead #5, ½" plywood with ¾" x 1½" fir frame and cleats.

11. Transom ½" plywood with ¾" frame.

(Set up bulkheads, bottom-up, at approximate height and spacing indicated, bracing them lightly so they can be easily moved later; stand cut-out and as-

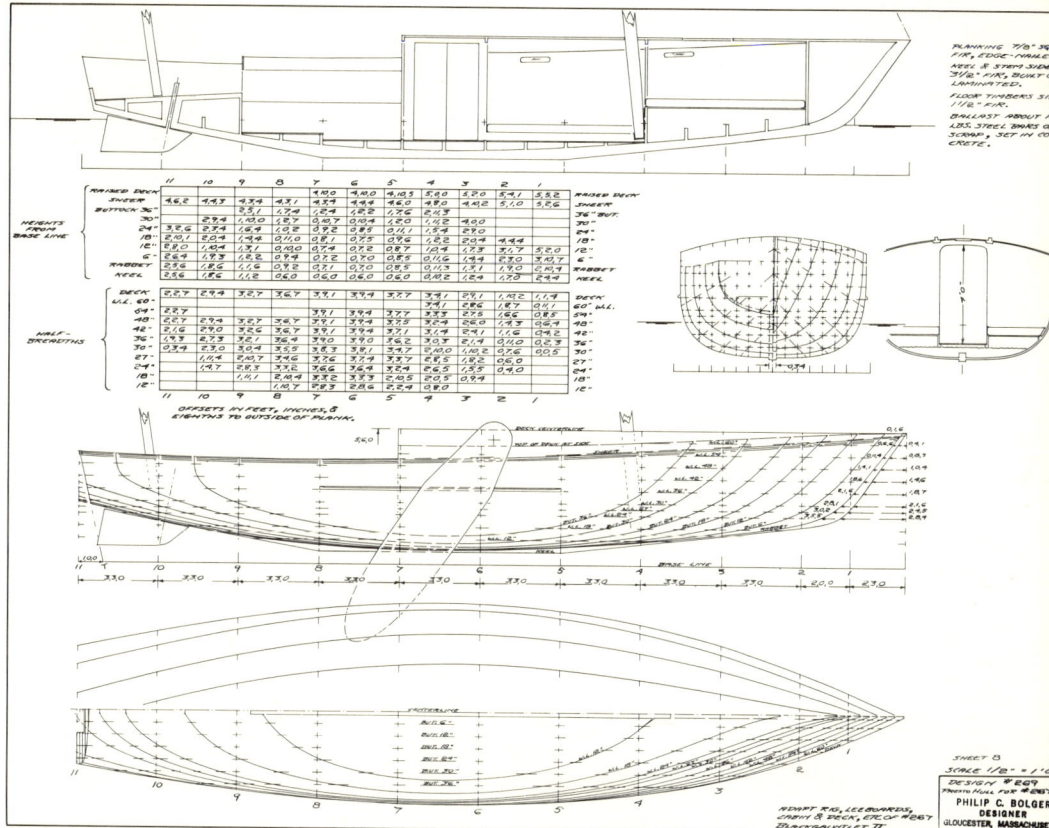

sembled full-length side sheets on edge on each side, and glue and screw together at the stem, being very careful to get them correctly aligned with the two stern ends at the same height. Spring the sides in around the bulkheads and brace temporarily together at the transom. Tap and wedge the bulkheads into position against their marks on the side sheets and flush with the bottoms of the side sheets. One by one remove bulkheads, spread glue, and screw permanently back in place, finishing by permanently fastening the transom. Sides and bulkheads will now have assumed the final shape of the hull; brace the assembly at stem and transom, after making sure that the bulkhead centerlines are in line, amidships; if necessary to make it rigid, at each bulkhead.)

12. Chine logs 1½" x 2½" fir, sprung along the edges of the side sheets, glued, clamped, and screwed from inside; better bevel the edges of the sides first so as not to have to allow for the bevel in putting the logs on. (The bevel is constant the full length and can be done at the first cutting if desired.) Bevel the logs as soon as the glue sets up, to take the hull bottom sheets.

13. Clamps 1½" square fir, glued, clamped, and screwed to inside of sheets.

14. Bottom double ½" plywood with butts staggered; butts may be riveted, clinch-nailed, or bolted, strength of fastening being important only till the glue sets; slobber the glue on and don't spare expense or mess, because if there are

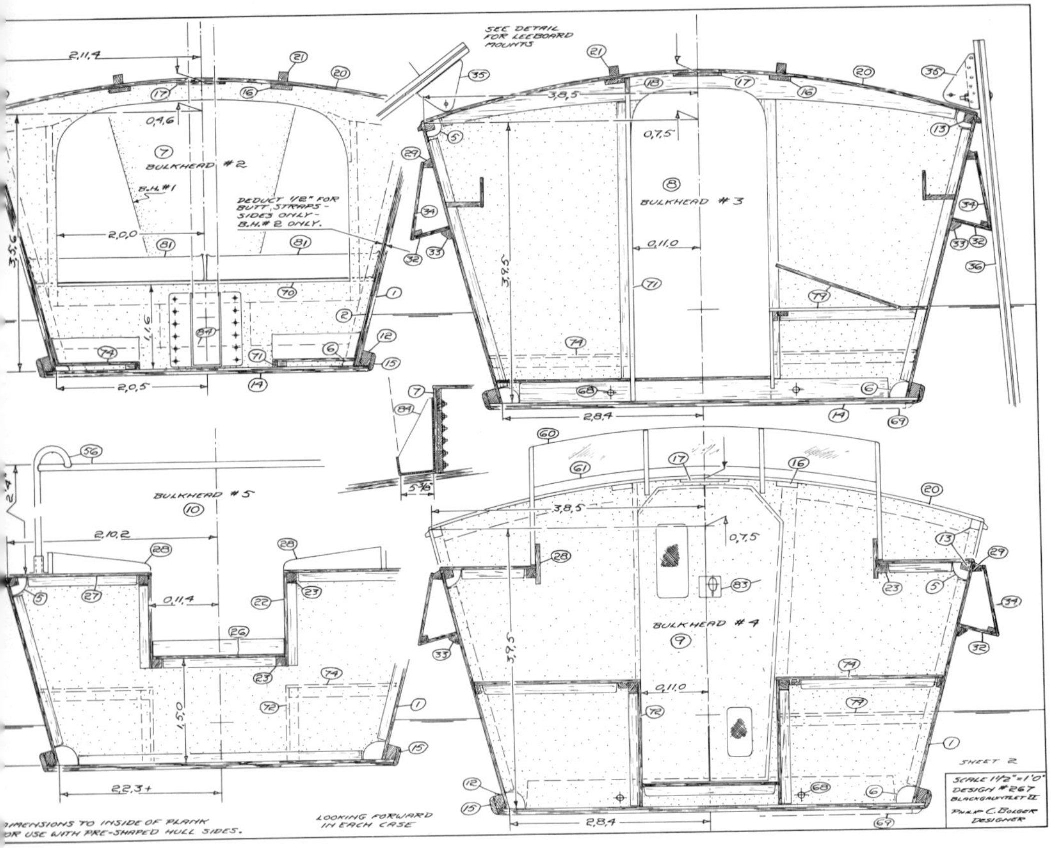
SEE DETAIL FOR LEEBOARD MOUNTS
BULKHEAD #2
B.H. #1
DEDUCT 1/2" FOR BUTT STRAPS - SIDES ONLY - B.H. #2 ONLY.
BULKHEAD #3
BULKHEAD #5
BULKHEAD #4
DIMENSIONS TO INSIDE OF PLANK FOR USE WITH PRE-SHAPED HULL SIDES.
LOOKING FORWARD IN EACH CASE
SHEET 2
SCALE 1 1/2"=1'0"
DESIGN #267
BLACKGAUNTLET II
PHILIP C. BOLGER DESIGNER

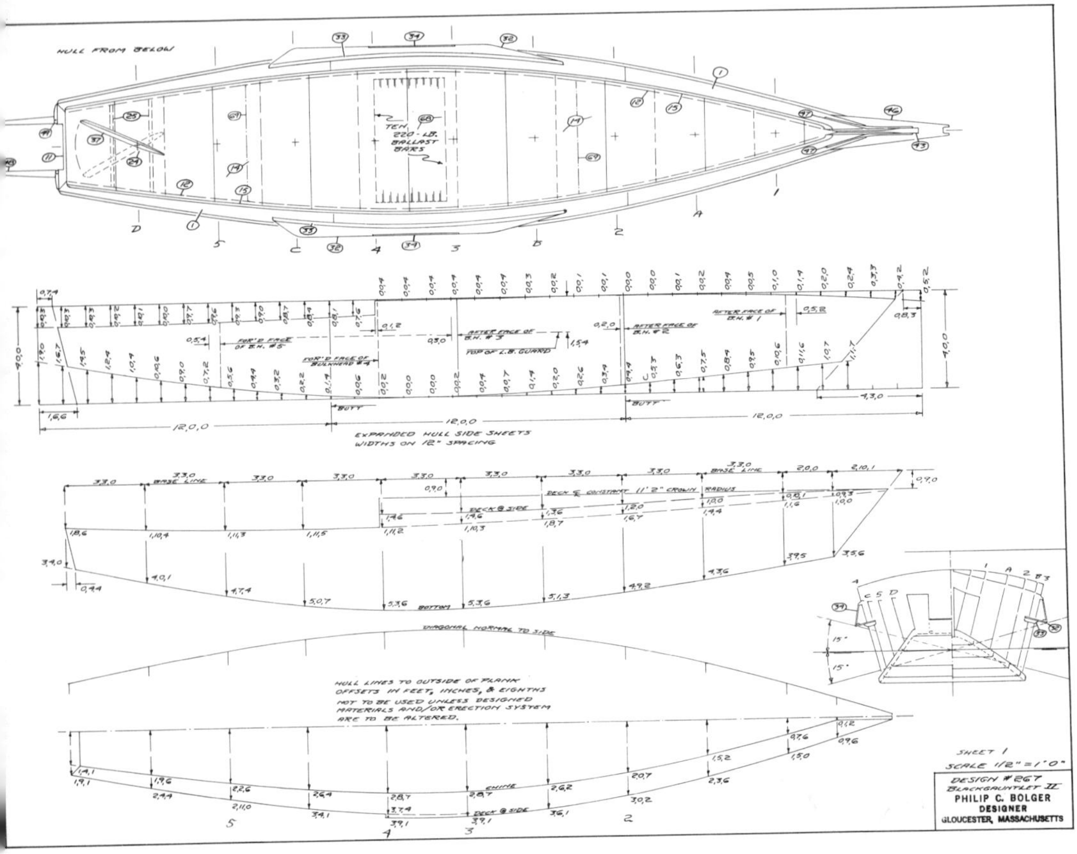
HULL FROM BELOW
TEN 220-LB. BALLAST BARS
FOR'D FACE OF B.H. #5
FOR'D FACE OF BULKHEAD #4
AFTER FACE OF B.H. #3
TOP OF L.B. GUARD
AFTER FACE OF B.H. #2
AFTER FACE OF B.H. #1
BUTT
EXPANDED HULL SIDE SHEETS WIDTHS ON 12" SPACING
BASE LINE
DECK ℄ CONSTANT 11'2" CROWN RADIUS
DECK @ SIDE
BOTTOM
DIAGONAL NORMAL TO SIDE
HULL LINES TO OUTSIDE OF PLANK
OFFSETS IN FEET, INCHES, & EIGHTHS
NOT TO BE USED UNLESS DESIGNED MATERIALS AND/OR ERECTION SYSTEM ARE TO BE ALTERED.
CHINE
DECK @ SIDE
SHEET 1
SCALE 1/2"=1'0"
DESIGN #267
BLACKGAUNTLET II
PHILIP C. BOLGER
DESIGNER
GLOUCESTER, MASSACHUSETTS

any dry places left between the sheets, rot will quickly start up there. From outer sheets drive 2½" screws to chine logs, bottom frames, etc., spaced 4" or thereabouts, plus three or four ¼" flat-head bolts each at bulkheads #3 and #4; inner sheets secured first with 1" screws spaced 6" or whatever it takes to hold them for gluing.

15. Chine caps ¾" x 3⅛" fir, glued and screwed in place and well rounded off. Bottom may be sheathed now with one, two, or more layers of glass cloth, dynel, etc., and polyester resin, wrapped around chine caps to finish on top of chine logs; designer doesn't think sheathing on the sides is worth the trouble and expense, but if the sides are to be sheathed, the internal angle between chines and sides ought to be filled in and coved out on as big a radius as is convenient.

(Hull can now be turned right-side-up, with ends blocked up so as not to stress the glue and fastenings till the decks are on.)

16. Raised deck stringers ¾" x 3½" fir, from bulkhead #1 to #4.

17. Raised deck butt strap ½" plywood, about 8" wide, placed flat and planed to fit crown of deck.

18. Fore and aft beam at toilet room door ¾" x 2½" fir.

19. Forepeak filled solid with expanding foam or blocks cut up to fit neatly; other foam-filled spaces are marked to be dealt with as convenient; if they are all properly filled with a good-quality foam, the boat will not only be fully buoyant, but self-righting when flooded.

20. Raised deck ½" plywood with butt on centerline; after part from 12' sheets, forward part can be one 12' sheet, or there can be a transverse butt, not shown, just abaft the stem to get it out of an 8' sheet; may be sheathed at builder's option.

21. Exterior deck stringers from 1½" square fir, from bulkhead #1 to just short of windshield; ¼" carriage bolts through internal stringers on about 12" spacing, and glued.

22. Sides of watertight cockpit ½" plywood, carried by edges of transom in way of motor cut-out.

23. Afterdeck and well carlines 1½" square fir.

24. Blocking for rudder stock from 5½" x about 18" long, fir; height about 9¾" but fit exactly to height of well sole carlines.

25. Two 1½" x 3½" fir bottom frames from side to side each end of rudder blocking.

26. Well sole ½" plywood; if sheathed, cove out the corners on about 1" radius; cut scuppers through transom flush with sole.

27. Afterdeck ½" plywood, with strapped butts about a foot ahead of bulkhead #5. Put some blocking under it before installation to take the gallows sockets.

28. Coamings ¾" x 6½" mahogany.

29. Sheer moldings bevelled from 1½" square fir to ¾" face.

30. Raised deck moldings from ¾" x 1" fir, stopped short at forward end as shown and deck edge rounded off as much as possible to minimize visual effect of "powder-horn sheer". (This type of sheer line can't be avoided without a hard-to-build distortion of the deck plywood.)

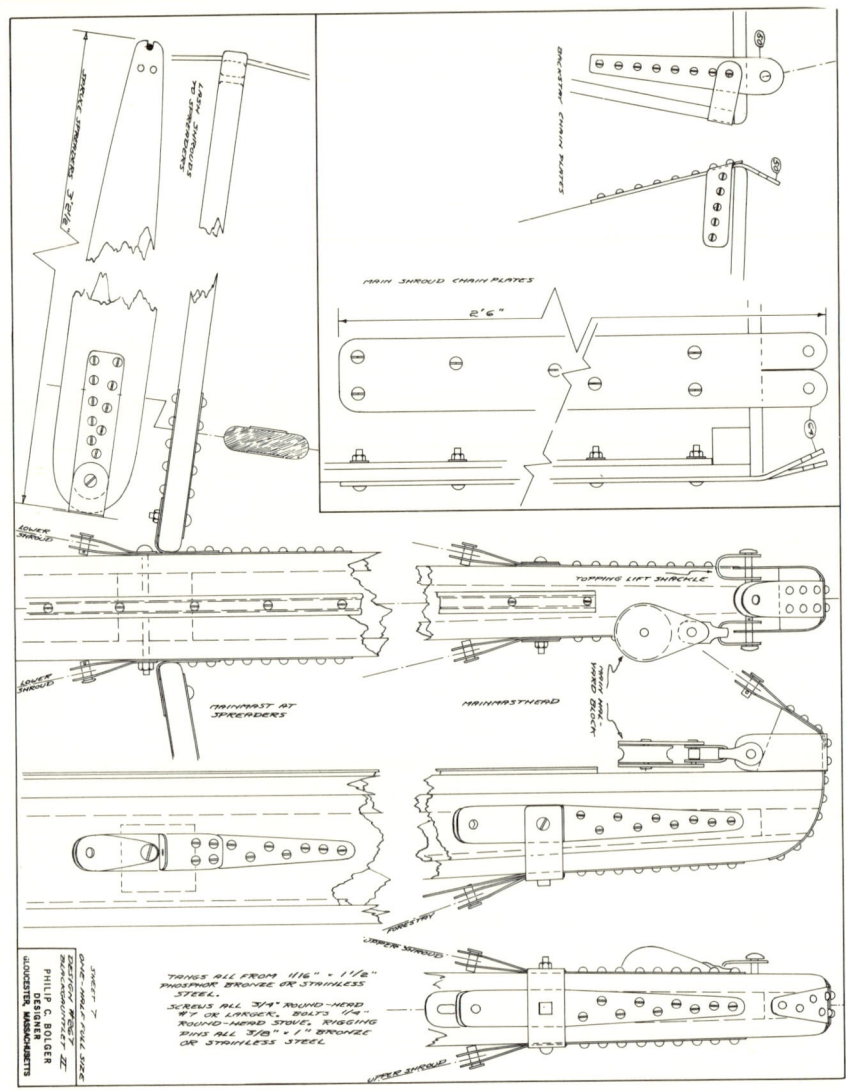

31. Toe rails from ¾" square fir, stopped at section A as shown.

32. Leeboard guards ½" plywood mounted square to hull side and standing 6½" off the sides at bulkheads #3 and #4.

33. Leeboard guard fastening cleats from 1½" square fir sprung on and tapered off at each end; ¼" bolts on about 12" centers through hull sides, or 1½" screws from inside on 4"-6" centers with a bolt at each end; 1½" screws and glue from guards to cleats.

34. Guard braces ½" x 13" x 3'6" plywood; 1½" screws to ¾" x 1½" fastening cleats on edges of guards, and to sheer moldings which are planed off flat in way of the braces.

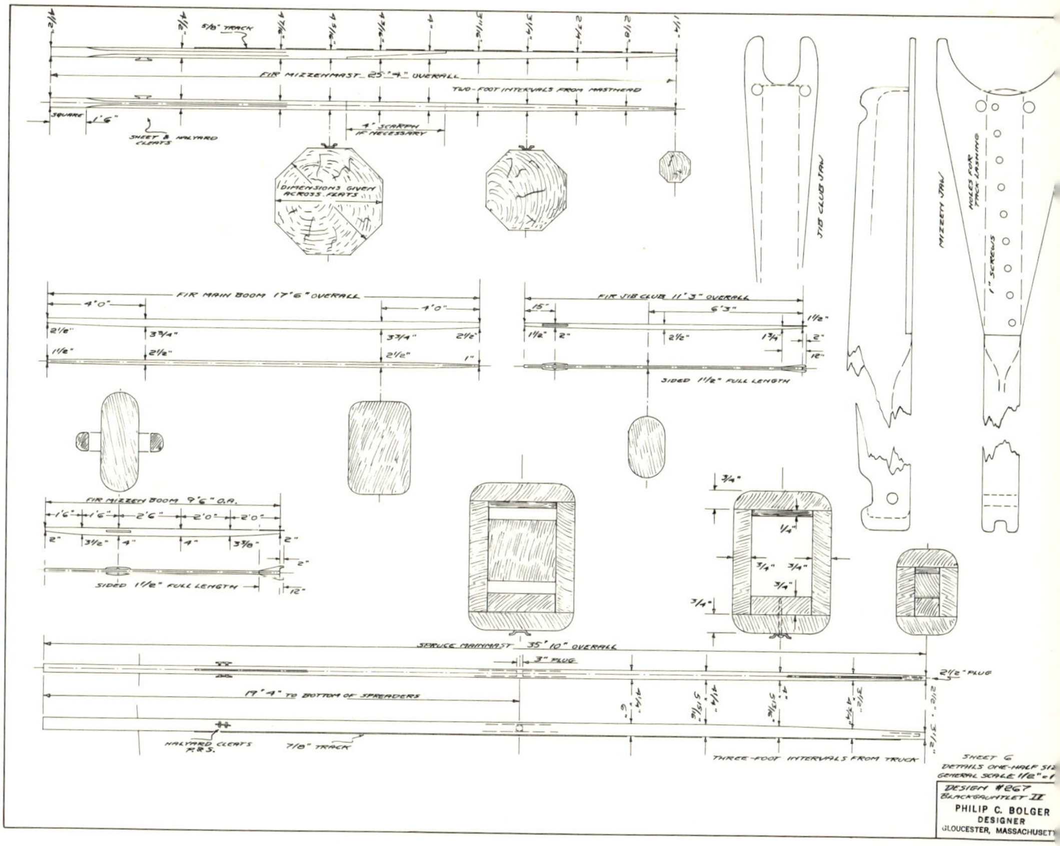
FIR MIZZENMAST 25' 4" OVERALL
TWO-FOOT INTERVALS FROM MASTHEAD
5/8" TRACK
SQUARE
1'6"
SHEET & HALYARD CLEATS
4' SCARPH IF NECESSARY
DIMENSIONS GIVEN ACROSS FLATS
JIB CLUB JAW
MIZZEN JAW
HOLES FOR TACK LASHING
1" SCREWS
FIR MAIN BOOM 17'6" OVERALL
FIR JIB CLUB 11'3" OVERALL
SIDED 1 1/2" FULL LENGTH
FIR MIZZEN BOOM 9'6" O.A.
SIDED 1 1/2" FULL LENGTH
SPRUCE MAINMAST 35' 10" OVERALL
3" PLUG
2 1/2" PLUG
19' 4" TO BOTTOM OF SPREADERS
HALYARD CLEATS P.&S.
7/8" TRACK
THREE-FOOT INTERVALS FROM TRUCK
SHEET 6
DETAILS ONE-HALF SIZE
GENERAL SCALE 1/2" = 1'
DESIGN #267
BLACKGAUNTLET II
PHILIP C. BOLGER
DESIGNER
GLOUCESTER, MASSACHUSETTS

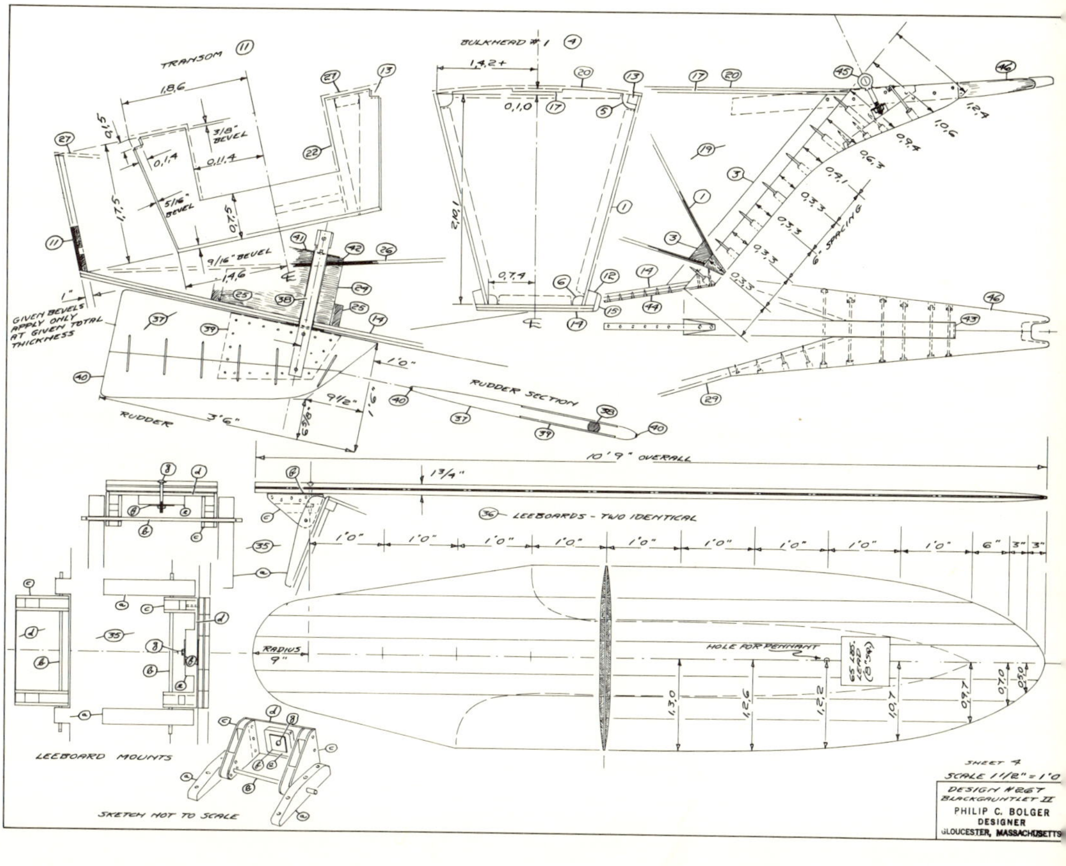
TRANSOM (11)
BULKHEAD #1 (4)
3/8" BEVEL
5/16" BEVEL
9/16" BEVEL
GIVEN BEVELS APPLY ONLY AT GIVEN TOTAL THICKNESS
RUDDER 3'6"
RUDDER SECTION
6" SPACING
10' 9" OVERALL
LEEBOARDS - TWO IDENTICAL
RADIUS 9"
HOLE FOR PENNANT
65 LBS. LEAD (EACH)
LEEBOARD MOUNTS
SKETCH NOT TO SCALE
SHEET 4
SCALE 1 1/2" = 1'0
DESIGN #267
BLACKGAUNTLET II
PHILIP C. BOLGER
DESIGNER
GLOUCESTER, MASSACHUSETTS

35. Leeboard pivots: a. deck mounting blocks 2½" x 2½" x 15" fir, ¼" bolts and glue to deck; b. pivot rod ½" x 2'2" galvanized or brass; c. brackets double ½" plywood cored with 1½" fir blocking, glued and screwed and/or bolted together and to — d. facing ½" plywood; e. backing block 1½" x 7½" square fir; f. bearing plates about 4" square ⅛" galvanized or brass; g. pivot carriage bolt ½", set up slack to turn easily in bearing plates.

36. Leeboards ¼" plywood cheeked out each side with ¾" fir planking glued to the plywood; see drawing for dimensions, fairing, and ballast.

37. Rudder sided 2" fir in three sections, ahead and abaft stock, and bottom, with ¼" x 6" galvanized drift rods.

38. Rudder stock 2" diameter bronze, with sides flattened off to 1½" in way of blade; top can be either squared or with keyway for tiller fitting.

39. Rudder plates ¼" bronze or stainless steel, about 11" x 18" set flush with blade; two ⅜" bolts through stock; 1" flat-head screws around perimeter to blade.

40. Stainless steel half-oval band along edges of rudder blade ¾".

41. Bearing plates ⅛" bronze or stainless about 6" square, an easy fit to stock.

42. Fir block 2½" x 7½" x 2'6", glued and screwed to cockpit sole to form rudder support, mizzenmast step and rack for fuel tank; make sure mast step hole is drained both sides.

43. Stem cap and false head sided 2½" oak or other very hard wood, faired to ¾" face; 3" screws deeply countersunk, or drift rods, to stem, plus plenty glue.

44. Stainless band ¼" x 1" x 1'6" with 1" screws to bottom, 3" to cap.

45. Shoulder eye bolt ¾" x 4½" for forestay.

46. Bowsprit in two sections, seam on centerline, each side 2½" x 4⅞" x 4'4½" fir; seven ¼" bolts through head, cap, and stem, and different-length screws to hull sides, to form knees for head; faired out at the end more or less as shown to form chocks for anchor rode.

47. Ornamental trail knees bent on ¾" square fir with a fillet in the angle of stem cap and hull side.

48. Mizzen sheet boomkin from two 2½" x 3½" x 4'11" oak or other strong, hard wood, connected by a ⅜" diameter rod at the outboard end for a traveller horse; about a 2½" lag bolt at each inboard end.

49. Cleat 1½" x 2½" x 10" glued and screwed to transom each side to take ⅜" x 5" bronze carriage hold-down bolts of boomkin.

50. Backstay chain plates ⅛" x 1½" x 8" bronze or stainless steel, with $\frac{1}{16}$" x 1" x 6" straps brought around the sides as shown; 1" screws.

51. Mizzen partner ½" plywood mounted on a ¾" x 1½" cleat each side, with four 3" screws to cockpit carlines each side plus glue; 1½" x 3½" fir beam on forward and after edges.

52. Portable fuel tank about 6 to 8 gallons.

53. Motor is owner's choice; 3 h.p. will drive her 3 or 4 knots in dead calm and smooth water but is not really enough. Five horse is adequate, seven and a half ample; transom structure as designed won't stand more than about 10 h.p. for long. Use a three or four blade low-pitch prop.

54. Tiller about 1½" square tapered to 1" round, 3' long, with ¼" bronze straps.

55. Main sheet traveller horse ⅜" bronze or galvanized rod flattened out each end to screw to outside of sides; provide stops for traveller.

56. Gallows 1" standard pipe bent and welded to forward diagonal braces; note flange and eye for lifelines to mast; galvanize after welding.

57. Leeboard outriggers 1½" x 2½" x 1'5" oak or other hard wood, with two or three ¼" bolts through carlines and deck; strap for leeboard block at outboard ends.

58. Cleats may be bronze or hardwood, at least eight or ten required; all can be six-inch, but main sheet and some others could be eight-inch.

59. Aluminum or galvanized bow for cockpit hood.

60. Windshield clear plastic ¼", with four ¾" x 3½" fir braces on after side.

61. Windshield coaming 1½" square fir.

62. Cockpit hood dacron, laced to gallows, snapped to windshield; includes, in one piece, side curtains to snap outside coamings, or fold across top to leave one or both sides open; a separate two-piece curtain for the after end would be useful.

63. Cowl ventilators with about 5" throat diameter; mounted on water trap boxes with same-diameter screened deck pipes about 4" above deck; drain deck boxes under #21 deck stringers.

64. Main shroud chain plates from 3/16" x 3" x 2'6" bronze or steel; split at top to take upper and lower shrouds; nine ¼" x 1½" bolts each through sides and butt straps.

65. Jib sheet horse ⅜" x 4' bolted through deck.

66. Forward hatch ½" plywood with 1½" square fir stiffeners on top; double coaming as shown incorporating deck stringers; continuous hinge across after edge; solid latch working from below.

67. Jonesport mooring cleat from 3½" x 5½" x 1'6" hardwood; glue and use four ⅜" bolts through deck.

68. Ballast cast in ten bars of lead with high antimony content; all cast in same mold 2½" wide at bottom, 3½" at top, 5'0½" long at top, 4'11½" at bottom; weight of bars 220 pounds each; about 15" from each end of each bar drill a hole to take a 1" diameter steel round bar fore and aft through all the ballast bars and the bulkheads at each end, to make sure the bars don't move around and to take some of the load off the hull bottom.

69. Alternatively, and in some ways better, the middle part of the bottom can be sheathed with two layers of ⅜" steel plate (preferably corten steel) bolted up through the bottom with ¼" bolts on about 6" spacing around the edges and on a 16" or 18" grid over the whole plate area; if the plating is shaped to be the width of the inside of the bottom and is 13'6" long fore and aft, it will be about seventy square feet in area with a total weight of 2100 pounds. Fillet around the edges with soft wood to smooth the flow. This arrangement should be cheaper and much stronger than the internal lead bars and about equally good for stability, but a boat so arranged will probably be slightly slower on account of the weight being carried more toward the ends of the hull; the steel should be very

thoroughly bedded in seam compound to minimize rusting of the bolts and risking rot in the plywood.

69b. Cabin and cockpit soles ½" plywood, lightly screwed down in five separate sections to be fairly easily removable.

70. Forward berth flat ½" plywood (or thinner if the foam under it is dense) permanently screwed down.

71. Facings of seat-berths and frame of toilet enclosure, ¾" fir.

72. Facings of cockpit seats ½" plywood stiffened at the top with ½" square fir, fixed in place; these facings are supposed to stiffen the bottom of the hull as well as to enclose storage space.

73. Floor timber from side to side 1½" x about 6¼" fir.

74. Seat and berth flats ½" plywood, laid loose, stiffened and held in place with ¾" x 1½" fir cleats round the edges; the same glued and screwed to hull sides and bulkheads for the flats to rest on there.

75. "Portapotti" or similar portable holding toilet.

76. Double-hinged door of toilet enclosure ½" plywood framed with ¾" x 2½" fir; arrange hooks under deck inside and out to hold the door shut.

77. Sink is an ordinary plastic dishpan set in a hole in the dresser.

78. Stove any two-burner alcohol or kerosene type, or bottled gas with the bottle boxed on deck; in view of the tendency of this type of boat to sail at a large angle of heel, a gimballed stove would be a worthwhile improvement.

79. Dresser ½" plywood, formica-sheathed, with a removable panel giving access to storage space.

80. Shelves ¾" fir with 4"-high ½" plywood coamings.

81. Mattresses 4" urethane foam.

82. Deadlights ¼" clear plastic screwed and glued to inside of hull.

83. Cabin doors double, see 1½"-scale drawing of bulkhead #4; screened vent openings top and bottom; any good standard knob and lock; arrange to hook back each side, or, better if suitable hinges can be found or made, to lift off and stow under cockpit seats. Slant of port side is only to provide more shoulder space and can be put up straight if a different galley layout calls for it.

84. Mainmast step welded of ¼" steel, galvanized; the backing plate is 12" square with twelve ¼" bolts through the bulkhead (note that the step has to be in place before the space ahead is filled with foam, and that the bolt nuts must be pinned to be secure against backing off without inspection). There should be about a ½" diameter drain hole on each side of the step.

85. Lifelines ¼" stainless 7 x 7 wire, spliced to gallows flanges and set up with pelican hooks to $\frac{1}{16}$" x 1½" x about 19" stainless strap around forward side of mast; length eye to eye about 15'8", but measure on the boat as built; lifelines should be slack to minimize stress at ends.

13
RONDO II

$39'6'' \times 6'8''$

Rondo II was derived from the Folding Schooner, not *Blackgauntlet*. She's a much smaller boat than she looks at first glance, weighing only a couple of tons on close to forty feet overall. Her thick bottom serves her as ballast, but it's relatively light compared with the ton of lead in *Blackgauntlet*. She sails at a comparatively small angle of heel, the point of maximum power, when the weather chine emerges, being on the order of ten degrees; she'll sometimes pound thunderously in a head sea in consequence. The upright stance is possible because in spite of being narrow for her length, she's wide for her depth under water.

She feels ponderous under way, something like the big coasting schooners whose proportions she resembles in hull and rig, and strangely different from the spirited flightiness of the actually much heavier *Blackgauntlet*. You can walk up to the bow and back before she takes notice that you have let go of the tiller, and she will easily sail herself beating and reaching. She doesn't like to be pinched, possibly partly because her bilgeboards are on the small side, but given a good fill she hangs on well and is perfectly reliable in stays. (In passing, it's worth remarking that the relationship between lateral plane area and sail area is inverse; an undercanvassed boat, one which has a lot of resistance in proportion to her sail area, needs more lateral plane than she would with more driving power.)

The swinging rudder has a good, firm feel, but becomes very heavy with the blade swung aft; when you put the engine in gear the prop stream has a tendency to kick the rudder back and up, whereupon the tiller is suddenly as stubborn as a mule.

The cabin reflects the theory that it's best to economize there first about as far as possible; there's absolutely nothing built into it. Fitted out with air mattresses, sleeping bags, portable toilet and curtain, camp stove, table, and ice box, it's surprisingly pleasant and comfortable as long as you

Rondo II *in Essex Bay.*

plant yourself in one place and stay there. Moving around is a bit cruel if you're much above five years old.

The end wells, open to the sea, for motor and anchors, work out well, though without the clamshells the forward scuppers will fountain six feet high when she stamps on a head sea.

Needless to say she goes easily and fast under power and handles well.

Though shallow and lightly ballasted, her high and flaring sides give her a great range of stability. I've never seen her rail down, but of course sooner or later she'll get a knockdown in a squall that will flood the open cockpit. When this happens, the watertight cabin bulkhead, with the sill of the companionway up at deck level, will keep the water out of the cabin, the foam built into her after quarters will float the motor head well clear of the water, and the buoyancy of the raised deck will lift her back onto her feet. Quite a bit of water will spill out through the motor well; the rest will have to be bailed out with buckets.

Bradford Story built her, exactly as here specified. He cut out and assembled the sides, bottom, and deck in 178 working hours, working alone most of the time in a hot July. He's a very skilled boat carpenter, getting good results quickly; I doubt anybody will do the job much faster. By the time she was finished, rigged, and launched there were 480 hours on the bill; the material cost was $2,032 including $477 for the epoxy resin with which all the plywood was treated. Over and above those costs the sails were $631; the engine $519; and camping and other equipment cost an

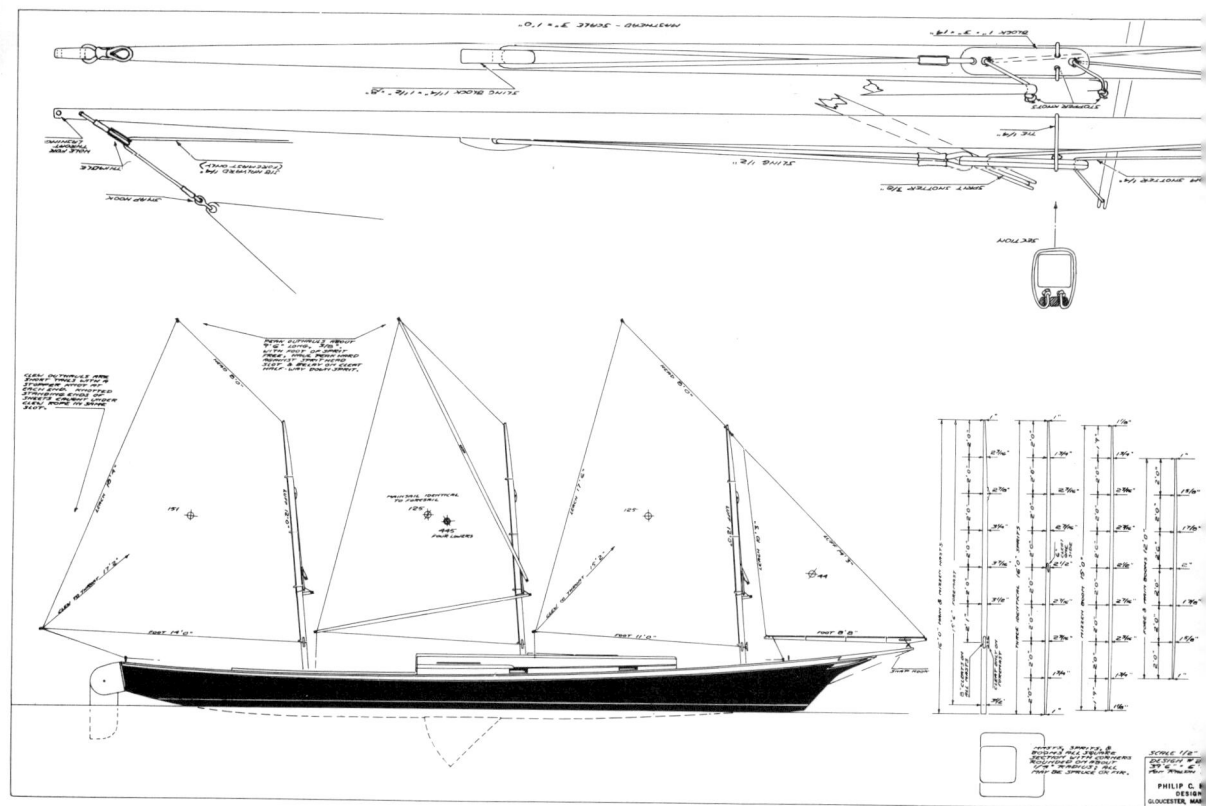

amount not known to me. Say she spoiled $8,000, about what a twenty-five-foot fiberglass sloop sold for that year with roughly similar finish.

I was proud of the rig, thinking it something of an exploit to get so much power without an inch of wire or a single block, or any spar I couldn't pick up and step in my two hands. I tend to take my own strength as a standard for mechanical advantage, on the theory that any man far into middle age can do what can be done by an office worker, who never was athletic. Perhaps, unfortunately, I'm still quite a bit stronger than many women, and moreover I knew that there was a trick to shipping those sprits which needed practice. Craig Hills didn't like the sprits at all, had apparently distrusted the rig in the first place, and after trying it out was not interested in half-measures such as lifts and snotter purchases. After considerable argument I drew, and Brad built, the alternate gaff rig. With it, each mast is more than six feet longer and I can't handle one alone. It took ten blocks and about four hundred feet of line that the sprit rig would function without. I have to grant that the gaff sails are more docile to take in and set, and not much more trouble any of the time, except in a jibe when the booms fly up in the wild old way. I guess the performance is about the

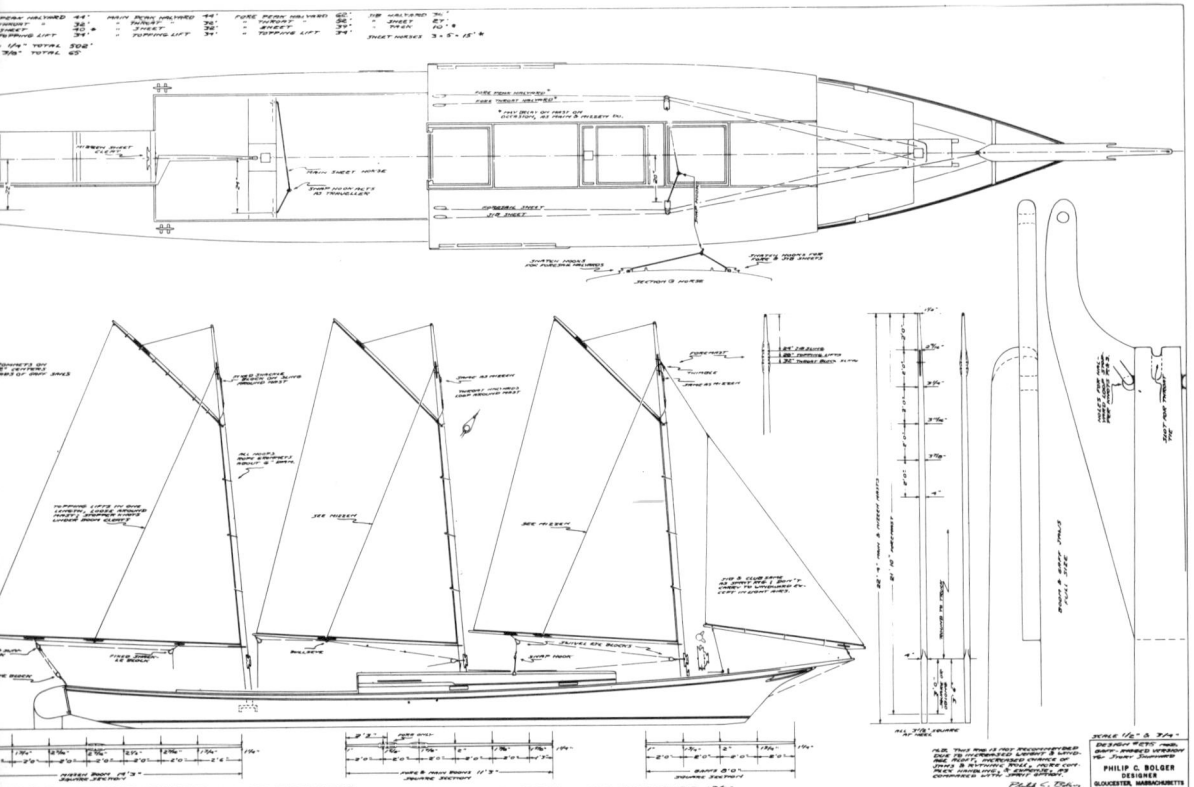

same with one rig as the other; the gaff rig has more weight aloft, but the sails are set better most of the time because the halyards don't stretch as quickly as the sprit snotters. I still think the sprit rig is better, because it's cheaper and the masts are so much easier to get down on deck. Nothing to do with machismo.

KEY TO PLANS

All plywood is supposed to be ½" in 4' x 8' sheets; it's thought that thirty-eight sheets will do the job if craftily used (bottom cuts to less waste from 10' sheets). Natural wood according to availability: any mahogany, or Douglas fir, will serve for any of it; spruce, cedar, and pine will serve in most places such as the bulkhead frames; oak is not to be used at any glued joint but would be good for the shoe, motor board, false head, and tiller if available in good quality.

1. Hull sides ½" plywood to pattern given.
2. Butt straps ½" x 6".
3. Stem from 1½" square.
4. Bilgeboard case faces ½" plywood.
5. Headblocks 1¼" x 2½".
6. Top plugs 1¼" x 1½".

7. Outside stiffeners from $1\frac{1}{2}''$ x $2\frac{1}{2}''$.
8. Log and header $1\frac{1}{2}''$ x $2\frac{1}{2}''$.
9. Bulkheads (including webs and transom) all $\frac{1}{2}''$ plywood with fastening frames sided $1\frac{1}{2}''$ and molded $1\frac{1}{2}''$ and $2\frac{1}{2}''$.
10. Temporary braces on B and E bulkheads.
11. Drain limbers in C, D, G, and H, *not* in A or F.

(Stand completed hull sides with bilgeboard cases in place, on edge, bottom up, each side of E and F bulkheads; true up bulkheads to their marks and set them reasonably square across; glue and screw sides to bulkheads, being especially careful not to have any holidays at F. Pull sides in to transom, placing G and H bulkheads on their marks as you go, and secure them. Pull forward sides' ends in to stem same way, using stem to perfect alignment; secure on marks, bulkhead A being the one that has to be perfectly watertight.)

12. Chine logs finished $1\frac{1}{2}''$ x $2\frac{1}{2}''$; if the curve aft is too hard, rip horizontally or otherwise laminate; glue and screw (or nail) to sides and smooth up the bevel.
13. Hull bottom to finish $1\frac{1}{2}''$, triple $\frac{1}{2}''$ or double $\frac{3}{4}''$; butts athwartships well staggered; glue throughout and try to avoid holidays.
14. Shoe $1\frac{1}{2}''$ x $2\frac{1}{2}''$.
15. Stiffeners or fillers along outside bottom of bilgeboard cases from 1 5/16" x $2\frac{1}{2}''$ (see full-size section).
16. Opening for motor lower unit about $1'0''$ x $2'6''$.
17. Motor board braces from $1\frac{1}{2}''$ x $7\frac{1}{2}''$. (Turn hull rightside up.)
18. Bowsprit heel beam from $1\frac{1}{2}''$ x $7\frac{1}{2}''$ (see dimensions).
19. Breasthook $1\frac{1}{2}''$ x $7\frac{1}{2}''$.
20. False head sided $1\frac{1}{2}''$.
21. Raised deck centerline butt strap $\frac{1}{2}''$ x $12''$.
22. Raised deck $\frac{1}{2}''$ plywood.
23. Raised deck stringers and hatch coamings $\frac{3}{4}''$ x $1\frac{1}{2}''$.
24. Hatches $\frac{1}{2}''$ plywood with $\frac{3}{4}''$ x $1\frac{1}{2}''$ frames; all these hatches are loose and each is to have two reasonably strong hooks to hold it shut, also an outside latch for a padlock on the after one. Note that the middle hatch has two positions, to clear or cover the mainmast partner hole.
25. Forward deck $\frac{1}{2}''$, with $\frac{1}{2}''$ x $12''$ butt strap on top and a third $\frac{1}{2}''$ layer at the partner.
26. Vent opening, screened, $6''$ x $12''$ with water trap inside.
27. Companionway slide $\frac{1}{2}''$ with $6''$ x $12''$ screened vent openings; $\frac{3}{4}''$ x $2\frac{1}{2}''$ retaining cleats.
28. Deadlights $\frac{1}{4}''$ clear plastic glued and screwed to inside.
29. Mast steps $\frac{1}{2}''$ plywood on $1\frac{1}{2}''$ x $2\frac{1}{2}''$ feet (note that mainmast step has a block at each end as well as at the sides); mizzen step is $12''$ x $14''$; main $8''$ x $12''$; fore $12''$ x $18''$. Locate step and partner holes exactly as dimensioned, taking pains; size of holes to provide a loose but close fit to masts to obviate wedges.
30. Thwart $\frac{1}{2}''$ x $12''$ with double $\frac{1}{2}''$ x $12''$ pad for partner as shown; $1\frac{1}{2}''$ x $2\frac{1}{2}''$ beam at forward edge.
31. Sides of motor well $\frac{1}{2}''$ plywood.

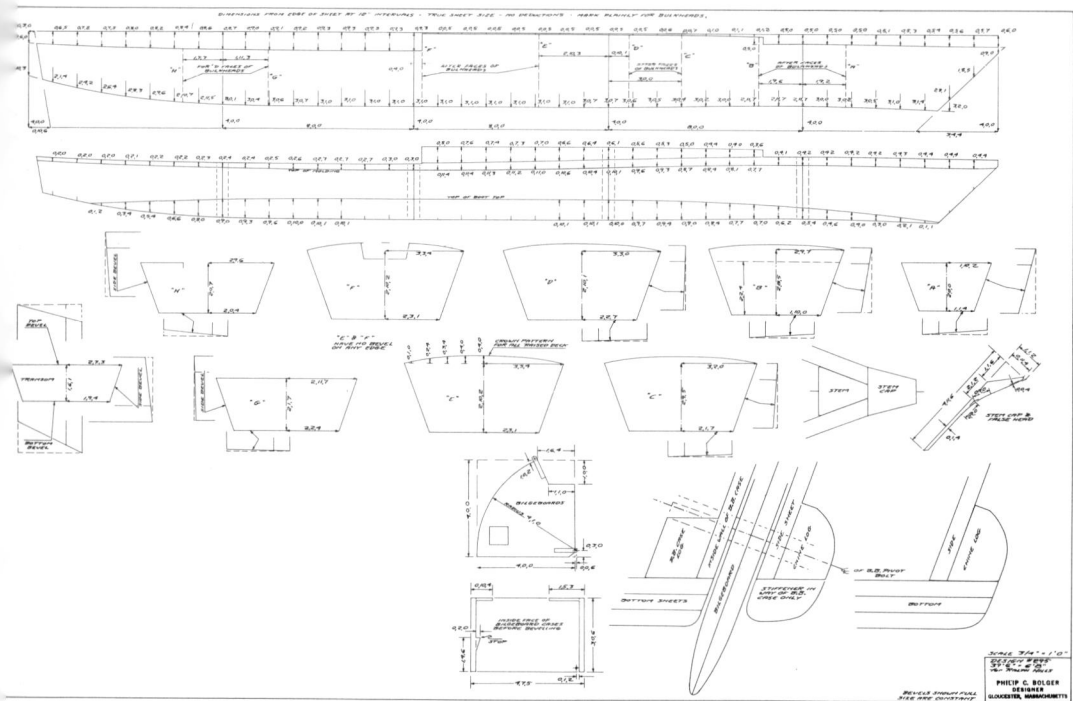

32. End and bottom cleats 1½" square.

33. Carlines ¾" x 1½".

34. Foam buoyancy, preferably urethane, expanded or cut blocks; about ten cubic feet each side for a total positive buoyancy of about 1200 pounds; if cut blocks, cleat up off the bottom to make sure of clear drainage.

35. Knees or brackets sided ¾".

36. Carlines, coamings, and afterdeck clamps ¾" x 1½".

37. Afterdeck ½" plywood.

38. Rudder double ½" plywood.

39. Rudder blade ½" x 18" x 48"; top rounded on 9" radius; ½" pivot bolt with the biggest wing nut that can be found.

40. Four gudgeons, galvanized or stainless, with a ¼" x 20"-plus rod through all.

41. Slot for tiller 3" x 12".

42. Tiller brackets plywood with ¼" x 1½" x 8" tongues to take link toggles (note that the link terminals must have toggles to take up the vertical movement due to raking rudder axis); the link can be about 1" aluminum tube with ends flattened out; radius of tillers from centerline of gudgeons to centerlines of toggle pins, 11".

43. Tiller tongue ¾" x 6" x 2'0" with pintles and gudgeons about as shown.

44. Tiller 1½" x 2½" x 3'10" with ⅛" x 1½" x 1'6" straps and ⅜" pivot bolt.

45. Motor board 1½" x 7½", with 1½" x 2½" cleat each side.

46. Motor O.M.C. 9.9 horsepower with three-blade low-pitch prop. One or two six-gallon portable tanks between motor and bulkhead H. Note that all the

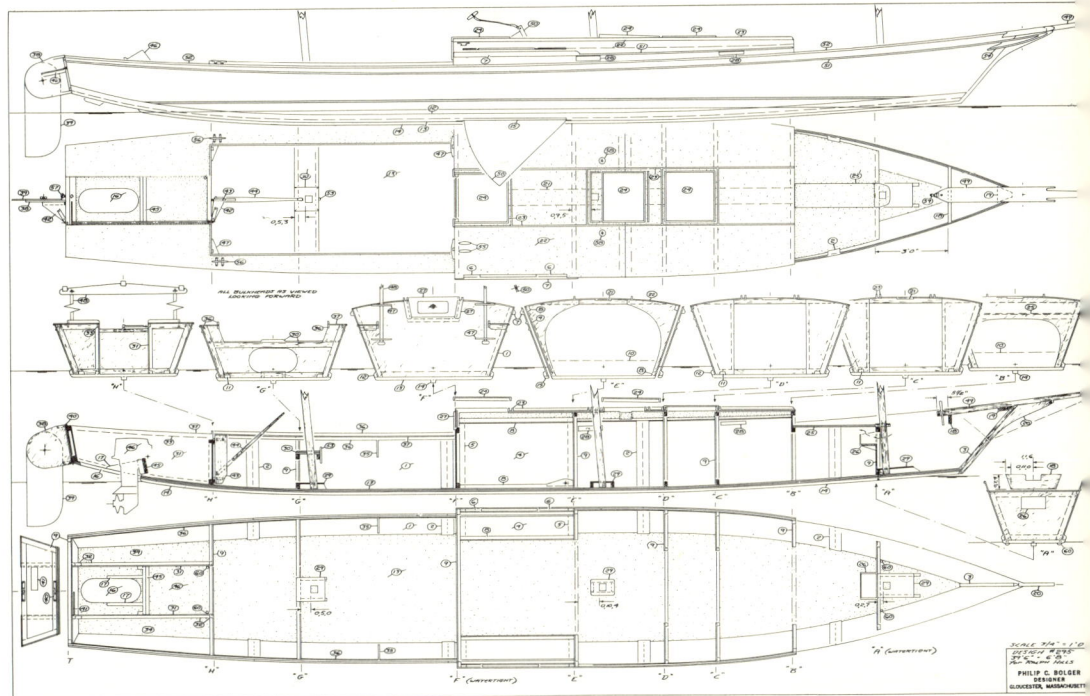

motor well area is watertight but not self-draining; gluing at sides and forward end must be done with as much care as any part of the hull.

47. Brackets for tent stanchions, eight in all.

48. Tent frames 3/4" x 5½" x 5'3", shaped to take the three sprits as shown; stanchions 4'10" overall, 3/4" x 1½", pivoted at top to fold up into compact packages. The tent itself is a square sheet about 13'4" each way including the side curtains.

49. Bowsprit from 2½" x 7½" x 7'0" overall, bolted down to breasthook and heel beam; 3/4" x 12" belaying pin for mooring.

50. Bilgeboards double ½" plywood; (see diagram and full-size section for edge fairing); 1/4" x 2" x 12" stainless straps engage 3/4" pivot bolt and head stop; a short lanyard with a wooden toggle, and a pin on a lanyard to fit several holes in the board suited to various depths.

51. Raised deck and lower trim moldings 3/4" half-rounds.

52. Main sheet molding 1" half-round.

53. Main sheet cleat.

54. Trail knees carved to fill angle of side and false head in a hollow curve to carry lower trim moldings and 3/4" square lower trail molding.

55. Cleats for jib and foresail sheets.

56. Quarter cleats 8"; one takes mizzen sheet.

57. Lanyard with stopper knot and 3" thimble is fairlead for mizzen sheet.

58. Pad eyes for standing end and lead thimble of foresail sheet.

59. Thimble for jib sheet lead.

60. Drain holes for motor well and forward well 1" diameter, covered outside with small, aft-facing clam-shells.

14
THE PARI-MUTUEL SCHOONER PROJECT

Dear Bill:

I've elected to show you a pure sharpie model rather than the scow type I judge you had in mind; I nearly gave up on it while sketching the scow, because being wide she had to be shingle-shallow to keep under 100 gross tons, yet still needed a fairly big rig with four tall masts instead of the five short ones; this set of proportions struck me as dangerous, as I mentioned on the phone; if overpowered she would flip bottom-up, suddenly; not likely, but possible. Besides, she'd be horribly noisy and bumpy in a head sea. Now this sharpie is a type I've designed many of and owned and sailed myself for years, and I don't think the giant scale of it negates the experience. They have a good range of stability, heel enough to be soft in a head sea, have an easy roll, and turn so short that I much doubt the bow thruster is needed, nor do I think she needs twin screws either to handle her or to keep the prop immersed. They're also good sailers and fairly graceful to look at, and can use all-precut plating. If anything, they are more economical of steel than the scow. Maintenance would be easier because more of the bottom can be reached without special facilities.

As to the power, it seems to me that since it makes sense to generate alternating current with an engine running steadily, the best arrangement would be to give her a sizable single engine both for propulsion and for electric power. One of the weaknesses of all light, flat-bottom types is that they lose their way in short turns and in general don't carry way well (this is an advantage if you need to stop her suddenly, by the way) but with a variable-pitch prop turning over gently all the time she should behave like a J-boat. On the other hand she doesn't need full motorship power because she always has some boost and stabilizing effect from her sails, so she can use a moderate-size engine and have plenty of power available for generating off the front end; in a crisis you could cut out the generator and devote all the power to the propeller in high pitch.

Foresail, mainsail, mizzen, spanker, and driver are loose-footed and brail up to the standing gaffs and masts, being secured semipermanently to jackstays. The driver has a permanent topping lift over the peak of the gaff, as you suggested, and sheets to a horse outside the stern. The other

THE PARI-MUTUEL SCHOONER PROJECT

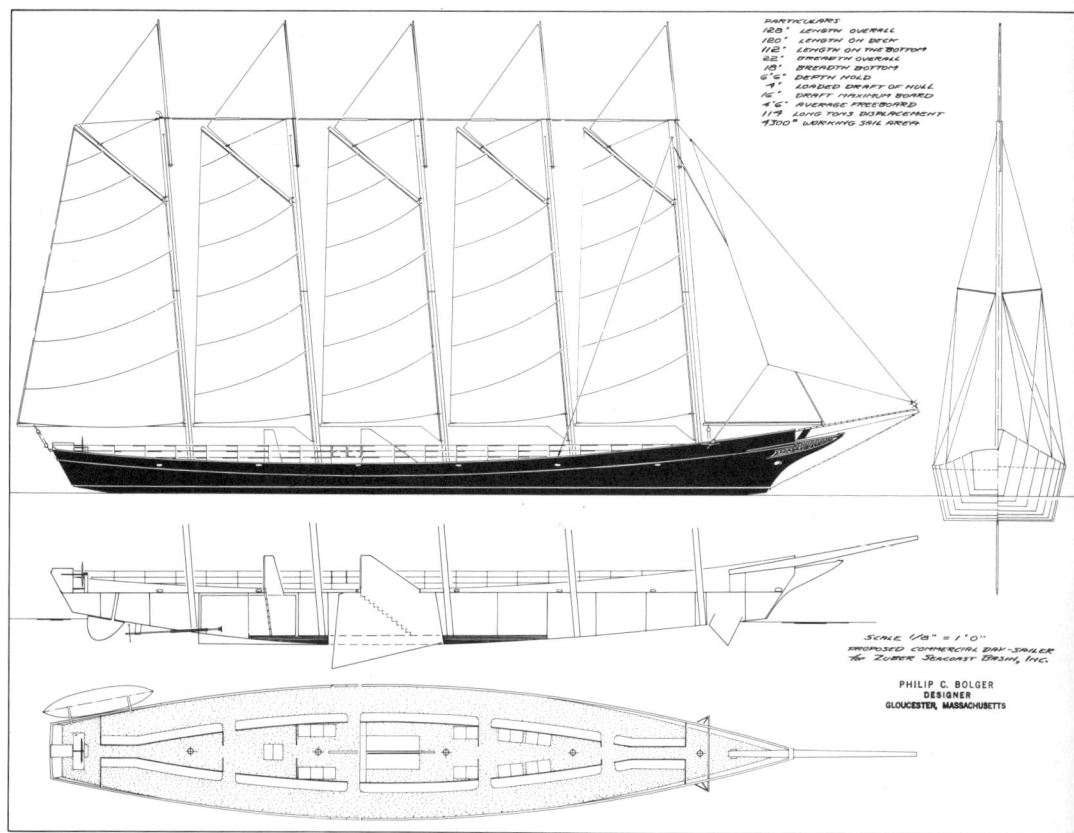

four have booms fixed in one plane to stand their own weight and hold down against the lift of the clew; the object is to keep them clear of heads and make it possible to sheet them with a single part to a centerline block on the next mast, so as to have minimum snarls and least chance of entangling the paying guests. These sails have about 673 square feet area each as drawn, with booms only nineteen feet long; not as lethal as a glance at the study might suggest — a big plus for the five-master over one with fewer masts, hence for the relatively narrow vessel. The forestaysail is conventional; jib has a wire luff and no stay, and is small enough to roll up easily. The topsails, of light cloth set on light, unstayed masts, are mostly for the taking of publicity photos, when they ought to look very pretty; they're set flying from the deck.

The mastheads are strutted together with aluminum tubing taking the small forward thrust of the after four masts to the permanent backstays of the foremast, resulting in a rig both simpler and stiffer than the usual coaster staying plan.

The deck plan is laid out about as you suggested, with passengers kept away from most of the centerline part of the deck so that there's a fairly small distance to fall for people who lose their balance. Extreme bow and stern are fenced off for crew stations, with good access forward and aft; a sizable power winch or windlass is on or by each mast, plus there is one at each end for anchor chains. The centerboard hoists to a gallows across the booby hatches leading down to the toilets. There's plenty of room below for quite roomy crew quarters and I'd think it would be well to have some so as to be able to take her south winters with minimum trouble and expense; I see no reason why she can't make any kind of ocean passage in perfect safety and considerable speed. The high sides at the ends will keep her dry and the open rail amidships will spill any heavy water she might ship.

I've drawn bench seating for 112 people; even regarded as an ordinary head boat she has rail space for about 100 at 30 inches apart. Lifejackets stow under the benches; inflatable rafts are indicated, plus a quarter boat for pursuing swimmers at short notice.

Now I think if we plan carefully and imaginatively you will be able to build two of these for the quarter-million you mentioned, and should, so people will have the other one to look at while they sail in one, besides other obvious advantages of a pair. But this leads to the thought: Instead of just a casual sail, why not race them? Twice a day over a fifteen-mile triangle laid out as might seem most interesting, reserving the evening calms for a gentle excursion with a band. Engines would be used as suggested, to make sure of completing the courses as scheduled, but with governed revolutions, and as one vessel or master tends to outsail the other they can be handicapped by adjusting the allowed engine speed. It'd be easy to fake the race, but much better to keep it honest and encourage people to bet on it. Maybe we have a new mass sport here; if it were carefully set up and promoted it could end with huge fleets of these things racing, the greatest spectacle on earth available on a daily basis, the best skippers more famous than any ballplayer, to say nothing of jockies, and more money bet than on the horses because with these the bettor can ride the horse of his fancy. Every place on board would be signed up months ahead, and the worse the weather the greater the spectacle. The franchises would be worth more than baseball or football clubs, and the investment quite a lot less. The more you think about it, the more glittering vistas open up.

Sincerely,
Phil. Bolger

(This letter was the result of a commissioned study; it was meant to be, and was, taken seriously. I still think, several years later, that the business opportunity is real, though no doubt it would take phenomenal talent and enterprise to get it off the ground.)

15
PROA

$$39'6'' \times 19'6''$$

The man who commissioned this design ran out of money, or maybe just lost his nerve, so it wasn't built and I've no idea how much tinkering would be needed to make it work. The dubious points include the strength of the outrigger, which was supposed to be very flexible, and the strength and geometry of the tricky steering-and-lateral-plane arrangement.

This latter was the best I could come up with to meet a specification for a singlehanded capability. The idea was that to "tack" her, the helmsman would start her off with wind abeam and let go the sheet, as in any proa, but that all he'd have to do to get her going the other way would be to swing the skeg lever down, chock it and the tiller to hold the skeg and rudder up horizontally, out of water; then stroll to the other end, release the tiller and skeg lever there, and pick up the handiest part of the endless sheet to get way on her. The difference from the usual proa, with a fixed fin or daggerboard and a steering sweep, is that the sail needs no adjustment, except to the sheet, and that the steering, once in the lowered position, is a one-handed operation leaving a hand free for the sheet.

The raised skeg and rudder at the end functioning as a bow are angled to give some lift when the bow goes under a wave; Dick Newick, when shown this design, warned me that he had doubts about the strength of the assembly under that kind of stress; the whole thing is too complicated for my taste anyway, but I haven't come up with a scheme I like any better. I do think it was almost certainly a mistake to introduce that two degrees of toe-in in the skeg mounts; the idea was to give her a boost to windward that would allow the hull to go straight through the water with none of what's called yaw angle. If it worked exactly as intended, it might add quite a lot to her speed at times, but it's about as likely that it would produce a lee helm more often — not as disastrous in a proa as in a conventional fore-and-after, but still very bad for windward performance.

I suppose the smart thing to do would be to make up one of these

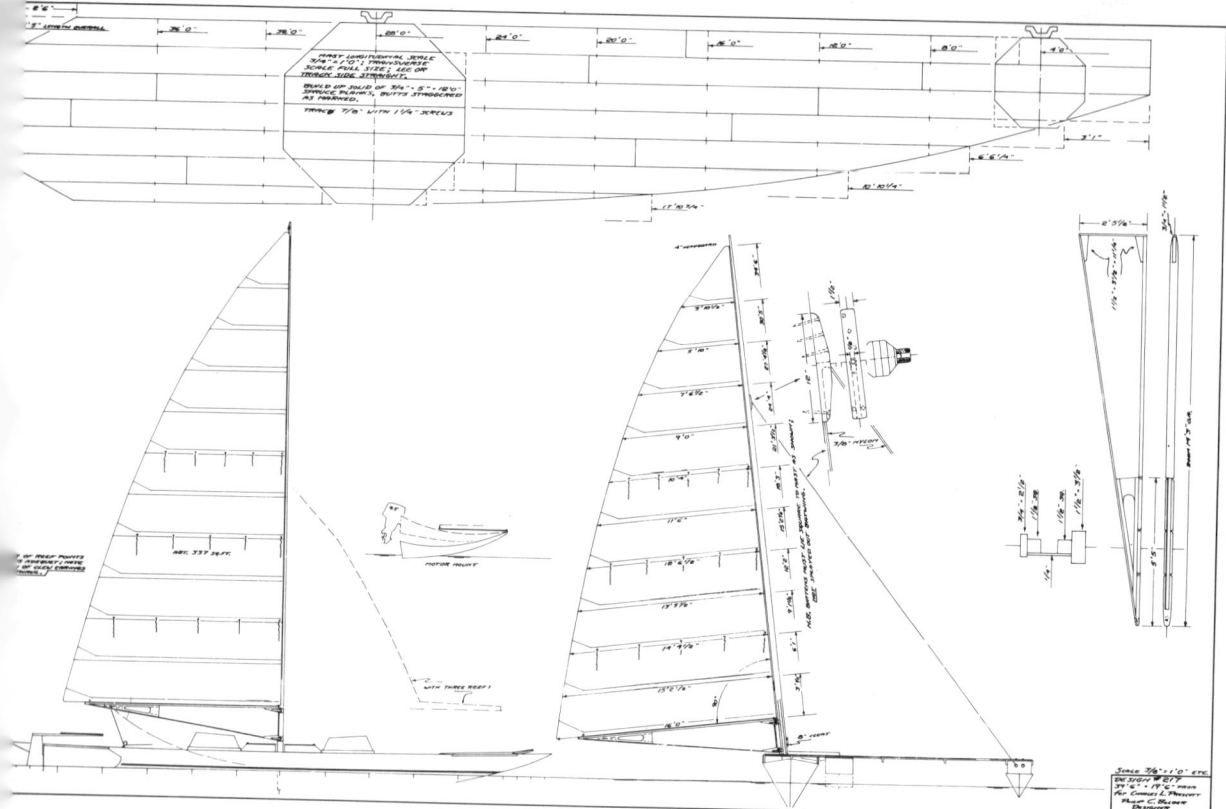

skeg-rudder assemblies and steer the other end with a big sweep in usual proa fashion until either it was established that the skeg-rudder worked properly, or an improvement was devised if it didn't. The sweep would be a two-handed affair, probably a heavy strain on the helmsman since it would have to function as a lateral plane as well as for steering with this rig. Somebody else would have to be along to sheet the sail. In fact, of course, she couldn't be driven hard without a second crewman anyway — the float is not heavy enough to be effective ballast when there's weight in the wind, unless somebody can walk out there and sit on it.

The general proportions and shape seem very good to me for fast sailing in open water. The rig is also attractive, especially the sail tracked on the lee side of the mast, which I think would produce magnificent thrust as there would be no interference with lee-side airflow. The mast is canted to leeward, at some sacrifice in power to carry sail, so that it'll hit the water in a knockdown before the outrigger goes over past vertical; i.e., she'd have a chance of righting herself. I suppose there ought to be a ladder built into the outrigger so somebody could climb the nineteen feet up to the float if she should hang on her side.

I can't figure out now (it's many years since I drew this) why I put the standing end of the stay on the float instead of aloft. It would seem more sensible to have the stay fast up on the mast and simply take it out to an ordinary (but strong) cleat on the float.

Though a horribly sprawling object, she breaks down fairly easily for storage. Her intended mooring in use was to have been in the open sea off a long beach without an inlet; I recall the owner and myself agreeing that, whether she could sail or not, he'd have a grand swimming float.

I've never sailed a proa, but every now and then, while maneuvering something more or less conventional under sail, I've thought about how to tackle the same circumstances with the proa configuration. You have permanent weather and lee sides and interchangeable bow and stern, and though you can luff straight into the wind, you can only turn one way when you've done so. What you can do, and it has to be a godsend at times, is to stop her short and start off again in either direction, beam reaching, without any risk of losing control. It seems to me that the proa principle has some interesting possibilities, but the only designer who's had a chance to learn much about them is Dick Newick, and I gather he finds that trimarans are both easier to design and easier to sell, as matters stand.

KEY TO PLANS

1. Backbone timber about 2 x 8, one side on centerline, one edge on base line, braced up to lie dead straight; fish to length from any number of sections.
2. Base timbers of frames about 2 x 4, one edge on base line, braced to floor or ground to stand plumb; set in notches in backbone.
3. Side frames extended to form legs screwed or bolted to base timbers; all ¾" x 2½" except the midships one which is 1½" x 2½"; brace diagonally to stand plumb to base line.
4. Deck beams ¾" x 2½".
5. Partner beam 1½" x 10½" replaces deck beam on midship frame.
6. Stiffening flanges on partner beam ¾" x 5½" screwed and glued to partner.
7. Midships floor timber built up of three courses of 1½" including the filler between the side frames, all glued and bolted together to form base for mast.
8. Gussets and bulkheads ⅜" plywood.
9. Bottom blocks of end frames from 3½" to 5½" x 9"; must be fitted neatly to allow plywood sides to bear and glue accurately.
10. Stems sided 2½" molded about 2¾", extended to rest in recess each end of backbone timber as shown.
11. Keel 1½" square; bevel as shown full size and spring over frames from stem to stem (sic); scarf as necessary or laminate.
12. Clamps, and supporting cleats for sole and cockpit, ¾" x 1½".

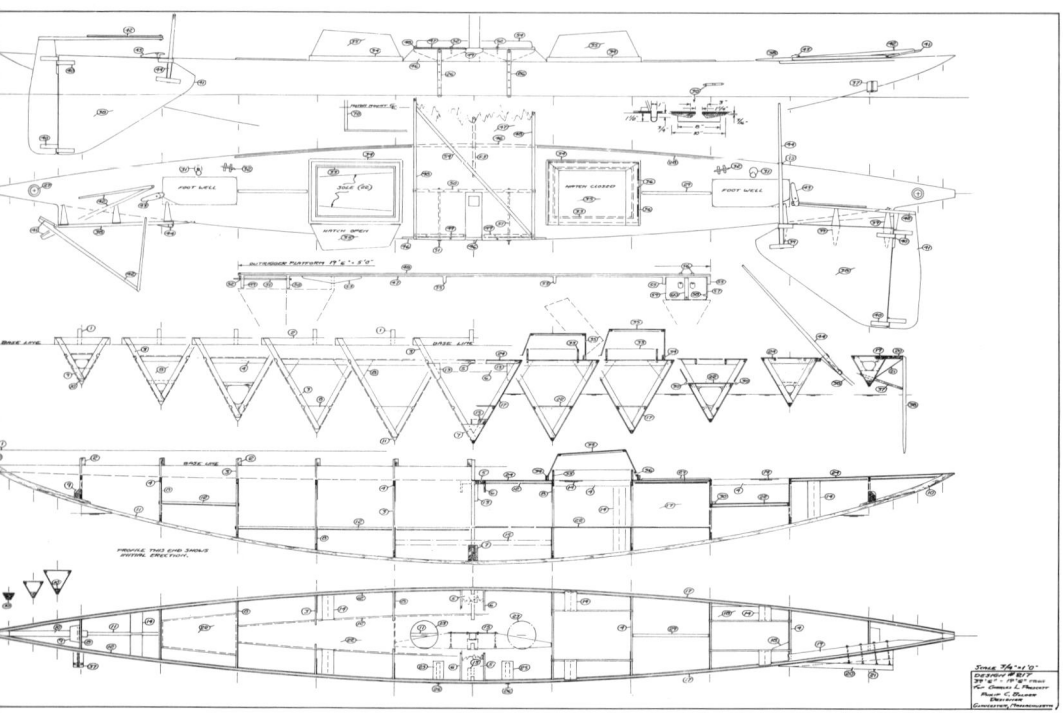

13. Supporting knees of partner beam sided 1½", one on each side on opposite sides of midship line as shown.

14. Butt straps ⅜" x 6" plywood.

15. Mast step sawn from 2½" x 7½" x 6'5"; retaining strap for heel of mast ¼" x 2" x 24" galvanized or stainless with four ¼" bolts through timber; bolt the strap before putting on the plywood hull sides.

16. See to drainage before plywood is put on, cutting limber holes as best serves to clear fastenings, etc., in all frames.

17. Hull sides ⅜" exterior-grade fir plywood, a twelve-foot sheet spanning the midsection, two eight-foot sheets each side, each end.

18. Deck blocking for cleats, etc., ¾".

19. Backing timbers for fin flanges from 1½" x 3½" x 5'7"; fit tightly to inside of clamp and make sure the deck bears closely on their tops.

20. Fin flanges built up in two sections of 1½" as shown; four ¼" galvanized bolts through backing block as shown; rabbet tops of flanges to take edge of deck well beyond hull side.

21. Bracing straps of fin flanges ⅛" x 2".

22. Foot well and cuddy soles ⅜" plywood.

23. Access holes to bilge.

24. Deck ⅜" plywood; six eight-by-four sheets required but there ought to be enough left in corners for all the bulkheads and gussets.

25. Backing blocks of chain plates ¾" x 5½".

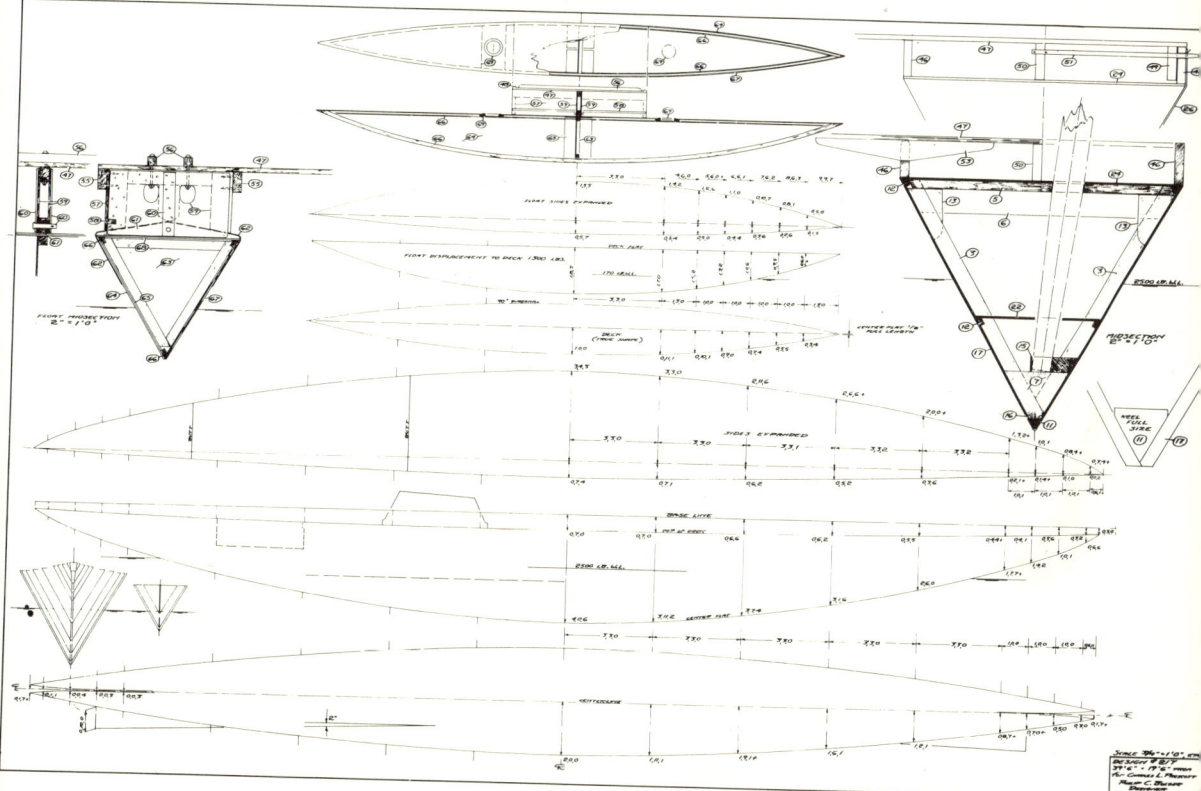

26. Chain plates ¼" x 2" x 24" galvanized or stainless; five ¼" bolts each through sides.

27. Four-inch diameter deck plates for ventilation when laid up.

28. Toe rails ¾" square.

29. Deck stiffeners ¾" x 1½" over and under deck.

30. Foot well scuppers, two to each well, with $\frac{1}{16}$" venturi shroud to pressure-drain in either direction.

31. Swivel-eye deck plate blocks; about 4" bronze or plastic shell.

32. Bronze 8" four-bolt cleats.

33. Hatch coamings ¾" x 5½".

34. Outer hatch coamings with drain holes at each corner, 1½" x 2½".

35. Hatch covers ⅜" plywood hinged to center coaming along "lee" side.

36. Ventilating slots 1" x 6" cut in each hatch on sides facing ends of hull.

37. Strut bracing fins when in down position about ¾" diameter pipe plugged and driven through hull from side to side in way of block #9; make a drive fit and flange or pin on "lee" side; fair up with a streamlined wood strip each side, strapped across pipe and pinned to prevent twisting.

38. Fins built up of 1½" square strips edge-nailed and glued; fair in on leading edges from 8" to ⅜" face and round off; fair trailing edges to about 1" face.

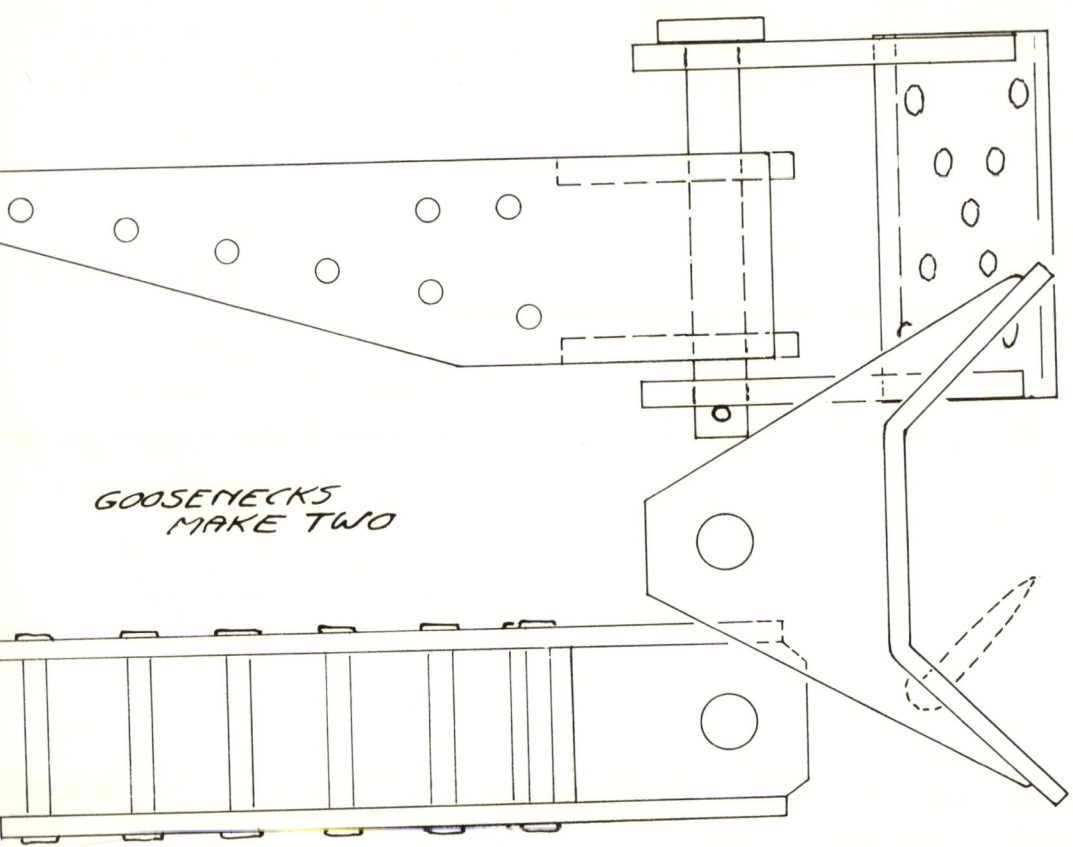

GOOSENECKS MAKE TWO

39. Heavy 10″-leaf strap hinges, galvanized.
40. Special pintles and gudgeons; see detail.
41. Rudder blades 1″ square strips edge-nailed and glued.
42. Tillers from 1½″ x 2½″ hardwood bolted and glued to rudder heads as strongly as possible; swinging extensions as shown.
43. Pivoting hardwood cleats to hold tillers and rudders at the indicated angle when fins are in the "up" position.
44. Lever arms from 1½″ square by 6′0″ hardwood, fitting loosely into strapped recesses in fins.
45. Steel hooks to secure lever, i.e., to hold fins in "up" position.
46. Outrigger mounts at sides of deck from 1½″ x 6½″ x 5′11″; bevel off at ends to match curve of deck in plan view.
47. Outrigger built up of ¾″ square strips edge-nailed and glued; turn each strip so annual rings of wood lie vertically, i.e., the stiff way.
48. Outrigger toe rails from ¾″ x 1½″.
49. Outrigger hull end timbers from 1½″ x 5½″ x 2′2″.
50. Outrigger beam at hull centerline 1½″ x 5½″ x 5′0″.
51. Galvanized steel rods ½″ diameter driven through beams #49 and #50 and pinned in place; to engage chain plates #26.

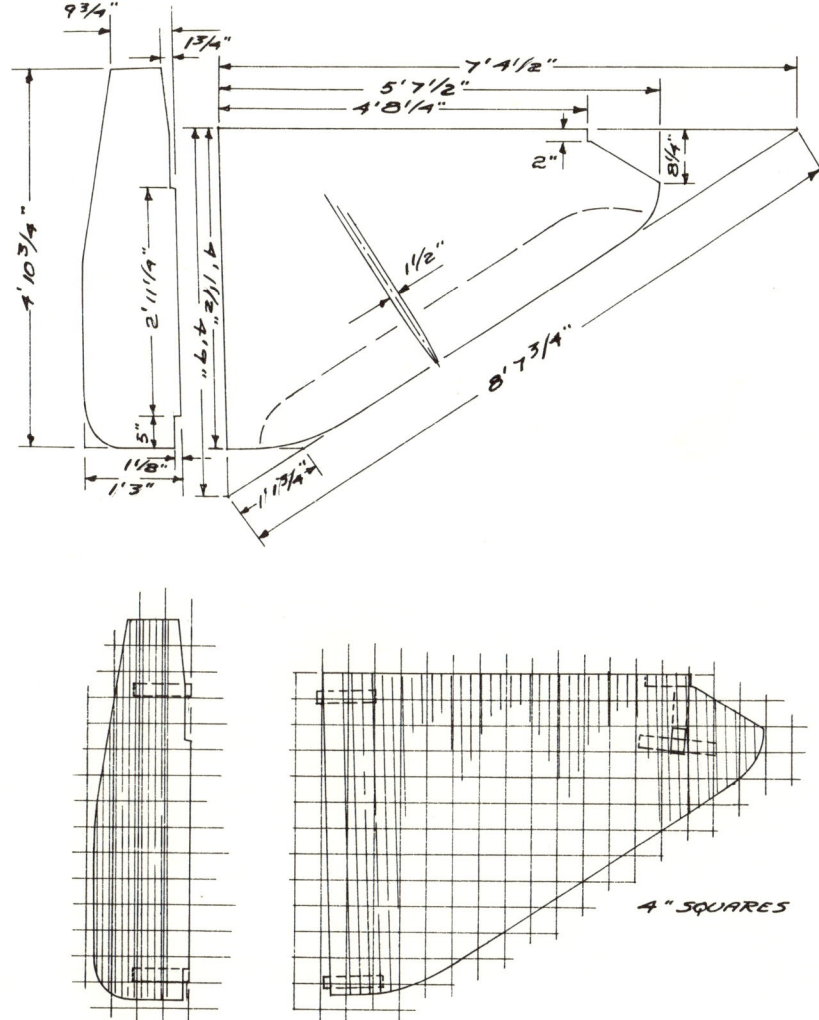

52. Retaining pins ½″ diameter with large heads; loose fit.

53. Cleat to hold outrigger against fore and aft movement, from 1½″ x 3½″ x 2′6″; screwed to outrigger; lies in slot in mount #46.

54. Diagonal brace for motor mount #70 1½″ x 3½″ x 7′3″.

55. Outrigger cross beams 1½″ x 3½″ x 5′0″.

56. Cleats 1½″ square by 4′9″ to spread stress of two ⅜″ bolts shown.

57. Web ⅜″ plywood to prevent outrigger twisting over float; ¾″ x 1½″ legs at ends.

58. Cleat ¾″ x 1½″ x 5′0″ to stiffen web fore and aft.

59. Thwartships web a sandwich of ⅜″ plywood faces spaced by 1½″-thick filler blocks as shown to take bolts from #56 and screws from #55 (N.B. — The sandwich is open at the bottom to drain and to engage the float deck flange #61.)

60. Steel straps $1/4'' \times 2'' \times 11''$ to take $3/4''$ diameter steel pin; pulling this pin disengages float from outrigger.

61. Float deck flange from $1\frac{1}{2}'' \times 2\frac{1}{2}'' \times 2'0''$.

62. Float chain plate strap $\frac{1}{16}'' \times 1\frac{1}{2}'' \times$ about $44''$.

63. Float frame $1/4''$ plywood with $1\frac{1}{2}''$ square fastening frame; in laying down this frame note deduction for thickness of butt straps.

64. One side of hull cut out of two $2' \times 10'$ sections of plywood butted at midlength; lay out flat from expansion furnished.

65. Butt straps for sides and deck $1/4'' \times 12''$ plywood.

66. Clamps and "keel" $3/4'' \times 1\frac{1}{2}''$ attached to one side laid out flat.

67. Other side of hull same as "one side" but without keel piece.

68. Deck $1/4''$ plywood butted at midlength.

69. Deck plates $6''$ diameter set in $3/4'' \times 10\frac{1}{2}''$ deck reinforcements.

70. Motor mount; see separate drawing.

16
TIGER LILY

$$\boxed{45'0'' \times 10'3''}$$

The magazine *Motorboating & Sailing* offered prizes for the best designs combining high speed with small fuel consumption in a straight powerboat. The only restriction on the designs was the requirement that they accommodate two couples with an enclosed toilet room and workable galley. Like most designers I find it intriguing to study boats that can be driven fast with relatively little power, so I worked up and entered this study. The competition rules didn't require a buildable plan, or I probably wouldn't have taken the trouble to enter: I've learned over the years that when a powerboat owner becomes troubled about fuel economy, he hardly ever thinks of changing to a radical-type boat; he decides to run at a lower speed, or simply moves the boat around less. I did lay the boat out in such a way that she represented a comparatively low-cost proposition for one-off building, in case some individualist turned up interested in having the design completed and built. I saw no cheaper way to build a solitary boat than with sheet plywood; the sacrifice of performance was minimal on the proportions I had in mind, and at about that time there began to be signs that plywood could be treated with epoxy in such a way as to make the consequences of neglect a good deal less disastrous than it had been.

My presentation to the competition judges was as follows:

> I would sum up the main qualities leading to high speed with low fuel consumption thus:
> 1. Light plane loading; the boat long or wide for her weight.
> 2. Easy flow lines, minimum frontal area and wetted surface.
> 3. Center of gravity in moderate aft location.
> 4. Power developed with a minimum number of cylinders.
> 5. Engine run low on its propeller-load curve; i.e., cruising speed much less than maximum speed.
> 6. Propeller with a minimum number of blades, large diameter, high pitch ratio, large tip clearance, and moderate shaft angle.

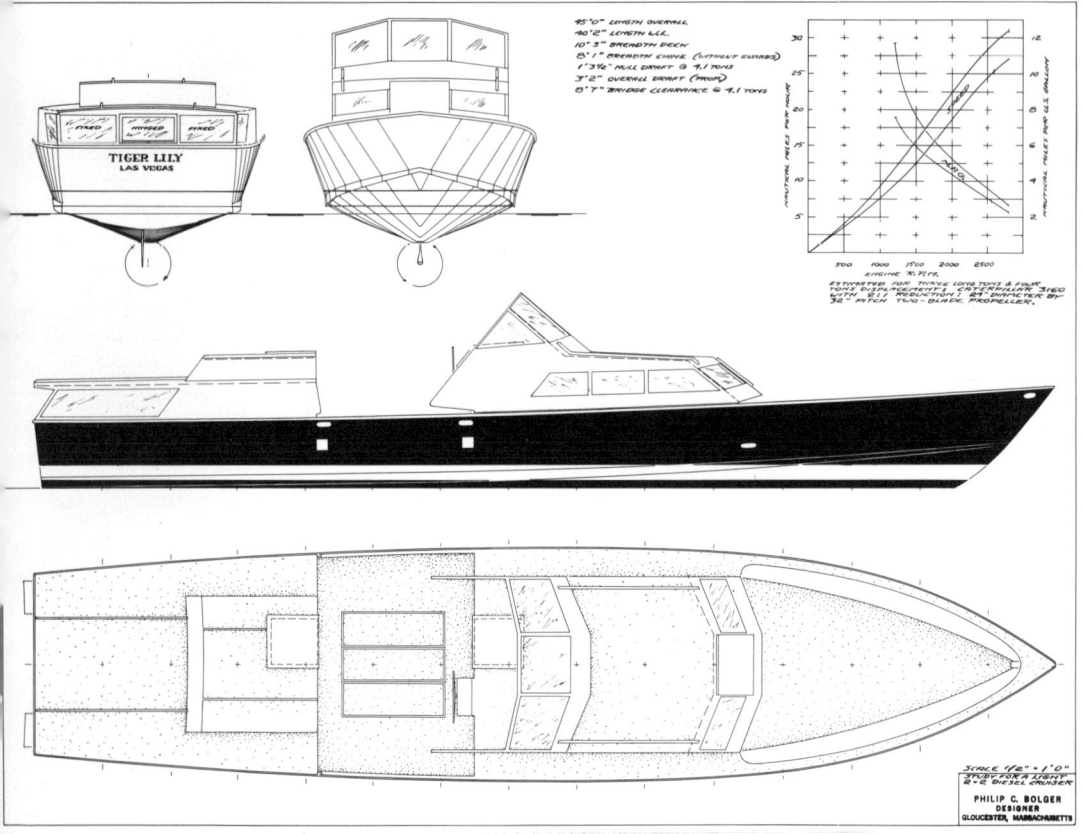

   The upper of the two given curves for estimated speed and fuel consumption, that for three tons displacement, would be achieved only in a stripped version with little or no accommodations. The four-ton curve can be met in the cruising layout shown by taking pains with structural design, using all joinerwork as web reinforcement with expanded foam backing over most of the bottom area (as shown she could run and maneuver with every compartment holed); sheet plywood epoxy-treated construction; thin plastic windows without frames; coldplate refrigeration and fresh water distillation off the main engine to avoid carrying large weights of water and ice; inflatable dinghy towed on a semi-rigid hook (also serves as breakdown power); little or no electronic gear, and a continual watch kept on personal accumulations. Reward of taking this much trouble, five miles per gallon at sixteen knots, or four miles per gallon at twenty knots, with a top speed of twenty-seven knots. Range, 390 nautical miles to dry tanks, in twenty-four hours at sixteen knots; in case of miscalculations, mileage can be stretched to seven miles per gallon by slowing to ten knots, and some reserve fuel could be carried in the towed tender with negligible increase in drag.

   It may be observed that this would not be a very expensive boat for the amenities offered. Her nominal length is somewhat misleading, as some fourteen feet for the bow amounts to no more than a combined cutwater and pulpit, which could even be made removable without much trouble. I think the performance curves offered are quite conservative, and that she would make an ex-

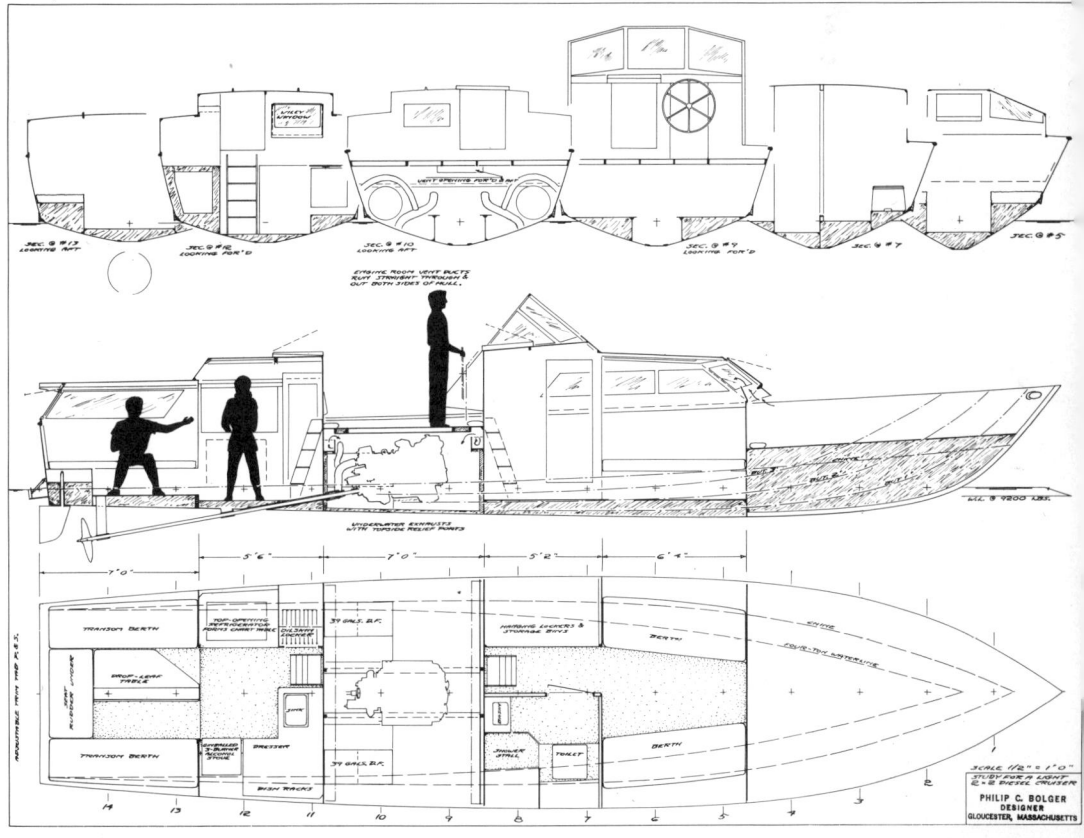

tremely nice boat in many ways; there are means of protecting a propeller located like this one, but since the devices required have to be retractable or removable to allow the performance sought, I have not cluttered the drawing with any of them.

The board of judges awarded me first prize in the competition, and the proposal was duly published. Perhaps two dozen people were intrigued enough to write me about it; of those, several did not grasp that the estimated speed-for-power was based on leaving out a good many customary things — such as a permanent full skeg and a deck saloon with a flying bridge on top, and twin engines — and wanted to put these things back into the design. Several others suggested using a smaller engine than the expensive Caterpillar specified, and accepting somewhat less speed, which I think is an excellent idea but not quite in line with the original concept. There were two or three who thought they liked the design as it stood, but I had to advise them that in view of how few of them there were, it seemed to me that the boat was likely to be almost impossible to sell, and might encumber their estates. They retired to consider the matter, and so far none of them has been back.

(The woman in the galley is not cooking for the two men; she's the navigator and is charting a course to give the helmsman.)

17
THE PLYWOOD TRIREME

A motel proprietor approached me to design a "pirate ship" as a tourist attraction. I thought there were already too many such stage sets, and in this case the lake to float it in was so hard to get to that it wasn't practical either to build a sizable vessel nearby, or to carry her to it complete.

I suggested the Greek trireme, period of Salamis, because it would make something highly visible that lent itself to prefabrication, adding that his rooms would be full of scholars come to sneer at my reconstruction. The lake was just about big enough to get the machine up to full speed and stop it again, any time you cared to assemble a hundred and sixty-eight oarsmen. My thought was that it wouldn't be hard to do that once, as the woods would be full of college oarsmen eager to say they'd rowed in a galley; they could come once, get in a few hours of practice, and make one or two speed runs; from then on she'd be a swimming platform, with still and moving pictures of her under way for entertainment.

For some reason the motel man wasn't roused to enthusiasm by this businesslike scheme; nothing came of it except that I got hooked on trireme design. I was already a classical Greece buff of sorts. By way of excuse for pursuing the theme I got up a plan for a feminist movie about Queen Artemisia of Halicarnassus, who commanded the municipal squadron at Salamis, and (by audacity and sheer gall) came away from the battle with all of what little credit there was on the Persian side. According to Herodotus, if her advice had been followed, Xerxes would have won the war, Athens would have been moved to Sicily, and you can play world history to taste from then on. Somebody certainly ought to make this movie; it'd be a surefire hit; but I had no more luck promoting it than I did selling a trireme to the motel man. Just a case of vision unappreciated. . . .

The immediate point is that the script was going to call for three functional triremes, for which the drawing here was the preliminary study.

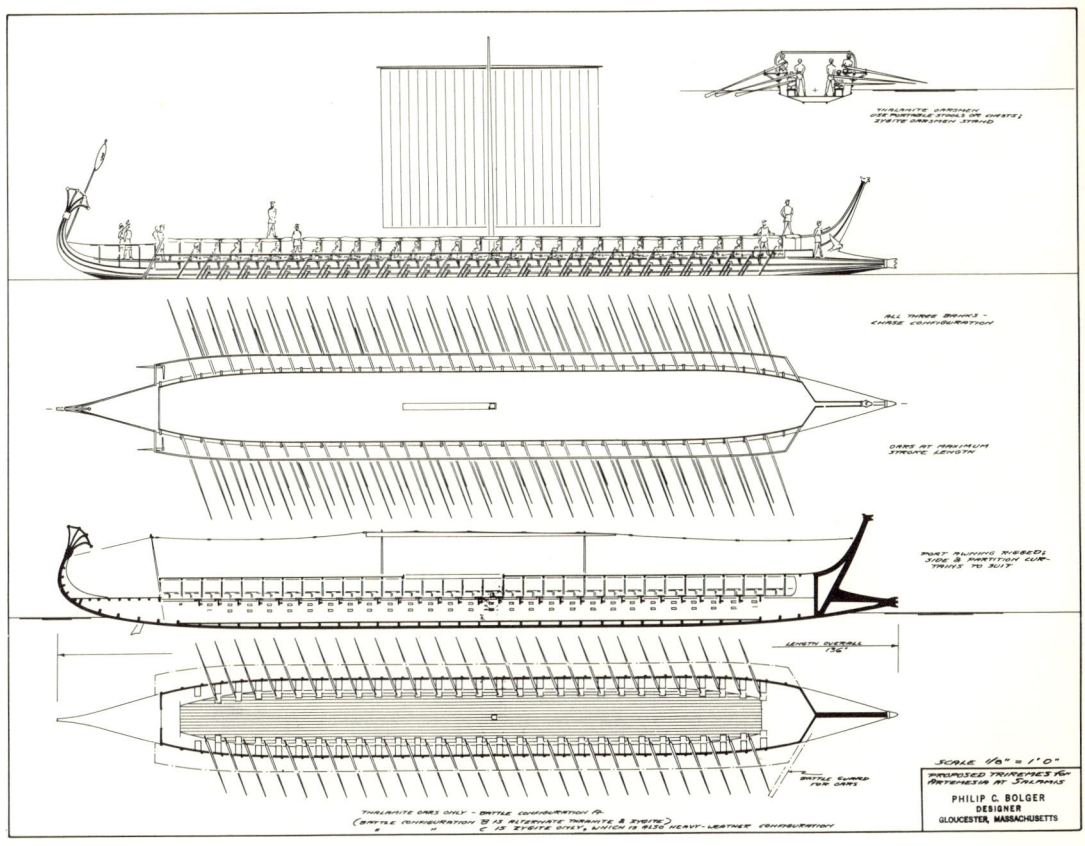

I think it's the only trireme reconstruction in which functional practicality takes precedence over scholarship. The current doctrine among the scholars has no place for the short lower-bank oars, and insists that the banks were staggered diagonally. I'll grant that a well-known marble carving does plainly show them that way, but I tell myself that Phidias was a land-bound hoplite and the carving a standing joke in the fleet. I see no excuse for staggering one-man oars if they're at markedly different levels, numerous objections to it show up as soon as the sweep of the grips is diagrammed in three dimensions, and none of the scholarly reconstructions, even Björn Landstrom's beautiful ones, look to me as though they could get out of their own way under oars. Most of them are literally unworkable, oars or men fouling each other if they move.

This one would at any rate work, and could cope with anything described by Thucydides if you assume that his word usually translated "sunk" or "foundered" could also mean swamped. For that matter, it could be ballasted, but considering how much live ballast had to be on hand I can't see why the builders should have done so and doubt that they did.

If anybody wants a cruising rowboat with a lot of accommodations, please let me know; I'm set to work it up. Slaves aren't needed, the galley slave of legend being an invention of upwards of a thousand years later. Athenian oarsmen were free voters as I understand it, and I surmise that a lot of them were also fighting men, as it seems obvious that there'd never be more than two of the three banks of oars manned in combat.

18
YACHT TENDERS

> 7'9" x 3'10" and 2.3m x 1.06m

Chris Petty gave me a midsection of fair lines around to 7'9" overall length. His idea was the sound one — that the thing to go for in a boat of that length was maximum initial stability and capacity. A perfectly rectangular section would be optimum, but he wanted to get it out of a one-piece mold; also, at that time sandwich construction was in its infancy, so some kind of curves and kinks were desirable to stiffen the limp fiberglass surfaces. After a couple of false starts I came up with the drawing shown, and boats on this model have been in fairly steady production ever since in various hands — by Ryder of Bristol, Rhode Island, the last time I took notice. Owners tell me without enthusiasm that they serve well enough; no complaints.

When Canadian John Bain came along ten years later I'd had time to reflect on the matter. The foam-sandwich and partial-sandwich stiffening system, or several systems, had come into fairly general use, so there wasn't the same need to drag in extraneous curves. Bain was also agreeable to using a split mold, which allowed more freedom in sectional shape. We decided to go all-out functional, the object being the most stable under-eight-foot dinghy possible with a reasonably light weight, and also the most reserve stability (that is, the ability to heel over far without capsizing or swamping) that we could get without actually decking her in.

The shape that suggested itself put me in mind of the big sloops that used to haul granite blocks from hereabouts to Boston: a box for the hold, rounded off at each end just as bluntly as seemed possible if it were still to be steered more or less reliably. By rounding in the corners I tried to make it possible to step anywhere in the boat and have the boat stand up to the weight, on the theory that most dinghy capsizes come from putting weight in the bow without anything aft to hold her down, and that the water in

Chris Petty's yacht tender.

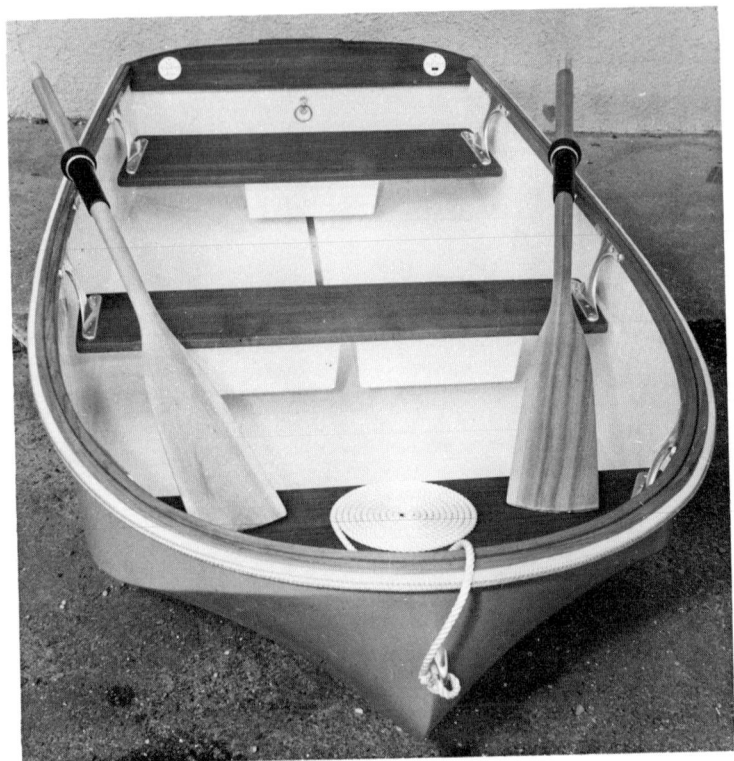

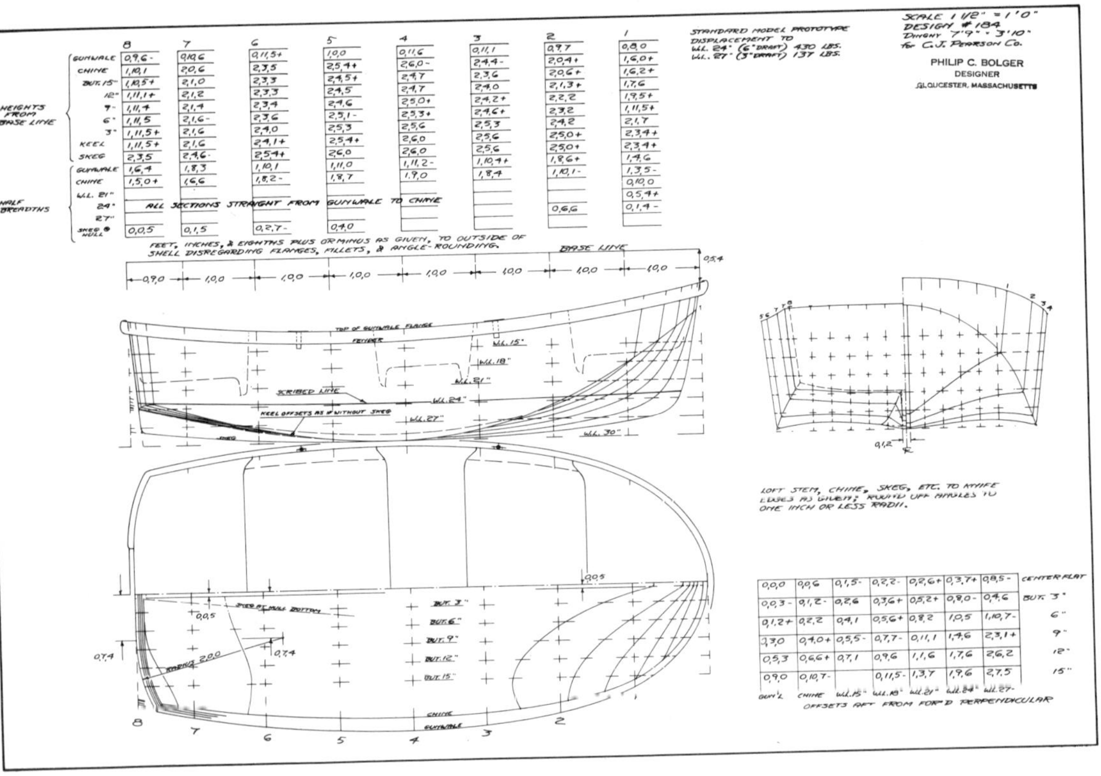

		8	7	6	5	4	3	2	1
HEIGHTS FROM BASE LINE	GUNWALE	0,9,6-	0,10,6	0,11,5+	1,0,0	0,11,6	0,11,1	0,9,7	0,8,0
	CHINE	1,10,1	2,0,6	2,3,5	2,5,4+	2,6,0-	2,4,4-	2,0,4+	1,6,0+
	BUT. 15"	1,10,5+	2,1,0	2,3,3	2,4,5+	2,4,7	2,3,6	2,0,6+	1,6,2+
	12"	1,11,1+	2,1,2	2,3,3	2,4,5	2,4,7	2,4,0	2,1,3+	1,7,6
	9"	1,11,4	2,1,4	2,3,4	2,4,6	2,5,0+	2,4,2+	2,2,2	1,9,5+
	6"	1,11,5	2,1,6-	2,3,6	2,5,1-	2,5,3+	2,4,6+	2,3,2	1,11,5+
	3"	1,11,5+	2,1,6	2,4,0	2,5,3	2,5,6	2,5,3	2,4,2	2,1,7
	KEEL	1,11,5+	2,1,6	2,4,1+	2,5,4+	2,6,0	2,5,6	2,5,0+	2,3,4+
	SKEG	2,3,5	2,4,6-	2,5,4+	2,6,0	2,6,0	2,5,6	2,5,0+	2,3,4+
HALF BREADTHS	GUNWALE	1,6,4	1,8,3	1,10,1	1,11,0	1,11,2-	1,10,4+	1,8,6+	1,4,6
	CHINE	1,5,0+	1,6,6	1,8,2-	1,8,7	1,9,0	1,8,4	1,10,1-	1,3,5-
	W.L. 21"								0,10,0
	24"								0,5,4+
	27"							0,6,6	0,1,4-
	SKEG @ HULL	0,0,5	0,1,5	0,2,7-	0,4,0				

ALL SECTIONS STRAIGHT FROM GUNWALE TO CHINE

GUN'L	CHINE	W.L. 15"	W.L. 18"	W.L. 21"	W.L. 24"	W.L. 27"	
0,0,0	0,0,6	0,1,5-	0,2,2-	0,2,6+	0,3,7+	0,8,5-	CENTER FLAT
0,0,3-	0,1,2-	0,2,6	0,3,6+	0,5,2+	0,8,0-	0,4,6	BUT. 3"
0,1,2+	0,2,2	0,4,1	0,5,6+	0,8,2	1,0,5	1,10,7-	6"
0,3,0	0,4,0+	0,5,5-	0,7,7-	0,11,1	1,4,6	2,3,1+	9"
0,5,3	0,6,6+	0,7,1	0,9,6	1,1,6	1,7,6	2,6,2	12"
0,9,0	0,10,7-		0,11,5-	1,3,7	1,9,6	2,7,5	15"

OFFSETS AFT FROM FOR'D PERPENDICULAR

most swampings gets in over the corners of the stern. The lines aft were cocked up enough to trim the bow high when the boat is in tow, with enough of a skeg-shape aft to keep her going more or less straight. The mold plug for this boat was built using strip planking for the deadflat area in the middle of the boat, with the curved ends built up bread-and-butter

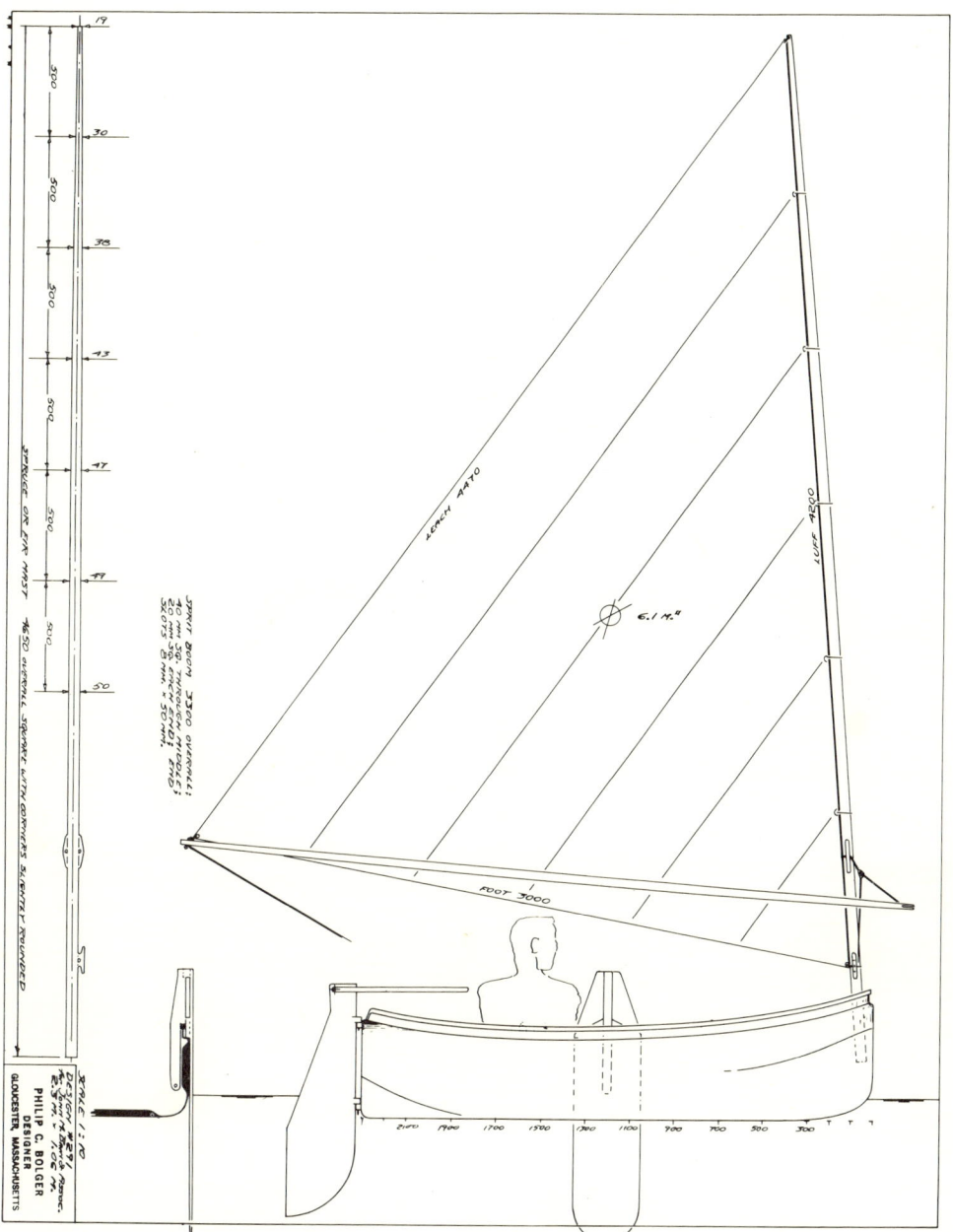

		2300	2200	2100	1900	1700	1500/1100	900	700	500	300	200	100
HEIGHTS FROM BOTTOM/BASE LINE	GUNWALE		486	465	439	426	SEE	434	451	478	516	538	566
	SHEER		424	405	379	366	DRWNG	374	391	417	459	477	504
	KNUCKLE								221	243	300	338	381
	BUTTOCK 450	276	212	157	014	023	004						
	400	248	184	130	050	009	000	000	012	071	233	324	
	350	229	167	113	038	005			004	044	186	297	
	300	215	155	102	031	003				025	143	260	373
	250	204	146	096	027	003				014	104	219	356
	200	197	141	092	026	003				007	071	170	328
	150	193	138	090	026	003				002	043	122	283
	100	190	137	089	026	003				000	023	073	204
	50	189	136	089	026	003				000	010	035	100
	CENTERLINE		000	000	000	000	000	000	000	000	006	019	044
HALF-BREADTHS	GUNWALE		334	408	478	504	510	509	506	492	448	402	303
	W.L. 400	411	418	424	478	504	510	509	506	512	469	426	339
	350	489	496	504	520	528	530	530	526	512	469	426	237
	300	476	498	509	522	528	530	530	526	512	469	355	165
	250	403	484	506	522	528	530	530	526	512	416	286	127
	200	222	432	490	522	528	530	530	526	496	363	230	098
	150	047	280	442	519	528	530	530	522	472	308	179	074
	100	038	038	286	482	518	528	526	509	433	244	128	050
	50	032	032	032	400	491	515	509	473	362	164	071	018

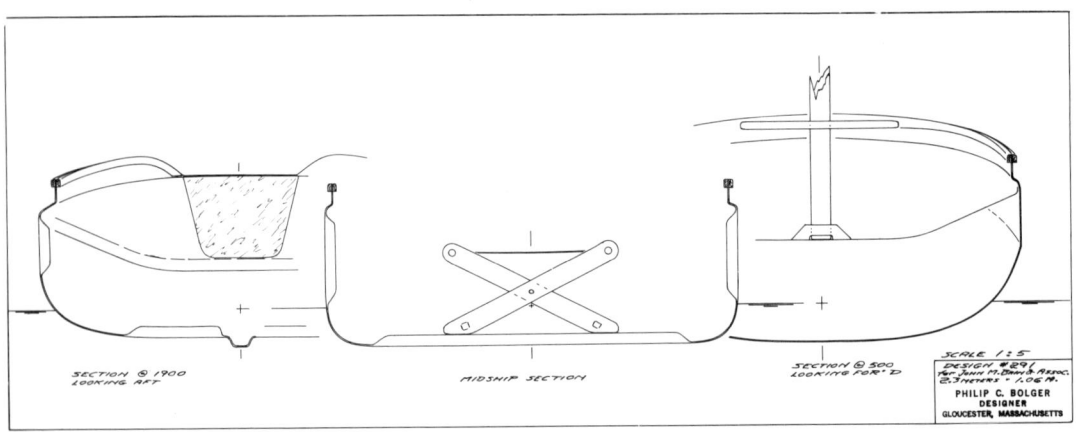

fashion and carved out of the solid wood like a model boat; we thought of using styrofoam and epoxy, but concluded that there would be more trouble caused getting a really good finish than would be saved over carving wood.

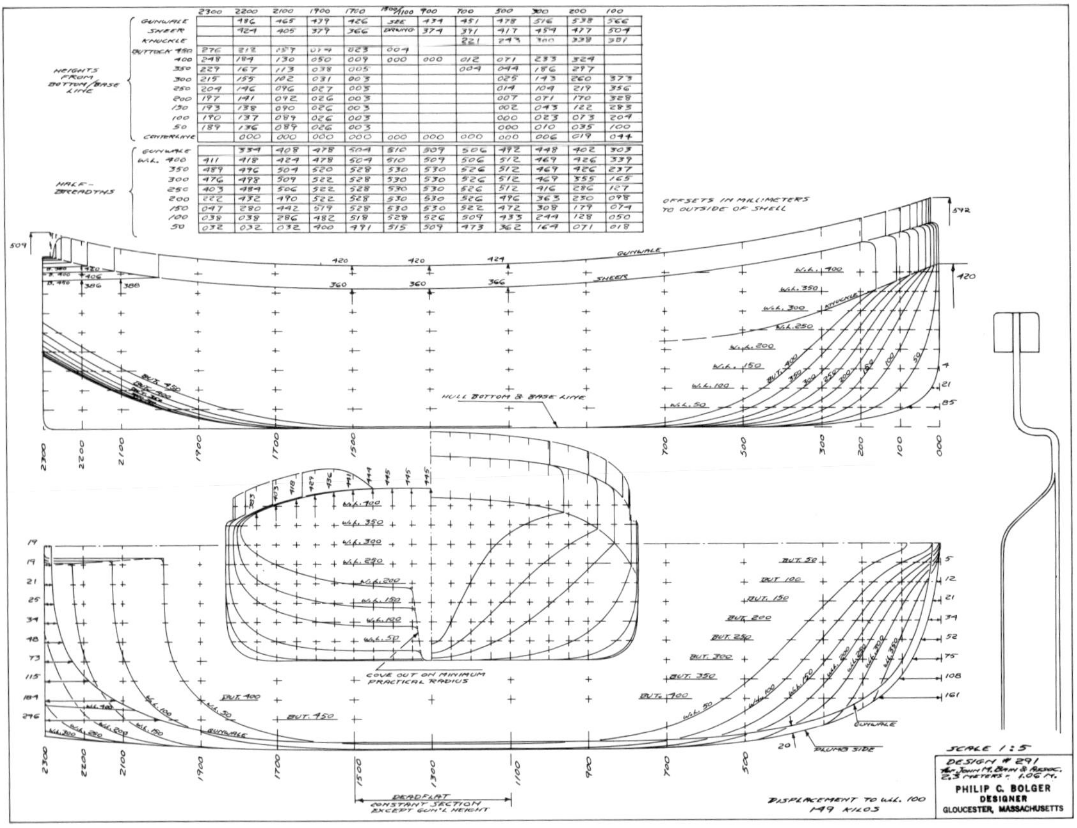

YACHT TENDERS 109

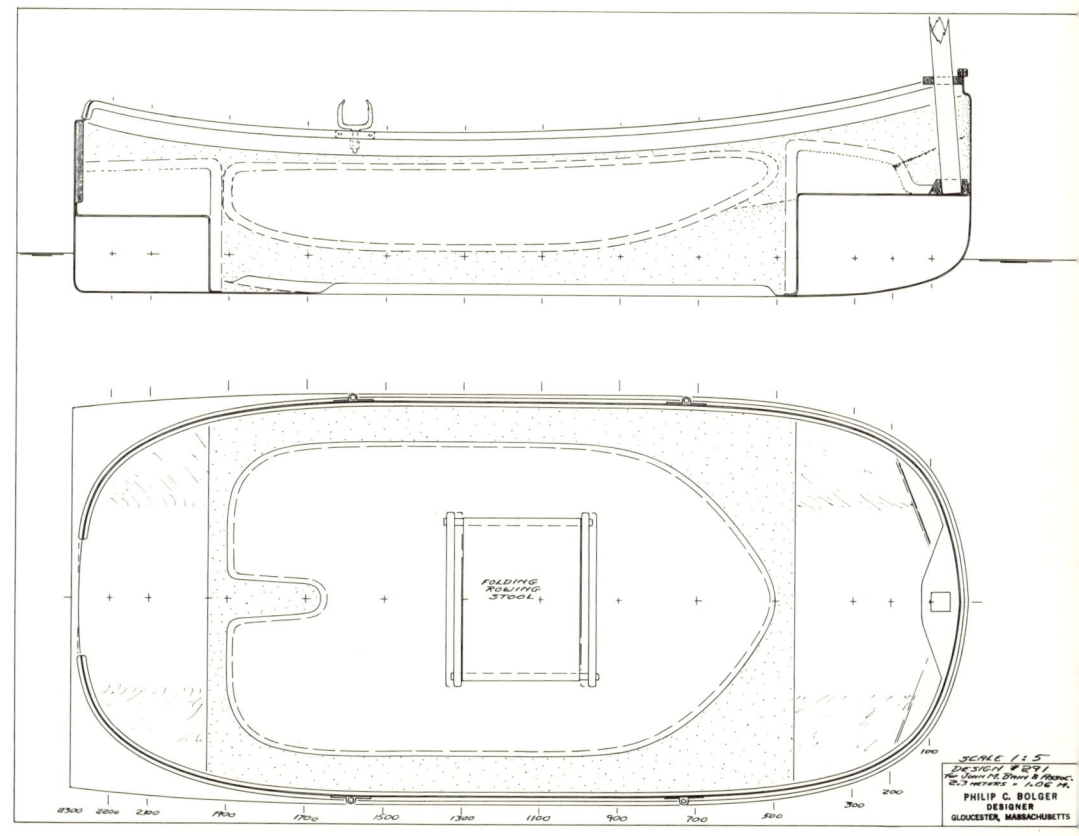

You might think that this is a bad shape, or no shape at all, either to row or sail, but it's not so simple. You have a given length and breadth, so with any given load, finer lines simply mean she'll float deeper, which is never good. I figured that we'd get the stability we were after by making the bottom flat over as big an area as possible, and that by the same token, with a light or moderate load she'd float so lightly on top of the water that as long as the water was fairly smooth she'd still row and sail respectably. As for what happens when it's not smooth, she's still better than, or rather not as bad as, a deeper floating boat, and anyway d'ya want an egg in your beer?

19
LITTLE SUPERIOR

10'3" x 5'0"

Larry Dahlmer had been working for a company that failed building rough ferrocement workboats, and he wanted to do some nice woodwork for a change. He had, for the time being, a very small space to work in. We talked of this and that, and decided to work up a keel sailing dinghy something like a tiny yawlboat plan we found in Chapman's eighteenth century *Architectura Navalis Mercatoria,* but with a rather deeper keel and hollow garboards to contain the bilgewater.

We thought we'd save some trouble by using glued strip planking: a mistake; we should have stayed with the original sawn frames and steamed oak planking. Anything on such proportions as these is bound to be hard to plank, but the strip boat proved to be an absolute bitch to get fair. The plank sequence had to be changed from the one specified, most of the strips had to be pre-steamed, the sheer kept trying to get lost; oh my! Larry persevered all winter and won through with his equable disposition intact, but we agreed that it'd have been easier to carve her out of a solid block. The construction plan is printed as designed; take it as an instructive exercise in how to drive a builder out of his mind.

Once afloat, we had a lovable craft. She moved well with two or four oars, handled and balanced well under sail, carried light loads without treachery and heavy ones without spitting spray all over them. As long as there were no tacking she could out-sail anything around here anywhere near her size. Used as intended, as a 50-50 row-sailer, she covered as much as thirty miles in a day, including narrow, twisty creeks and low bridges.

The dipping lug rig was my experiment. I badly wanted to get a cheap trial with this rig because I've long thought it ought to be reintroduced as an auxiliary sail plan for motorsailers and motorboats. I offered to buy the sail if Larry would put up with its impracticality in a sailing dinghy,

Little Superior *(photo by Becky Garland)*.

and he agreed, more from scientific interest, I think, than as an economy. Manchester built the sail for me, as far as I know the only pure lug built in North America this century; it has a lovely flow and pulls like a stallion mule.

As long as you stay on one tack, this sail is docile, light to sheet and has no tendency to trip the boat when eased in an overpowering puff. Reefed, it sets and balances well. There were no complications once we got the grommet around the mast big enough to avoid binding; it's specified too small, and as far as I can see there's no reason not to have it extremely large and loose. The only time the rig gave us a fright was once when we tried to get more power running before the wind by taking the tack off the stemhead and guying it out to one side like a squaresail. The big Scots luggers, some of whose sails were as much as 1,600 square feet, are supposed to have done this, and I've seen it mentioned as an advantage of the rig, though after my attention was engaged I looked at scores of photos of them under sail and have not found one in which the tack is outside the boat, though I've found a couple in which it was fastened to the rail abreast the mast. Be that as it may, when we tried it we couldn't hold the

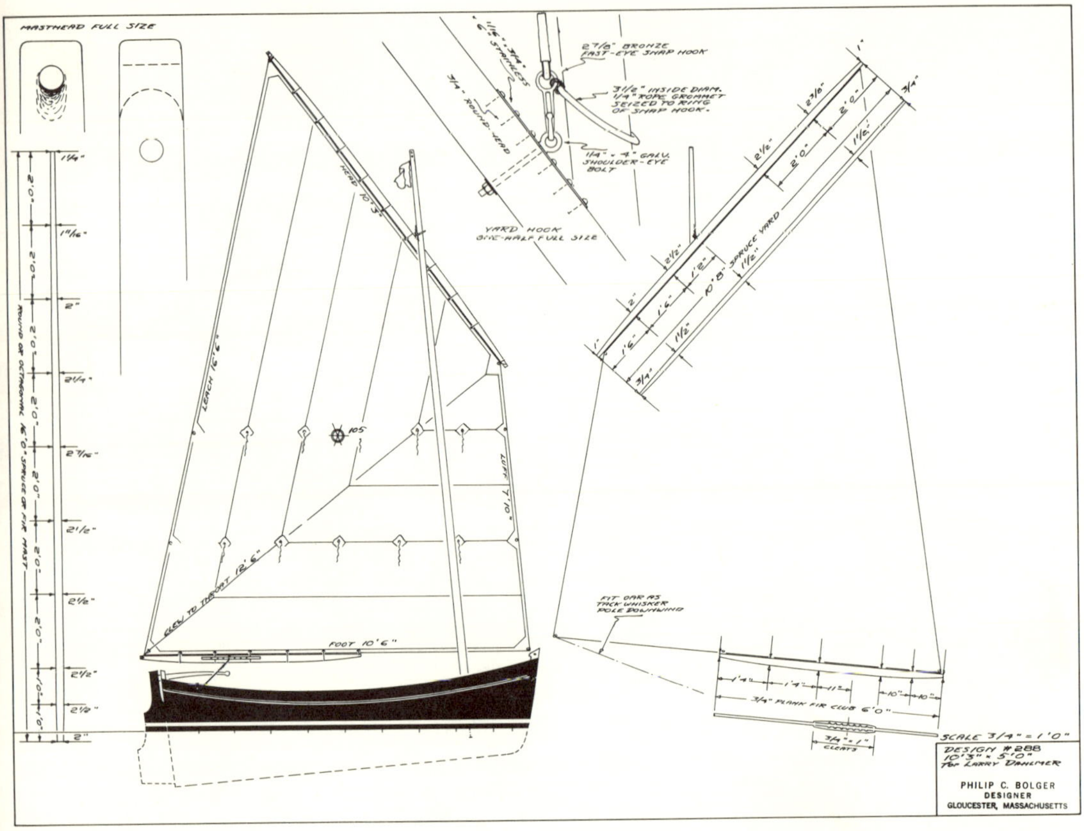

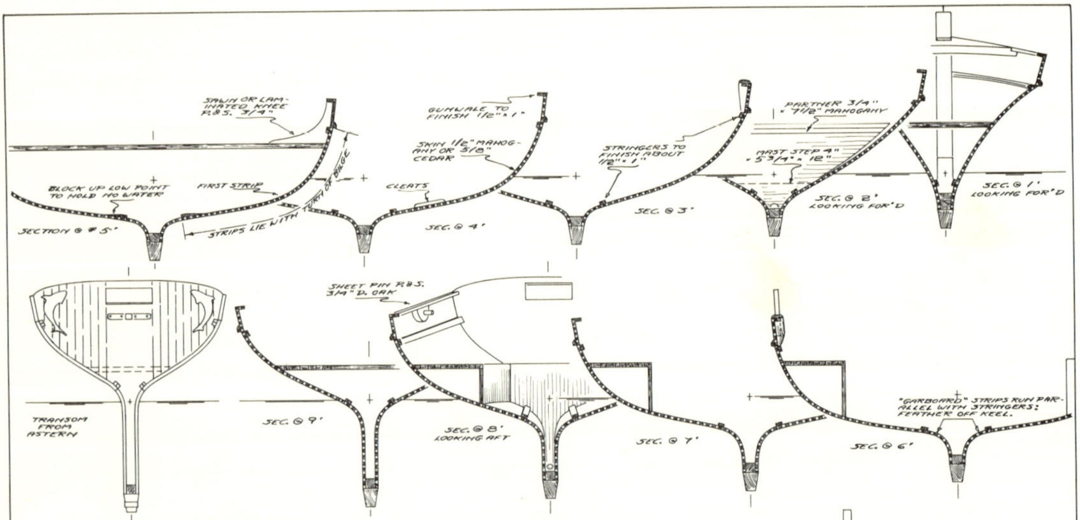

		10'	9'	8'	7'	6'	5'	4'	3'	2'	1'6"	1'	6"
HEIGHTS FROM BASE	GUNWALE	2,11,2	2,9,2	2,7,7	2,7,0	2,6,6-	2,6,7-	2,7,4	2,8,6	2,10,4+	2,11,6	3,1,0	3,2,4-
	KNUCKLE	2,7,3	2,5,2	2,3,6-	2,2,5-	2,2,1-	2,2,1+	2,2,6+	2,4,0	2,5,6-	2,6,6	2,7,7	2,9,2
	BUT. 21"			1,9,6	1,5,4	1,3,2	1,2,6-	1,3,7	1,7,4-	2,2,6			
	18"		2,1,3	1,7,5+	1,4,0	1,2,0+	1,1,5+	1,2,5+	1,5,5	2,0,0-	2,4,6+		
	15"	2,7,3	1,10,7+	1,6,2	1,3,0	1,1,3	1,1,1-	1,2,0-	1,4,2+	1,9,5-	2,2,2	2,7,5	
	12"	2,3,1	1,9,2	1,5,1	1,2,3+	1,0,7	1,0,5-	1,1,3	1,3,2	1,7,4	1,11,4+	2,5,4	
	9"	2,0,6	1,7,6	1,4,1-	1,1,6	1,0,3+	1,0,1	1,0,6+	1,2,3	1,5,6	1,9,0	2,2,6	
	6"	1,11,0-	1,6,2+	1,3,1-	1,1,1+	0,11,7+	0,11,3+	1,0,2-	1,1,4+	1,4,0	1,6,4	1,11,1-	2,7,2
	3"	1,9,0	1,4,5-	1,1,6	1,0,0-	0,11,1	0,11,0-	0,11,3-	1,0,4	1,2,2-	1,3,4+	1,6,1	2,1,7
	RABBET		0,3,6	0,4,6	0,5,6	0,6,6	0,7,7	0,8,7	0,10,0-	0,11,0	0,11,4	1,0,0	1,5,0
	SHOE		0,0,6	0,1,6	0,2,6	0,3,6	0,4,6+	0,5,7	0,6,7+	0,8,0	0,8,4	0,9,0	0,9,7-
HALF-BREADTHS	GUNWALE	1,4,0	1,9,5	2,1,6	2,4,3	2,5,5	2,6,0	2,5,5+	2,4,3-	2,0,5	1,9,3-	1,4,5	0,10,1-
	KNUCKLE	1,3,0	1,8,6	2,1,0+	2,3,6	2,5,0+	2,5,3+	2,5,1-	2,3,4	1,11,5	1,8,1	1,3,2-	0,8,3-
	W.L. 30"	1,2,2									1,7,2+	1,0,5	0,5,0-
	27"	0,11,7-	1,7,3	2,0,6+					2,3,0+	1,9,2	1,4,0-	0,9,2	0,3,3
	24"	0,7,6+	1,4,4	1,11,0+	2,2,6	2,4,3+	2,4,6+	2,4,1	2,1,2+	1,6,0	1,0,4	0,6,5+	0,2,4
	21"	0,3,0	0,11,5	1,8,0	2,0,6+	2,3,1	2,3,4	2,2,4	1,10,7-	1,2,2	0,9,0	0,4,4+	0,1,6
	19 1/2"	0,1,6	0,8,4	1,5,6	1,11,4+	2,2,1	2,2,5	2,1,3	1,9,0+	1,0,0	0,7,2-	0,3,6-	0,1,4
	18"	0,1,3+	0,5,2	1,2,4	1,9,6-	2,0,7	2,1,4	2,0,0+	1,6,6	0,9,5	0,5,4-	0,3,0-	0,1,2+
		10'	9'	8'	7'	6'	5'	4'	3'	2'	1'6"	1'	6"

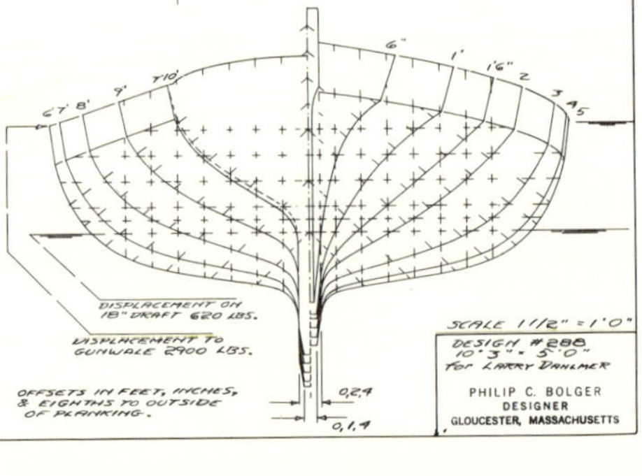

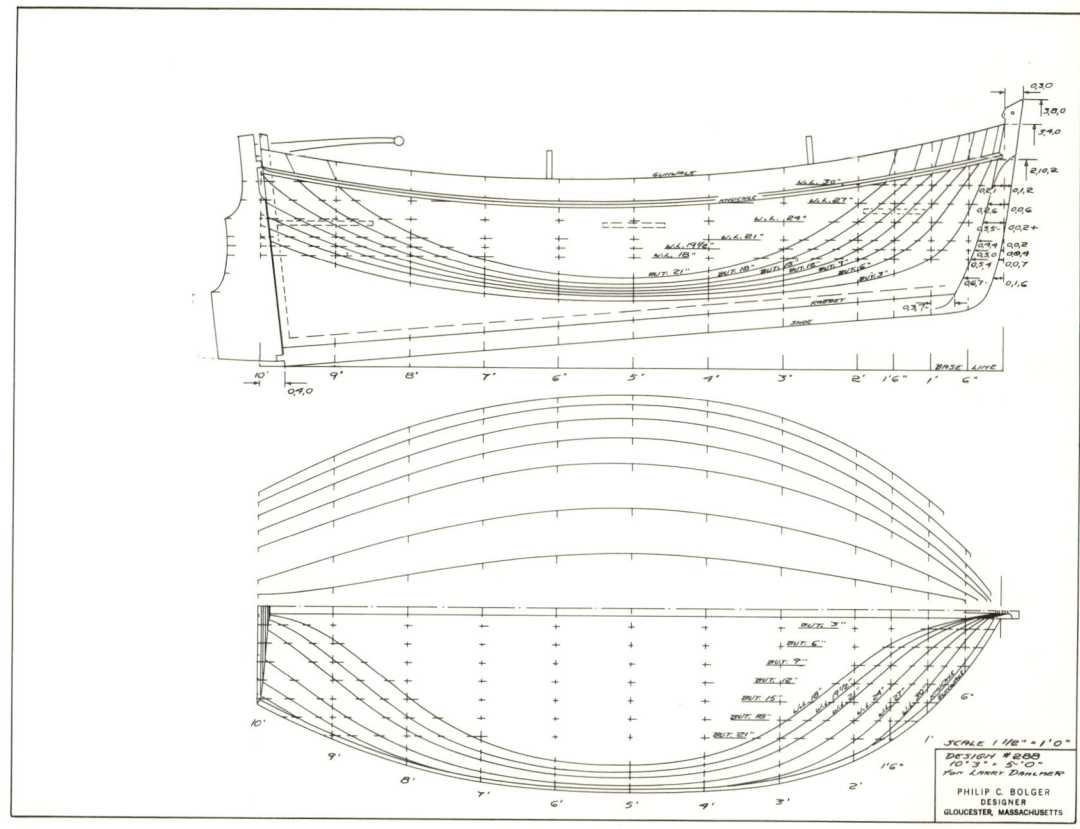

tack down hard; since the luff of the sail is what keeps the yard peaked-up, the head of the yard dropped some and went forward a lot, producing a great twist in the sail and a steadily-increasing rhythmic roll that almost capsized us before we could let go the halyard. I surmise that if they actually did do this in big luggers they must have had a vang or heel rope on the yard, probably brought in to the mast about where the tack would be in a standing lug, or some such arrangement. With the tack on the stem, her downwind manners were good.

Larry sailed her singlehanded quite a lot, including some breezy days, but I wouldn't care to do it myself if I could help it. It took him about three-quarters of a minute to tack her, from putting the tiller down to getting steerageway on the new tack, which calls for thinking some distance ahead of the boat. With two men it's not so bad, partly because the boat isn't so bouncy and the stern can be kept down in the water better, but a long series of short tacks is a strenuous proposition. It's possible to make a hitch with the sail on the weather side of the mast, but in puffy conditions this feels risky and you can't count on being able to get back through stays again; I understand that trying this was a favorite method of getting into trouble in the Scottish fleet. If you want to get her around suddenly with no time to dip, the best system seems to be to put her about and start her off at once to at least a beam reach, finally wearing ship to get back on the right tack: not a racing maneuver but a reasonably safe one as this sail is gentle in the jibe compared with a boomed sail.

What the rig is good for is going from here to there in a straight line. For that it's more powerful for its cost, windage, and heeling effect than anything else I've ever tried (not a bad definition of efficiency). A big genoa jib has some of the same qualities, including the drawbacks, but the lug will stand with a much shorter mast and less complicated and expensive rigging, and is somewhat lighter to sheet home; it can be lowered and stowed faster, with less chance of a jam, than any sail I know except possibly a balance-club jib. Incidentally, it presents a handsome and shipshape effect to the eye.

(*Little Superior* was dismasted her second season. She was being driven hard at the time with three men hiking out, and the break was at a kink in the grain of the spar. Nevertheless, it's clear that the mast diameters given are marginal.)

20
VECTIS

5.0m x 2.37m

After a season with *Little Superior* Larry Dahlmer started to talk about a new boat. He'd been much taken with an English cutter that hauled out here that winter, and had the notion of trying a miniature one, to see how he liked it and in the meantime have something that could be sailed without keeping such a sharp eye on the weather as was desirable in the open lugger.

I'm not an enthusiast for cutter-type hulls myself, though I grant that a good one has some nice qualities and I do think there's a lot in Claud Worth's position (expounded in *Yacht Cruising*) that it's the most efficient rig for heavy weather. But I thought five meters was plainly too short to make a decent cutter of the usual type. I've seen it tried and thought the result was a dirty, wet slug.

What I did have, in various reference books, was quite a collection of lines of Itchen Ferry Boats — the Solent fishing type — including two by Dan Hatcher himself. These had the rig Larry wanted to try, adapted to to a short, stubby boat, and they had the deep forefoot he liked. The breadth on such a short length would make one hard work to plank, but there wasn't all that much twist in the planks, and after *Little Superior* he was trained to cope. Besides, in the meantime he'd produced a scheme for going lobstering under sail, so the added stability looked attractive when it came to standing up and hauling by hand with the boat hove to; all the sailing lobsterboats I know of were of powerful model.

The result has really fine and fair lines for five meters overall, enough buoyancy to be tolerably dry in spite of her weight, a big powerful sail plan and the ability to carry it. She has to be fast in moderate weather, and the large lateral plane ought to ensure hanging on well to windward. She'll

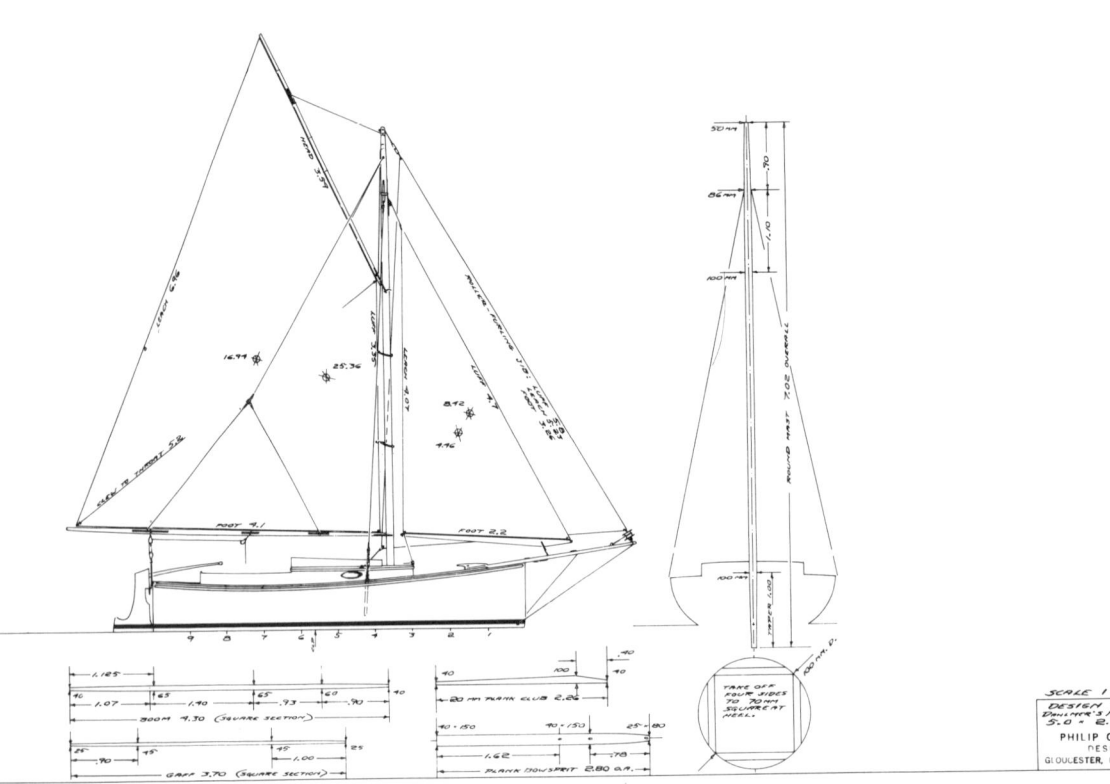

carry her way well and tolerate pinching, a combination that could save embarrassment in crowded anchorages since the boat is still not too heavy to be stopped or fended off by hand or foot.

A lead casting of 825 kilos is expensive, but at the time lead seemed to be less inflated in price than most things, so might be a good investment; better than gold, for instance, which just then was causing great pain to everybody who'd bought any recently (not that gold wouldn't make a good ballast keel, but this particular one would have cost four and a quarter million dollars at the time).

I did throw out the idea that a lot more freeboard might make her abler, a lot more roomy, and probably not much slower. You could have the same cockpit depth and width, enough to sit down inside instead of clinging on top, and still make it drain at a moderate angle of heel, which it won't as designed — the drains are for rainwater accumulated when she is on her mooring, though they would shed a lot of water under way if

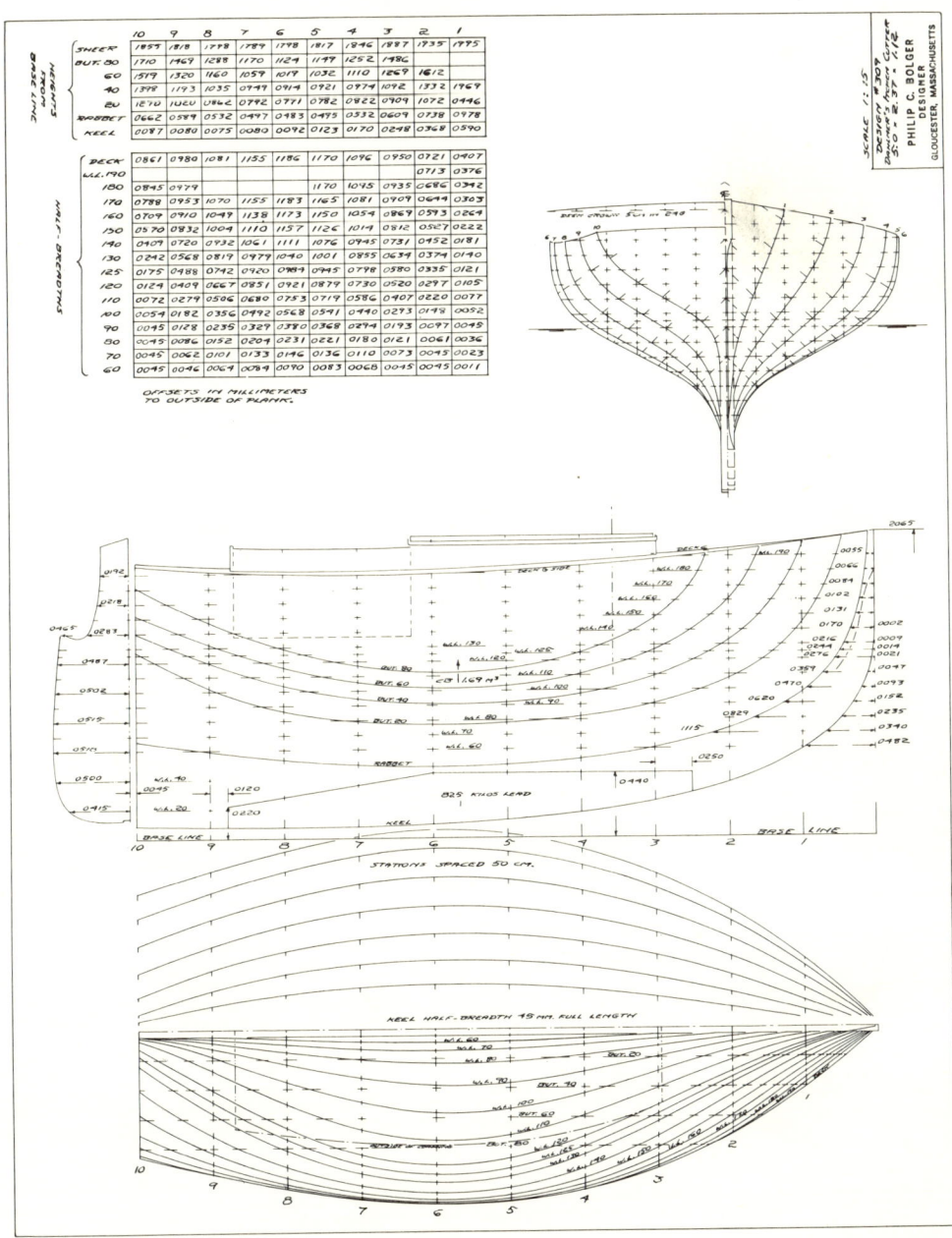

you pulled the plug while luffing or running off. Probably space could be found in the high-sided boat for full positive buoyancy, which I don't think is practical as designed. At any rate, Larry didn't like the looks of the added freeboard and thought it less suitable for his lobstering. I suspect him of lacking true faith in the possibility of a fool-proof boat; I certainly know of at least one boat that foundered because it was overloaded with safety equipment.

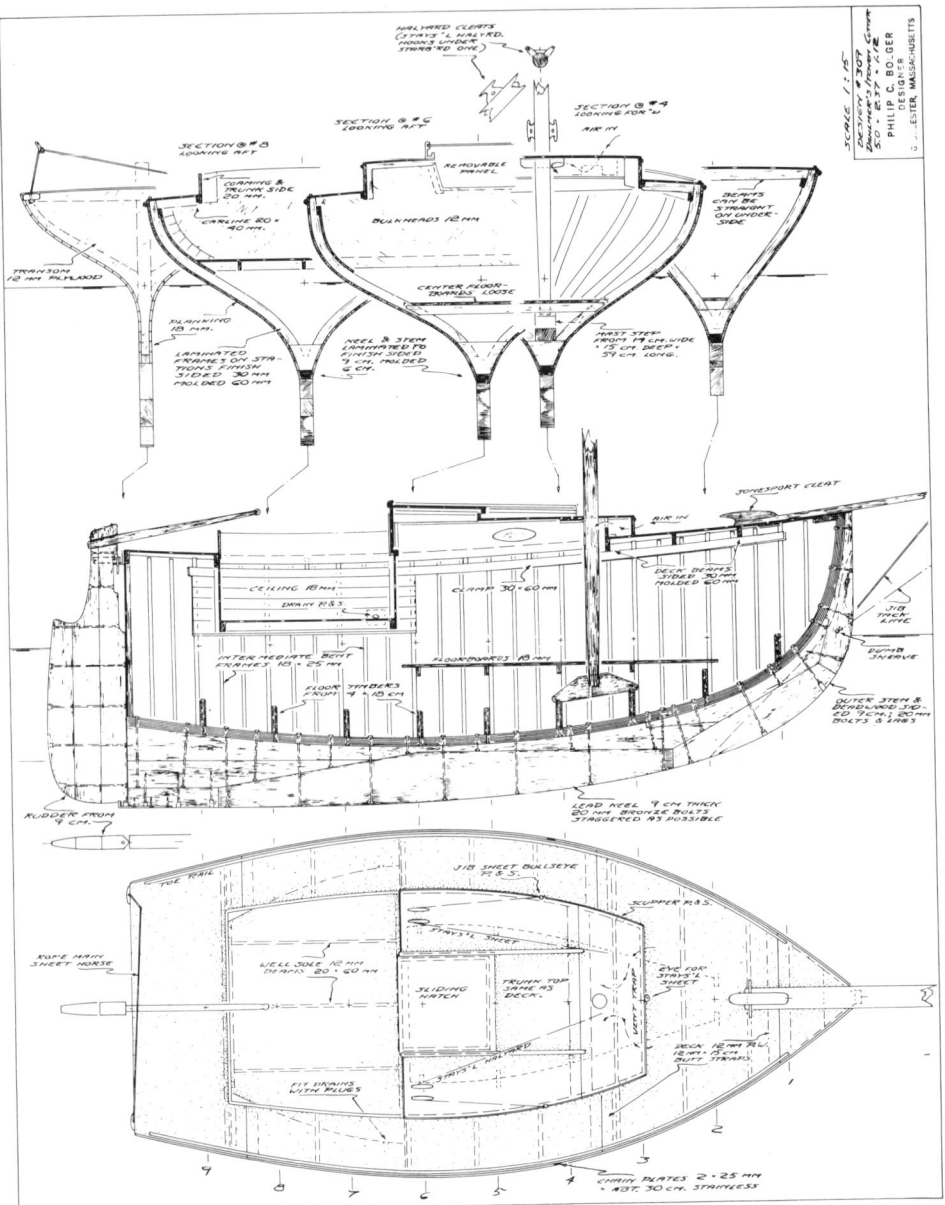

I only put about five working days into these plans once we agreed on how it should be. I took it just far enough to order materials and get started, and wasted little time on small details which I figured we would work out as she came along in construction. I often think that an owner-builder might know what he wants better than I can tell him, or could buy John Leather's *Gaff Rig* (International Marine Publishing Company, Camden, Maine) and read that instead of a specification which would say about the same except for the addition of personal quirks of mine.

21
RECREATIONAL ROWBOAT

13'9" x 4'0"

I keep arguing that one reason rowing boats aren't more popular is that most people insist on turning rowing into an athletic event. That's all very well for athletic people at times when they're feeling ambitious, but it's not the half of the possibilities. A rowboat can be an ideal place to relax, as good as gentle walking, better if you have things to carry.

It occurred to me that it would be good to get up a design for a rowboat with more initial stability than is usual; one with her feet wide apart, that wouldn't have to be trimmed carefully and wouldn't leave a novice with the usual impression that rowboats are tiddly and maliciously on the lookout for a chance to drop one over the side. I used to think this wasn't possible, but it developed that if you didn't insist on rowing fast, you could make a stiff boat that would row easily at a gentle pace, say three miles an hour. After all, there are a lot of lakes and harbors with pleasant and interesting things to look at within a three-mile radius of some convenient starting point, and nowhere to go that's farther. What's more, such places can take just so many water-skiers before they start to cut each other and the bystanders to bits, so encouraging the rowers is a means of coping with a crowded locality; it's Socially Responsible.

One penalty of opting for large stability is that the boat is harder to plank than the fine-lined and slack-bilged types, especially if it's to be good in rough water, as it ought to be: if the boat is to relax in, people shouldn't be expected to keep hair-trigger alert for dragger wakes and squalls. I didn't worry much about it because I was thinking mostly in terms of one wooden prototype by an expert, and thereafter molded hulls; I had a vague notion of interesting some entrepreneurial type in the design. The strip construction indicated seems to be best suited to use for building a mold plug, though I'm not as convinced as some that it's an easy way to build.

120 RECREATIONAL ROWBOAT

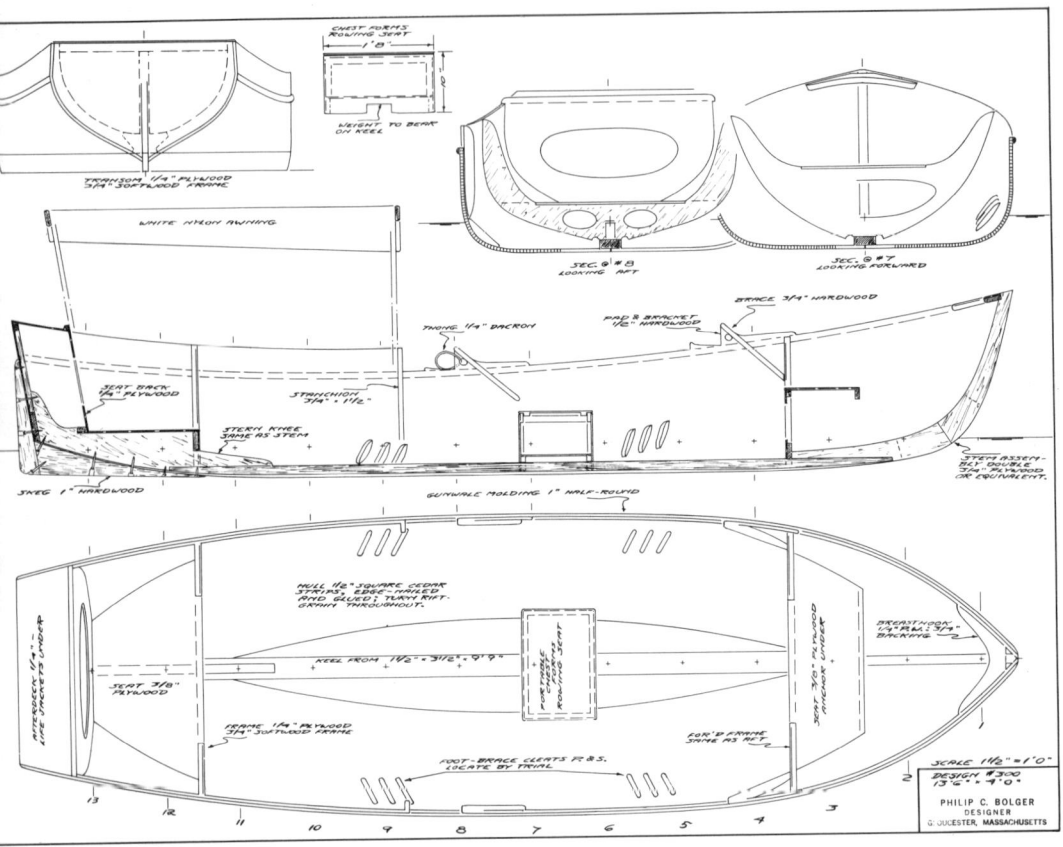

The shape is not fit for an inexperienced builder in any construction, and an experienced one can go ahead and use lapstrake or foam-core plastic or whatever he's used to; for that matter, one of these might not make a bad dry run for a ferrocement project.

The awning was an afterthought, a turn in the shade being pleasant on a summer day. It could be extended over the rowing positions, but in that case it ought to be arranged to be quickly removable; a full-length awning might be an embarrassment in a hard squall. The short one shown would probably swing her around bow to the wind before it would knock her over. Besides, it reminds me pleasantly of ceremonial barges to be seen in old pictures and European museums.

The middle part of the boat was kept clear, with a movable rowing seat, to allow napping and sun-bathing at full length. I know of people in England who make fairly long river and canal cruises in such boats, camping quite decently with an overall tent, which strikes me as a big improvement on camping ashore and chancing property-owners or rattlesnakes according

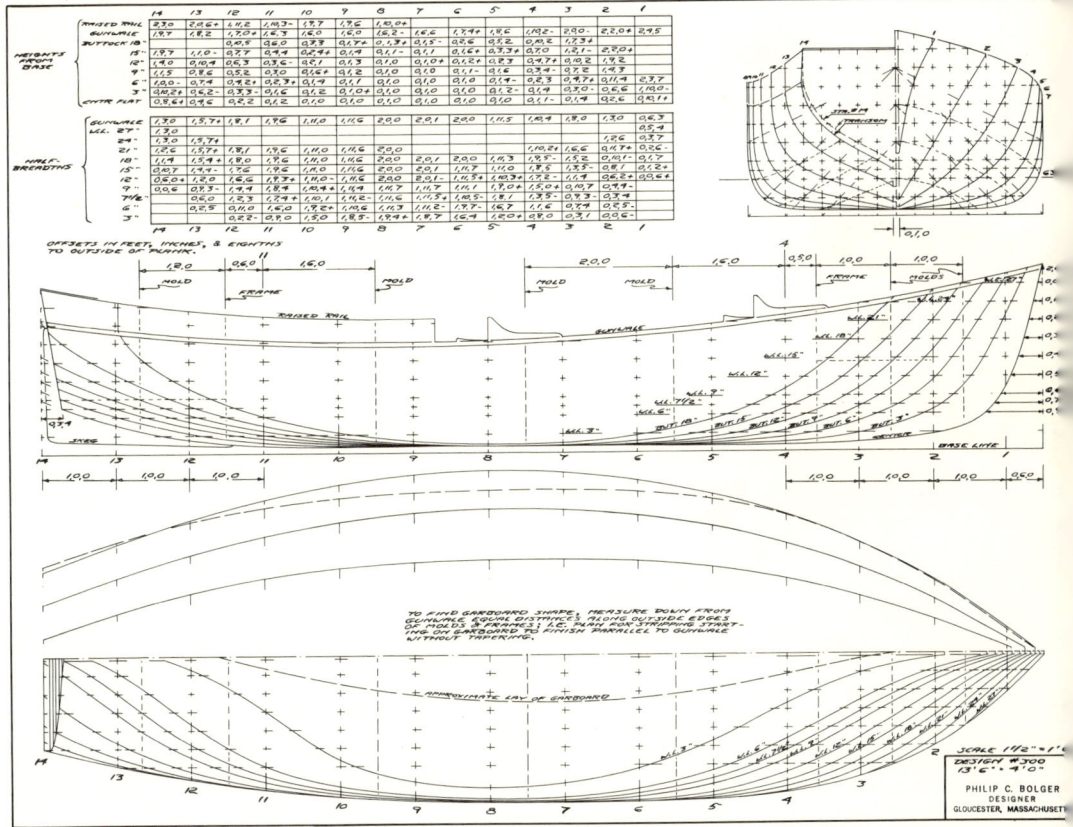

to locality. This idea, plus wanting to provide buoyancy enough to float three or four people with a good reserve, determined the length of the boat.

No doubt it would be foresighted to remark now that this is a poor design for a sail or motor boat, being modelled for a slower speed than you're entitled to expect of either. Motors and sails are too expensive and troublesome to be added to everything you come across as a habitual reflex, and both are only in the way if this boat is put to the use it was meant for.

22
HARBINGER

15'0" x 7'1"

When Brad Story started to talk of building himself a catboat to replace his Thomaston Galley, I dug out a set of plans made by Fred Goeller in 1911 and another by Edson Schock in 1907. Very nice catboat designs (see *Rudder* Magazine December, 1907, and February, 1911); "They got it right," I said; "Goeller especially. Why go through it again?" But no; the Galley had spoiled him with its nice rowing qualities, and it's a fact that Essex River and Bay are mean places for a straight sailer; the tide runs hard over flats, around hairpin bends, and through tight guts. For eight or nine months in the year I think it's one of the world's most beautiful places in a quiet, restful way, but swarms of mosquitoes, greenheads, and gnats think so, too; it's as much as your life and sanity are worth sometimes to have to lie over a tide without screens.

So, I designed Brad a catboat that can be rowed fast and far, relatively speaking, and incidentally produced one that doesn't need as big a sail plan as the usual hard-bilged Cape model; she's more on the New York model, the kind that developed into the sandbaggers. I call this a really sweet model, fair and easy, no great problem to frame and plank. For some reason the dish shape of the sections isn't nearly as noticeable in the wood as it is on paper; there's nothing abnormal about her looks. Nor is she tender, as the slack bilges might suggest, though of course she does roll when you step on the side in boarding her.

The rig is no different from the 1900's type, except for the elimination of a lot of unnecessary blocks; it used to be customary to show three- and four-part halyards on small gaff sails in which a single part in a dumb sheave is a one-handed operation. Apart from that, I can't see that anybody's come up with a clear-cut improvement on this rig. Jib-headed cats balance badly when reefed, and contrary to what some have written, raking the mast

Harbinger *at her builder's landing.*

makes it worse, not better. This one has the gaff peaked up more than is ideal from a reefing standpoint; an overcanvassed boat that will be sailed reefed a lot of the time should have a squarer head to keep the area above the reef points more in line with the full sail.

Brad wanted the bottom of the rudder cut up above the line of the skeg, for obvious reasons. I didn't think it would hold her reaching at that depth. We concluded I would draw it my way, he would build it his, and I could say "I told you so" if I happened to be along when she turned around and looked him in the eye, cat-fashion. Then construction was put off for a year while he built an auxiliary and a power cruiser for paying customers, and in the meantime it occurred to me that if we put about a four-inch plate along the bottom of the shallow rudder to keep some of the flow of water from eddying off the bottom of the blade, it might work at his depth after all. The sail plan shows the profile shape; look at the *Moccasin* design for a detail of a similar rudder, and at the text about *Blackgauntlet II* for some discussion of this matter of end-plates and rudder effectiveness, which is technically somewhat interesting.

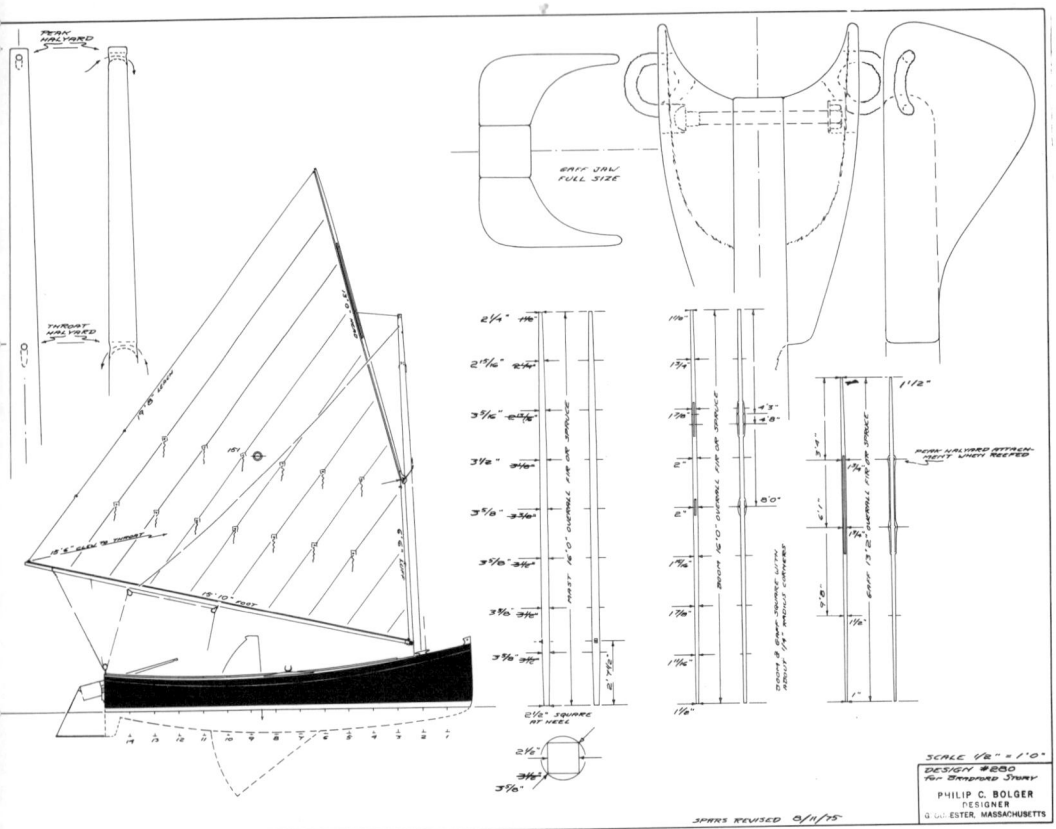

KEY TO PLANS

1. Keel in two logs, each sided 2½" mahogany, rabbeted for centerboard trunk sides which are to be installed before keel is assembled.

2. Centerboard trunk sides ½" marine plywood; 1" screws to keel, headblocks, etc.

3. Headblocks of centerboard case 1½" x 2½" mahogany.

4. Top blocking and flanges of centerboard case 1½" square mahogany.

5. Keel filler blocks forward and abaft centerboard case sided 1½" mahogany; ¼" bolts through keel and cheeks.

6. Horn timber cheeks sided 1½" mahogany.

7. Skeg sided 1½" mahogany; round off leading edge smoothly.

8. Transom 1¼" mahogany, fir or cedar, edge-drifted with ⅜" galvanized rods; two 1½" square vertical stiffeners as shown; no frame.

9. Stem and foregripe sided 2½" mahogany, halved and bolted and/or screwed together; stem needs about 10½" breadth. Drive stopwaters clean through in way of a backrabbet. Brass pin about ½" x 6" through stemhead for a mooring cleat.

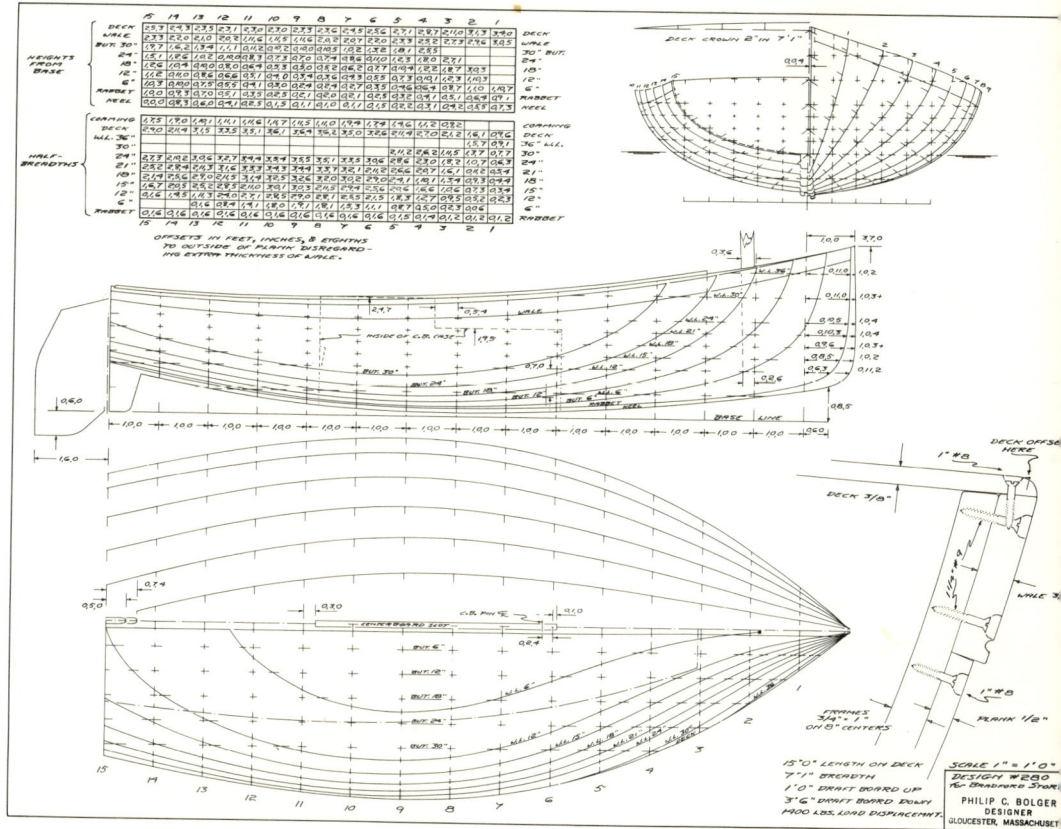

10. Breasthook from 1½" x 5½" oak or mahogany; ⅜" bolt through stem.

11. Keel shoes sprung on from 1" x 1½" oak.

12. Stop-block in centerboard case to take jog of centerboard and prevent board from ever dropping through.

13. Floor timbers sided 1½" oak or mahogany; ⅜" bolts through backbone structure; in way of centerboard case, ⅜" x 5½" lag screws to keel.

14. Floor timber forming mast step sided 2½", cut down as shown to hold heel of mast.

15. Mast heel bracket in two 1½" sections, oak; one forward of mast molded 1½", one abaft mast 2"; four ¼" bolts through floor timber and frame.

16. Three sawn frames in bow sided ¾", molded about as shown, including deck beams; #2 has ½" plywood gussets to beam.

17. Bent frames ¾" x 1" oak on 8" centers.

18. Planking ½" cedar; 1" #8 Everdur screw fastenings.

19. Sheer strake ¾" mahogany; 1¼" #9 screws.

20. Deck beams and short beams sided ¾", molded about as shown, fir or mahogany; ¾" x 1½" struts to frames and floors, as far inboard as stowage of oars will allow.

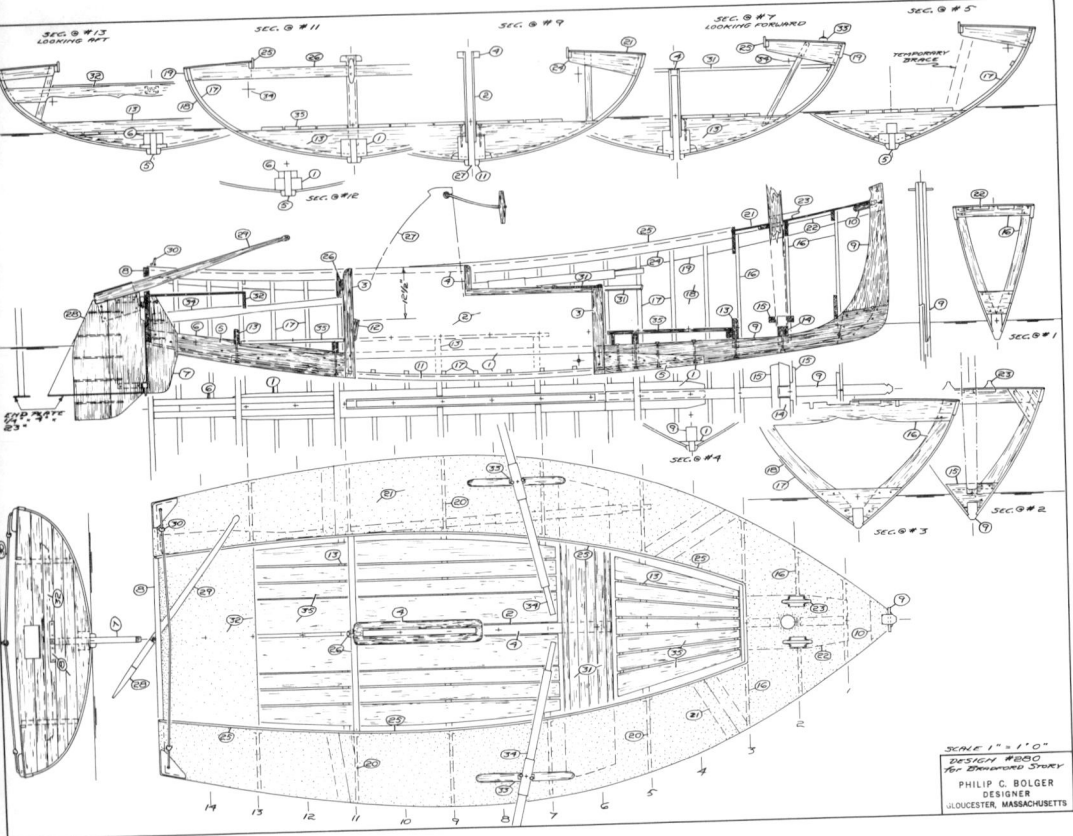

21. Deck ⅜" marine plywood, with butt straps of the same not under 6" wide.

22. Partner blocking ¾" fir.

23. Halyard cleats oak; two ¼" bolts each through partner blocking.

24. Deck carlines ¾" x 1½" fir.

25. Coamings ½" x 2½" mahogany.

26. Deck beam extended across cockpit to brace after end of centerboard trunk; 6" wood cleat for main sheet on after side; ¾" x 2½" doubling on forward side of exposed part of beam.

27. Centerboard 1¼" thick oak or mahogany; see diagram for dimensions and layout; hoist with 12" pennant and handle; provide holes and pin to hold in fully raised and two or three intermediate positions; ¾" bronze pivot pin.

28. Rudder 1½" oak or mahogany dowelled together; bronze pintles and gudgeons; $\frac{1}{16}$" brass or stainless steel sheet bent over top to take tiller in a loose fit, with round head screws to blade.

29. Tiller from 1½" x 2½" x 4'2" oak or mahogany; note that rudder can't come off gudgeons unless tiller is first removed.

30. Traveller horse ¾" rope or ¼" wire, threaded through deck and 1½"

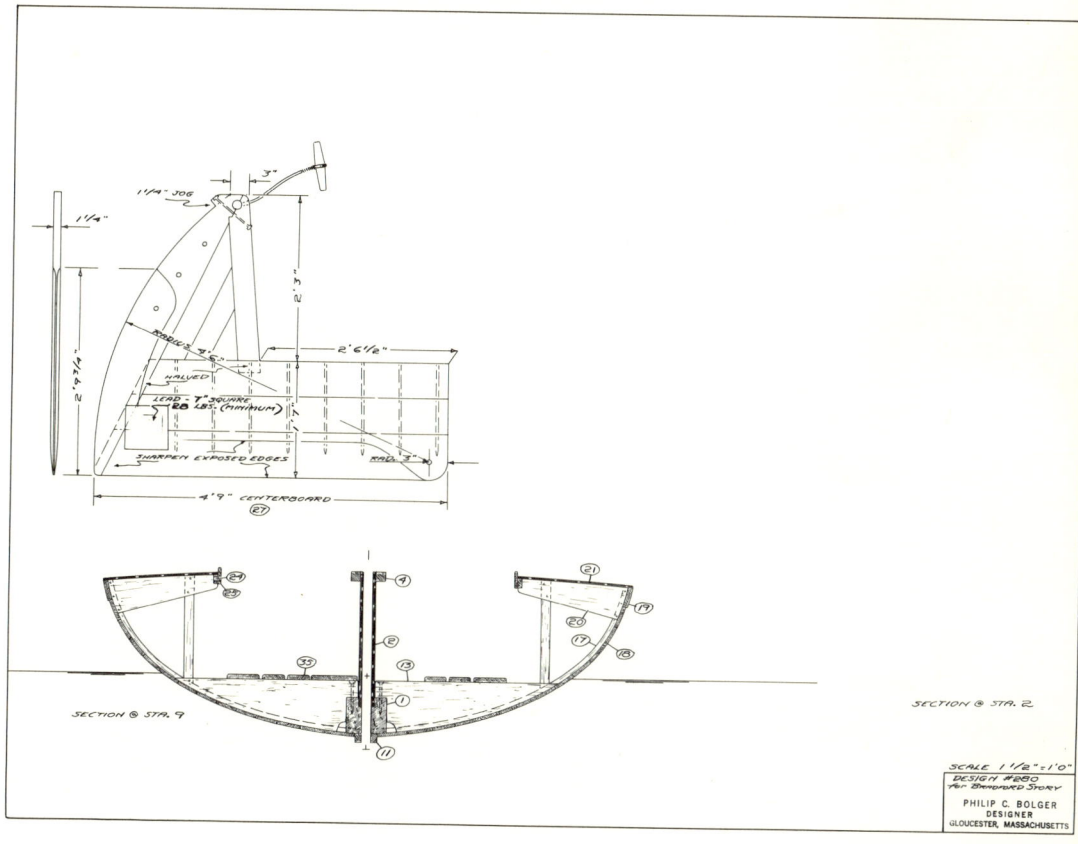

blocks on top of deck; note stops to prevent sheet blocks from jamming at ends of horse.

31. Rowing thwart mahogany or teak, four strakes ½" x 2¼" and two strakes ¾" x 1½"; all edge-nailed, and screwed down to top of centerboard case; ¾" x 1½" cleats over four frames support ends at hull sides.

32. Stern sheets beam from ¾" x 3½", shaped to clear oars and to taste; sternsheets ⅜" plywood cleated to transom.

33. Rowlocks bronze, flush socket type, raised off deck on 1½" x 2" x 2'0" mahogany spacers about as shown to bring bottom of locks about level with top of coaming.

34. Oars 10' ash straight-blade, leathered without buttons.

35. Floorboards ¾" teak or mahogany; separate forward section lightly screwed down, outboard side planks firmly secured, one broad strake each side of centerboard case left loose.

36. Buoyancy: unballasted wood hull is of course unsinkable and in smooth water can be bailed out afloat even if swamped; designer nevertheless thinks it would be good to use urethane foam blocks sawn up to fit as neatly as possible in space ahead of frame #2 and all along sides of hull outboard of short beam

struts; should be possible to get about ten cubic feet each side and four or five in the bow, with which she will have stability enough to be sailed (after a fashion) when swamped, and can be bailed even in very rough water.

37. Ballast: the boat will sail best without ballast, but because of the slack bilges and narrow waterline she will feel tender at rest, and may benefit in comfort by the use of anything up to eight or ten fifty-pound sand bags placed each side of centerboard case. (N.B. — only if buoyancy is installed as in #36.)

38. Solid grown spars, preferably fir but may be spruce; mainmast round to given diameters, planed off square at heel; allow about $\frac{1}{8}''$ over diameters for partner hole, to step through easily but need no wedges. Boom and gaff square with corners just slightly rounded; see full-size detail for gaff jaw. Boom uses a plate spinnaker pole fitting and socket in place of a gooseneck, as boom and gaff must be readily detachable from mast to clear space for rowing. No hoops or lacing are needed for the luff. Running rigging, one sheet, two halyards, and two topping lifts, all $\frac{1}{4}''$ manila or dacron. No standing rigging.

23
WINDFOLA

21'0" x 7'1"

Victor Hopwood had an old-time boat carpenter for a neighbor, who could advise about lapstrake construction. There's almost nothing in his boat that would have looked remarkable to a member of the Humber Yawl Club a hundred years ago unless he'd been pleased to allow that she's an unusually good-looking example of her breed. If the lay of the planking comes off well, this ought to be a real beauty; to my eye there's hardly anything as pretty as a white-painted lapstrake hull with nicely lined-off planking.

She's meant for day-sailing and camping in the waters around Auckland, New Zealand. Captain Cook's journals for the time he was in those waters report many days of gentle breezes interspersed with occasional screaming horrors. I haven't looked up a more recent account of the weather than this two-hundred-year-old one, and it could also be that what the skipper of a brick backhouse like Cook's *Endeavor* would call a gentle breeze might seem otherwise to a singlehanded canoe sailor. The owner said to give her a big rig with good reefing qualities.

A singlehander ought not to be too flighty, and this is a sizable boat, meant to displace three-quarters of a ton when loaded for cruising. She's a shape that won't slow down much or steer badly at considerable angles of heel, and she can plug along on the wind under short sail without being badly knocked about by a steep chop. With the long keel and yawl rig it ought to be possible to let go the tiller long enough to get a pipe lit, in moderate weather. This kind of keel also tends to make a boat lie steadily to an anchor, an improvement both in comfort and safety over the kind that walk nervously back and forth till you let go a second anchor in desperation.

It's to be hoped that she has enough lateral plane to sail on all points reliably, but she will certainly be slow hard on the wind without her lee-

SCALE 1/2" = 1'0"
DESIGN #311
21'0" x 7'1"
for Victor Hopwood
PHILIP C. BOLGER
DESIGNER
GLOUCESTER, MASSACHUSETTS

MACHINED BLOCK
& WELDED ARM
A LOOSE FIT ON
VERTICAL SHAFT
EXTENSION TILLER
SOCKET & ARM
DECK
SHAFT A DRIVE FIT
THROUGH DECK.

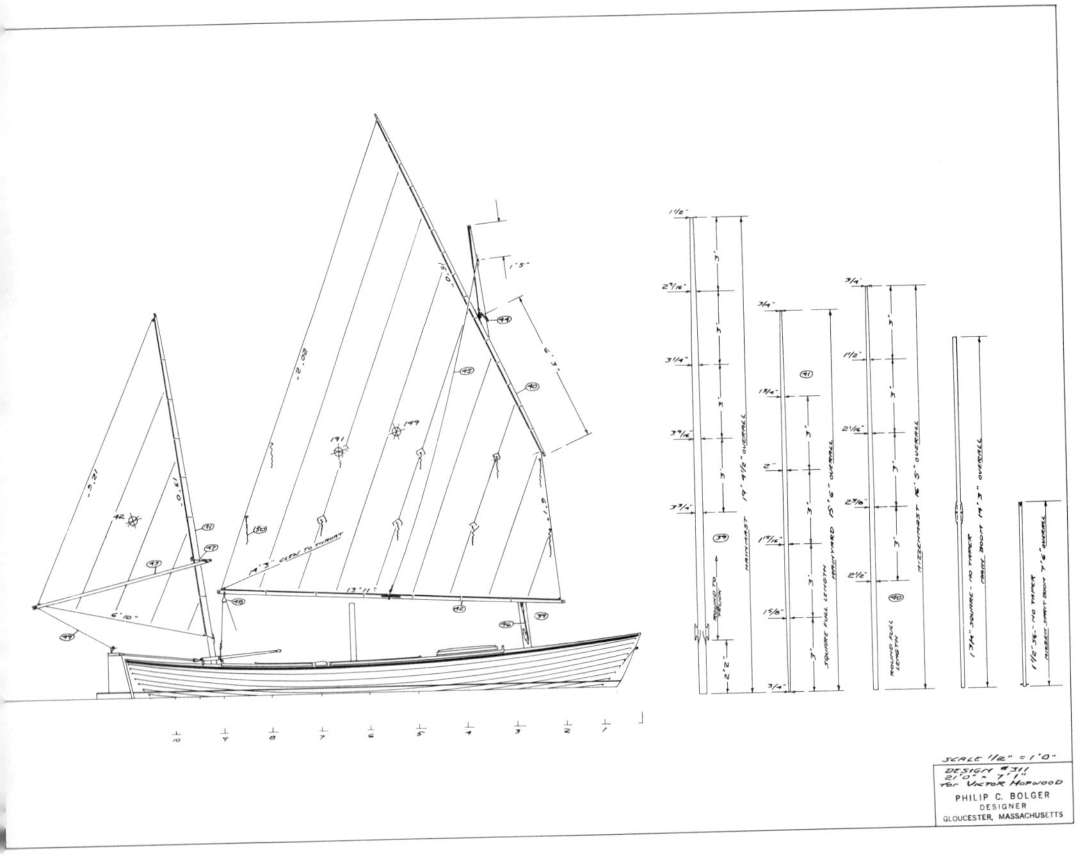

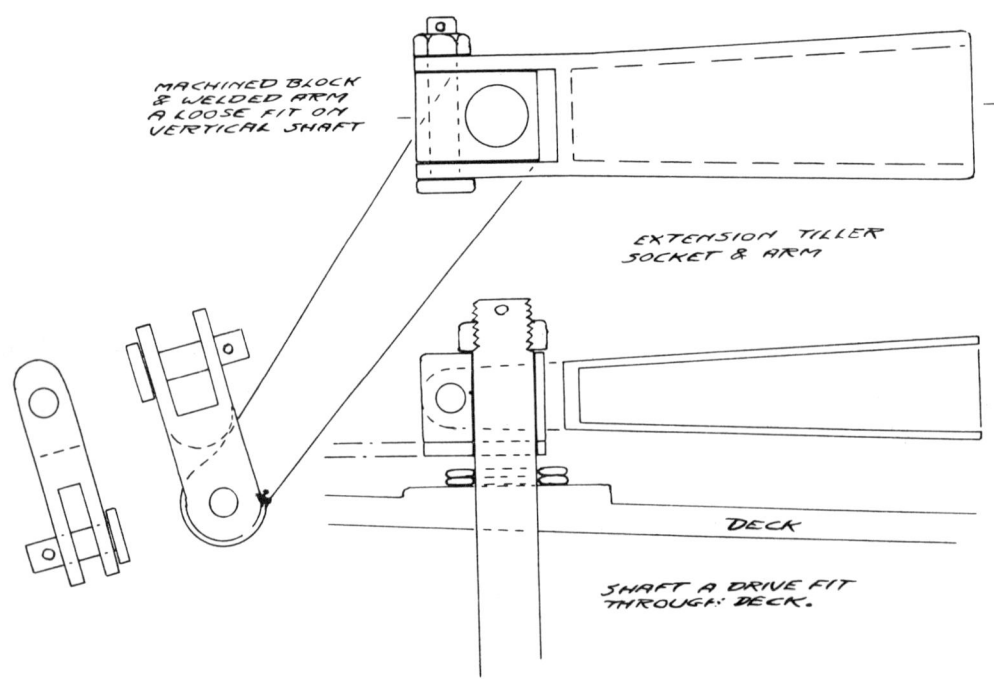

board. The idea is that maneuvering is done with the board stowed, and when she's all in order and settled on course, the leeboard is dropped over the side to let her point up and stop crabbing. Reaching and running, there's no need of it.

The oars are strictly auxiliary, though it's surprising how far you can get in a boat this big and heavy if you don't lose patience and wear yourself out pulling too hard. Even in some wind, provided you get the masts down on deck, a short, quick stroke will keep her moving, enough to get clear of a beach or into some narrow creek.

For those who don't happen to know an English boat carpenter, the shape would be good for one of the one-off plastic constructions, or for that matter a production job using a full female mold if a little sectional taper were worked into the keel. I wouldn't recommend using her as the basis for more of a cruiser, though.

KEY TO PLANS

1. Keel, stem, and sternpost all sided 2″ mahogany or equivalent (fir will serve any part of the boat except possibly the bent frames); ⅜″ bronze or galvanized bolts; 6″ lags amidships; end posts would be best if natural crooks but well-seasoned straight-grain stock will serve well enough to obviate any need to laminate crooks.

1a. Keel apron from ¾″ x 3½″ bevelled by trial and sprung in.

2. Shoe ½″ x 2″ x about 17′6″ galvanized steel (weight about 60 pounds); may be bronze or lead if preferred.

3. Bulkheads ⅜″ plywood with ¾″ x average 2″ fastening frames around edges; I suggest that these be lofted and set up as molds to plank on, jogging for the laps as planking progresses, to get them perfectly watertight.

4. Floor timbers sided 1½″.

5. Bent frames ¾″ x 1″ on 12″ centers; the bend is easy enough to allow use of other wood than (preferred) oak, ash, or elm (see #6).

6. Planking ½″ finished, not less than ten strakes to a side, with glues or adhesive seam compound at the laps; top four or five strakes should have at least one butt, that in the sheer strake well aft; if natural wood rather than plywood is used for planking, the frames should be shimmed to bear on the whole width of each plank near the turn of the bilge through the middle part of the boat (to reduce risk of splitting planks).

7. Clamp 1″ x 1½″.

8. Deck beams, including short beams, sided 1″, molded about 2″.

9. Deck ½″ plywood with ½″ x 6″ butt straps.

10. Sheathing, in way of cockpit only, a strong ½″ laid up tight seam; make sure that butt blocks don't block drainage and air circulation between frames behind sheathing.

11. Carlines ¾″ x 2½″.

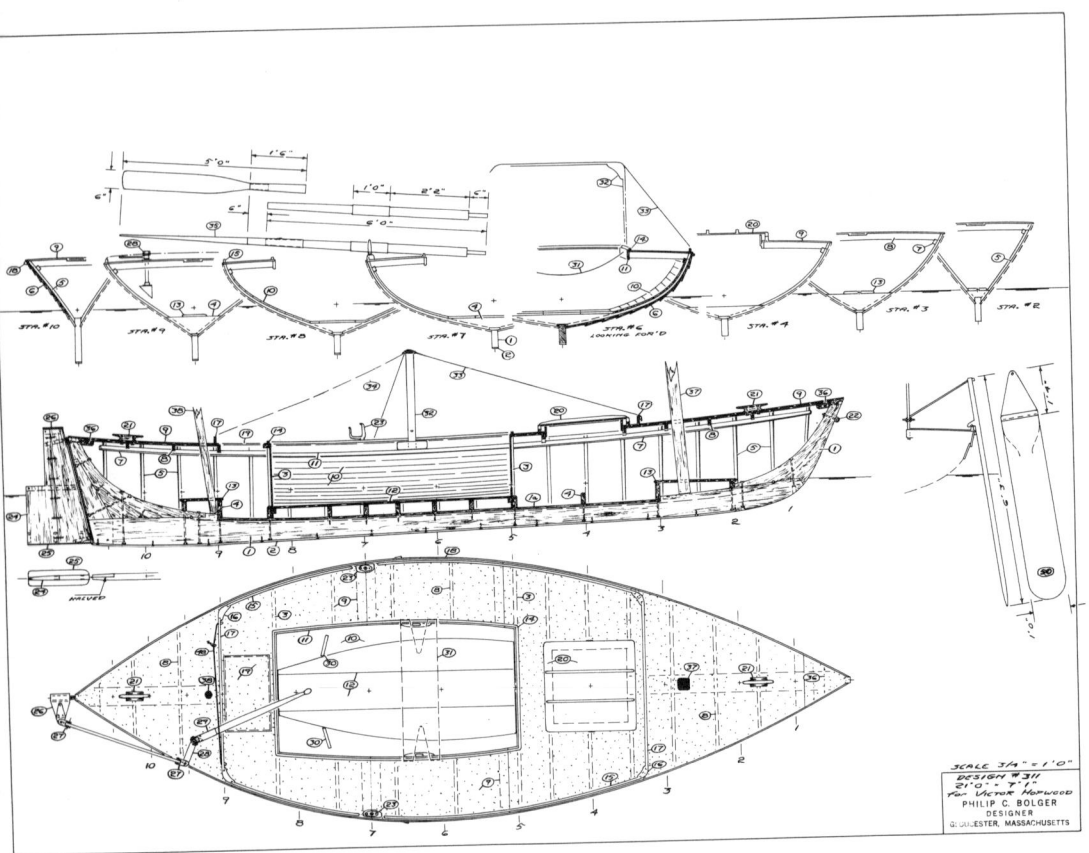

12. Cockpit sole ¾″; may be plywood; removable 12″ wide along center.

13. Mast steps ¾″ plywood, glued and with three lags each to floor timbers; holes for masts a loose fit.

14. Cockpit coaming ¾″ square.

15. Toe rail ¾″ x 1¼″; best cut scuppers about stations #6 and #8 besides openings at #7.

16. Corner blocks sawn out, with rabbets for toe rails and splash boards.

17. Splash boards from ¾″ x about 3″.

18. Sheer moldings about ¾″ x 1″, tapered at extreme ends.

19. Flush hatch to "wet stowage" (anchors and rodes, bailer, fresh water); provide a lanyard and hooks (not shown) to hold it in place.

20. Hatch to "dry stowage" (especially bedding) with double coaming; ½″ top with ¾″ x 1″ stiffeners; to keep in place I suggest a stopblock in each corner of the underside of the top, to bear against the inside angles of the inner coaming, with a swiveling hook each side to outer coaming to hold it down; also a lanyard to make sure it's not lost entirely. The bow compartment can have slat sheathing or underdeck nets to keep dry items off damp planking, or use waterproof bags.

21. Ten-inch cleats hardwood or metal bolted through centerline butt strap.
22. Stem eye something like $3/8''$ bronze with $3/4''$ opening.
23. "Thames Crutch" oarlocks shown have to be special castings or weldments; on reflection I think ordinary single thole pins with lanyards around the looms would make more sense, in which case the raised base blocks should be somewhat higher and extend aft as a base for the oars.
24. Rudder blade from $1\frac{1}{2}''$, faired to $3/4''$ at trailing edge; $3/4'' \times 1\frac{1}{2}''$ stiffener each side just above water.
25. Rudder base plate $1/4'' \times 5''$ galvanized or stainless steel, secured with tabs up sides of rudder; make sure it's fastened for keeps, as while its function is to improve the effectiveness of the shallow rudder, it'll inevitably be used as a step some day.
26. Rudder arm $3/4''$ plywood with $1/4'' \times 3''$ stainless steel tip to give $8''$ radius; mount arm on $3/4'' \times 1\frac{1}{2}''$ cheek each side of rudder head.
27. Toggles to accommodate drop in rudder linkage; drag link can be a metal tube or solid $1''$ square hardwood.
28. Eight-inch arm.
29. Tiller socket; see detail for this fitting; tiller about $1\frac{1}{2}'' \times 2'' \times 3'4''$.
30. Foot braces about $3/4''$ square; locate by trial.
31. Fabric sling rowing seat hooked outside coaming.
32. Gallows $1'' \times 2\frac{1}{2}''$ solidly fixed to carlines; note belaying pins for leeboard.
33. Spray hood of reasonably waterproof white fabric; to pass over top of gallows and lash under it; it bundles up against gallows in fine weather, with straps attached for the purpose; the after corners snap or tie outside the toe rail, and each forward corner has a tail passing through a hole in the splashboard corner block to a jam cleat inside so it can be instantly released to get forward to the halyards. This hood is not supposed to keep all water off the deck, just enough so the small lip coaming can handle the rest.
34. After cockpit cover similar to spray hood and one piece with it; also bundles against gallows when not in use.
35. Oars of spruce or similar light, stiff wood, in two sections each so they can be racked or slung under deck at sides of cockpit; loom diameter about $2\frac{3}{4}''$; normal leathering, with buttons if desired; brass or stainless steel tapered sleeves with spring catches to hold shaft to blade. (Better not use hooked blades as they're likely to be used for poling, sculling, and fending-off as well as rowing.)
36. Breasthooks $1\frac{1}{2}'' \times 5\frac{1}{2}''$ with $1/4''$ bolts through posts; make sure the deck is neatly bedded on these, otherwise certain rot.
37. Mainmast Douglas fir or equivalent; see diagram; square or with slightly rounded corners at and below deck; round above; may taper slightly from deck to heel to step easily; fit to need no wedges at step or partners.
38. Mizzenmast fir; see diagram; round full length with blunt conical heel to rotate easily; loose fit at step and partners.
39. Mainsail cut to sailmaker's taste, not necessarily as shown; reef points at least $9''$ long, but no more of them than shown; luff strongly roped or taped; no roach, no battens.

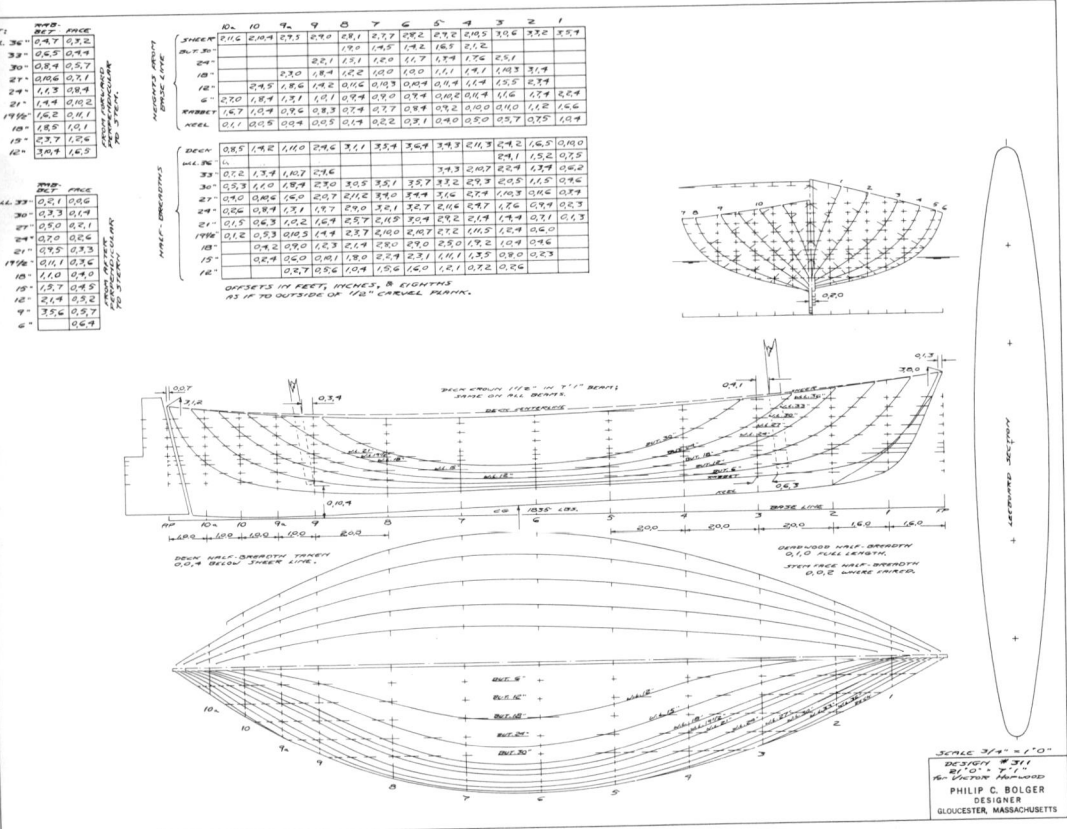

40. Main yard fir, see diagram; lash head of sail to it with separate ties, not a lacing.

41. Mizzen rolls up around rotating mast; lash stiffly at head and tack, tight ties up luff; rope luff in way of snotter (see #47); make clew and foot very strong.

42. Main boom, see diagram; fir.

43. Mizzen boom, see diagram; fir; $3/8'' \times 2''$ slot in outboard end for sheet and clew rope; hole and belaying pin at inboard end for standing end and fall of snotter respectively.

44. Halyard attachment a $3/8'' \times 2\frac{1}{2}''$ bronze shoulder eye bolt through the yard, with about $\frac{1}{16}'' \times 1'' \times 6''$ stainless strap and four or more $1''$ screws on top of yard under bolt (to take diagonal stress on bolt); a very large ($3''$ or $4''$) bronze snap hook engages the eye bolt with $1/4''$ nylon halyard spliced into eye of hook; lashed to the eye of the hook is a $1/4''$ rope ring about $6''$ inside diameter or whatever it takes never to jam up; halyard passes through athwartships dumb sheave in masthead and falls to a cleat on port side of mast near deck.

45. Topping lift $1/4''$ nylon passing through a smooth eye on forward side of masthead; snap hook each end engages a loop in a short rope tail on each side of boom, adjusted with stopper knots under the boom.

46. Downhaul ¼" nylon or shock cord from eye bolt under boom to a big smooth cleat on starboard side of mast. (This has to be set up hard or the peak will sag, but needs some spring to accommodate swing of boom.)

47. Snotter ¼" dacron or manila; standing end fast with a stopper knot through hole in end of sprit boom; passes around mast, through reinforced hole in luff of sail (so it won't slip down), and back to belay on pin through boom; remove from mast before rolling up sail.

48. Main sheet ⅜" nylon; snap hook on standing end engages ⅜" rope traveller horse outside splashboard; up through a single block slung on boom end, down to hand; this gives enough mechanical advantage, but some kind of cleat or hook each side on deck or carline, to catch the fall under on the lee side, would be convenient but is best placed by trial.

49. Mizzen sheet ¼" nylon; standing end a stopper knot caught in boom slot; runs through a big thimble on the rudder head to a pin or cleat on the mizzenmast.

50. Leeboard mahogany or equivalent; see diagram; 1½" x 2½" x 12" gunwale stop; ⅜" rope from head to gallows pin. This board is to improve speed close-hauled and need not be used unless and until convenient; fix a rack for it under the deck in way of cockpit.

24
DOVEKIE

6.52m x 1.82m

In the beginning, boats were paddled and consequently had to be lowsided though they could be very long and weren't necessarily narrow. At a date not very accurately known but upwards of four thousand years ago, a genius with a blinding flash of insight made a very long paddle, set it against a fulcrum, and put the strength of his back and legs into his stroke. The next several thousand years were spent spreading the word of how well this notion worked, and refining the technique. It allowed much heavier and bulkier vessels, though it had its drawbacks and never caught on among leads in ice, or up jungle creeks.

The next brainstorm was that of using the expansion of a heated gas or vapor to turn a shaft on which paddles could be mounted, whereupon the oar went out of fashion again. It never disappeared entirely, any more than the paddle had in the age of the oar, but its use declined until few people understood its potential. A time came when hardly anybody thought a boat without expanding-gas-driven paddles was useful or even prudent. Athletes worked out in strange oar-driven machines, and children played in toys maneuvered (hardly driven) with vestigial oars, but all serious movements, such as taking the dog ashore from the moored cruiser, depended on the mechanical paddles, though they, too, have their drawbacks, as follows:

They're expensive, costing ten or more times as much as oars.

They're complex and temperamental, needing much care and forethought to be reliable; they don't get this care and forethought and tend to stop working at inconvenient times.

They need periodic refueling, and grow very heavy and bulky if designed to extend the intervals by carrying more fuel or by use of nuclear fission.

Dovekie *steering herself, but feeling the weight of a large man in the lee bilge.*

Dovekie: *the relaxed singlehander.*

Below: *About to put up* Dovekie's *mast.*

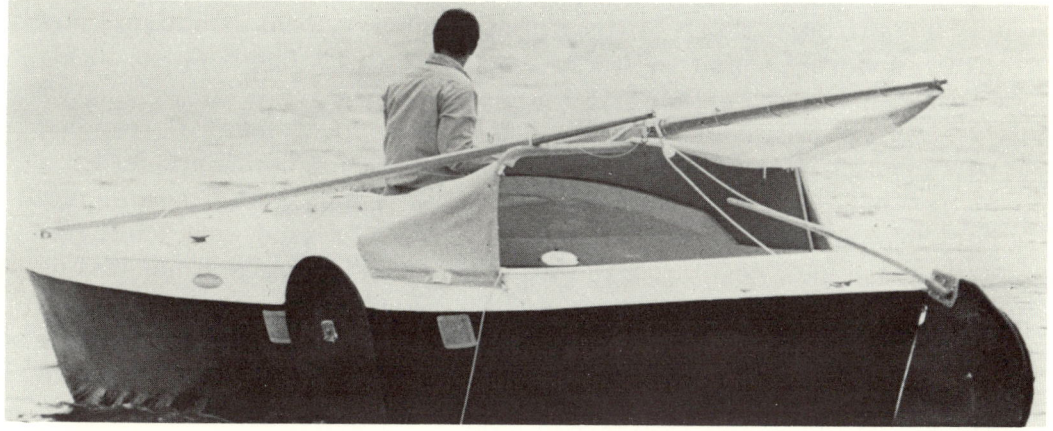

DOVEKIE

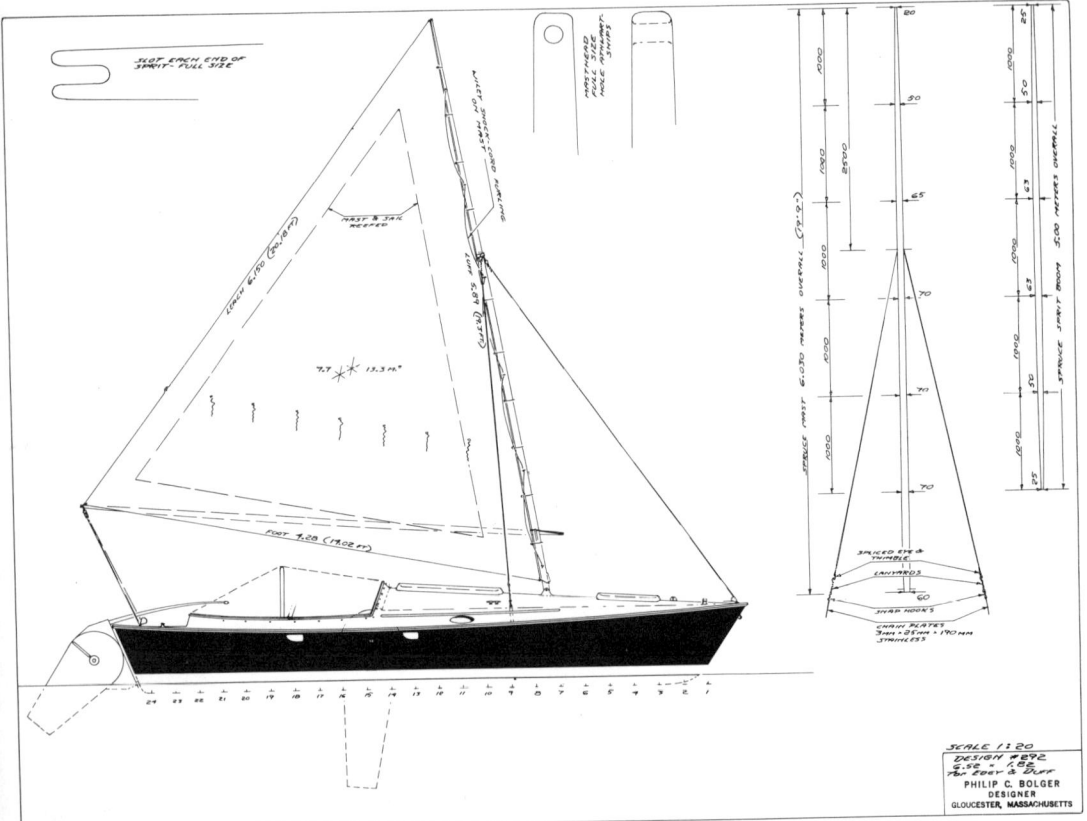

They're attractive to thieves in a time in which it's unusual to do anything cruel to a thief.

They're awkward and ugly objects, laborious to carry around, and they interfere with various good qualities, such as an ability to sail well.

They're messy things to come near, the best of them exuding oil and grease; many of them are also noisy enough to cover sounds which, in fog or darkness, it is well to hear.

Dovekie is a strenuous attempt to produce a popular family recreational boat that will function without an engine. For this she plainly needed a high enough performance under sail, and tight enough control, to go under sail wherever there is wind and minimum space. Secondly, she must row well enough, in a calm, to make rowing her a mild satisfaction not leading quickly to frustration or exhaustion; this meant among other things that there could be no underwater surfaces or excrescences not absolutely necessary to float her, and that she must be as low to the water and streamlined as possible, certainly having no spars or wires sticking high in the air.

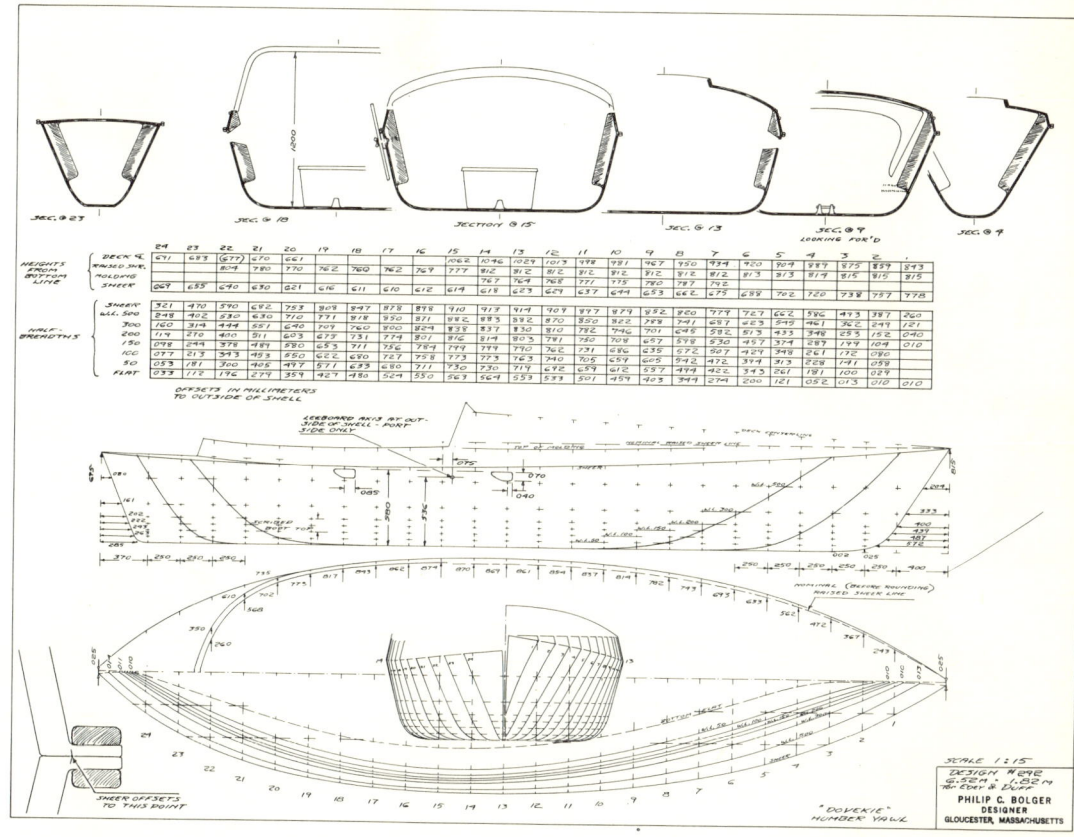

She was built as a joint experiment with Edey & Duff of Mattapoisett, of Airex foam-sandwich construction. The hull and deck assembly, stripped, weighs four hundred pounds. With normal equipment her displacement without crew is on the order of six hundred pounds. Another five or six hundred pounds of people doesn't seem to affect her performance much, other than making her much stiffer under sail and harder to start *and stop* under oars. So loaded she draws about four and a half inches of water, whereas empty she floats in about three inches. This sort of draft and upright stance aground were bonuses of the dead-flat bottom, which was mainly meant to give maximum stability for her weight and enough flat surface inside for four people to lie down. The raised keelson inside is to keep the rowing seats, and the crew, from sliding into the lee bilge when she heels; it's not needed for stiffening with this construction and could be eliminated if somebody wanted a pure rowing version, which would be a vast sum cheaper, as something like half her cost is devoted to the sailing capability.

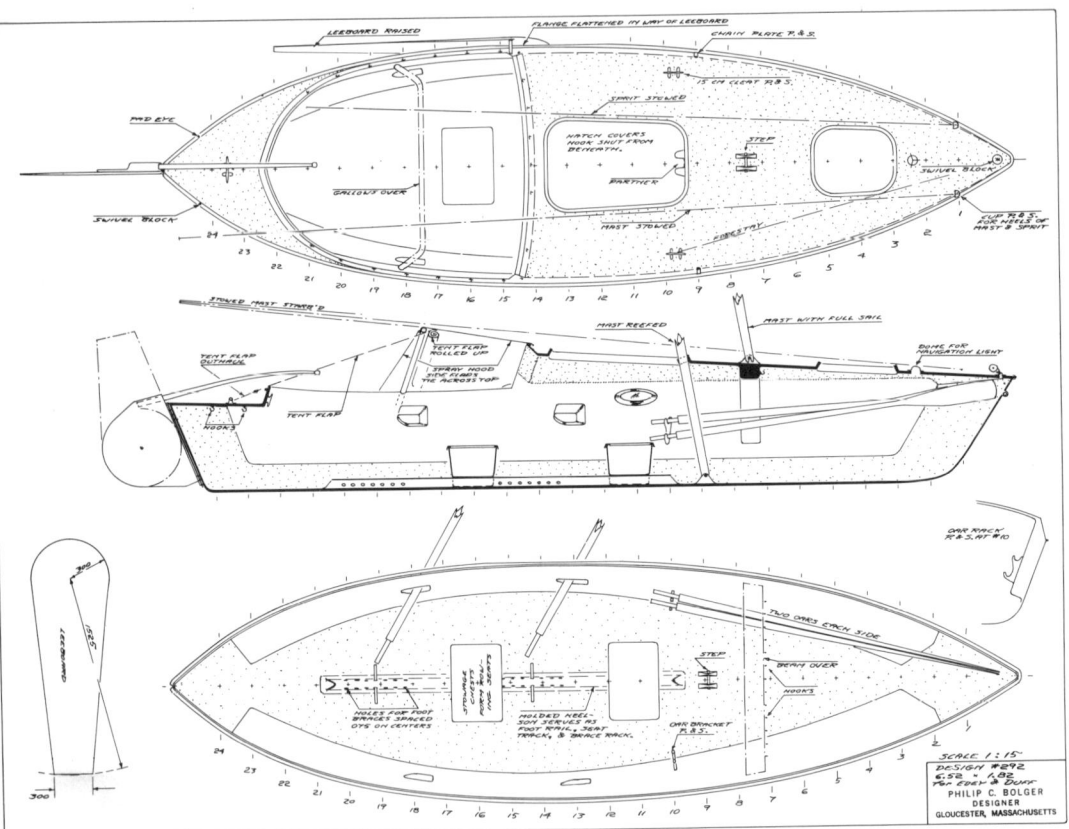

It's a fact, not an opinion, that *Dovekie* is a technical success. Everyone who has sailed her has been impressed. She is fast on all points, having for instance sailed thirteen nautical miles in two hours, nearly close-hauled, singlehanded, in choppy water. She's extraordinarily close-winded, not losing headway or making leeway when sailed three points from the true wind (of course she goes very slowly when thus pinched). She's the most perfect boat to steer I've ever handled, razor-sharp and instant in response to every movement of the tiller, yet steady on course. There's no tendency to roll or yaw downwind, even in strong gusts. I wish I was sure how this thoroughbred behavior was produced, so I could count on delivering it on demand. The long sprit boom obviously has something to do with it, but I have an uneasy feeling that the cut and flow of her Harding sail has as much to do with it as my design.

She has, in fairness, three failings: she sails around her anchor in an infuriating way; she's easily overpowered by strong winds with a light crew; and she pounds, not heavily but noisily, in a head sea. The second failing is partly remedied by the reefing arrangement, which about halves the sail

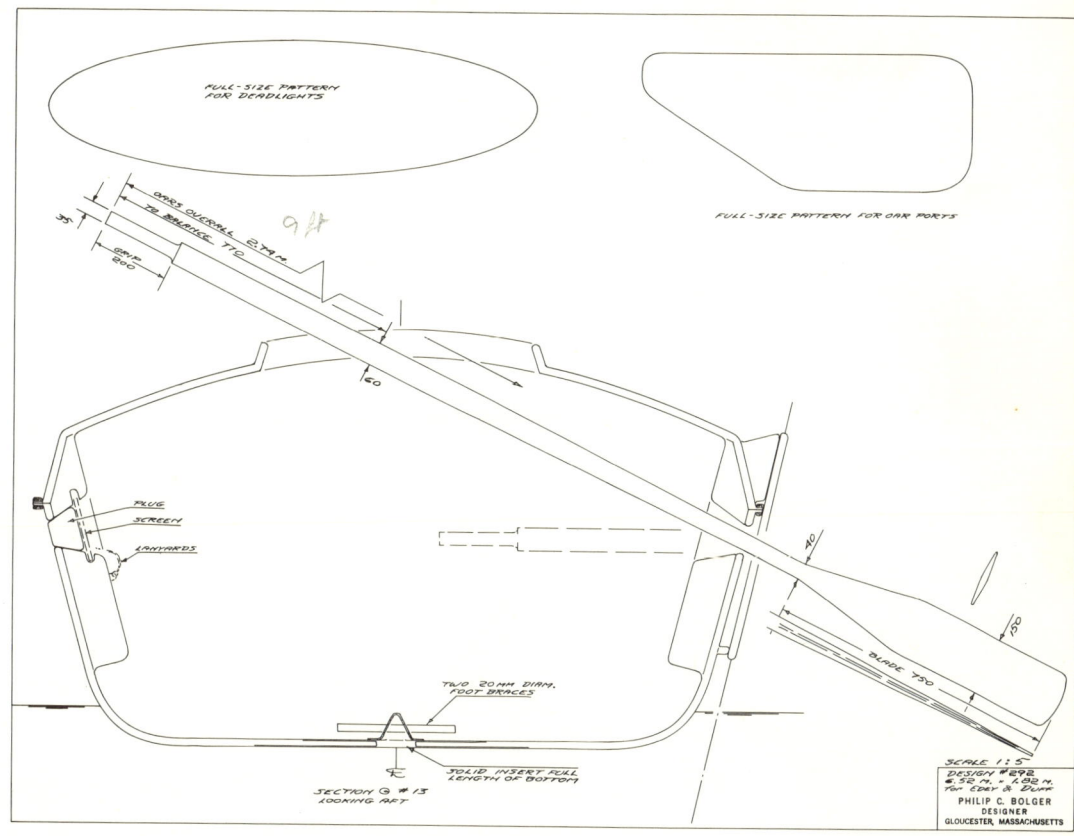

area and lowers the whole mast by upwards of a meter. The reduction is too drastic at one step to be ideal, but it came in handy one day of testing when the papers talked of fifty-knot gusts (on top of some thousand-foot tower, no doubt, but it really did breeze on fresh), and I was able to nurse her a few miles to windward before returning at a furious pace.

As to the rowing: I've rowed her as much as five miles in two hours without more effort than it would take to walk the same distance in the same time. (But the walker couldn't carry two or three other people while they rested; with a crew of three taking turns, *Dovekie* could be rowed something like twenty-five miles on a windless summer day.) She carries way well between strokes and is no trouble to keep straight. One man can't quite get her up to three knots even with a strong effort, but he can make useful progress against a stiff breeze by keeping his stroke short. Rowing downwind is apt to be more laborious than going into it, as the stern is blown around and demands hard pulling with both hands on the weather-side oar; a second person along to drop the rudder and steer is a great help at such a time.

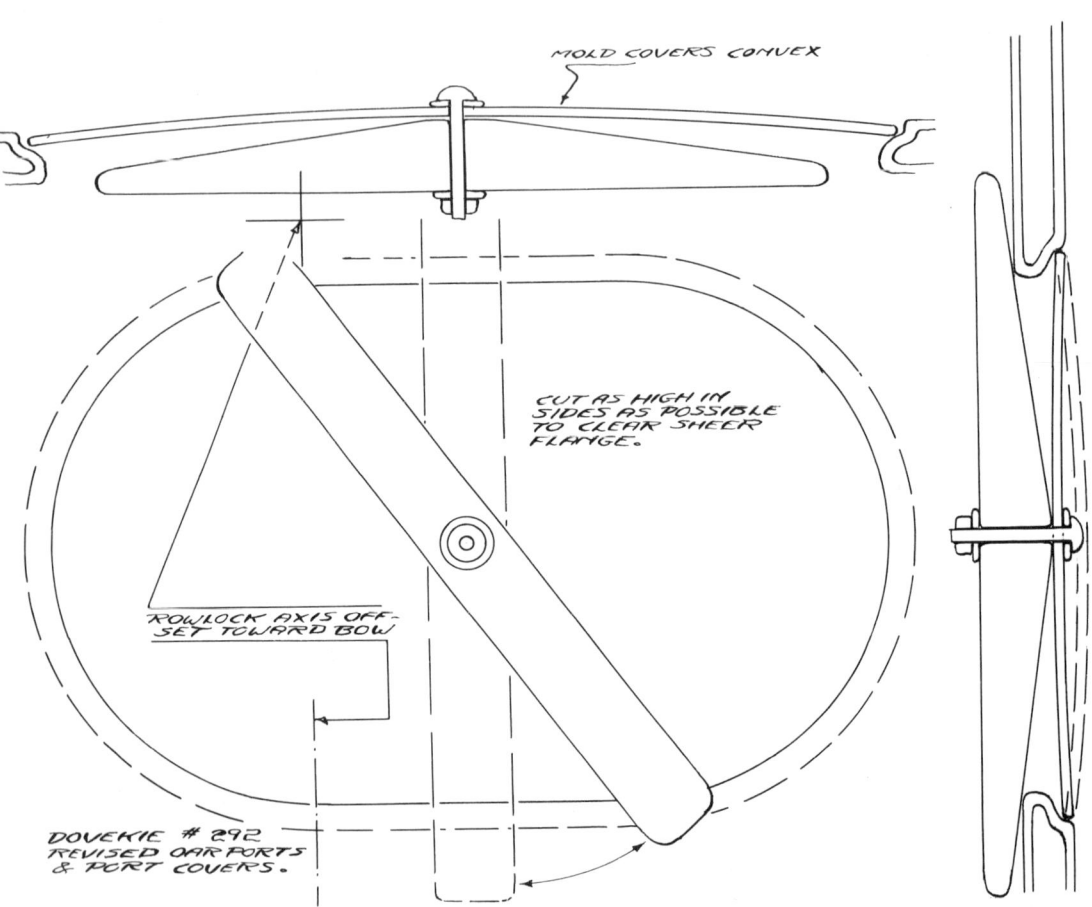

It's illuminating to try to row her with the leeboard and rudder in the sailing position. There's a sensation as of trying to drag a parachute, and if the mast is left standing as well and there's the slightest breath of wind, she becomes quite helpless with a single oarsman.

The oar ports work well in normal use, though the covers aren't perfectly watertight and must be redesigned. There's an echo of galley warfare, however, in the twenty-foot span she needs under oars To get an oar inboard out of the way as now arranged the blade has to be swung down into the water while extended straight out athwartships, and, since it has a limited swing fore and aft, it's not hard to get jammed up against a float (for instance) in such a way that you've got an embarrassing problem. Having had my nose rubbed in this problem a few times, I think I see means of at least mitigating it in a production version by using larger and differently shaped ports and a different type of lock.

Dovekie is an open boat to make all her volume available either for day-sailing, or for camping. An incidental bonus is that you're *in* her, not on top of her, almost waist-deep even when handling an anchor. There's no need to perch on the rail, ever, as sitting lounged in the turn of the bilge has as much or more effect on her stability. She tents in quite tightly, ventilated through the oar ports. I've spent up to five days and nights aboard in perfect comfort, even during hard rain with temperatures in the forties. She wouldn't be a bad substitute for a tent ashore. She can be rowed with all the canvas in place except the cover of the midships standing room. I often took her for a short row up and down the river on a calm evening. The effect from outside is odd as the rower is almost invisible, but in fact he can see very well all ways except straight astern.

In the test boat, no positive buoyancy was installed outside of the structural foam. In capsizing trials, once the mast was released she was easily rolled upright and bailed out, in smooth water; I don't think I'd want to count on doing it in a seaway; a production boat would have some added buoyancy, though probably less than the plans show. It would be easy to add enough ballast and buoyancy to make her self-righting (though not self-bailing) but it would increase the trailer weight correspondingly and does not seem to me necessary.

The single leeboard, used to save hardware and reduce adjustments, has the drawback that its length shifts the lateral plane appreciably aft as it comes up; she carries an unacceptable lee helm on the wind unless it's down nearly vertical, so she can't sail well in very shallow water. It could be that two shorter boards would work as well in other respects, and better in this one. There's been considerable discussion while sailing her about which tack is better, my own impression being that she likes it on the weather side. If there really is a difference, it's a slight one. The designed board was ¾" plywood with two layers of glass-cloth sheathing; it bent alarmingly from the first and finally broke at the pivot while being driven hard with a heavy crew. It was more heavily stressed when it was on the weather side, of course. The new board was laminated of two courses of mahogany, both laid lengthwise but slightly canted to each other, finished 1¼" thick, unsheathed and carefully foil-shaped. It shows no weakness.

Whether *Dovekie* will be marketed in quantity is undecided at this writing, to say nothing of whether she'll sell if she is. The doubtful points are psychological rather than technical. It seems to me that she has some singular advantages for some people's use, and ought to be especially interesting to people now using smaller straight sailboats. I hope that there are also people now using small outboard-powered auxiliaries who'd be open to a demonstration of how to dispense with some of their irritations. There may even be some who'd find the skill of getting the most out of the oar power a sporting proposition. I'm devising an involved and elaborate curse on the heads of the prohibitionist types whose instant reaction will be to forbid the use of the oars in racing. Such people are an international plague in sport and politics, always combining their urge to forbid everything they can't compel with a barren desert where their imaginations ought to be.*

SAILING DOVEKIE

1. Remove canvas covers and forward oar port covers; leave rowlocks in stowed position. Cast off and push clear of float or mooring.

2. Lift lee side oar grip from bracket and bring grip up, back, and out center standing room; swing oar athwartships and pass blade out port as far as neck of oar; erect rowlock around neck of oar and pass oar outboard to rowing position. Repeat with weather side oar.

3. Row to deep water, through low bridge, etc. Row gently and steadily; don't try to row fast. Use shorter stroke in stronger wind. Speed $2\frac{1}{2}$ to 3 miles per hour depending on conditions.

4. Allow to drift if there's sea room, or come to anchor. Bring weather oar in, passing grip out through standing room, blade forward to extreme bow, and grip to bracket. Repeat with lee side oar. Close oar port covers!

5. Swing leeboard and rudder blades down until vertical, rudder past vertical, and set up tension to hold them. Ship tiller.

6. Free main sheet; should have stopper knot in fall. Cast off all but lowest furling cord loop from sail. Carry mast and sail aft and turn over to bring mast forward side upward, making sure to turn it the right way to show a clear lead of shrouds from chain plates to tangs. Place mast heel slot on deck step bar. See that tail of forestay-halyard is within reach of center standing room.

7. Grab mast and sail in both hands at after end of center standing room and put it upright as far as shrouds will allow in one smooth heave. Don't stop half-way! Holding mast against shrouds with one hand, seize halyard, take up slack, hook under cleat (either side as convenient), and sway taut. Belay.

8. Pull boom off stem bracket and slide it ahead until outboard end is within reach of center standing room. Free and unroll sail, keeping hold of clew; shackle clew to boom end.

9. Grab stopper knot of snotter at mast block, take up slack, take a bight through slot at fore end of boom, and set up tension (the stronger the wind, the tighter); belay on boom cleat.

10. If anchored, pick up anchor, hanging fluke on the deck with shank down forward standing room. Fill away and sail; time from closing oar ports, ninety seconds plus time to deal with anchor.

To reef (may be done on any point of sailing but is easiest before the wind if sea room permits):

*After much discussion, it's been reluctantly concluded not to market her, or invest in production design or tooling.

1. Free snotter; unshackle boom and stow.
2. Holding clew, with tension on leech, roll up sail tightly from leech in to mast; pass lowest furling cord loop.
3. Cast off halyard; grab mast and sail as high as possible, and lower down aft in a smooth sweep. Don't stop half-way! Free and unroll sail.
4. Tie up foot of sail to reef tack (luff) grommet, leaving tack of sail fast. Tie up reef points in sequence from luff, tying clew loosely to last one or two points.
5. Roll up sail and pass second-from-bottom furling loop.
6. Unshackle shrouds from chain plates and tie them up loosely to mast.
7. Transfer snotter to upper mast block and retie stopper knot.
8. Slide heel of mast off deck step bar and aft; lift mast from after cockpit and slide heel of mast under deck at forward end of midships standing room.
9. Put heel slot down on hull bottom step bar.
10. With halyard in reach, swing mast up against partner knees at forward end of standing room and set halyard up hand tight to hold it there.
11. Cast off furling loop, unroll sail, shackle in clew reef grommet to boom end, and set up snotter (boom will stand far ahead of mast but will clear forestay-halyard). Time five minutes, with practice.

25
OCEAN-CROSSING ROWBOAT

$$33'0'' \times 6'0''$$

Some years ago John Zeigler had me do a study for a boat to be used to row the Atlantic. His approach to the exploit was careful and realistic, not the usual kind that leads to fiasco, but I was still somewhat relieved when he went off to do a hitch in the Navy instead. There it seems he came across a couple of other men who were taken with his idea; among them they got up a scheme to row across the Pacific. Consulted about it, I argued that it made no sense to deny themselves sails arbitrarily, since the rowing boat has to allow for the wind in any case. They commissioned a study, and presently I sent them the drawings shown here and the following letter:

> Thanks for the go-ahead. I started out with the premise that she had to carry ninety days' supplies for three men, which I understand by current technique and accepting a monotonous diet can imply about 1,800 pounds of food and drink in various combinations; the men themselves with minimum personal gear for the tropics, 600 pounds; stripped hull say 1,500 pounds for the sake of argument at this stage, leaving 500 pounds for rig, anchors and drogues, charts and navigating gear, and casual bilgewater, if she's to float about as shown (but she could go a lot deeper or rather heavier, if it so happens, without much harm; allow 800 or 900 pounds per inch immersion).
> Next I laid out arrangements to pull two long oars or two pairs of shorter sculls (the oars are shown 12 feet because on this breadth that length allows centerline rowing seats adaptable to the sculls for one-man rowing) with seats having 20 inch slide and everything as close to optimum heights and angles as possible. It's my opinion that in a dead calm and perfectly smooth sea, two men can row this craft about two and a half knots, sustained, and three or a

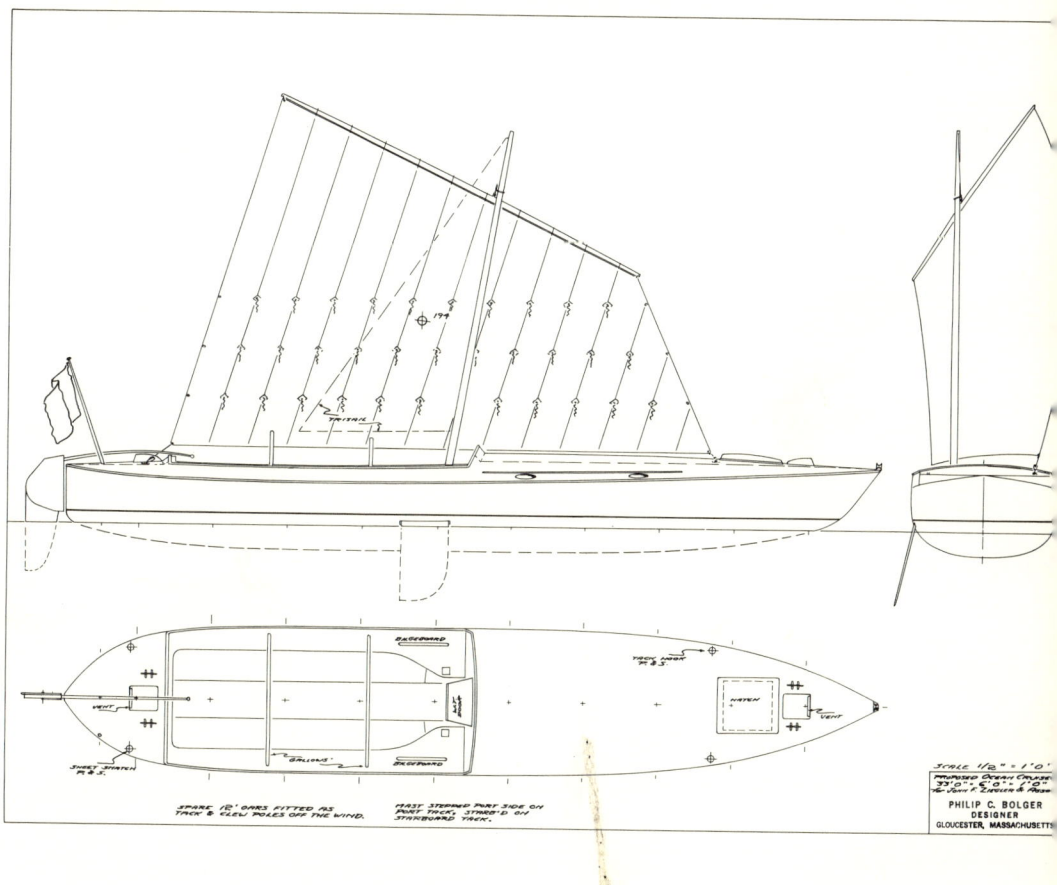

little better briefly, and can maneuver her and make some progress in a fair breeze of wind by heavy effort. I doubt one man pulling a pair of sculls can make her do more than one knot, or do anything with her in wind, but I'd carry the sculls because on occasion one knot might be much better than nothing. I've placed the oars low for best smooth-water efficiency on the theory that she would get nowhere under oars when it's rough in any case.

I've studied how a shorter boat, 26 feet by 8 feet, would serve; the weight saving seems to be on the order of 300 pounds, and the wetted surface about 18 square feet less. Since wave-making wouldn't seem to come into the matter at all at the rowing speeds in question, there's not much doubt that such a boat would row more easily, but I guess that the difference would be quite small, maybe six percent. The long boat would be much faster under sail, probably have an easier motion, and be so much more comfortable at sea or in port that I'd think there would be no comparison. I think at least one of three men cooped up in the 26-footer would be eaten by the other two before the voyage ended.

The rig may be a bit startling to modern eyes. The point to hold on to is that this is a rowboat. The mast is set up and the sail

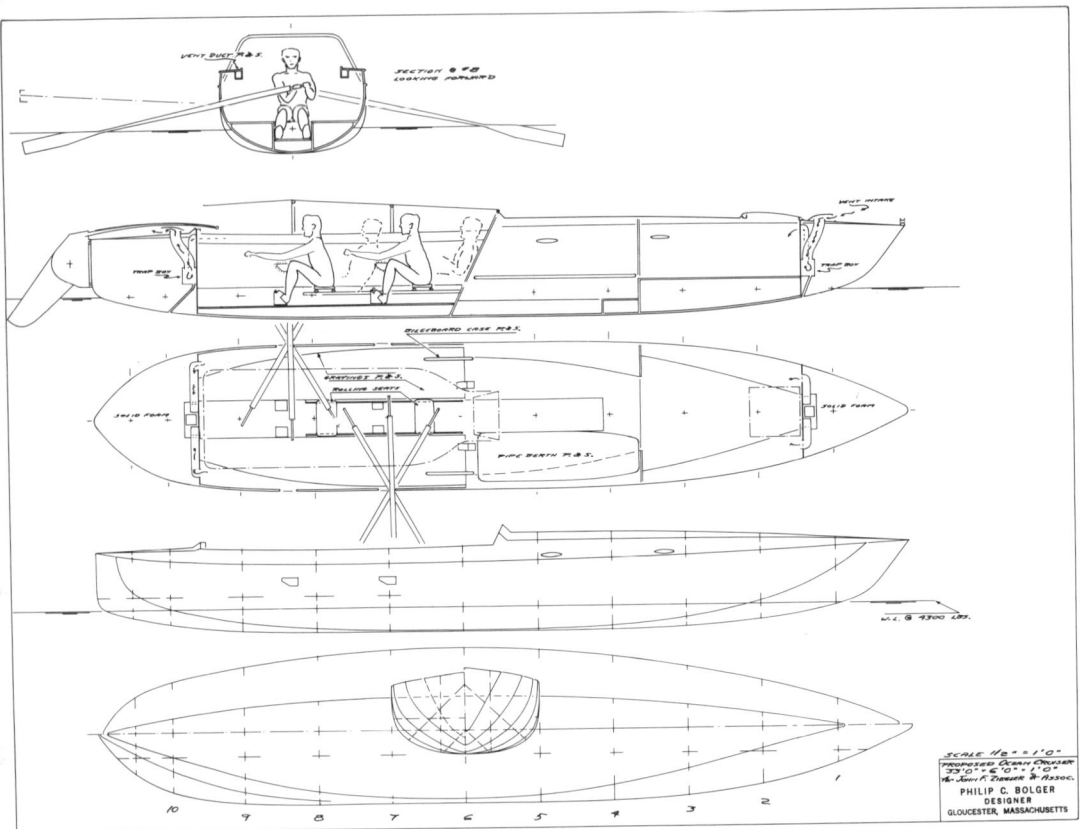

set when and as the wind serves, and the whole thing struck down when the time comes to maneuver. There's no spar you can't put up on end and lift to its step in your two hands; the mast is out of the way, stepped or struck, and interferes only slightly with the awning and not at all with keeping the cabin dry, or with using any combination of oars. Nevertheless, the rig has great power and she would be capable of fast passages, and is likely to be fast to windward as long as no tacking is involved. If the wind shifts abruptly when the helmsman happens to be off his guard, she may be caught aback and could be knocked down flat. As she can't sink, or even really swamp given some precautions, and would right herself as soon as the sail can be bundled up, the consequences aren't lethal, at least if you stick to warm seas. The ventilators would ship little water even in a complete barrel roll. In a gale she would ride to a drogue, well streamlined with spars stowed, cockpit hood pulled down tight on all sides, and rudder blade swung up vertical and lashed to serve as an aerodynamic stabilizer; given sea room, she might not need the drogue. Supposing the hood blew away, things would be much less comfortable, but you could still breathe and should come to no harm. It might be well to connect the big Edson bilge pump inside the cabin with suction either way; as you may know, these things will shift a lot of water and won't choke on anything short of dead rats.

Stores are under gratings at the sides in cockpit and cabin; probably some of the centerline at first; I haven't figured the actual volume involved. All must be packaged to stand immersion, no more than good sense anyway. The point is that there's no double bottom to float her upside-down; the deck floats more than the bottom. You can take full advantage of the lightening as you expend consumables instead of having to take on ballast.

It seems to me you might make a spectacularly fast passage in this machine in the light weather zones, as from Panama (Costa Rica, Ecuador) to Tahiti by way of the Galapagos and maybe Easter Island. Thence on among the islands to Australia. According to what I read, this would be a superb boat to use along the Great Barrier Reef, and it's possible that, though she'd be an expensive proposition to get built, you might show a profit on her thereabouts.

26
CHICAGO COBLE

$25'1'' \times 6'0''$

John Rowe is a Chicago boatbuilder who thought the squatty boats with huge engines he saw used as day-fishing boats there could be improved on. His idea was that a modified Yorkshire Coble, with its easy entrance and clean run, would go at good speed with a small engine, could be sailed after a fashion if the engine gave out, and might even be rowed a little way. The tumblehome upper sides of the Coble would serve the same function as a deck in providing reserve buoyancy and have the added advantage in a slim boat that nobody would be able to step far out from the centerline and claim the boat was tender because it heeled.

All this was much to my taste and I took a lot of trouble working it up, with many versions so there'd be something for everybody as they were to be built semi-custom, at least at first. Rowe built a rough full-size hull of expendable materials for a trial, which by all accounts ran very nicely, as it could hardly help doing on these proportions.

It was interesting to hear about the reactions of potential customers. There were some sensible suggestions: the drawing showing her with movable seats to sit on facing outboard came from one. But the main theme seems to have been a demand for more power and speed, both inboard and outboard, disconcerting to a builder who'd hypothesized a demand for economy and simplicity. Granted that this was before the uproar about a fuel shortage, it was still remarkable.

There *was* a definite demand, which I'd suspected for a long time, for a light diesel boat. I specified that a forty horsepower diesel should be maximum power, for around sixteen miles per hour top speed. As it turned out this was about the *minimum* power that anybody Rowe approached seemed willing to even contemplate; most insisted on much more. His

CHICAGO COBLE

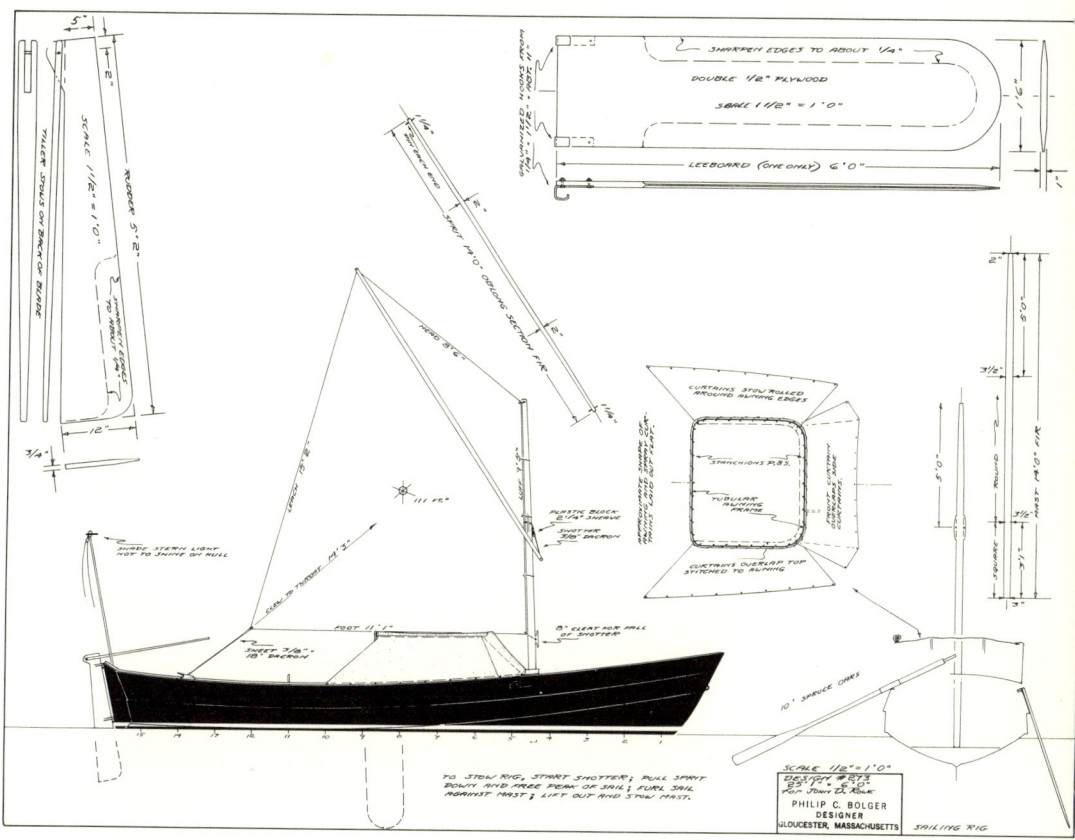

original and (I thought) sensible idea of standardizing on something like ten h.p. for eight miles per hour, drew no interest at all, though it's to be hoped that there was somebody skulking around unnoticed who would have liked it.

Oddly enough, there does seem to be some demand for really slow motorboats on scaled-down fisherman hulls (obsolete-model fishermen at that), but next to none for a boat that can slide along much faster with very little more power, or even the same power. I've been out in a boat designed by the late William Atkin that looked and ran like a destroyer with a tiny, old-fashioned Couach two-cylinder, and I've seen the late L. Francis Herreshoff sweep by in a boat at fifteen knots hardly leaving a wake on the water, but their demonstrations met with total indifference. This kind of performance calls for very long boats, and I can see why many people object to extra length on account of storage and docking expenses, but it seems to me there ought to be many others, somewhere, to whom storage and docking are no problem: yet they're not to be found.

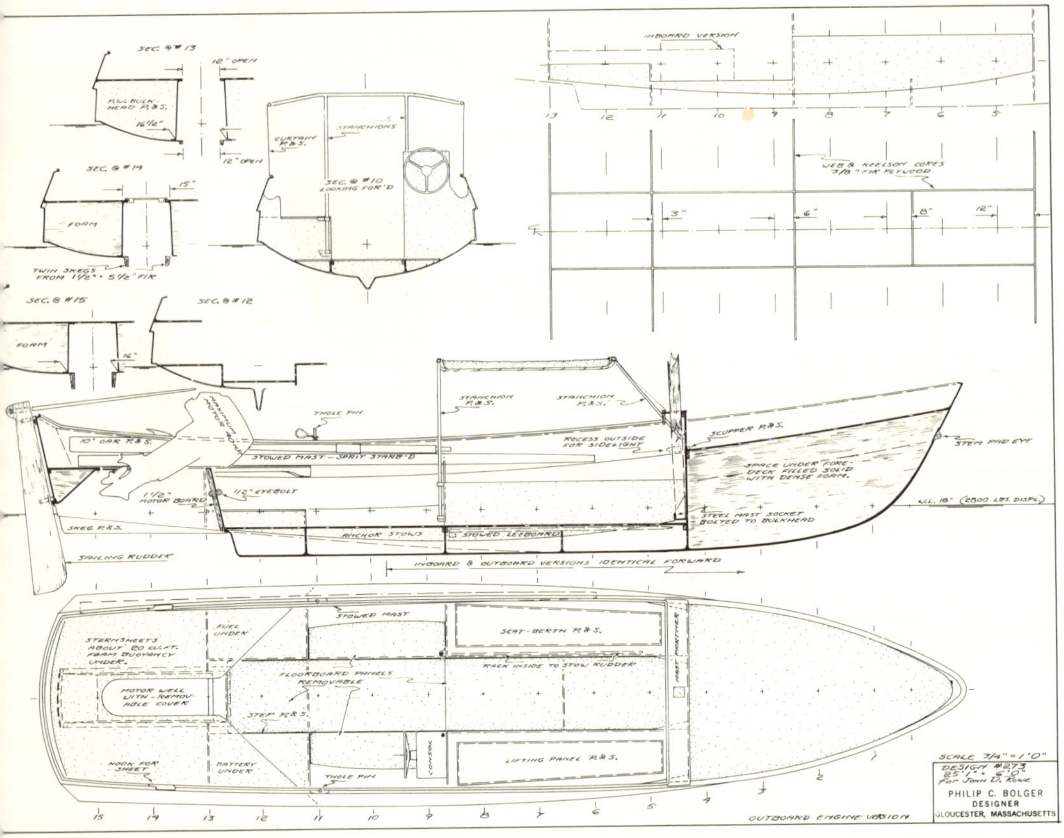
SEC. @ #13
12" OPEN
PLY. BULK-HEAD R.&S.
16 1/2"
12" OPEN
STANCHIONS
CURTAIN R.&S.
SEC. @ #10 LOOKING FOR'D
SEC. @ #14
15"
FORM
TWIN SKEGS FROM 1 1/2" × 5 1/2" FIR
SEC. @ #15
SEC. @ #12
FORM
16"
INBOARD VERSION
WEB & KEELSON CORES 3/8" FIR PLYWOOD
3"
6"
8"
12"
STANCHION R.&S.
STANCHION R.&S.
THOLE PIN
10' OAR R.&S.
STOWED MAST - SPRIT STARB'D
RECESS OUTSIDE FOR SIDELIGHT
SCUPPER R.&S.
STEM PAD EYE
SPACE UNDER FORE-DECK FILLED SOLID WITH DENSE FOAM.
1/2" EYEBOLT
1 1/2" MOTOR BOARD
SKEG R.&S.
ANCHOR STOWS
STOWED LEEBOARD
STEEL MAST SOCKET BOLTED TO BULKHEAD
W.L. 18" (2800 LBS. DISPL.)
SAILING RUDDER
INBOARD & OUTBOARD VERSIONS IDENTICAL FORWARD
STOWED MAST
FUEL UNDER
STERNSHEETS ABOUT 20 CU.FT. FOAM BUOYANCY UNDER.
SEAT-BERTH R.&S.
FLOORBOARD PANELS REMOVABLE
RACK INSIDE TO STOW RUDDER
MAST PARTNER
MOTOR WELL WITH REMOVABLE COVER
STEP R.&S.
CONSOLE
HOOK FOR SHEET
BATTERY UNDER
THOLE PIN
LIFTING PANEL R.&S.
SCALE 3/4" = 1'0"
DESIGN #273
25'1" × 6'0"
For John D. Rowe
PHILIP C. BOLGER
DESIGNER
GLOUCESTER, MASSACHUSETTS
OUTBOARD ENGINE VERSION

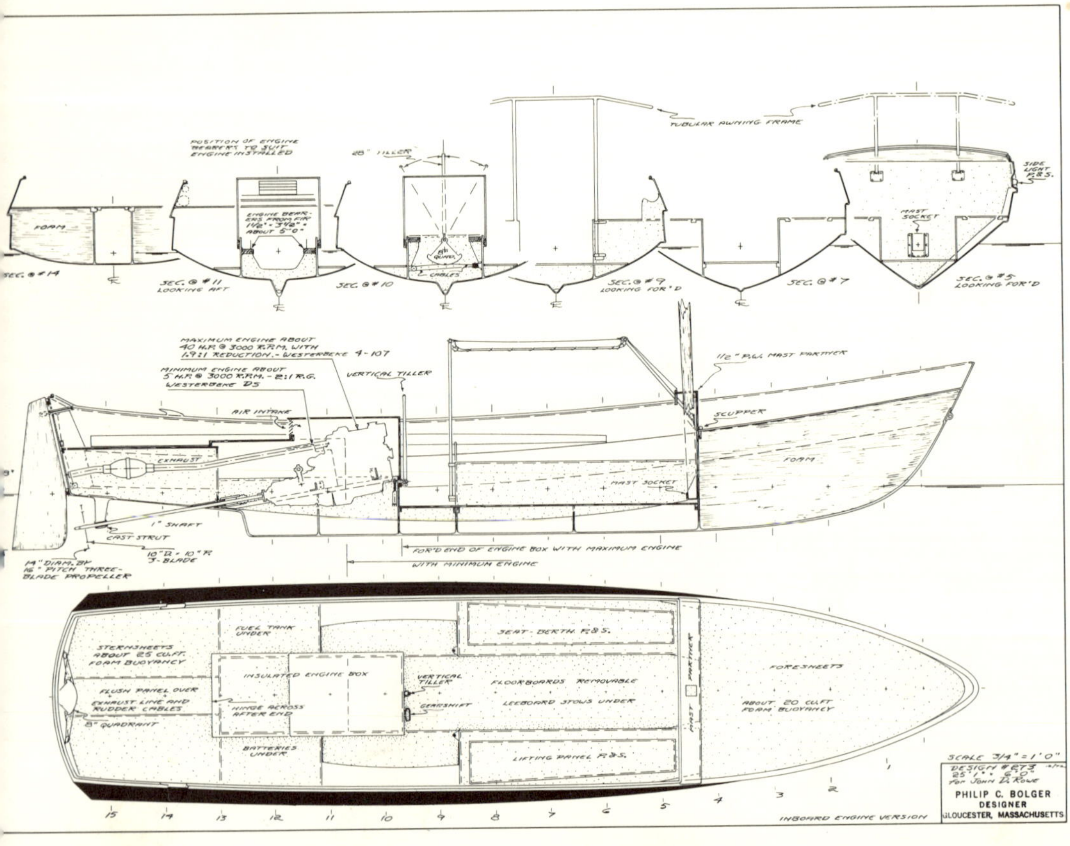
TUBULAR AWNING FRAME
POSITION OF ENGINE BEARERS TO SUIT ENGINE INSTALLED
28" TILLER
SIDE LIGHT R.&S.
FORM
ENGINE BEARERS FROM FIR 1 1/2" × 3 1/2" ABOUT 5'0"
MAST SOCKET
CABLES
SEC. @ #14
SEC. @ #11 LOOKING AFT
SEC. @ #10
SEC. @ #9 LOOKING FOR'D
SEC. @ #7
SEC. @ #5 LOOKING FOR'D
MAXIMUM ENGINE ABOUT 40 H.P. @ 3000 R.P.M. WITH 1.92:1 REDUCTION. - WESTERBEKE 4-107
MINIMUM ENGINE ABOUT 5 H.P. @ 3000 R.P.M. - 2:1 R.G. WESTERBEKE D5
VERTICAL TILLER
1/2" PLY. MAST PARTNER
AIR INTAKE
SCUPPER
EXHAUST
FORM
MAST SOCKET
1" SHAFT
CAST STRUT
10" D × 10" P 3-BLADE
14" DIAM. BY 16" PITCH THREE-BLADE PROPELLER
FOR'D END OF ENGINE BOX WITH MAXIMUM ENGINE
WITH MINIMUM ENGINE
FUEL TANK UNDER
SEAT-BERTH R.&S.
STERNSHEETS ABOUT 25 CU.FT. FOAM BUOYANCY
INSULATED ENGINE BOX
VERTICAL TILLER
FLOORBOARDS REMOVABLE
FORESHEETS
FLUSH PANEL OVER EXHAUST LINE AND RUDDER CABLES
HINGE ACROSS AFTER END
GEARSHIFT
LEEBOARD STOWS UNDER
MAST PARTNER
ABOUT 20 CU.FT. FOAM BUOYANCY
8" QUADRANT
BATTERIES UNDER
LIFTING PANEL R.&S.
SCALE 3/4" = 1'0"
DESIGN #273
25'1" × 6'0"
For John D. Rowe
PHILIP C. BOLGER
DESIGNER
GLOUCESTER, MASSACHUSETTS
INBOARD ENGINE VERSION

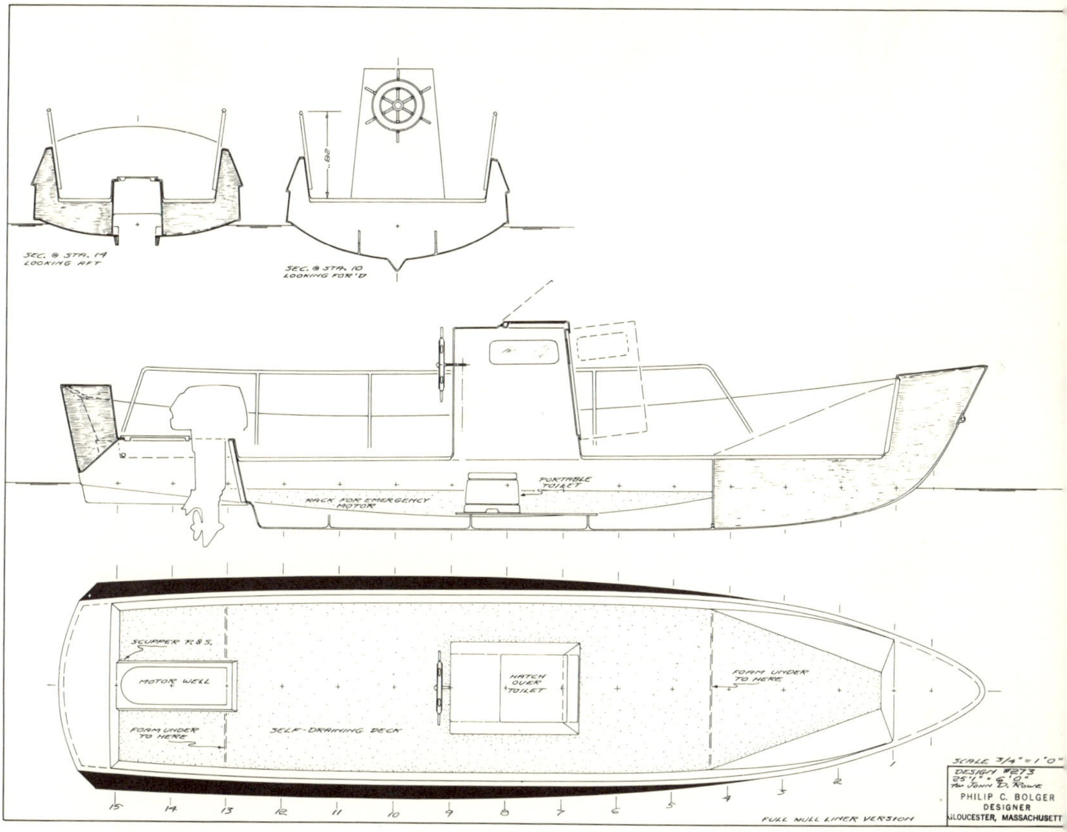

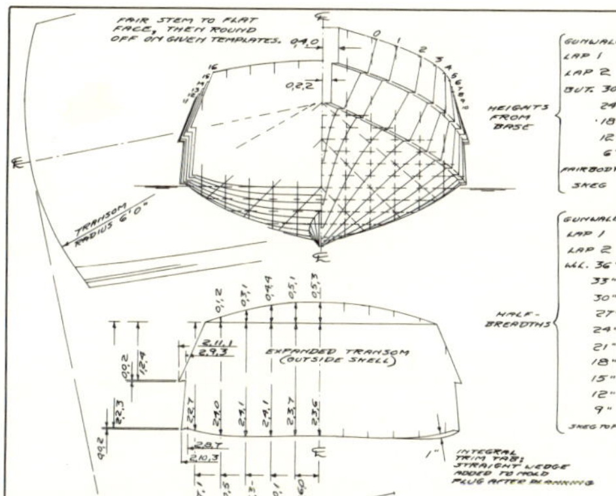

		16	15	14	13	12	11	10	9	8	7	6	5	4	3	2	1	0	
HEIGHTS FROM BASE	GUNWALE	3,10,4	3,8,1	3,6,2	3,5,0	3,4,2	3,3,7	3,3,7	3,4,2	3,5,0	3,6,0	3,7,2	3,8,7	3,10,4	4,0,5	4,2,7	4,5,3	4,7,1	GUN'L
	LAP 1	2,8,6	2,7,4	2,6,4	2,5,6	2,5,2	2,5,0	2,5,1	2,5,4	2,6,2	2,7,3	2,8,7	2,10,5	3,0,6	3,3,1	3,5,6	3,8,5	3,10,5	LAP 1
	LAP 2	1,8,6	1,8,1	1,7,4	1,7,0	1,6,6	1,6,6	1,6,7	1,7,3	1,8,1	1,9,3	1,11,0	2,1,0	2,3,2	2,5,6	2,8,4	2,11,4	3,1,5	LAP 2
	BUT. 30"	1,8,3	1,7,4	1,6,4	1,6,5	1,4,6	1,4,0	1,3,6	1,4,0	1,5,2	1,7,3	1,10,4							30" BUT
	24"	1,6,7	1,5,5	1,4,4	1,3,2	1,2,1	1,1,1	1,0,4	1,0,4	1,1,2	1,3,0	1,5,6	1,9,6	2,2,7					24"
	18"	1,6,2	1,4,5	1,3,1	1,1,5	1,0,1	0,11,0	0,10,1	0,9,7	0,10,2	0,11,2	1,1,4	1,4,7	1,9,5	2,3,7				18"
	12"	1,6,0	1,4,2	1,2,4	1,0,6	0,11,1	0,9,5	0,8,4	0,7,6	0,7,5	0,8,2	0,9,5	1,0,0	1,3,6	1,9,3	2,5,4			12"
	6"	1,6,0	1,4,1	1,2,2	1,0,3	0,10,4	0,9,0	0,7,4	0,6,3	0,5,6	0,5,6	0,6,2	0,7,4	0,9,6	1,1,4	1,7,6	2,7,2		6"
	FAIRBODY	1,6,0	1,4,1	1,2,2	1,0,3	0,10,4	0,8,7	0,7,2	0,5,7	0,4,6	0,4,0	0,3,6	0,3,7	0,4,3	0,5,4	0,8,0	1,1,6	2,0,5	FAIRBODY
	SKEG					0,3,4	0,3,4	0,3,4	0,3,4	0,3,4	0,3,4	0,3,4	0,3,6	0,4,3	0,5,4	0,8,0	1,1,6	2,0,5	SKEG
HALF-BREADTHS	GUNWALE	2,3,2	2,4,6	2,6,0	2,7,0	2,7,4	2,7,6	2,7,7	2,8,0	2,8,1	2,8,0	2,7,6	2,7,2	2,6,2	2,4,0	2,0,7	1,6,2	1,1,2	GUN'L
	LAP 1	2,7,4	2,8,3	2,9,2	2,9,7	2,10,3	2,10,5	2,10,6	2,10,6	2,10,3	2,9,6	2,8,6	2,7,2	2,5,0	2,1,6	1,9,2	1,2,6	0,9,3	LAP 1
	LAP 2	2,7,0	2,7,5	2,8,2	2,9,0	2,9,4	2,9,7	2,10,0	2,10,0	2,9,4	2,8,3	2,6,4	2,3,7	2,0,3	1,7,7	1,2,5	0,8,4	0,3,7	LAP 2
	W.L. 36"																	0,3,1	36" W.L.
	33"																0,7,0	0,2,1	33"
	30"															1,0,4	0,5,4	0,1,4	30"
	27"													2,0,1	1,5,1	0,10,1	0,4,2	0,0,7	27"
	24"												2,2,6	1,8,5	1,2,2	0,8,2	0,3,1		24"
	21"										2,8,0	2,4,2	1,11,1	1,5,3	0,11,6	0,6,5	0,2,2		21"
	18"	(1,0,0)	2,1,3	2,4,5	2,7,0	2,8,3	2,9,1	2,9,1	2,8,4	2,7,0	2,4,3	2,0,3	1,7,4	1,2,2	0,9,2	0,5,1	0,1,4		18"
	15"			1,4,6	1,11,1	2,2,1	2,4,0	2,4,6	2,4,2	2,2,7	2,0,0	1,8,1	1,3,5	0,11,2	0,7,0	0,3,5	0,0,6		15"
	12"					1,5,0	1,9,2	1,10,6	1,11,0	1,9,6	1,7,2	1,3,6	1,0,0	0,8,3	0,5,0	0,2,2			12"
	9"						0,6,7	1,2,0	1,3,5	1,3,2	1,1,4	0,10,7	0,7,7	0,5,2	0,2,7	0,1,0			9"
	SKEG TOP		0,0,4	0,0,4	0,0,4	0,1,5	0,2,5	0,2,7	0,2,5	0,1,7	0,1,1	0,0,5	0,0,4	0,0,4	0,0,4	0,0,4	0,0,4	0,0,4	SKEG TOP
		16	15	14	13	12	11	10	9	8	7	6	5	4	3	2	1	0	

OFFSETS IN FEET, INCHES, & EIGHTHS TO OUTSIDE OF SHELL.

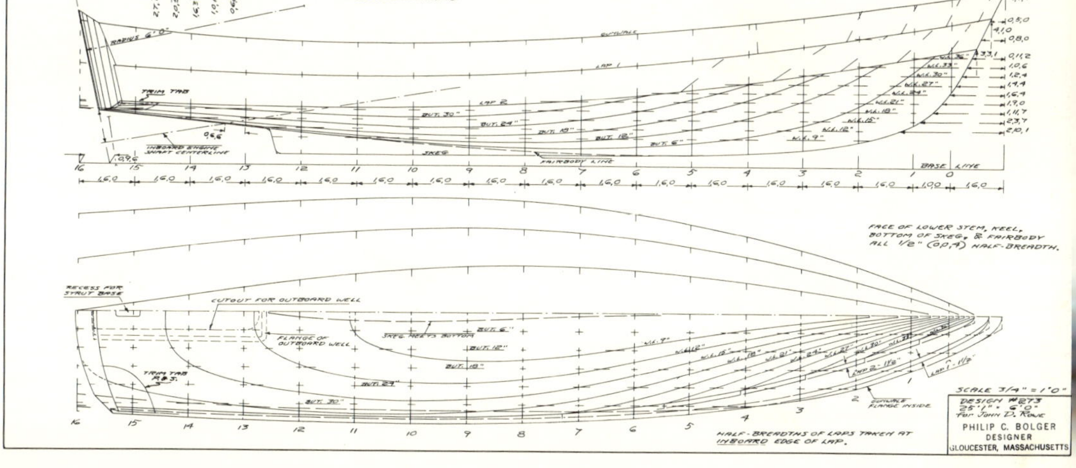

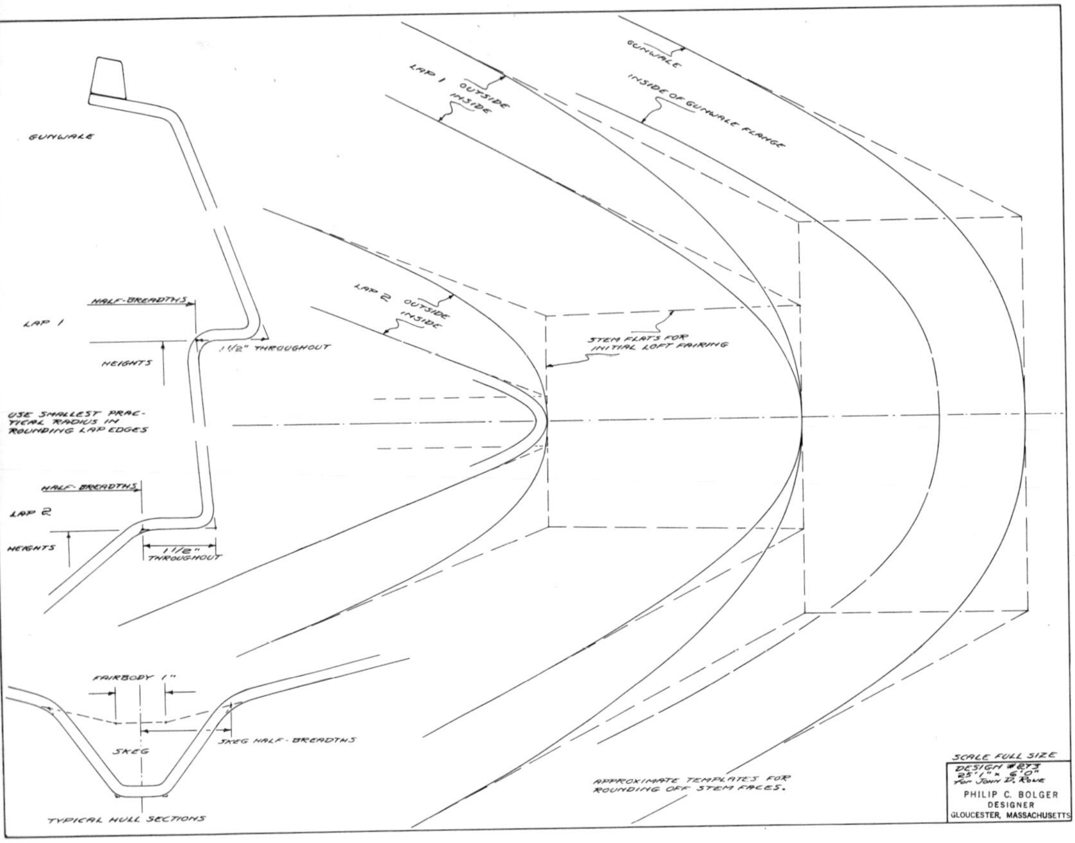
GUNWALE
LAP 1 OUTSIDE
INSIDE
GUNWALE
INSIDE OF GUNWALE FLANGE
HALF-BREADTHS
LAP 1
HEIGHTS
1 1/2" THROUGHOUT
LAP 2 OUTSIDE
INSIDE
STEM FLATS FOR INITIAL LOFT FAIRING
USE SMALLEST PRACTICAL RADIUS IN ROUNDING LAP EDGES
HALF-BREADTHS
LAP 2
HEIGHTS
1 1/2" THROUGHOUT
FAIRBODY 1"
SKEG
SKEG HALF-BREADTHS
TYPICAL HULL SECTIONS
APPROXIMATE TEMPLATES FOR ROUNDING OFF STEM FACES.
SCALE FULL SIZE
DESIGN #273
25'1" x 6'0"
for John D. Rowe
PHILIP C. BOLGER
DESIGNER
GLOUCESTER, MASSACHUSETTS

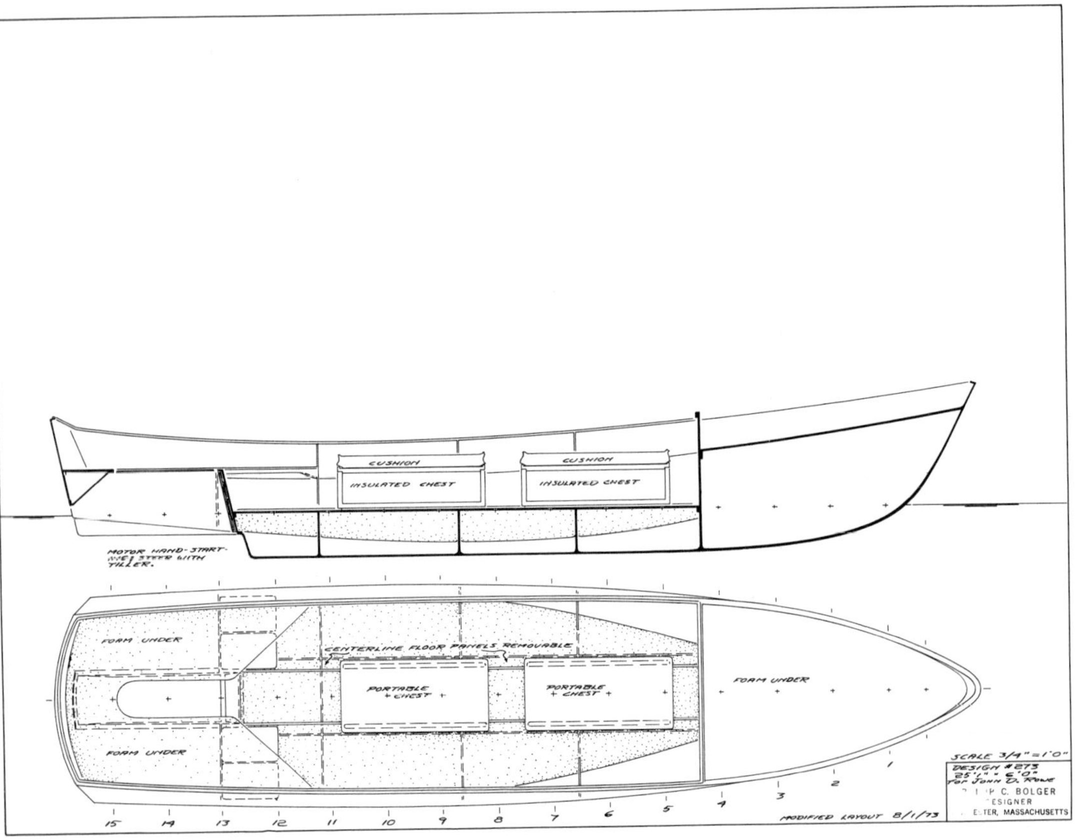
CUSHION
CUSHION
INSULATED CHEST
INSULATED CHEST
MOTOR HAND-START-ING; STEER WITH TILLER.
FOAM UNDER
CENTERLINE FLOOR PANELS REMOVABLE
PORTABLE CHEST
PORTABLE CHEST
FOAM UNDER
FOAM UNDER
15 14 13 12 11 10 9 8 7 6 5 4 3 2 1
MODIFIED LAYOUT 8/1/73
SCALE 3/4" = 1'0"
DESIGN #273
25'1" x 6'0"
for John D. Rowe

27
MOCCASIN

36'9" x 9'10"

Stanley Woodward wrote that he was thinking of having a Francis Herreshoff *Nereia* ketch built for short cruises around the Balearic Islands, and what did I think of raising her freeboard somewhat? I said, surely, that would be an improvement, but why not do something about that highly impractical galley and off-center companionway while you're at it, and I went on to suggest changes in construction, hull form, ballasting, and deck layout, ending up by transposing her masts to make a schooner. All perfectly valid suggestions taken one by one, though I was slipping over from irony into sarcasm towards the end.

The point is that Herreshoff's designs are full of technical weaknesses easy to seize on, but he was a great artist; a really great one; up in the class of Leonardo da Vinci, not merely by comparison with the run of boat designers, as William Fife was and Olin Stephens is. Tamper ever so slightly with one of Herreshoff's designs and you're apt to find you've lost the art and kept the failings.

Stanley is an artist himself of a pretty high order. He understood me perfectly and was amused rather than irritated at the way I put it. The upshot was that I designed him *Moccasin,* to suit his functional needs with as much art as I'm capable of. He oversaw her construction on Mallorca where there are first-class boat carpenters.

She's to be used for day-sailing and short cruises based on the east side of Mallorca. The bays on that end of the island run shallow, but her underbody design had two other objects: to be easy to haul out and store without elaborate equipment, and to be suitable for being hoisted to a ship's deck and taken to exotic places like the Persian Gulf, or the Great Barrier Reef, or Chesapeake Bay. A realistic capability of that kind makes for colorful daydreams at the least.

Moccasin's *owner enthusiastically reports her a paragon of all the virtues. Her designer remarks that careful selection of owners is a major factor in successful boat design.*

The shoal body and light displacement relative to her breadth make a combination that can be sailed at a small angle of heel, and a fairly dry boat, though anything this fast is bound to bring her bow spray aft at times. High sides and outside ballast make her self-righting. She's strongly built; I'm not fond of sawn frames myself, but good bending stock is not to be had on Mallorca, and sawn frames do make a good, rigid structure. She's naturally slow in stays, the price of good rough-grounding protection and her ability to sail as well as float in shoal water.

I favored a cat-yawl rig. Stanley demanded headsails (he's a demonic sail-carrier; I vividly recall beating out of a narrow inlet in his old *Belisarius* with a huge mizzen staysail taken in and reset every tack). I suggested the log canoe topsail as more appropriate to the unstayed mast and more effective as well. He liked that, but in addition to the jib and, later, the masthead reaching jib-cum-spinnaker as well. I never knew him to carry anything away and expect that he'll always take in that ballooner *just* before the top of the mast would otherwise break off. She can set over twelve hundred square feet of sail and should be a great spectacle reaching in light airs. I expect that topsail will need some tinkering to stand well, and I don't especially recommend it to any and everybody, but in principle it's a much better sail for light weather than anything that can be set on masts that have more standing rigging in the way.

Apart from all the playful kites, this is a docile and cheap rig for its power. The full-batten standing lug mizzen can be left set night and day, to steady her on mooring or anchor, without taking much harm; I once left such a sail set for about six weeks continuously, before nemesis caught up with me in the form of a thundersquall with a ninety-degree wind shift while the boat was grounded out. For an impulsive daysail, one has only

Launching of Moccasin; her built-in gear is used. It's supposed to have a safety factor of about five, but I wouldn't stroll under her myself!

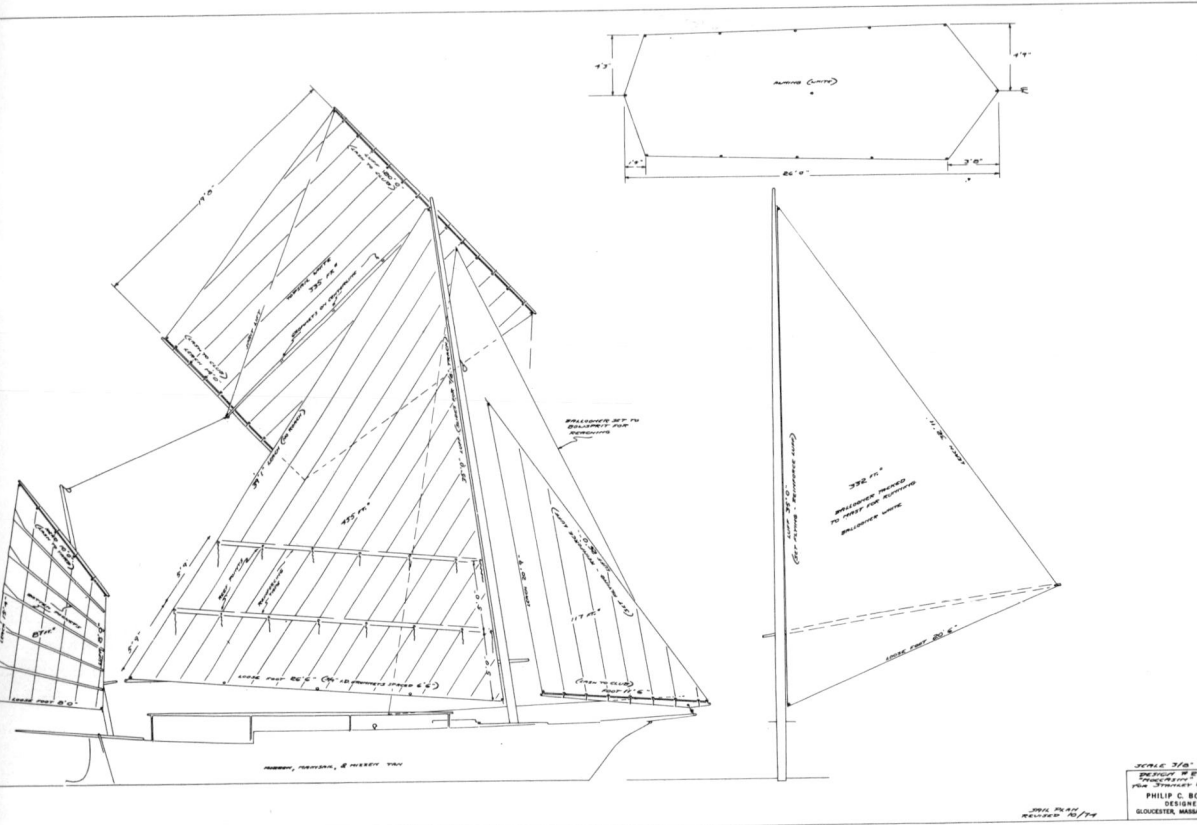

to haul on the main halyard and cast off the mooring pennant. The hazard of the long boom in heavy weather is mitigated by letting it run out ahead of the mast when reefed, since in this kind of rig the headsails would be off her long before you got around to reefing the main. The advantage of the long boom is that the broad sail has great power for its heeling effect, and sheeting and hoisting effort. It's rigged spritwise so the sail will swing out flat and not start her rolling downwind. Also, no effort is wasted sheeting *down,* on any point of sailing, and no traveller is needed.

She'll have respectable manners under jib and mizzen, with both backstays set up hard. This is why she has such a large mast step.

I think *Moccasin* is a remarkably nice boat. What's more, I think that if Francis Herreshoff had come into an anchorage and seen her, he would have come over for a friendly look. I don't recall that he ever put pressure on me, or others who looked up to him, to imitate him in design methods. He did naturally like to see people influenced by his philosophy, as both Stanley and myself have been, to our benefit.

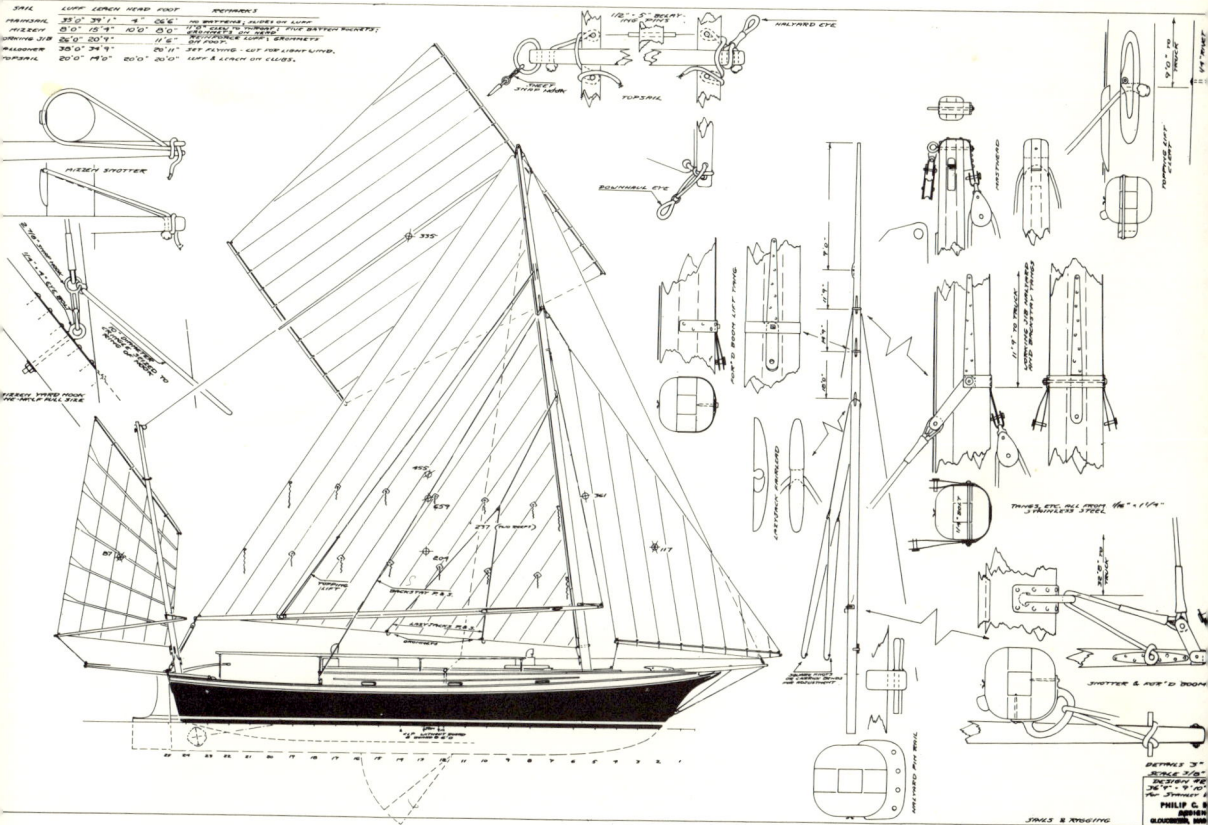

KEY TO PLANS

1. Ballast castings 3¾" thick (flat-sided, square-edged), 9" deep, 11'0" long overall with 3'0" jog each end as shown on the drawings, scrap lead (i.e., with normal antimony and other impurities); two identical, about 1,343 pounds each, with eight ½" bronze bolts each staggered about as shown.

2. Keel 6" deep iroko, width as given in offsets, composed of end logs with 2½" tongues reaching to centerboard case, and side logs 3¾" thick scarfed to ends.

3. Keel cheeks iroko 3¼" square, notched on bottom for frame ends.

4. Shaft logs above and below shaft hole iroko, splined together to form 8"-deep by 7½"-maximum-thickness shaft log.

5. Horn timber, bearing post, filler block, inner and outer sternposts iroko joined about as shown; thickness to offsets.

6. Horn timber cheeks iroko about 1½" x 5½" bolted through horn timber, inner sternpost, and shaft log; here and throughout, bolts indicated on plans are suggestive; no bolt needs to be more than ½", most can be ⅜" or in some cases ¼"; builder should judge.

MAIN SHEET PIN
SCUPPER
MIZZEN STEP
1" FORGED STEEL ANCHOR SHACKLE
HOISTING EYES
SECTION @ FRAME #23 LOOKING AFT
SECTION @ FRAME #15 LOOKING FORWARD
SECTION @ FRAME #2
SCALE 1 1/2" = 1'0"
DESIGN #297
36'9" x 9'10" x 2'0"
For Stanley Woodward
PHILIP C. BOLGER
DESIGNER
GLOUCESTER, MASSACHUSETTS
CONSTRUCTION SECTIONS

FALSE KEEL - FROM BELOW
UPPER TRAIL KNEE
LOWER TRAIL KNEE
STEM FROM BELOW
SCALE 3/4" = 1'0"
DESIGN #297
36'9" x 9'10" x 2'0"
For Stanley Woodward
PHILIP C. BOLGER
DESIGNER
GLOUCESTER, MASSACHUSETTS
CONSTRUCTION

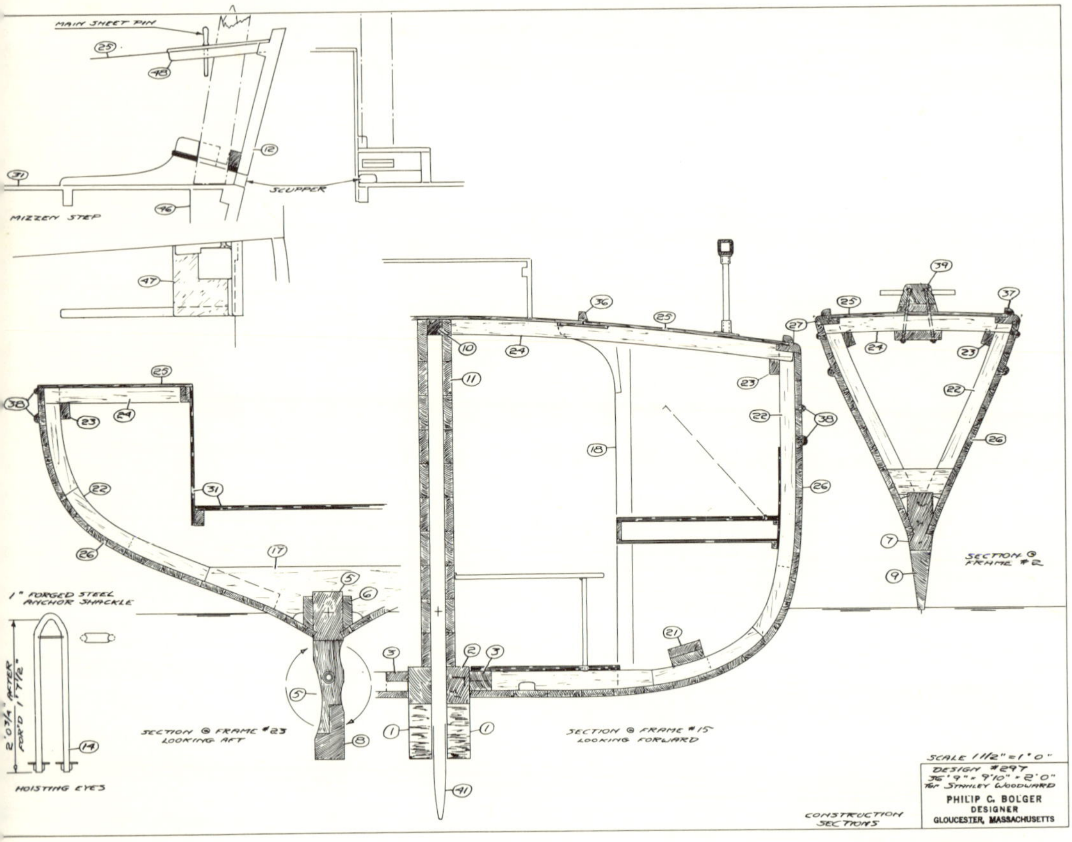

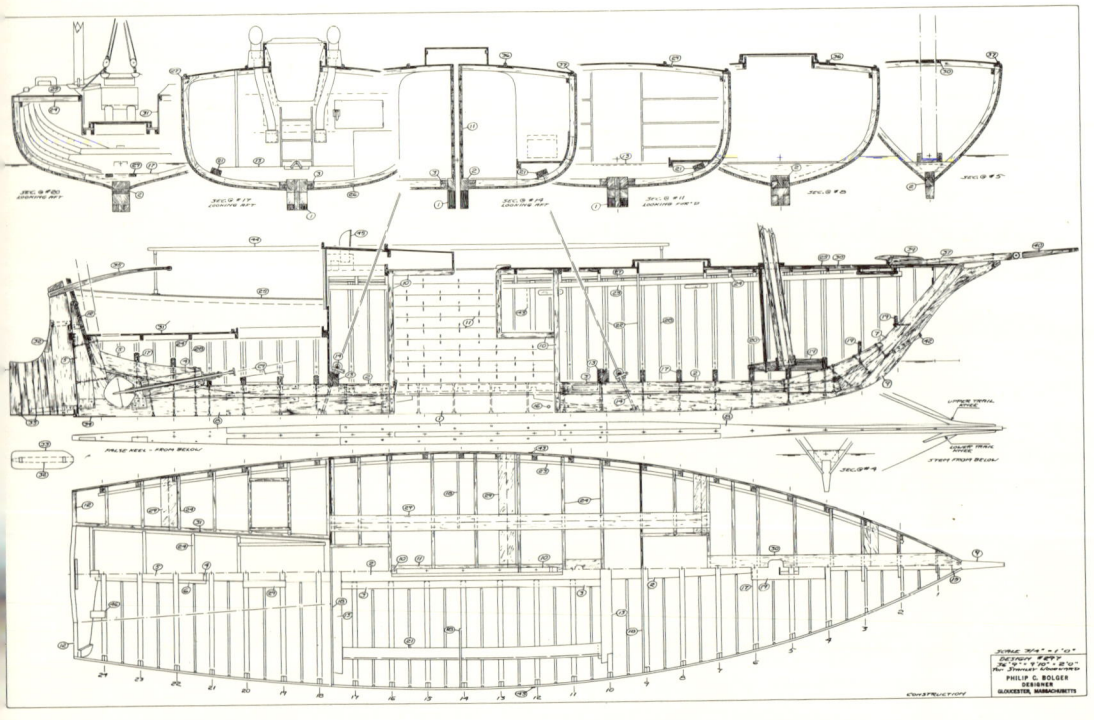

7. Stem and knee sided 4″ iroko.

8. False keel iroko 9″ deep forward and abaft ballast castings, tongued and scarfed similar to keel proper; halved to outer sternpost and propeller bearing post about as shown.

9. False stem and head iroko or mahogany screwed to stem, or may be tongued or splined, to be replaced with reasonable ease.

10. Centerboard case endposts and blocking iroko, 2½″ square; note stopper block at after end of case to prevent board dropping out.

11. Centerboard case sides 1½″ thick iroko or mahogany, rodded or dowelled together about as shown.

12. Transom mahogany, 2″ thick, rodded or dowelled together, with fastening cleats at the sides but no frame at the bottom.

13. Strong floor timbers sided 5½″ hard pine, forward one rabbeted to take frame #10, after one for ¾″ plywood bulkhead.

14. Hoisting eyes from 1″ stainless steel rod, with ends a drive fit through false keel; 3½″-diameter washers recessed into false keel as shown.

15. Cheeks on stem from deck down about two feet.

16. Centerboard pin 1½″ hard bronze or stainless steel.

17. Floor timbers in ends of hull sided 2½″, rabbeted to take lowest futtock of frames.

18. Bulkheads and partial bulkheads ¾″ plywood.

19. Mast step 5½″ x 12″ x 3′0½″ iroko or hard pine.

20. Tie rod ⅜″ steel in 1½″ square mahogany stanchion.

21. Bilge stringer double to finish 3″ x 5½″ hard pine or fir; extends from one heavy floor to the other, not beyond.

22. Sawn frames double to finish 2½″ square, hard pine (if laminated, may be smaller, not less than 2″ square); two or three single frames in bow, 1½″ x 2½″; frame #1 in extreme bow is ¾″ stock.

23. Clamp fir 1½″ x 2½″; ⅜″ bolts to frames and deck beams.

24. Deck beams fir, sided 1½″, molded 2½″; raised deck beams all to same crown diagram, see lines drawing; afterdeck beams not crowned.

25. Deck ½″ plywood, fiberglass sheathed or epoxy-saturated; 1¼″ screws to beams, shelf, etc.

26. Planking 1″ African mahogany; 2″ screws.

27. Raised deck shelf sawn or laminated to finish 1½″ x 4″ fir or mahogany.

28. Intermediate frames ¾″ x 1″ acacia; fasten to planking with 1½″ screws from inside.

29. Deck butt straps ½″ x 8″ plywood.

30. Centerline butt strap double plywood, to finish 1″ x 8″.

31. Foot well sole ¾″ plywood; sides of well ½″.

32. Rudder sided 2½″ mahogany, faired to about ¾″ trailing edge; cheeks for tiller 1½″; note removable block under upper gudgeon to secure against lifting off.

33. Rudder end-plate ¼″ x 9″ x 2′7″ stainless steel, secured with two or more inverted-U straps through slots in plate and up sides of blade.

34. Heel shoe ¼″ x 2½″ x 1′9″ stainless.

35. Tiller grown or laminated mahogany, 2½″ square at socket, about 5′3″ overall, tapered and curved more or less as shown.

36. Deck toe rail and stiffener 1½" square iroko or mahogany; starboard one built up near forward end of fore hatch to form an open fairlead for working jib sheet.

37. Toe rail 1" x 1½" mahogany, built up near stem to form strongly fastened chocks for bowsprit.

38. Moldings 1" and 1½" half-round (or may be more elaborate, with drip groove, to taste) mahogany.

39. Mooring cleat from 3½" x 5½" x 2'0" mahogany; two ½" bolts through 1½" x 7½" x 1'8" block under beams.

40. Bowsprit from 3½" x 10½" x 7'11" hard pine or mahogany; see deck and arrangement plans for shape, sheaves for jib tack line, etc.; ½" hold-down bolt to false head.

41. Centerboard sided 2" hard pine or mahogany, with edges faired to about ¾" and rounded off or shod with half-oval metal; see lines for shape; run in about 100 pounds lead ballast; ½" dacron pendant to three-part purchase on deck.

42. Stem straps ⅛" x 1½" x 1'4", with ½" pin for tack lead block.

43. Chain plates ⅛" x 1½" x 1'4" for ballooner sheet snatch blocks.

44. Hand rails hollow fir with four stanchions each, see spar plan.

45. Cowl vents with trap boxes, ducted through bulkhead to engine compartment.

46. Block under heel of mizzenmast 3½" x 7" hard pine.

47. Mizzen step ¾" plywood about 11" x 12" inboard edge glued and screwed to 1½" x 4¾" x 2'5" mahogany knee bolted to sole; fastening cleat against foot well side 1½" x 2½" x 7"; against (and bolted to) transom, 2" x 2½" x 1'0".

48. Mizzen partner ½" plywood screwed down to deck and to 1½" x 2½" x 1'2" cleat on transom; stiffen with 1½" x about 5½" laid along inboard edge.

Running rigging (boat has no standing rigging)

Main sheet: ½" x 175' dacron; standing end on becket of starboard swivel deck block; up through one of two single blocks hung on boom end bail; down through port deck block; up through the other boom block; down through starboard deck block to belaying pin.

Main halyard: ⅜" x 80' dacron; snap shackle to headboard; through swivel block slung on masthead eye bolt, down port side to pin rail.

Main lazyjacks: all parts ¼" nylon; upper part runs free in dumb sheave on forward side of mast, with a thimble eye each end; lower part one continuous loop led as diagrammed through the two thimbles and two grommets in foot of sail.

Main topping lift: ⅜" x 24' nylon; caught with stopper knot through hole in cleat starboard side of mast; ends in a big smooth thimble for first purchase; purchase caught in cleat port side of sprit boom, up through thimble on foot of lift, down through cheek block on boom, forward through one fairlead to purchase block running on a slide on the boom; second purchase fast in boom cleat, aft through sliding block and back to belay on same cleat.

MOCCASIN

MOCCASIN

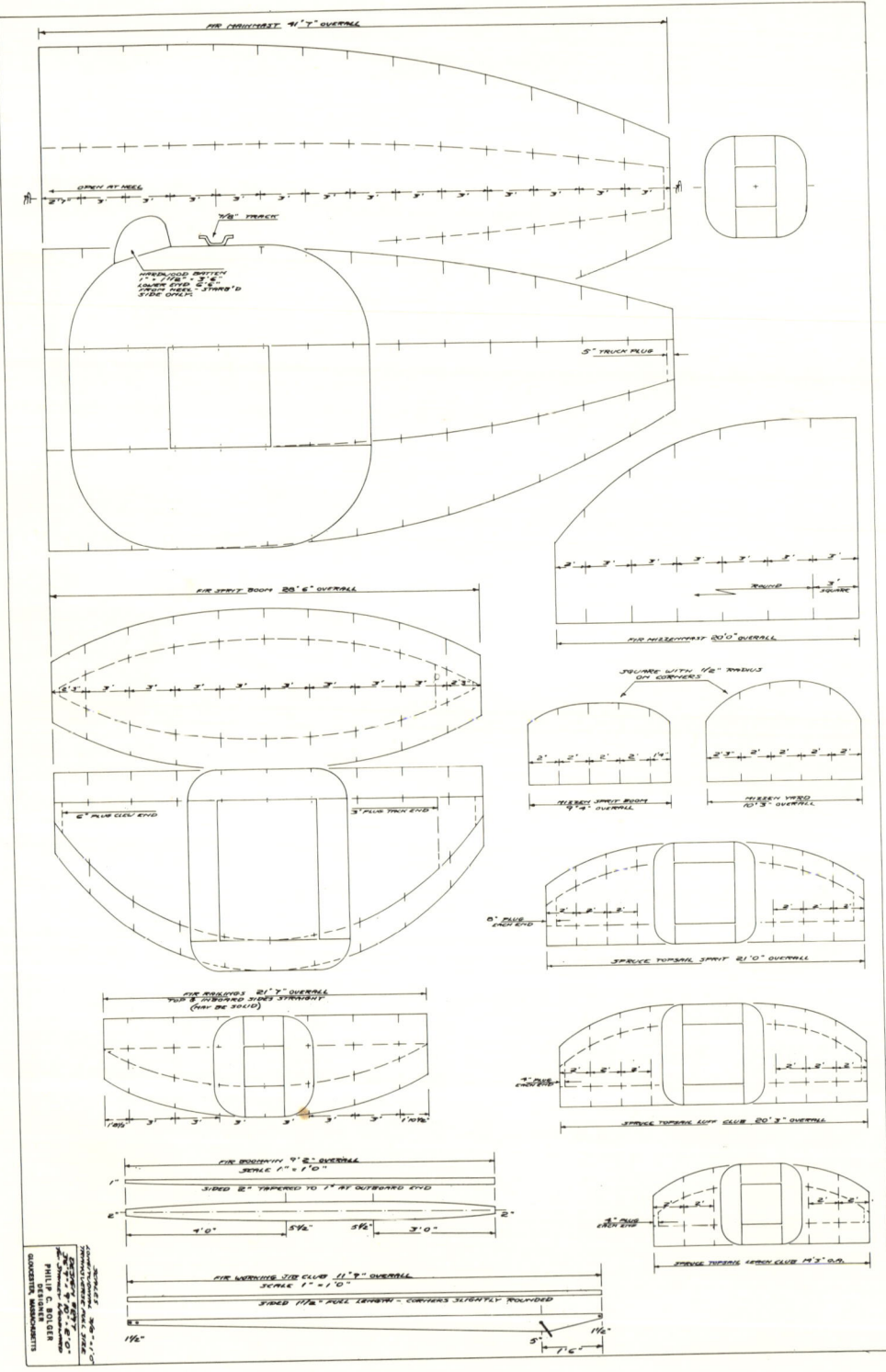

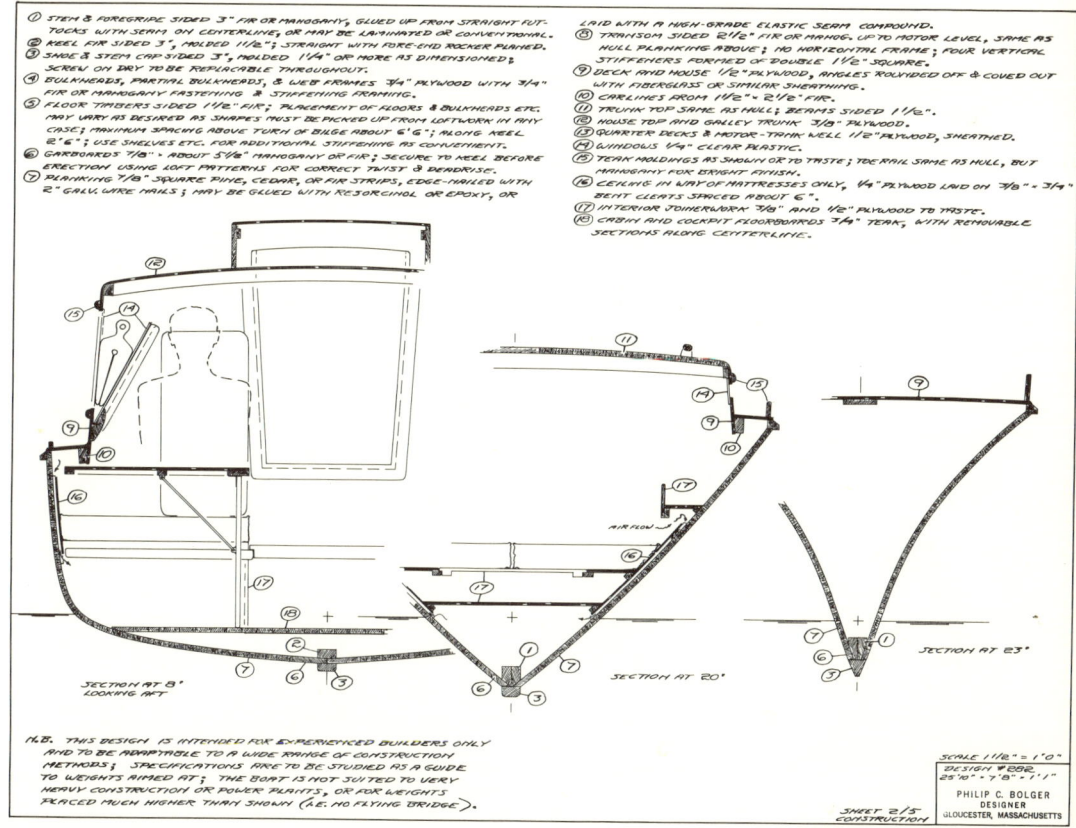

Main backstays (two): ½" x 34' dacron; eye splice to tang pin each side of mast; straight back to cleat on after side of break in deck; a light tail on each to secure to railing when not in use. (N.B. — The backstays are just to set up the luff of the working jib on the wind; they're not needed with started sheets or when short-tacking, nor should they be set up harder than can readily be done with a sway while luffing.)

Main boom heel lift: ⅜" x 18' dacron; eye each end, to mast tang and straps on heel end of boom.

Main boom snotter: ½" dacron, standing end spliced to same tang pin as lift; in through mast bail and back to belaying pin in boom. (N.B. — When sailing reefed and without headsail set, take reef clew earing to end of boom, let boom run out ahead of mast, and belay snotter to mast bail with a round turn and two half-hitches,)

Ballooner halyard: ⅜" x 75'; snap hook to head off sail; through swivel block on masthead tang and down to pin rail.

Ballooner sheets: ⅜" x 32' nylon (two); bend to clew grommet; through deck snatch block each side to cleats at break.

Working jib halyard: 3/8" x 50' dacron; snap hook to head of sail; up through block on mast tang, down to pin rail.

Working jib sheet: 1/4" x 35' nylon; snap hook to eye on club; through fairlead or tailed thimble on deck centerline, around open fairlead on toe rail starboard side, aft to cleat at break.

Working jib tack line: 3/8" x 27' dacron; snap hook to spliced eye 1'6" abaft forward end of club; through dumb sheave in end of bowsprit; down through block on forefoot straps; up through 4" sheave in bowsprit; in to mooring cleat or (later) a special cleat conveniently placed.

Mizzen halyard: 1/4" x 34' dacron; snap hook engages eye bolt on yard 4'0" from heel of yard; hook lashed to 10" inside diameter rope cringle running on mast; up through block slung at masthead; down outside sprit boom to cleat starboard side of mast.

Mizzen sheet: 3/8" x 20' nylon; snap hook to spliced eye on boom end; down through fairlead on end of boomkin; in to cleat on deck starboard side (see deck plan).

Mizzen snotter: 3/8" x 5'; standing end a stopper knot caught in slot cut in inboard end of sprit boom; in over shoulder on after side of mast, around mast and back to belay in boom end slot.

Topsail halyard: 3/8" x 80' dacron double-ended, rove through masthead slot lined with a stainless steel strap; bend standing end to seized cringle on end of topsail sprit; fall (from either side of masthead) to pin rail.

Topsail outhauls (two): 3/8" x 1'6" dacron; standing end caught with a stopper knot in hole in end of topsail sprit; use to lash clubs to sprit about as shown.

Topsail downhaul: 1/4" x 32' nylon; snaps into eye at lower end of luff club; take to leeward of ballooner when setting it as it need not be taut when topsail is on lee side of mainsail and will be clear to windward of ballooner after tacking; take to pin rail at first — later install a cleat for it each side when best location is clear.

Topsail sheet: 1/4" x 50' nylon; standing end snaps to eye on end of topsail sprit; through block slung at mizzen masthead and down to cleat on mizzenmast; put an eye somewhere on or near foot of mizzenmast to snap standing end into when topsail is not set.

To set topsail: Lash luff club to sprit with both laid on deck and leach club stopped up to luff; bring sheet standing end forward and snap on to end of sprit; bend on halyard and hoist in lee of mainsail until sprit is on end and clear of deck; belay halyard (if single-handed), break out sail and bend leach club to end of sprit; run up chock-a-block; set up downhaul loosely, to make sure topsail doesn't blow over leach of mainsail and jam aloft after tacking; take up slack of sheet as much as possible without curling leach of mainsail or pulling the mizzenmast up by the roots; sheet will need tending in conjunction with main sheet, and possibly, on account of offcenter mizzenmast, on every tack. To take it in, reverse process of setting it, except that it's just possible that under at least some conditions it would be more docile if brought down the weather side of the mainsail; i.e., take it in on the tack that brings it to windward.

28
ECONOMY MOTORSAILER

$$25'10'' \times 7'8''$$

This design was made as an entry in a design competition sponsored by *Motorboating & Sailing* magazine. "An economical cruiser for weekend and vacation use" was called for, with four berths, an enclosed toilet, and some galley facilities. I submitted the following explanation along with the plans:

>A powerboat type, because it can be lighter and more compact for a given accommodation than an auxiliary or straight sailer.
>
>Single main engine, because first cost, maintenance, and fuel economy are all better on a given performance. Outboard motor because it's cheaper to buy and lighter, and more convenient for major servicing. Auxiliary sail rig, because it works better than a second engine if the trouble is empty tanks, can be used to stretch the typically short range of an outboard boat, and is pleasant to use when in no hurry and under ideal conditions.
>
>Spritsail rig and single leeboard, very simple and crude, because while the motorboat hull will in any case not sail well by contemporary standards, this rig will move her tolerably well, including close reaches, is probably no more expensive than a second engine, can be erected quickly by one man, and stows with all components inboard and off the working spaces, with negligible windage. Steering oar instead of a sailing rudder because it stows more neatly, can be used to row her stern around (probably she couldn't usually tack under sail otherwise), and could be used to scull her a short distance.
>
>Designed for edge-nailed wood strip construction, because in most places it's the cheapest method of building a one-off boat except for plywood, which is not usually economical when depreciation is figured. She's well adapted to PVC foam sandwich construction, which, however, has usually been more expensive and less handsome than good woodwork, so far. Adaptability to fiberglass series pro-

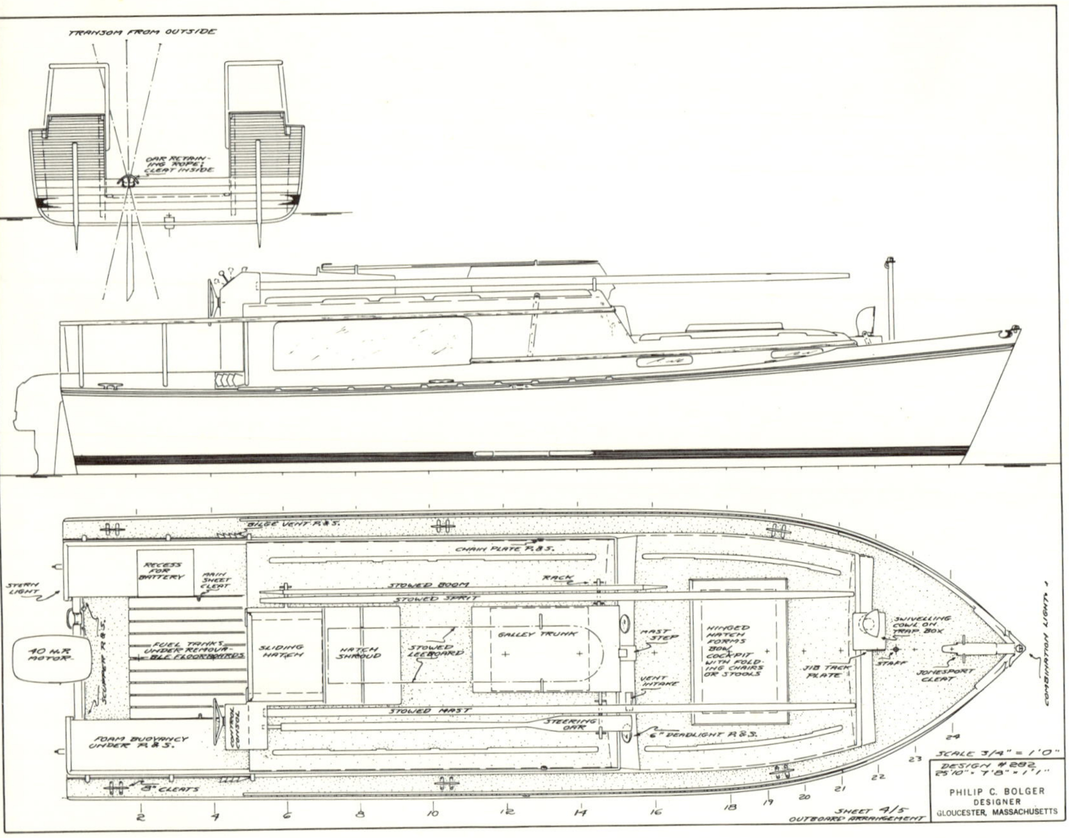
TRANSOM FROM OUTSIDE
OAR RETAINING ROPE; CLEAT INSIDE
BILGE VENT P. & S.
CHAIN PLATE P. & S.
RECESS FOR BATTERY
MAIN SHEET CLEAT
STERN LIGHT
RACK
STOWED BOOM
STOWED SPRIT
40 H.P. MOTOR
SCUPPER P. & S.
FUEL TANKS UNDER REMOVABLE FLOORBOARDS
SLIDING HATCH
HATCH SHROUD
STOWED LEEBOARD
GALLEY TRUNK
MAST STEP
VENT INTAKE
HINGED HATCH FORMS BOW COCKPIT WITH FOLDING CHAIRS OR STOOLS
JIB TACK PLATE
SWIVELLING COWL ON TRAP BOX
STAFF
JONESPORT CLEAT
COMBINATION LIGHT
STOWED MAST
CONTROL CONSOL
STEERING OAR
6" DEADLIGHT P. & S.
FOAM BUOYANCY UNDER P. & S.
8" CLEATS
2 4 6 8 10 12 14 16 18 19 20 21 22 23 24
SCALE 3/4" = 1'0"
DESIGN #282
25'10" × 7'8" × 1'1"
PHILIP C. BOLGER
DESIGNER
GLOUCESTER, MASSACHUSETTS
SHEET 4/5
OUTBOARD ARRANGEMENT

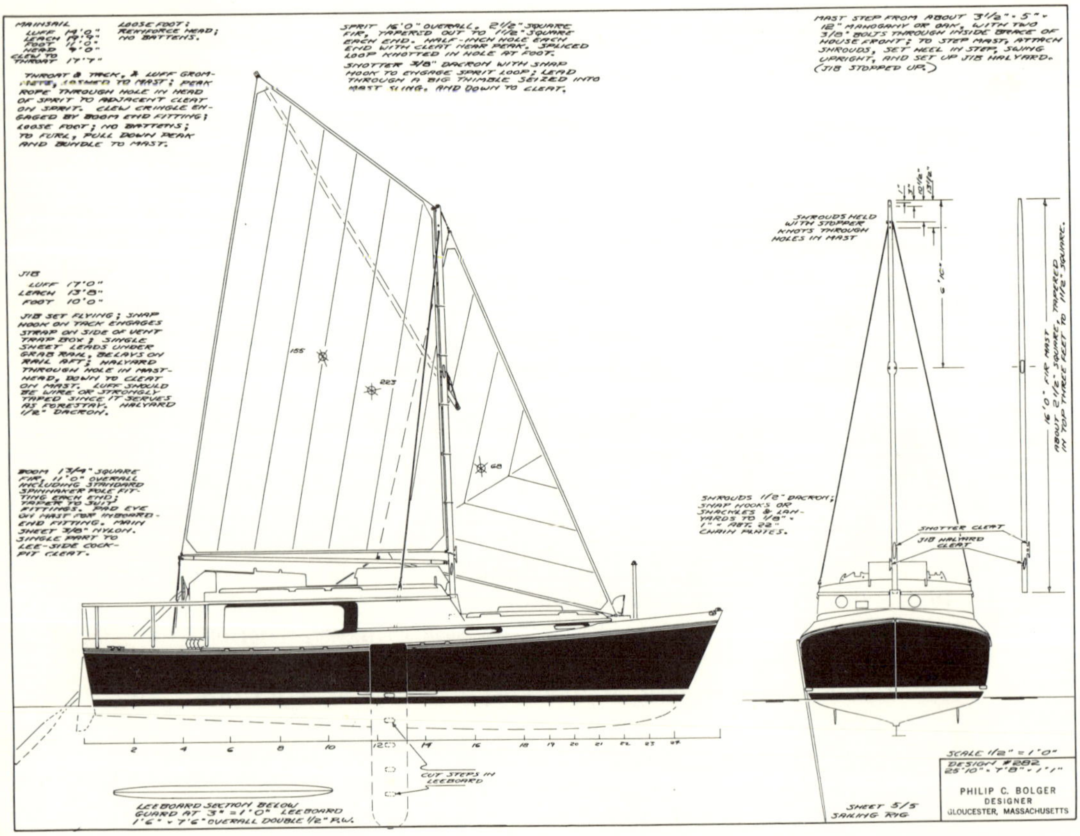
MAINSAIL
LUFF 14'0"
LEACH 19'9"
FOOT 11'0"
HEAD 9'0"
CLEW TO THROAT 17'7"
LOOSE FOOT; REINFORCE HEAD; NO BATTENS.
THROAT & TACK, & LUFF GROMMETS, LASHED TO MAST; PEAK ROPE THROUGH HOLE IN HEAD OF SPRIT TO ADJACENT CLEAT ON SPRIT. CLEW CRINGLE ENGAGED BY BOOM END FITTING; LOOSE FOOT; NO BATTENS; TO FURL, PULL DOWN PEAK AND BUNDLE TO MAST.
SPRIT 16'0" OVERALL, 2 1/2" SQUARE FIR, TAPERED OUT TO 1 1/2" SQUARE EACH END. HALF-INCH HOLE EACH END WITH CLEAT NEAR PEAK. SPLICED LOOP KNOTTED IN HOLE AT FOOT.
SNOTTER 3/8" DACRON WITH SNAP HOOK TO ENGAGE SPRIT LOOP; LEAD THROUGH A BIG THIMBLE SEIZED INTO MAST SLING, AND DOWN TO CLEAT.
MAST STEP FROM ABOUT 3 1/2" × 5" × 12" MAHOGANY OR OAK, WITH TWO 3/8" BOLTS THROUGH INSIDE BRACE OF HOUSE FRONT; TO STEP MAST, ATTACH SHROUDS, SET HEEL IN STEP, SWING UPRIGHT, AND SET UP JIB HALYARD. (JIB STOPPED UP.)
JIB
LUFF 17'0"
LEACH 13'8"
FOOT 10'0"
JIB SET FLYING; SNAP HOOK ON TACK ENGAGES STRAP ON SIDE OF VENT TRAP BOX; SINGLE SHEET LEADS UNDER GRAB RAIL, BELAYS ON RAIL AFT; HALYARD THROUGH HOLE IN MASTHEAD, DOWN TO CLEAT ON MAST. LUFF SHOULD BE WIRE OR STRONGLY TAPED SINCE IT SERVES AS FORESTAY. HALYARD 1/2" DACRON.
BOOM 1 3/4" SQUARE FIR, 11'0" OVERALL INCLUDING STANDARD SPINNAKER POLE FITTING EACH END; TAPER TO SUIT FITTINGS. PAD EYE ON MAST FOR INBOARD-END FITTING. MAIN SHEET 3/8" NYLON. SINGLE PART TO LEE-SIDE COCKPIT CLEAT.
155
223
68
SHROUDS HELD WITH STOPPER KNOTS THROUGH HOLES IN MAST
1" 3" 10 1/2" 13 1/2"
6'10"
16'0" FIR MAST ABOUT 2 1/2" SQUARE, TAPERED IN TOP THREE FEET TO 1 1/2" SQUARE.
SHROUDS 1/2" DACRON; SNAP HOOKS OR SHACKLES & LANYARDS TO 1/8" × 1" × ABT. 22" CHAIN PLATES.
SNOTTER CLEAT
JIB HALYARD CLEAT
2 4 6 8 10 12 14 16 18 19 20 21 22 23 24
CUT STEPS IN LEEBOARD
LEEBOARD SECTION BELOW GUARD AT 3" = 1'0" LEEBOARD 1'6" × 7'6" OVERALL DOUBLE 1/2" P.W.
SCALE 1/2" = 1'0"
DESIGN #282
25'10" × 7'8" × 1'1"
PHILIP C. BOLGER
DESIGNER
GLOUCESTER, MASSACHUSETTS
SHEET 5/5
SAILING RIG

ECONOMY MOTORSAILER

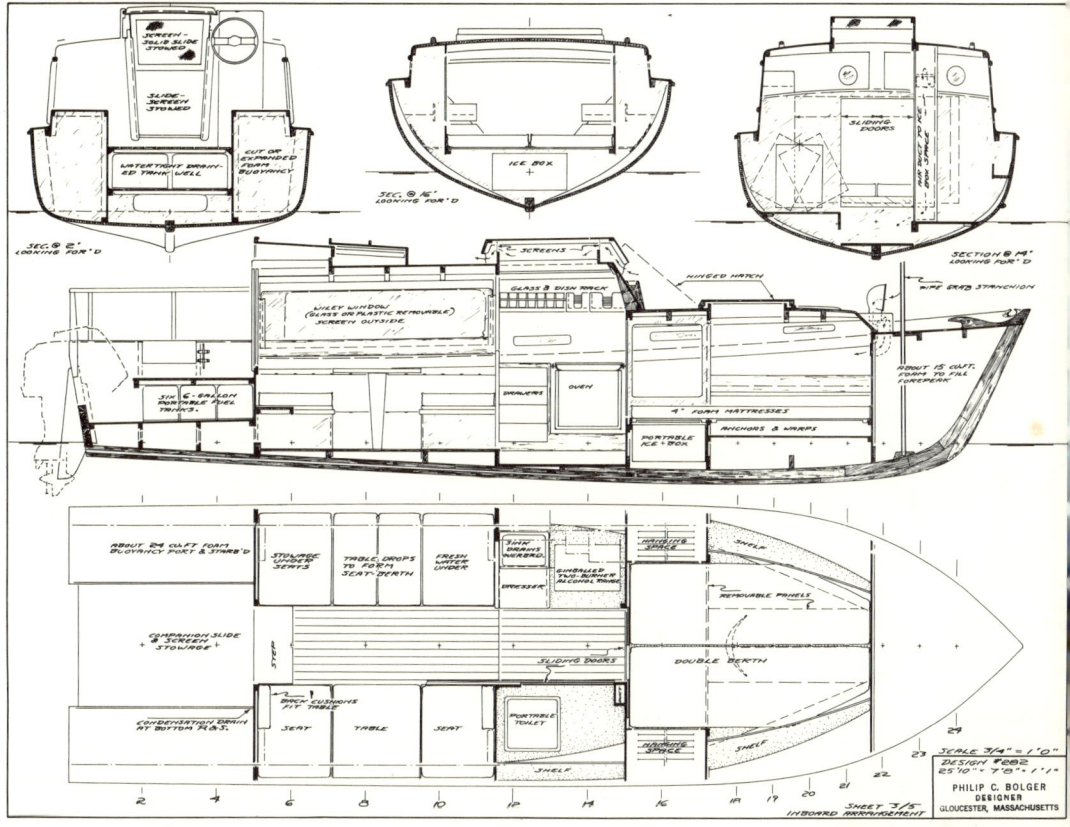

duction was kept in mind, but my experience is that it doesn't usually pay to try to use a prototype hull as production tooling. The most economical boat of all in the long run is the amateur-built, or otherwise labor-discounted type, of professional quality.

Styling very conservative, following that of the middle 1930's, the period widely regarded as the classical era of powerboat design; this to more or less immunize her against changes of fashion and so reduce depreciation.

Dimensions the least that can take the required cabin without false ingenuities; also works out about maximum for ordinary trailer use. (A trailer boat this heavy is not economical on account of the cost of the trailer itself and of the heavy and powerful tow car, but storage is cheaper and resale value improved by the capability.)

Hull form a shallow and fine-lined semi-displacement type with no pronounced planing point, to make a natural drift at economical speeds and lose comparatively little in progress or comfort in an ordinary summer chop. Speed, with the designed single 40-horsepower motor, 12 to 15 knots maximum, 10 to 12 cruising, more or less according to load. I would have less, perhaps an 18 hp with a lugging propeller, to cruise at 7 or 8 knots (still much better than

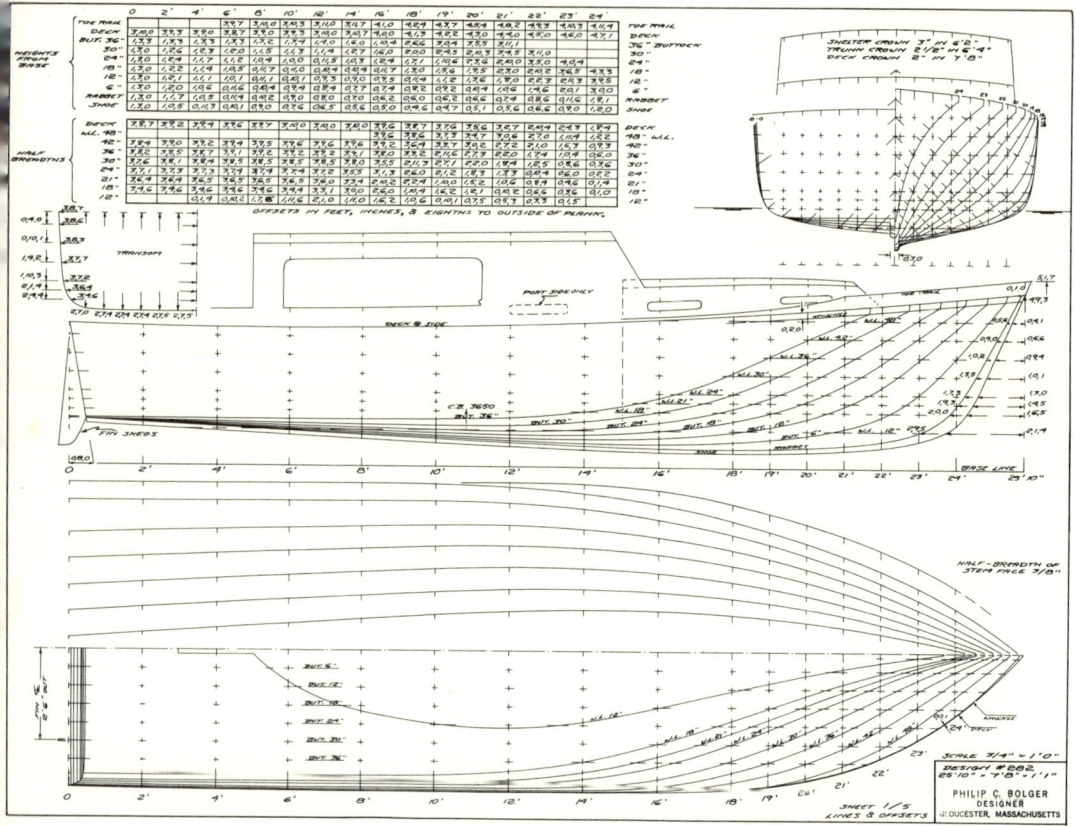

any relevant sailboat); she could handle more with slight modification if a subsequent buyer desired it, up to 100 hp or more for speeds to 30 knots, but not economically in any sense.

Cabin layout designed to be used sitting down except for the stand-up galley, headroom being expensive, tending to degrade open water capability, and not very compatible with a good view from below; fuel economy in this case depends on encouraging people to spread out and not congregate on the fantail, hence forward cockpit and the main cabin dinettes with large shoulder-and-eye-height opening windows. Besides attention to view, ventilation and compartmentation are laid out with rainy weather in mind, in such a way that even four people, in various mixes of age and sex, may not depend entirely on clear weather for a successful cruise.

She's as close to being seaworthy* as is readily possible in an unballasted outboard-powered boat. Her range of stability and reserve buoyancy is not bad, including when flooded. I see no reason why she couldn't cross the Straits of Florida, or any of the Great

---

*I think "seaworthiness" is strictly definable as "ability to keep the sea in all weather with reasonable safety."

Lakes, on a good weather report, and a more extreme capability would be uneconomical for her designed purpose.

This proposal is a slight enlargement of a boat I designed about twenty years ago that was a technical but not a commercial success. Perhaps its time has come around.

To this account I'll now add that the design got the second prize in the competition (the judges commenting that the rig might be crude but did not look simple to them), but that it then dropped into the void of indifference, its time apparently *not* having come around. I still think it would make somebody a nice boat, with or without the rig.

29
CALIFORNIA LOBSTERBOAT

$$30'0'' \times 7'10''$$

Dave Plumb had a plan to go after spiny lobsters on weekends, keeping the boat in his yard through the week. Saturday morning he would couple up, boom down the freeway to a launching ramp, thence skim over the Pacific fifty miles to a place where the lobsters congregated, start hauling his traps, sleep aboard Saturday night, finish hauling, and so go home by sea and road.

I was pretty skeptical about all this, although, as it turned out, for the wrong reasons. The idea of regularly launching and hauling something this size and weight with a road trailer struck me as horrible to think about, having seen enough grief of that kind to last a lifetime, but Dave swore there was nothing to it given experience and proper gear.

The technical problem at my end was to design a boat inside highway dimensions that could normally sustain twenty-five knots. Dave was willing to allow a fair amount of extra time for slower speed in bad weather, but it meant his losing sleep and so had to be infrequent.

The design is based on a race boat I designed in the early 1960s. I'd been highly discontented with her because her trim and spray pattern weren't what I'd expected, and I was convinced she would have been something like ten knots faster if I'd shaped her better. Still, she was a good sea boat and won the single-screw prizes in the Miami-Nassau and 'Round Long Island Races the year she competed. From some subsequent experience with models and fullsize hulls, I knew I could fix what ailed her.

Dave didn't like plywood, arguing among other things that if the surface maintenance was once let go it was gone for good; a sound point given willingness to do considerable extra work at the start. The bottom would've been strip in any case; for a given weight it gives the thickest skin and least vulnerability of any construction to minor scars and abrasion.

CALIFORNIA LOBSTERBOAT

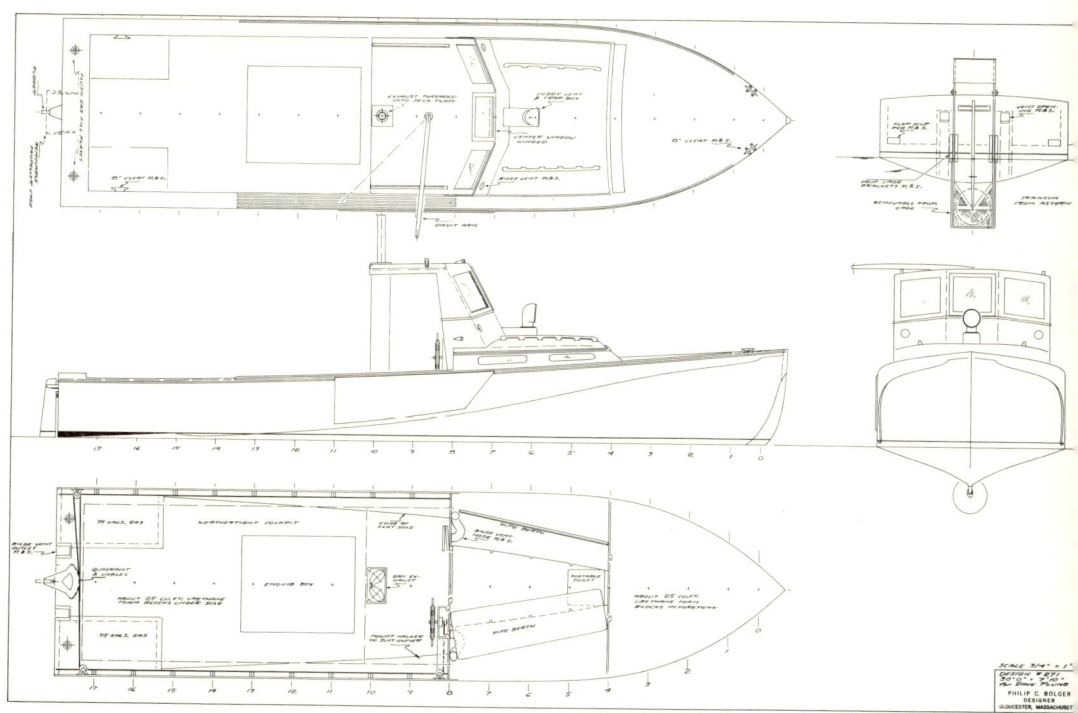

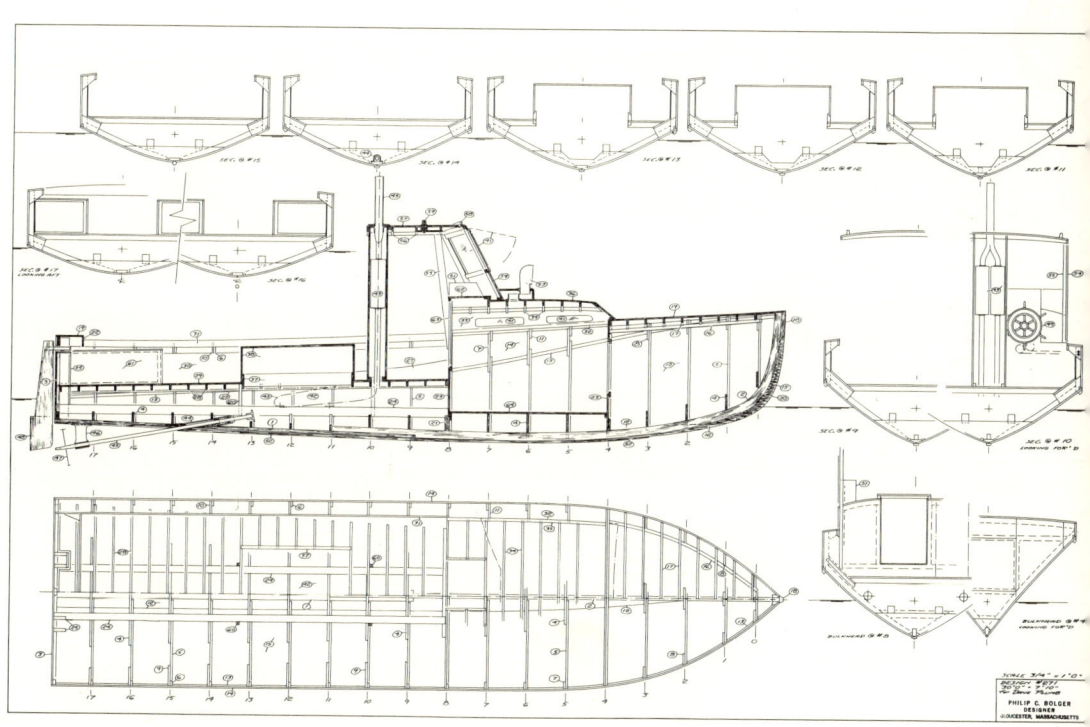

174 CALIFORNIA LOBSTERBOAT

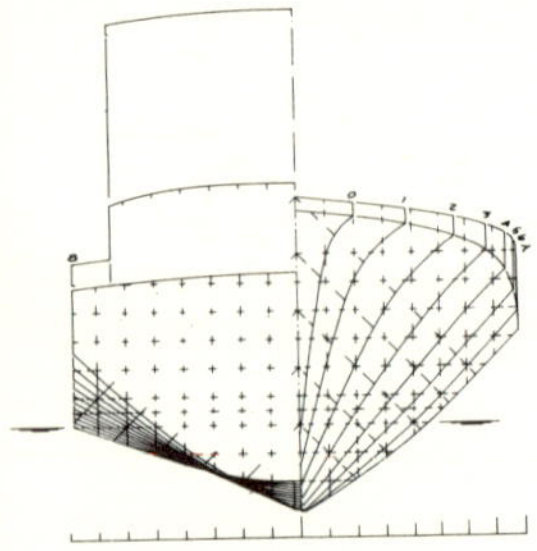

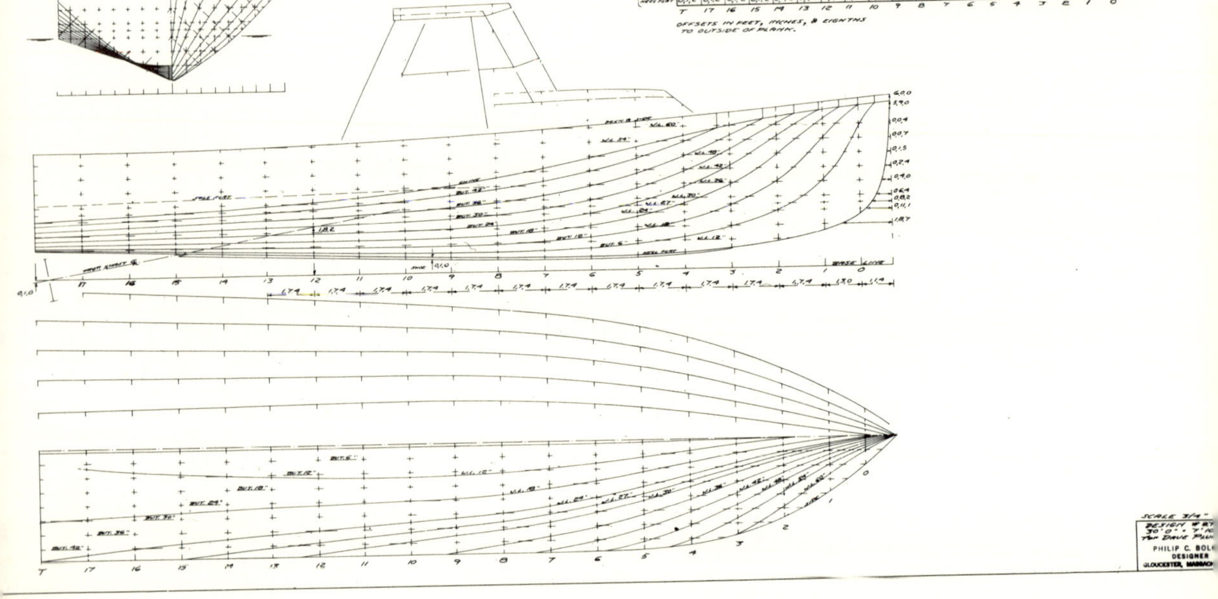

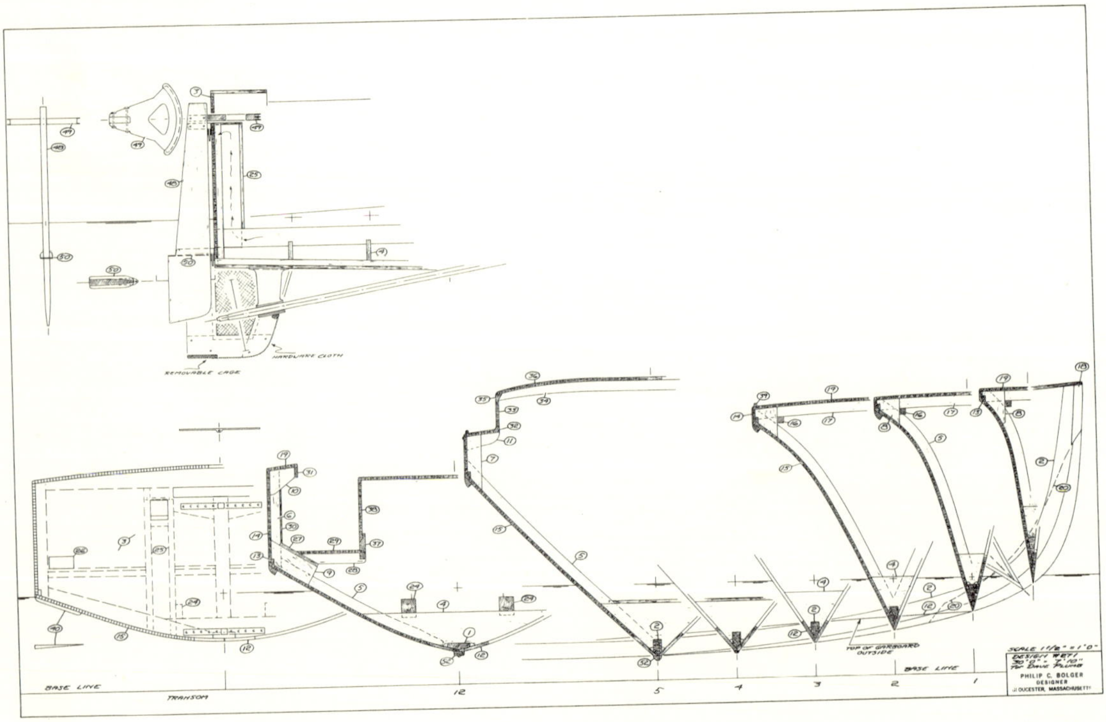

RX-1 in the race around Long Island, 1961. The progenitor of the California lobster boat.

The straight drive engine was supposed to need less maintenance than an outdrive. With the propeller so far aft, and the slope of the ramp said to be well designed, the special trailer could be arranged to accept the shaft and strut without much trouble. I never did think the usual skeg was effective protection against driftwood, which it's to be hoped would pass over the top of a prop in this position., The lobstering area was said to be full of kelp, hence the full cage dropped over the stern and pulled up to enclose completely the propeller when the boat arrived on the grounds and slowed down to work. It wouldn't have been much of a job to build this cage strong enough to support the hull aground, but the grounding would have to be anticipated as the cage couldn't be fitted once she was on the bottom.

This boat represents the most easily driven type in a steep sea that I know of, both in the sense of being smooth-riding for the sake of the crew's health and of needing little extra power to maintain speed when it's rough. This type is exhilarating to ride in a chop, rather than punishing. The price is that it's all bow, with no room to speak of inside, and tender, swaying and rolling when stopped or idling.

Incidentally, this stem profile, though homely compared with the usual long, sharky rake, is what I think is the functional optimum. The strong chin carries the deck above an on-coming wave-crest; thus it's not necessary to snub the waterlines.

About the time Dave was going to start building this boat, the late King of Arabia concluded that it was time to start rationalizing his oil production and prices; it seemed to me at the time, and still does, that everything he did was reasonable and moderate (if you take it for granted that an alliance with Israel wasn't in the political hand he'd been dealt) and that moreover he did us a very big favor in moving sooner rather than later; but however that might be, a project involving two 450-cubic-inch high-compression gasoline engines (including the one in the tow car) abruptly looked quite dubious economically, and was stopped short.

The design itself, given a powerplant with more future (and no more weight), is worth printing still, the shape and proportions being more suitable than most for moderate speed with good fuel economy.

30
ALL-WEATHER HOUSEBOAT

29'10" x 13'11"

This design was meant to be a test model of a production molded boat. She was to be similar in principle to one about the same size I'd done for Captain Alex Moffat, a makeshift on the hull of a Lang cruiser also of my design, which had worked out quite well, though widely considered the ugliest boat ever seen on Penobscot Bay. We hoped that the new one, starting from a clean sheet of paper, could be a little less perverted aesthetically and would represent a functional advance as well.

We had to assume that she would be very heavy; even if you build the hull light (which wouldn't be very sensible), a boat of this kind accumulates gear and appliances at a furious rate as the owners make themselves at home. With over ten tons designed displacement, I expected to watch this process with an easy mind. The great breadth makes this displacement possible in a boat that is still good and floaty. The shape and depth of hull allow quite a range of optional powerplants under the flush sole, leaving the whole boat for subdivision into apartments. Building the house right out to the hull sides contributes to interior volume, but it also gives her a tremendous range of stability; a boat of about these proportions, of my design, was dropped when a hoisting sling broke and she landed in the water almost bottom up. She flipped herself right-side-up so quickly that next to no water got inside her. I would be surprised if a boat like this, given Lexan or thick plastic windows, came to any harm from wind or wave.

As to wind resistance, this design has actually a lower profile than a very ordinary cruiser with a flying bridge. Moreover, I've noticed that it is never the high-sided powerboats that have windage troubles. I've looked over Marblehead Harbor after a hurricane, with the causeway to the Neck piled ten feet deep with the wreckage of lofty-rigged auxiliaries and racers, and seen the three-story Chris Crafts riding easily at their moorings. Its tall

ALL-WEATHER HOUSEBOAT

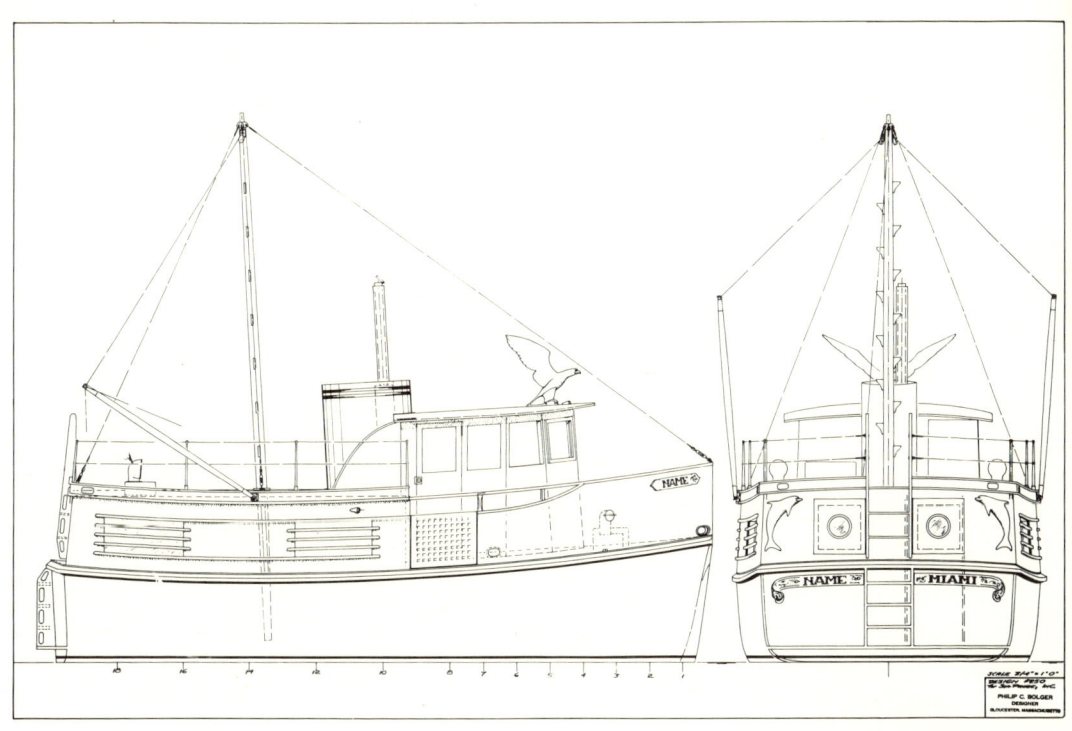

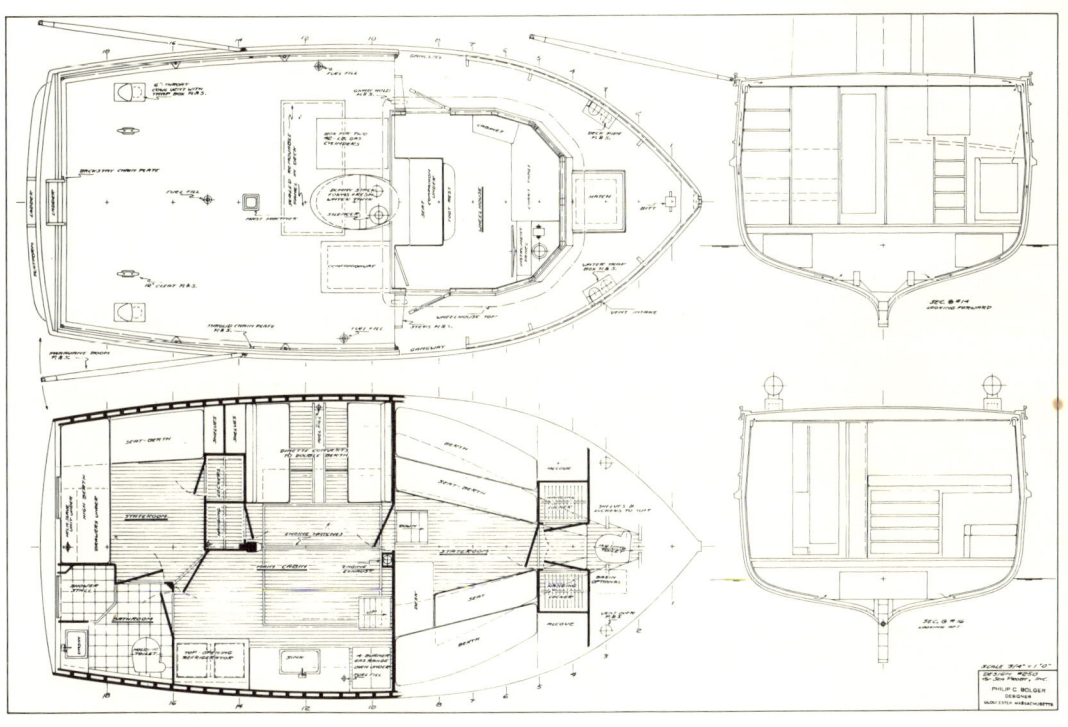

masts and rigging that tear up moorings, not freeboard and deckhouses. I'd say, with only a little hyperbole, that a foot on the top of a tall mast adds more effective windage than a foot of hull freeboard all along. A curve published by Frederick Fenger of wind velocity graphed against altitude shows why: the velocity close to doubles between ten and twenty feet of altitude, as the wind gets clear of the surface friction.

A failing of Captain Moffat's boat that I didn't see how to avoid in this one was a wild, bouncy motion in both pitch and roll, which is the reverse of the "buoyant, floaty" coin. The Captain said he hadn't been so seasick since he took a squadron of 110-foot subchasers to England in the first world war. He knew it meant safety and put up with it because he didn't use the boat for passages of any length. The promoter of the new boat hoped to tame her with paravane anti-rolling gear, with which he'd had experience in larger craft, but I was skeptical myself that it would work in a hull as powerful as this one. I agreed to go in her for a transatlantic passage as an expression of faith in her safety, and I had no qualms about making it in good time, but I did expect to arrive very tired indeed and with an impressive set of bumps and bruises. My idea was that she be seaworthy enough to go coastwise and between islands with an easy mind about whatever might blow up in the way of wind or sea, but she was not meant to be a passagemaker over oceans for the pleasure of it.

As for speed, we talked of ten knots and it's just possible she could be made to go that fast, but if I had a boat like this I'd plan to cruise her at seven or seven and a half knots, no more, and expect quite good fuel economy. After all, if you make a passage that fast in a comparable sailing cruiser, you boast about it for the rest of your life.

When the plans were done we rejoiced at having put fifty-footer accommodations in a thirty-foot hull, but when the bids came in to build her we were reminded that you don't get a fifty-pound package down to thirty pounds by rolling it up tightly. The bids averaged around forty thousand dollars, which as matters turned out would probably have been a good investment even disregarding the production follow-up, but which seemed astronomical at the time and caused the promoter to back away and reflect. While he hesitated, things got still more expensive and I think he must have concluded that bigger vessels were safer bets.

KEY TO PLANS

1. Main keel mahogany sided 5½", molded 7½", about 22'5" long overall.
2. Shoe mahogany or hard pine, 1½" x 5½".
3. Stem, foregripe, shaft logs, sternpost, and horn blocking all sided 5½" mahogany; note hood ends of planking in way of the shaft logs bevelled to about

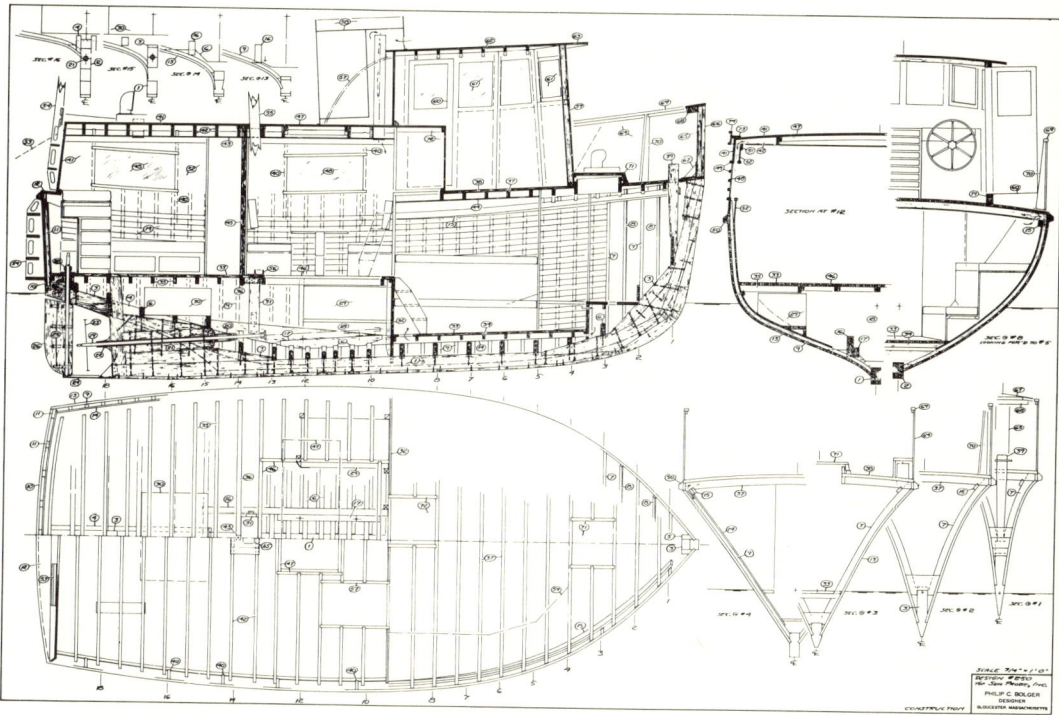

½" to reduce depth of rabbet and make room for bolts to pass shaft tube.

4. Horn timber cheeks sided 2½" mahogany; ⅜" galvanized bolts.

5. Stem cheeks sided 2½" mahogany; no breasthook.

6. Floor timbers sided 2½" mahogany; ½" galvanized drifts and through-bolts about as drawn.

7. Sawn frames on three foremost sections sided 1½" or more, molded about 3½" mahogany or hard pine.

8. Intermediate bent frames between sawn frames ¾" x 1½" mahogany, bent in after planking and fastened from inside.

9. Bent frames to finish 1¾" square, oak or laminated mahogany.

10. Transom 1¼" mahogany.

11. Transom frame 1½" mahogany; build transom on temporary radius beams to be removed after planking and decking.

12. Transom cap sawn from 1½" mahogany.

13. Planking 1¼" mahogany; 2½" #18 bronze screws bunged.

14. Hull ceiling ¾" mahogany; carry from transom to frame #3, from underside of clamp to below forecastle sole; make sure air circulation and drainage behind ceiling is nowhere blocked; e.g., butt blocks of planking not more than 1" thick and should not touch frames.

15. Clamps from main bulkhead forward, bent in double to finish 2½" x 3½" mahogany, hard pine, or fir; outboard course stops at frame #3, inboard course carried to frame #1.

16. Engine stringers sided 2½".
17. Engine beds (shape and position to suit engine mounts) sided 2½"; ½" galvanized bolts through stringers.
18. Engine to be selected by owner: configuration shown for Perkins 6-354M with Warner 3:1 reduction gearing; dry exhaust to truck-type muffler in stack.
19. Propeller shaft 1¾" diameter bronze about 8'6" overall.
20. Flexible neck stuffing box.
21. Lead shaft tube.
22. Bronze rectangular base stern fitting with rubber bearing.
23. Propeller (for 130 hp, 3:1 reduction Perkins) 28" diameter by 22" pitch three-blade medium speed type.
24. Rudder skeg bronze channel bolted to flange angle on stern post to be easily removable.
25. Rudder stock 1¾" diameter bronze about 5'8" overall, tapered and splined at top to take hydraulic helm slave unit.
26. Rudder blade 1¾" mahogany or hard pine; four ¼" x 1½" bronze straps with machine screws each side to stock.
27. Lead or bronze tube.
28. Bronze port, rectangular base.
29. Main fuel tanks 1'6" x 2'3" x 4'0", shaped to inside of ceiling; about 84 U.S. gallons each.
30. Auxiliary fuel tank (optional) 1'3" x 3'0" x 4'0", about 135 U.S. gallons.
31. Posts take thrust of mast to engine stringers.
32. Bulkhead, as near watertight as may be, double ¾" plywood, bolted to laminated belt frames inside ceiling.
33. Cabin soles 1½" teak, iroko, or rift-grain fir.
34. Forecastle sole beams 1½" x 2½" mahogany or fir.
35. Main cabin sole beams 1¾" x 3½" mahogany or fir.
36. Strong beam 2½" x 3½".
37. Foredeck beams sided 1¾", molded 3½" fir.
38. Foredeck 1½" teak, iroko, or rift-grain fir, or double ½" plywood fiberglass-sheathed; if plywood, vary crown of beams to eliminate the dip in the deck centerline forward.
39. Bitt 5½" square mahogany.
40. Side frames of raised afterdeck 1½" x 2½" fir or mahogany.
41. Sides, after end, and decking of raised afterdeck all double ½" plywood, fiberglass-sheathed.
42. Afterdeck beams sided 1½" fir or spruce, 6" depth at centerline; crown out from upper side, underside straight.
43. Sheathing under afterdeck beams ¼" plywood; screw strongly to beams, especially outboard, as these sheets are stressed as part of the deck structure; stop the sheathing not less than 1½" clear of clamp to allow air circulation behind ceiling as indicated by arrows on the drawings.
44. Sheathing under foredeck beams ¼" plywood; stop at #5 partial bulkhead.
45. Stanchion 2½" square mahogany; split to take ⅜" galvanized tie rod.

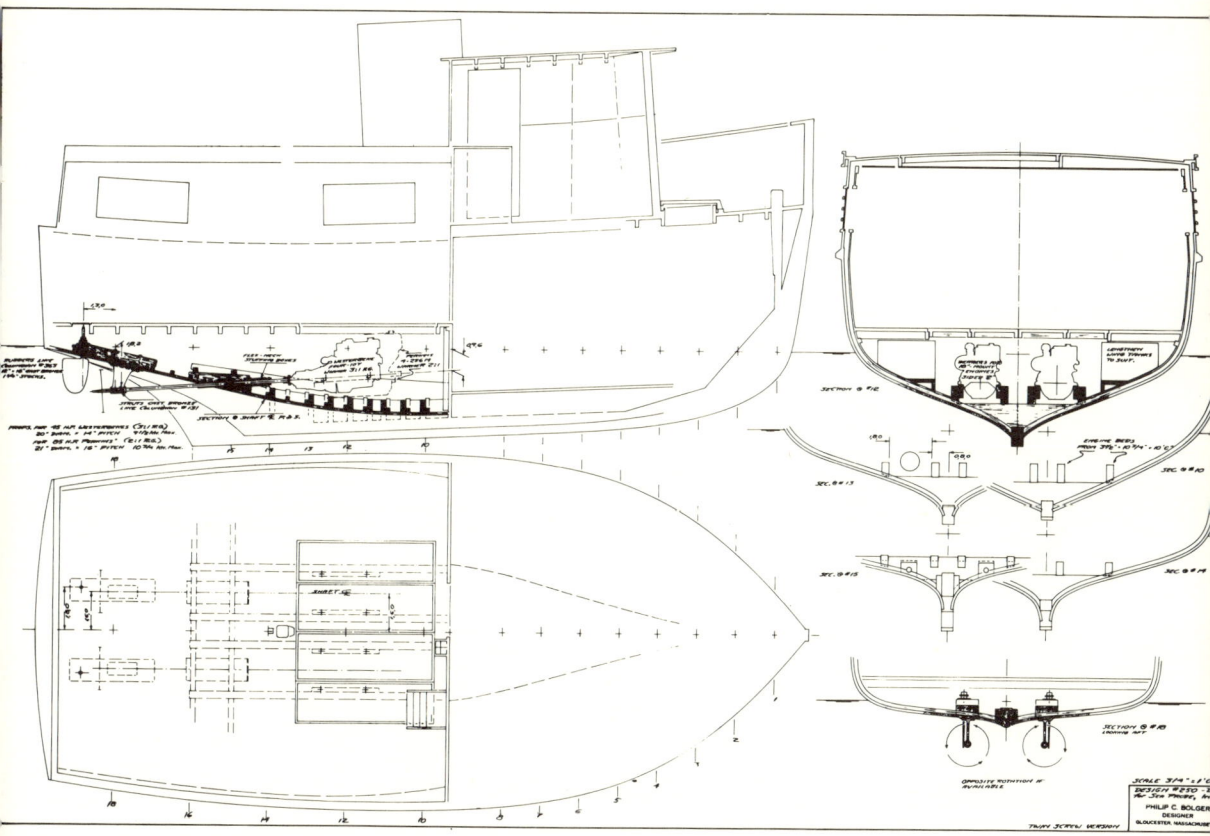

46. Engine hatches in four sections; a four-finger lifting ring (not shown) in one of the middle ones.

47. Flush panel in afterdeck, to open about 2′7½″ x 6′0″, for installation and removal of engine and other machinery and of prefabricated cabin furniture; the panel is screwed down on seam compound and its edges could be sealed with fiberglass tape.

48. Fixed windows of afterdeck ½″ laminated glass.

49. Moldings and protective bars of windows 1¼″ x 1½″ mahogany; cut away the bars crossing the windows by ¼″ to clear the glass.

50. Guard moldings from 2½″ x 5″ mahogany, shod with 2″ brass or stainless steel; cut a drip groove on the underside.

51. Clamp of afterdeck 1½″ x 3½″ fir or mahogany.

52. Sheathing of afterdeck sides ⅜″ plywood; leave open for air passage top and bottom of windows.

53. Square ports in after end of raised deck open about 23″ x 24″, hinged at the top and fitted with braces to hold them at any angle; about 11″ diameter fixed deadlights.

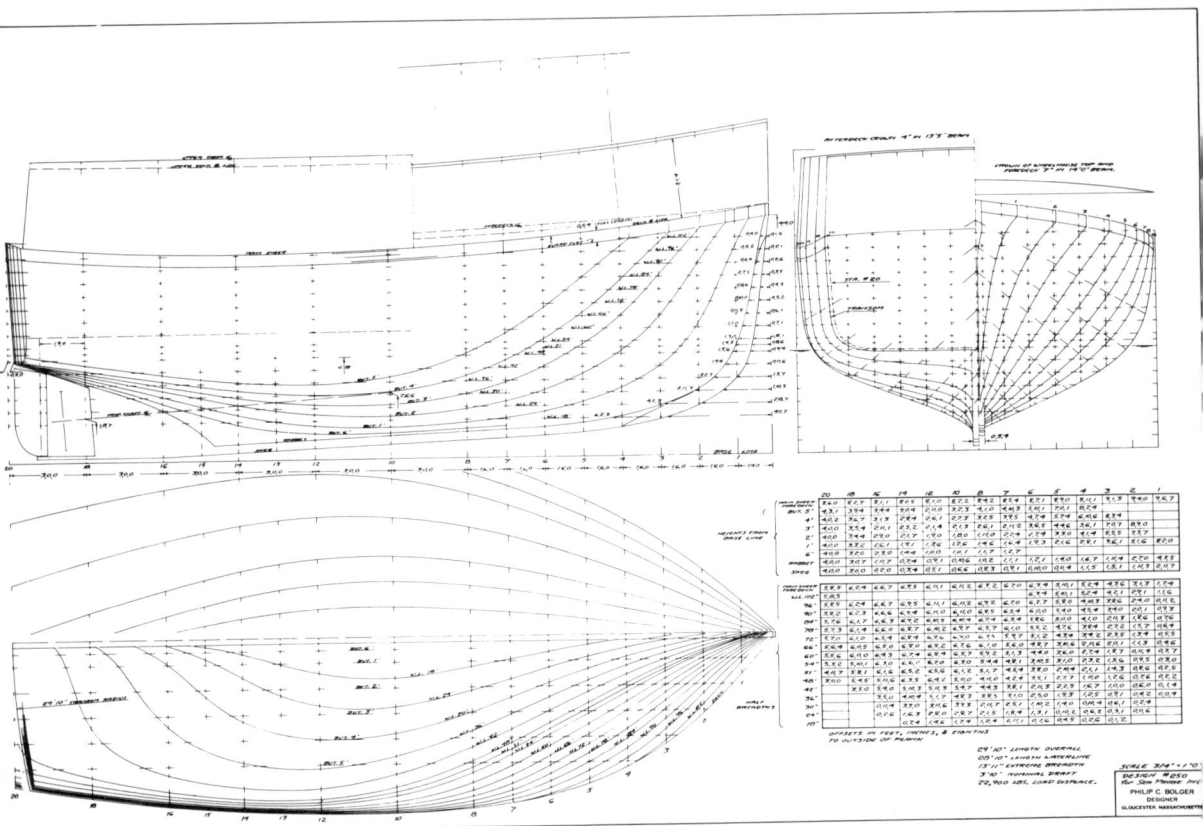

54. Stern platform and ladders about as shown on the outboard arrangement plan and profile.

55. Mast fir, 24'0" overall, 5½" square at deck, 4" square at heel, 3½" square below truck band; round corners on about 1" radius.

56. Mast step collar cast bronze, bolted through sole blocking.

57. Companionway shroud double ½" plywood; sides 1½" mahogany.

58. Dummy stack, elliptical section 30" x 48", $\frac{1}{16}$" galvanized or stainless steel, with tab flanges for four ⅜" bolts to afterdeck and two to wheelhouse top; three plates 3/32" steel form ends and front of 135-gallon fresh water tank connected in heads and galley for gravity flow; engine exhaust muffler starboard side; main cabin vent air intake (6" diameter) port side.

59. Wheelhouse walls double, ¾" plywood outside, ⅜" inside; about 1½" fir posts and filler blocking; make sure the voids in these walls are drained and vented.

60. Doors hinge forward, to swing clear around and hook back.

61. Wheelhouse glass ⅜" laminated (i.e., shatterproof); all fixed except the two inboard angled windows, which should be framed and hinged across the top.

62. Wheelhouse beams sided 1½", molded 2½" mahogany.

63. Wheelhouse top double ½" plywood, fiberglass-sheathed.
64. Bulwarks ¾" plywood.
65. Bulwark stem 2½" x 7½".
66. Bulwark stem cap 1¾" x 5½".
67. Bronze bracket for bulwark stem.
68. Bulwark breasthook side 2½".
69. Cap 1½" x 2½" teak or mahogany.
70. Stanchions sided 1½" mahogany.
71. Forward hatch 1½" teak or iroko.
72. Extension of afterdeck forms forecastle companionway shroud and view seat for wheelhouse; space to starboard, next to companionway, can be fitted as a locker opening either below or to wheelhouse.
73. Toe rail 1½" x 5" teak.
74. Toe rail facing (forms fake sheer line parallel with main sheer and conceals actual line of raised afterdeck; see outboard profile) ¾" plywood with about 1" x 1¼" teak moldings top and bottom; same across stern each side of ladder.

31
GILL-NETTER TYPE HOUSEBOAT

| 35'10" x 12'0" |

Leon Wallace ordered a lobsterboat from Nick Hemeon. Nick got into one of his "boatbuilding is for imbeciles — I'll go lobstering" moods and handed the order over to Dana Story, along with the half-model. Dana hired me to pick a set of offsets off the model, but I can't ever let anything alone, so I tinkered with the bow shape and moved the engine aft. While they were laying her down, Leon put the engine back where Nick had it and then some. When the molds were set up, you could see there was a place in the bow I'd drawn where the frames would go in hard, so Brad Story, the foreman-carpenter, shaved one of the molds quite a lot, and while he was at it he let the ribbands spring out along the topsides amidships to ease up the turn of the bilge, which made her about six inches wider. The transom was pulled out six inches or so and made curved instead of flat. Leon and Nick and Dana and I, besides Brad's helpers and casual bystanders, stood around and kibitzed while all this was in the works.

This is not quite the way a boat ought to be designed according to the textbooks, but as it happened the boat turned out good-looking, handy, fast, cheap, and very able. The lines drawing here represents, as near as I can make out, how she ended up. Nick built two more from the molds, except that I think he re-spaced the molds on one of them, and dropped the rabbet down somewhat in way of the shaft log.

Wallace's boat only cost about $15,000 with a Ford Six diesel, and it struck me that if she had a long house built on her, like a winter gill-netter but higher off the water, she'd be a very economical place for a migratory couple to live. I have in mind the sort who ease into some New England or New Jersey port in May; he takes a job on a head boat, gutting fish for the tourists, and she's a waitress in a seafood restaurant. In October, when

GILL-NETTER TYPE HOUSEBOAT

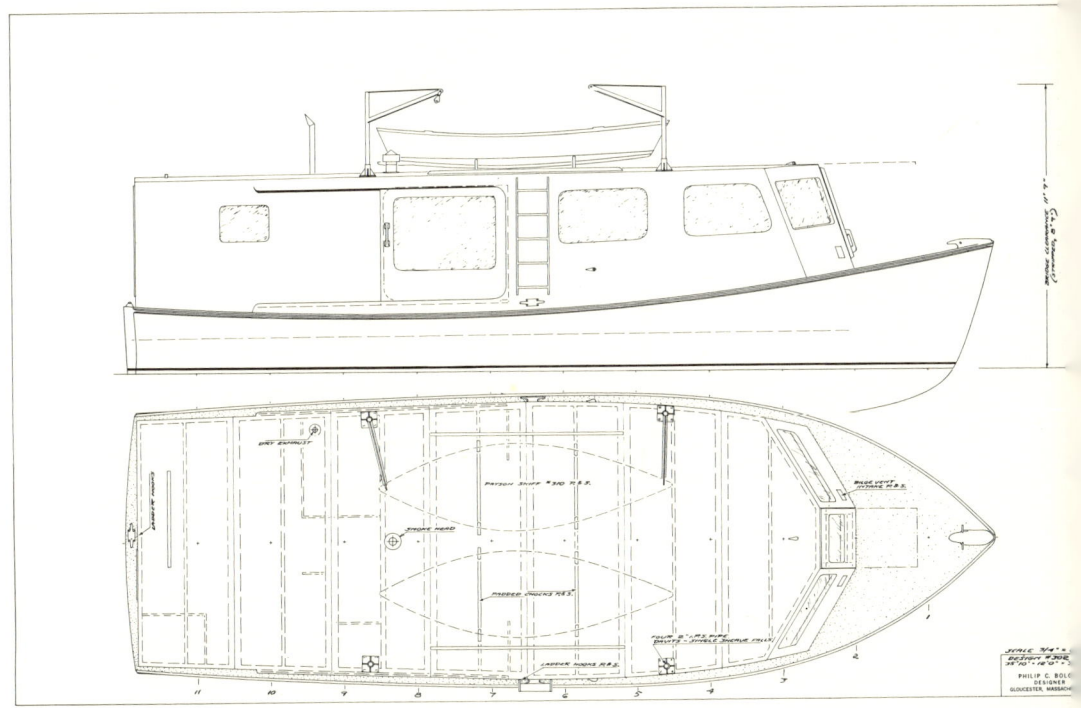

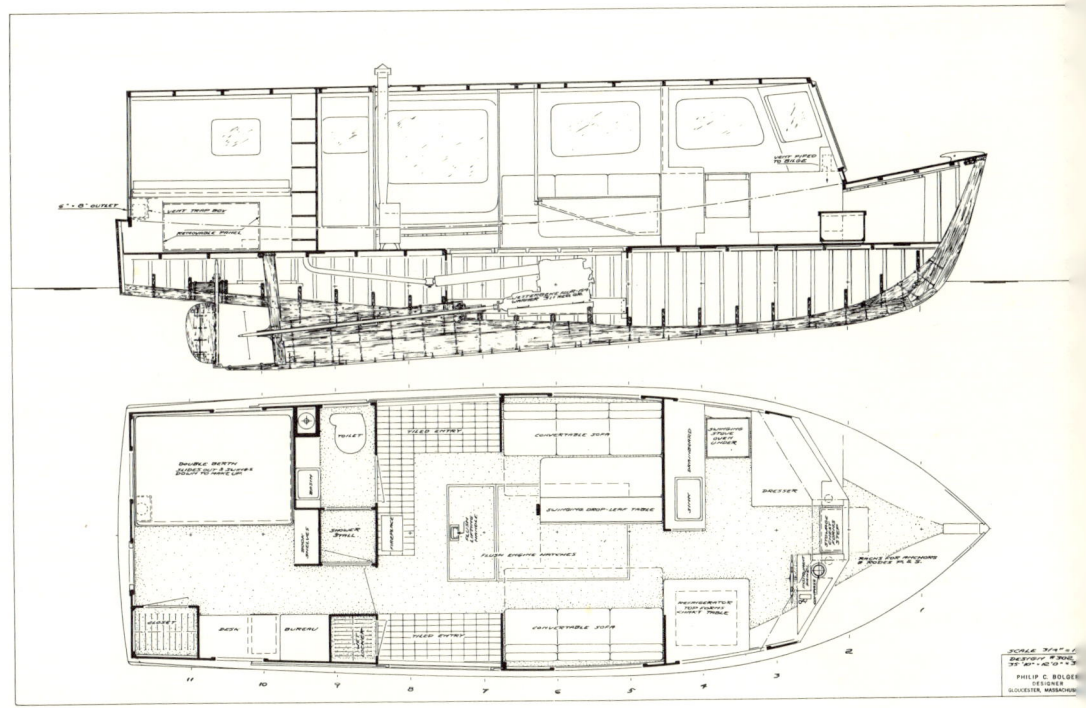

GILL-NETTER TYPE HOUSEBOAT

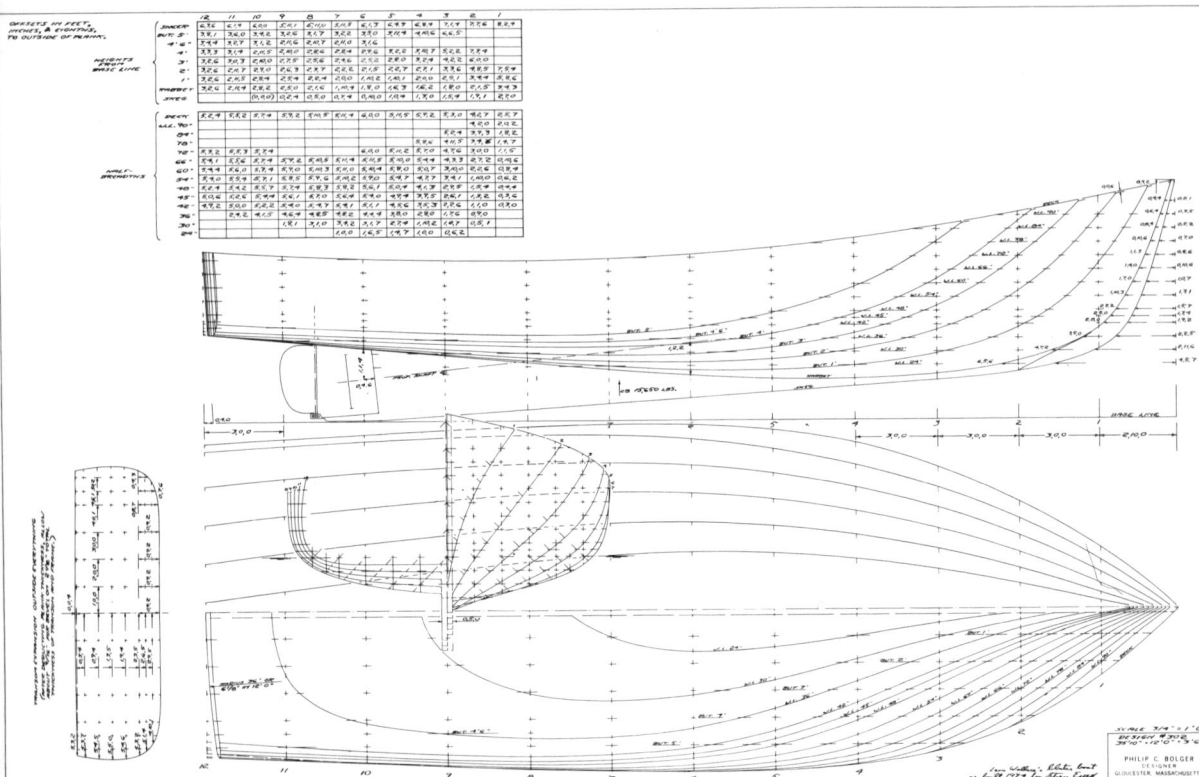

the summer jobs tail off, they head for Florida for winter work. Retired people do the same, but work less or not at all, and are apt not to come so far north.

It's getting expensive to tie up in marinas all the time, so I showed a pair of rowing boats good enough to commute a mile or two from an anchorage. These are from the plans back in Chapter 3 and also make a fair singlehanded sailing dinghy for recreation, or even for going after help if the house should break down or run aground in an out-of-the-way place. More likely she'd be tied up somewhere, with a couple of bikes racked on the side away from the float-stage. A real 'netter would only have the big sliding door on one side, but I liked the idea of the breezeway for the houseboat.

The galley is placed where the cook can keep the helmsman company in the inland waterway; outside with an autopilot the cook can be lookout while his partner gets on with maintenance. The engine is much smaller than the one in the lobsterboat to save on first investment, there being no special hurry in this kind of life. The boat is sufficiently able not to need speed for safety; nothing that would blow up before she could run to shelter

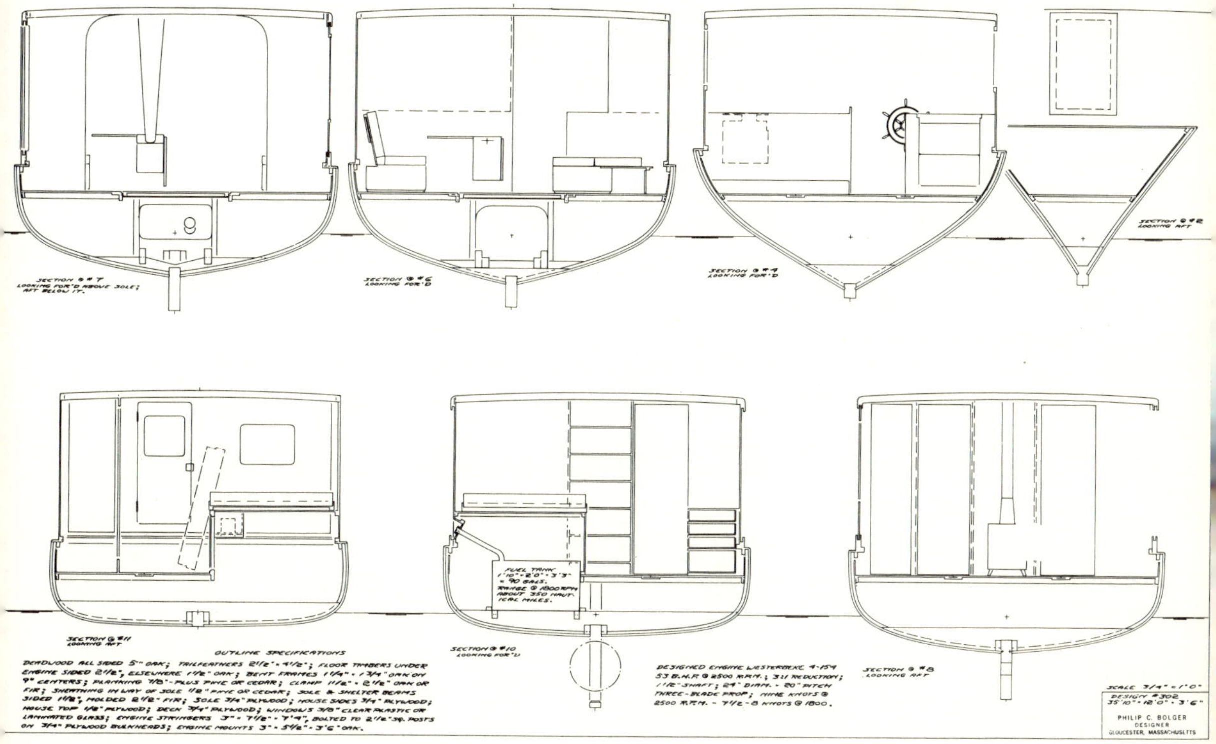

GILL-NETTER TYPE HOUSEBOAT

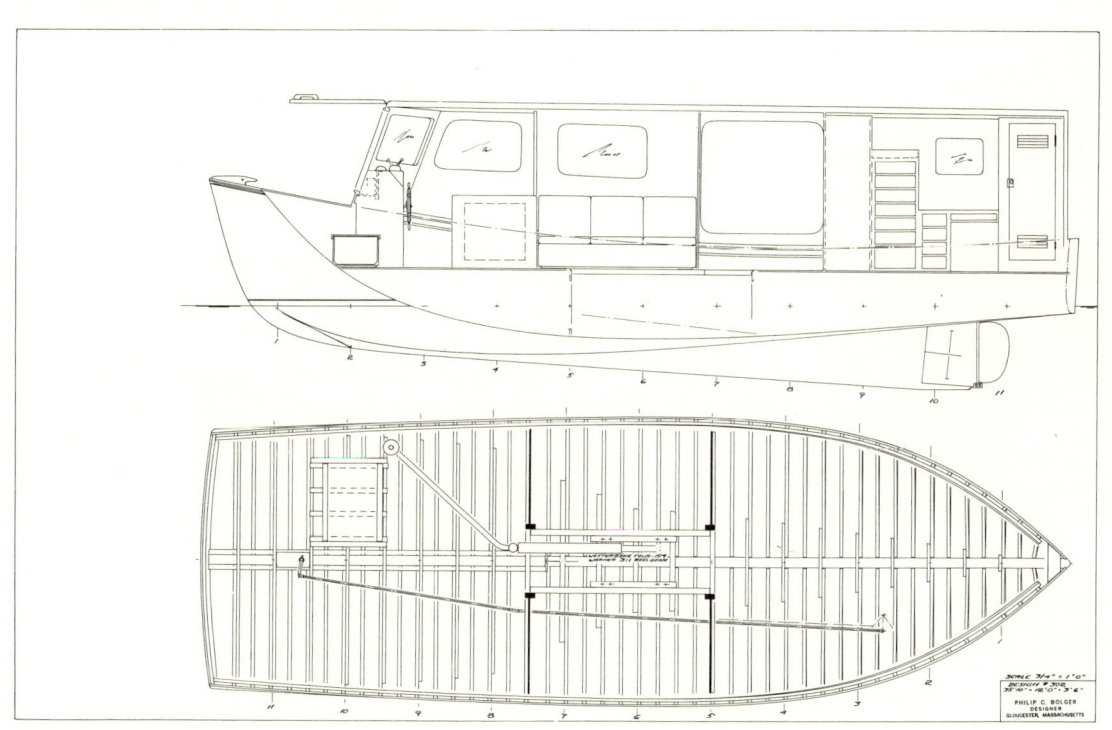

at seven or eight knots would be likely to give her trouble in the open. Before a real gale could build a sea she shouldn't have to cope with, she would have time to get in out of the wet.

Being a buoyant, corky sort of hull, the swing stove and table are almost necessary. She's also got a full-size double bed; most couples seem to like these, but as usually designed into boats they're impossible to make up decently. I learned bed-making from a Finnish mercenary soldier who'd studied the subject in at least three armies, and I've liked a tight, smooth bed and despised fitted sheets ever since. How well the scheme shown for tipping the bed up on edge to tuck in the far side will work remains to be seen; it might be an improvement on walking round.

The washroom is pretty well up to shore standards except for the door from the bedroom opening into the shower stall. This may not be a hardship.

Regarded as an economical place to live, this design looks quite efficient, which is about all that can be said for its looks. She has a good deal more room than a trailer of comparable cost, to say nothing of a motor home. If it comes to that, you can't buy much of a house for the same money.

32
RESOLUTION

$$48'0'' \times 11'0''$$

Resolution is the outcome of ten or twelve years of sporadic tinkering with the requirements. I wanted a cruiser that I could eventually live aboard year 'round. In my profession you don't retire in the usual sense: I mean to draw boats while I have wits and eyesight, but some day I have in mind to have no telephone, or automobile, or fixed address outside a postal drop or two.

She has to be a convenient place to live for a single man, or, what comes to the same thing, a congenial couple, of simple tastes and an addiction to more or less trivial books. She has to be capable of being handled by one man even if he's getting old, independence and privacy being the object.

I don't have any plans to go over an ocean, though it's nice to know she's capable if the spirit moves, but I do want to be free of anxiety about local weather. The fundamental point of the design is to be easy in mind: not to be hustled, not to be crowded, not to have to plan far ahead, not to worry about the consequences of impulses. I've been spoiled too long; it's been thirty years or more since I've had to do much that was distasteful, or been denied anything that I greatly desired, and with this boat I hope to prolong my singular good luck. Solon said, "Call no man happy till you know how he died."

A succession of shallow boats has ruined my piloting, and now I hate a boat that won't sail over any rock that doesn't show a swirl on the surface. I want to be able to lie on middle grounds and at the heads of slips where all the craft that don't dry out upright at low water won't come crowding me. If the tide leaves a boat dry an hour or two a day, it will be a long time before she grows foul, and when she does you won't have to clean her

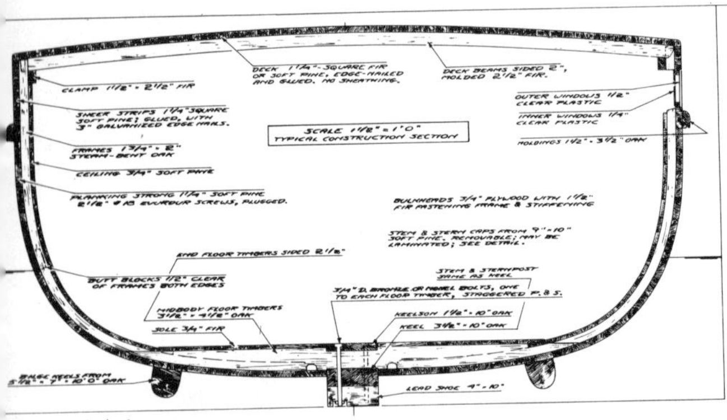

RESOLUTION

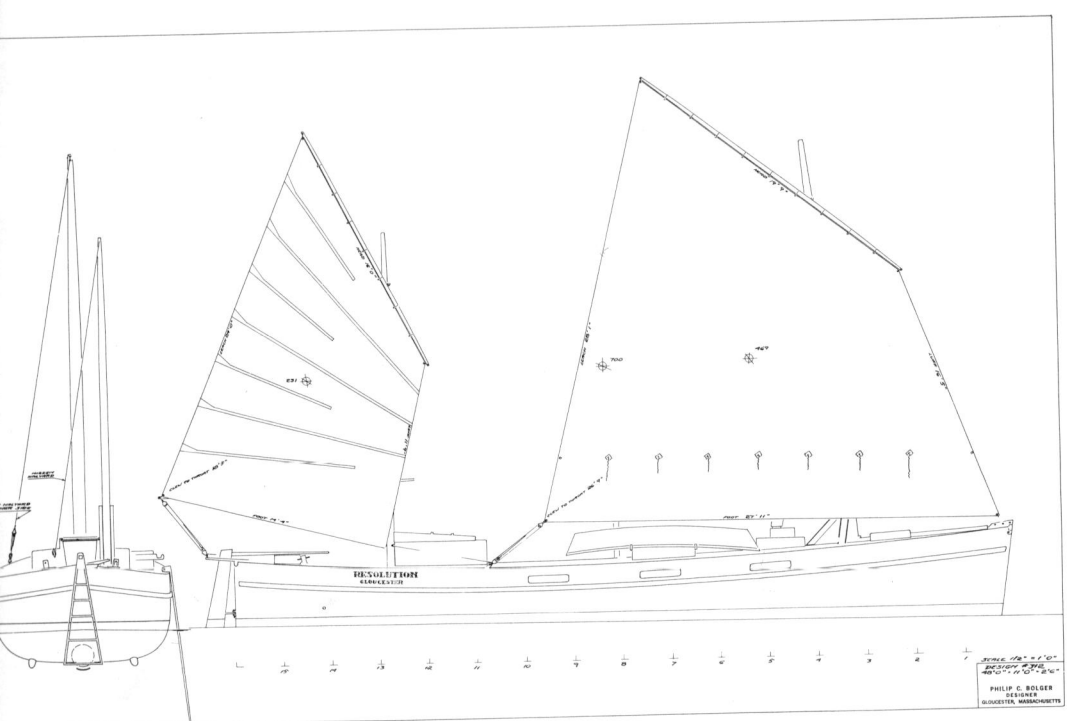

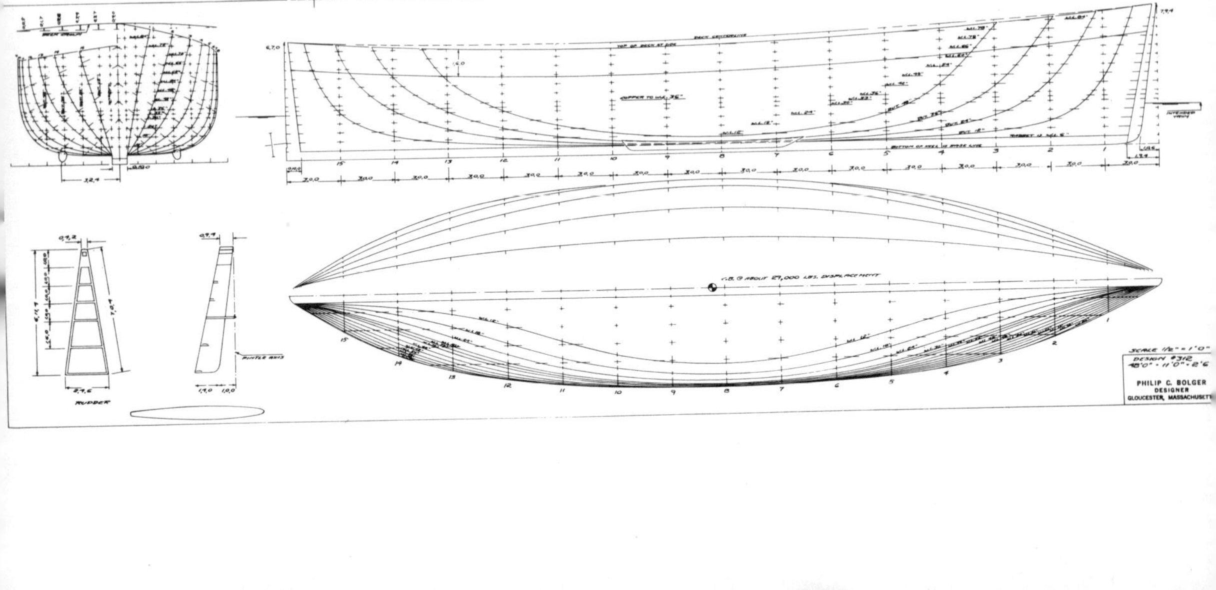

all at once. I have in mind to have *Resolution* copper-sheathed, which according to the old-timers makes scrubbings a pleasure.[1]

For a one-off boat this bent-frame and carvel plank construction is still the best way if you know the right builder; it's the least trouble to keep in good order and the pleasantest to live with. There aren't enough carpenters alive to build good production boats this way, or even many custom ones. Dana and Bradford Story have agreed to build *Resolution* in the old yard at Essex. They are the fifth and sixth generations of Storys to build vessels on that spot. They won't build two boats alike, or promise a delivery date, or quote a fixed price. I've reason to be sure I'll get good work produced in few man-hours, and intelligent execution, meaning the plans will be followed except for the mistakes and improvements.

Among the *Resolutions* that had phantom existence on paper were some as short as twenty-five feet and some as long as eighty feet. Some had no sails, others no engines. I settled on a motorsailer because I couldn't work out a straight sailing rig fit to handle alone that would drive the amount of space I judged necessary to do business. I'm not that fanatical about sailing in any case, rowing and paddling being what I like for recreation. I do think an effective sailing rig is better insurance by far than a second engine or any amount of spare parts. It also allows a diminution of fuel capacity that saves at least a couple of feet of overall hull length. The rig, almost a straightforward copy of a nineteenth century British drift fisherman, a Mounts Bay lugger[2] to be exact, is cheap and powerful. There's little to go wrong, and it folds down on deck, all inboard, with no special gear and minimum effort. The catch is that the mainsail has to be brought down on deck and shifted around the mast as you tack. I tried this rig on a small scale in *Little Superior,* and I'm satisfied that it's the optimum type for a boat that doesn't have to maneuver under sail. I may add a main trysail to her inventory later, and will have high-class and redundant ground tackle including enough, and heavy enough, chain to make what's on the far end almost irrelevant.

The mizzen will likely be used a lot more than the main, to steady and boost her in conjunction with the engine, and is the reason I expect to get away with such a combination of small engine and shallow propeller, which otherwise would mean trouble on a lee shore. The A-frame rudder has most benefit from the prop stream when it's hard over; it also forms a

---

[1]See Claud Worth *Yacht Cruising,* and *Yacht Navigation and Voyaging,* for first-hand comments on copper sheathing. My observation over the years is that Worth is never wrong and seldom outdated.

[2]See *Sailing Drifters,* by Edgar J. March, for a mass of data, photos, and plans of the Cornish, Manx, and Scots vessels that used this rig, also for the origin of the hull form. *Resolution* is a highly derivative and reactionary design!

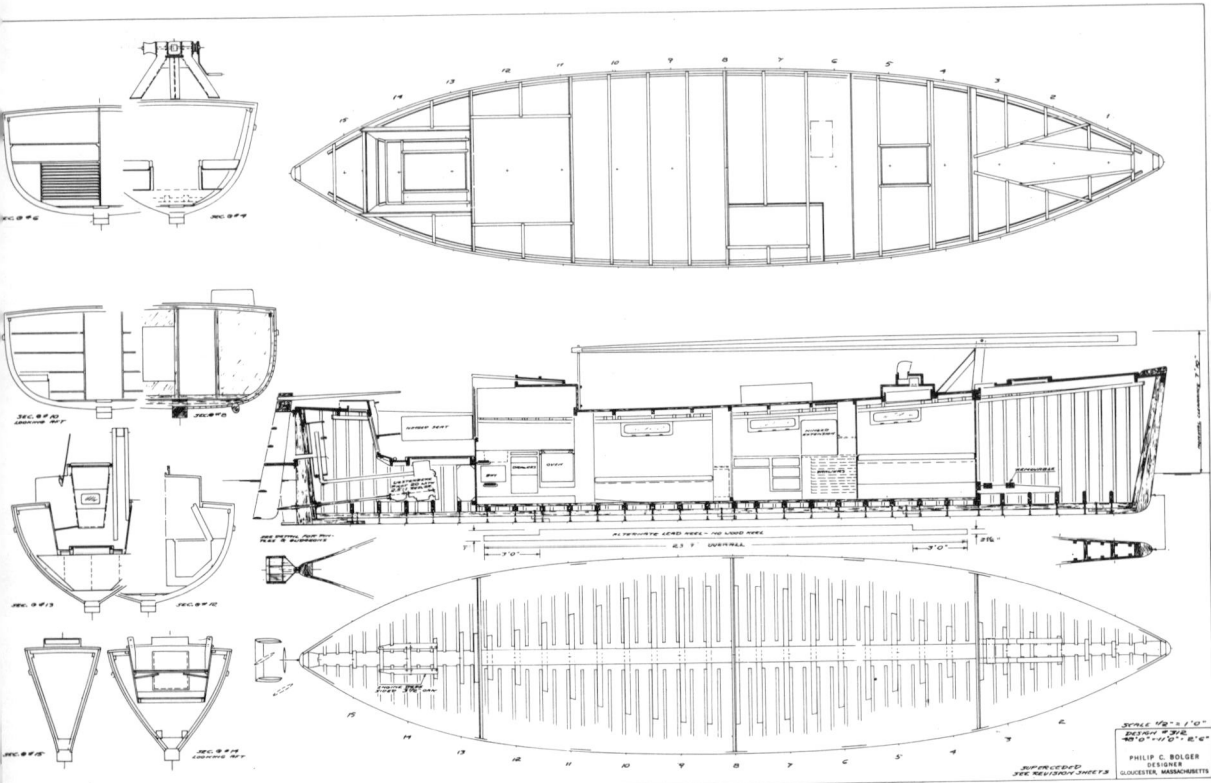

ladder to climb down when you need to unwind a rope from around the propeller.

    A long boat can be a coarse model and rig and still go at good speed, so the accommodations were arranged lengthwise instead of side-by-side or vertically; she was stretched further to allow bulkheading off the engine and tank at one end, and the bicycles and anchors at the other: being able to keep oil and mud out of the cabin is a real amenity. The breadth is what seemed to come naturally given her depth, freeboard, and length, neither pinched nor bulged. I aimed at an easy motion in pitch and roll, with as much steadiness at anchor and under way as could be had in such a shallow hull. She has enough salient keel to get by, even to windward under sail alone, I hope, without the crude leeboard being an urgent necessity.

    A galley has to be built to cope with spills and mess, so it's placed where it can also be used to take off wet oilskins and dirty boots. There won't often be enough people aboard to make squeezing past the cook a problem. The sleeping cabin is at the other end, to spare heating it in cold weather. Library, workroom, and washroom are set in a compact, low group around the wood-burning heater. The washroom is not a shower, but simply

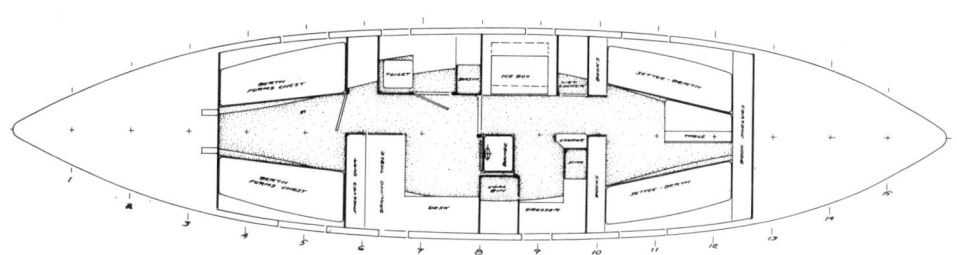

a watertight, hard-finish space where you can take a kettle of warm water and splash with no inhibitions; a sponge bath with a cloth of just the right size and texture is a sybaritic luxury in at least the same class as a good shower, requiring much less plumbing and water. She'll have a self-contained toilet for her initial use as a weekend and vacation cruiser; by the time I get around to living aboard, the permanent sanitation requirements ought to be clearer than they are just at present.

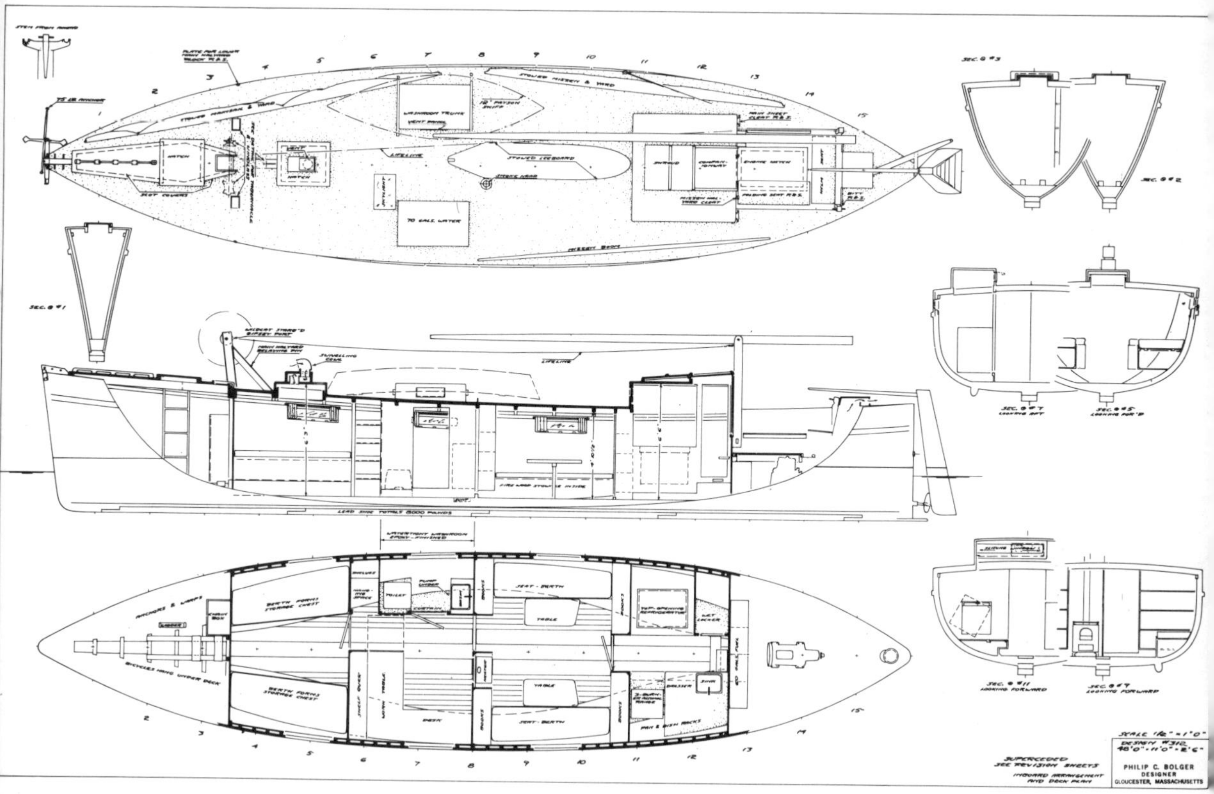

There'll be a mattress to fit the top of the worktable, or perhaps a Root berth over it; she can sleep five in three compartments, as might be handy once every few years.

(I looked at a 25 percent scale-up on the same proportions. It would measure 60′ in length, 13′9″ in breadth, and about 3′1″ draft, and would have good standing headroom in all the areas where I'll have to keep my head down besides being loosened up all over in the accommodations. But it would displace 25 tons, need at least 1,100 square feet of sail and a much bigger engine, and I simply don't need or want it even if I thought I could pay for it.)

The engine will be a two-cylinder, hand-starting diesel of around 20 horsepower, geared to swing a solid three-blade prop of 16 inches or 18 inches diameter. A Westerbeke Pilot 20, with a gear no longer offered, is shown; I'm still looking at Sabbs and Yanmars and possibly one or two others.[3] I expect eight knots tops and six knots cruise from whatever I settle on. Reaching in a breeze of wind under sail and power she ought to go more than ten knots, in clouds of spray and high excitement.

Above the copper sheathing she'll be painted an unrelieved flat white, sides, decks, spars, and interior. It may be a bit smudged underfoot sometimes, and I mean to touch up the spots that wear bare and never let it build elsewhere: fisherman finish. Inside there will be some nice colored fabric — blankets, curtains, and carpets — and several hundred books. Outside there will be the sun and the rain and her fine proportions.

Resolution won't perform any exploits. I see no way to record objectively the freedom from worry and irritation which is her reason for being. Subjectively, I don't think she will frighten me often, or bore me, ever.

[3] I've ordered a 22 hp Sabb with a 23″ variable-pitch propeller.

33
ANCHOR

Dovekie was supposed to have a fifteen-pound yachtsman anchor, but it turned out that the last company to make them had given them up. I think this was because forged arms were too expensive, and cast ones too unreliable. I took a plow (Taylor, CQR, Maxim) anchor because I'd never had one and disliked the Danforths I'd had. The plow turned out just as hard to clean as the Danforths and with the same habit of failing to take hold just when it's most needed.

"Nobody should buy a stockless anchor under fifty pounds," I muttered to myself (I'm a libertarian and *never* say "there ought to be a law"), and I designed an all-welded removable-stock anchor for a welder of my acquaintance to make. He made a neat job of welding, I had it hot-dip galvanized, and I had a neat-looking but exceedingly expensive little anchor.

We took it, and the plow, out in Tom Morse's 300-horsepower gillnetter and dragged them on a bridle in sand, mud, and the thick soup of fish scales and gurry typical of Gloucester's inner harbor. The pair of them together didn't even slow her down with her prop idling. Mine brought home the plow two out of three trials. As it was a couple of pounds heavier, and one of those times it turned out to be foul of a hundred-foot length of inch one-chain somebody had mislaid there, I was not very pleased. I'd expected it to win every time.

Wanting to see, and photograph, whatever was going on, I took the pair to a footbridge across a sandy creek, at low tide, set them in the sand backwards and on their sides, and hauled on the bridle with about a two-to-one scope.

On wet sand they both took hold at once, buried, and became equally immovable for small-boat purposes. On dry sand they were both unreliable, the plow having a tendency to skid on its side, and mine to drag on the tip

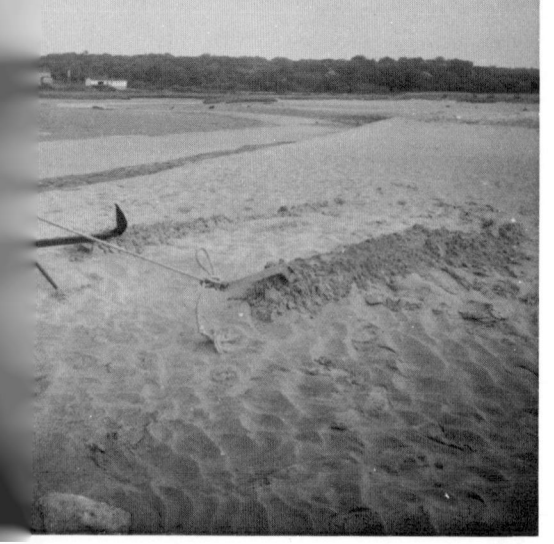

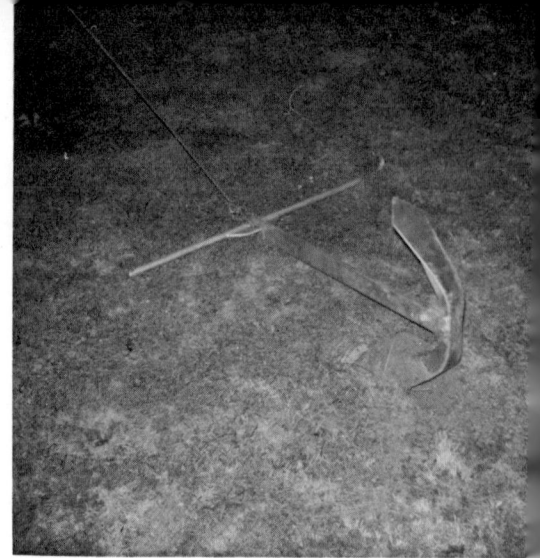

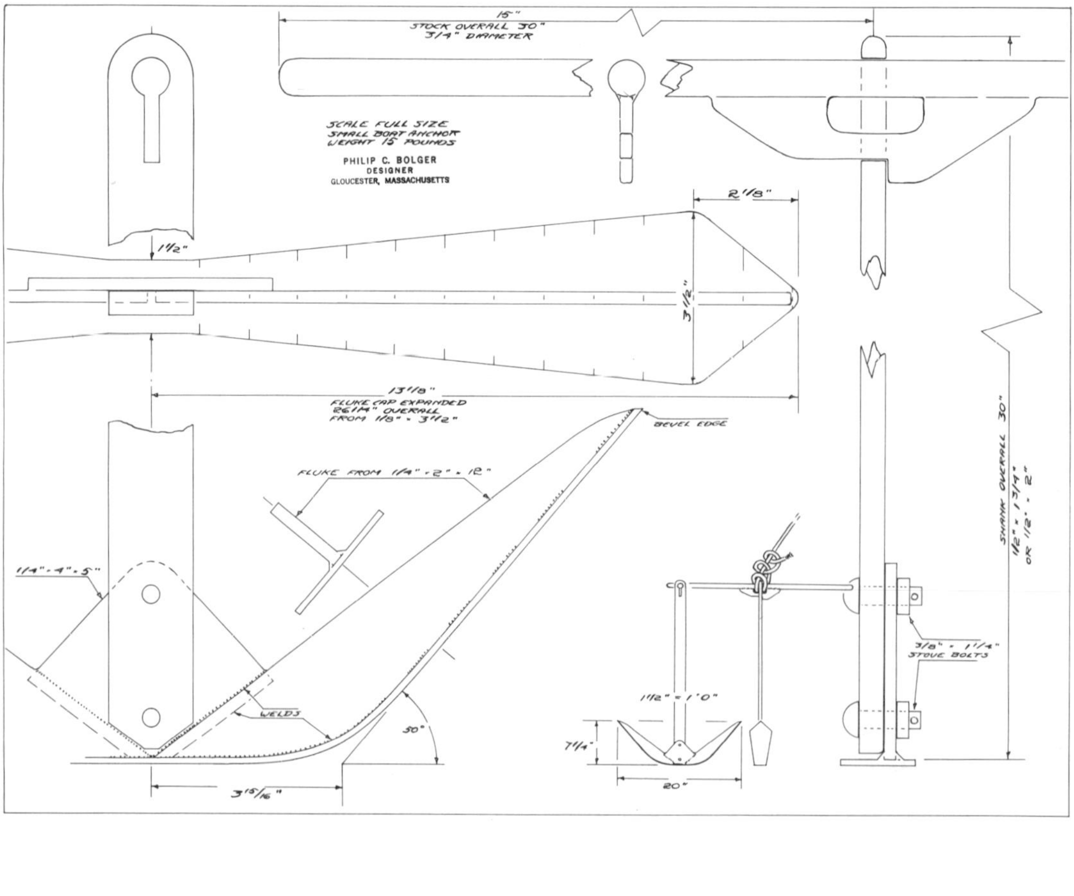
15"
STOCK OVERALL 30"
3/4" DIAMETER
SCALE FULL SIZE
SMALL BOAT ANCHOR
WEIGHT 15 POUNDS
PHILIP C. BOLGER
DESIGNER
GLOUCESTER, MASSACHUSETTS
2 1/8"
1 1/2"
3 1/2"
13 1/8"
FLUKE CAP EXPANDED
26 1/4" OVERALL
FROM 1/8" × 3 1/2"
BEVEL EDGE
FLUKE FROM 1/4" × 2" × 12"
1/4" × 4" × 5"
WELDS
30°
3 15/16"
1 1/2" = 1'-0"
7 1/4"
20"
3/8" × 1 1/4"
STOVE BOLTS
SHANK OVERALL 30"
1/2" × 1 3/4"
OR 1/2" × 2"

of its fluke and one end of its stock, without burying. My anchor had a better score, but no more than in proportion to its weight. I went home considerably chagrined and never got around to repeating the test with a Danforth. "Thought experiments" like the one Francis Herreshoff performed in *The Complete Cruiser* are more satisfactory. It seemed I had a perfectly good anchor, but if I hadn't tried to prove it was a superior one I could have gone on taking its superiority for granted.

Of course this testing didn't amount to much. No hard figures were produced. The Danforth wasn't tried, and my design here is not necessarily a fair substitute for a yachtsman, let alone a Herreshoff (though it has the same proportions and weight distribution). It seemed to me that sharper points and edges on the palms would be an improvement, and I even began to wonder if all that ailed the old, contemptible Navy stockless anchor was its bluntness. It had seemed obvious that the traditional stock anchor lay on the bottom with its palm in a more advantageous attitude than a stockless anchor, given a normal initial trend of the warp. The silly tests used in advertisements of modern anchors are so obviously unrealistic that it hadn't occurred to me before that a stockless anchor puts a higher proportion of its weight on the tips of its palms and that that might be some compensation for the light shank.

Francis Herreshoff objected to anchors with moving parts which might get jammed with mud. I had this happen to a Danforth once, but it'd been on the bottom all winter first. In any case, I've never been able to make a Danforth turn end-over-end. They always pivot around horizontally when the pull is reversed, and I think the risk of their turning over is much more remote than the chance of a folding-stock anchor coming unstocked, which happens fairly often, though it won't to my design for obvious reasons.

My present idea is that no anchor of any design weighing under sixteen or eighteen pounds is reliable for even the smallest boat, because it is too light to drive its bills into anything but soft mud. Weight for weight, I judge the two modern anchor types are almost if not quite as good as the traditional type with a short scope. On all very small anchors, needle points and razor edges may be the most important features for reliability when let go suddenly.

I used to think that the best arrangement for all occasions was a "backed anchor," a large anchor or simply a heavy weight, with another anchor fast to it by a warp equal to the depth of water plus the freeboard. If this arrangement is proportioned right, it has the combined advantages of a very long scope to the further anchor, and of a short scope to the nearer one; the former gives the anchor its best chance to bury, the latter steadies the boat best. However, when a boat has really ugly habits when riding to her anchor, as *Dovekie* for instance does, two anchors spread out are more likely to tame her than two of the same weight in tandem. At any rate no such boat ought to go cruising with only a single effective anchor, no matter how small and light she is.

The immediate effect of the experiment has been that I have abruptly stopped sneering at stockless anchors. If I stick with stock anchors, as I probably will with *Resolution,* it'll be for a number of petty reasons of which the most important is that it's easier to get all the mud off them. My storm anchor will be some imitation of a Herreshoff three-piece, because it will be stowed below decks and will weigh something like 120 pounds: I don't care to bring it on deck in one trip.

nylon type? or tin?

clamp